THE GARDENS OF SALLUST

THE GARDENS OF
SALLUST

A Changing Landscape

KIM J. HARTSWICK

UNIVERSITY OF TEXAS PRESS

AUSTIN

The publication of this book was made possible by a gift made
in honor of Lindsay Morehead Larkin and Mia Kleberg Larkin
and by generous grants from George Washington University
and its Department of Fine Arts and Art History.

First paperback printing, 2006

LIBRARY OF CONGRESS CATALOGING-IN-PUBLICATION DATA

Hartswick, Kim J.
  The Gardens of Sallust : a changing landscape / Kim J.
Hartswick.
      p.   cm.
Includes bibliographical references and index.
    ISBN-13: 978-0-292-71432-8 (pbk. : alk. paper)
    ISBN-10: 0-292-71432-7
    1. Horti Sallustiani (Rome, Italy)—History.   2. Gardens,
Roman—Italy—Rome—History.   I. Title.
    SB466.I83H675   2004
    712′.0937′6—dc21   2003007783

Dedicated to my parents

CONTENTS

ACKNOWLEDGMENTS

This study has been in the making for a number of years, and I have been fortunate to be able to pursue most of my research in Rome. The George Washington University offered me financial assistance through the University Facility Fund to spend part of the summer of 1994 in Rome, and in 1998 I was a Resident of the American Academy in Rome for ten weeks. It was there where most of this research was undertaken, and I am most grateful to all the fellows, residents, and employees of this wonderful institution. In particular, I thank Lester Little, the Director of the Academy, and Christina Huemer, the Librarian, for their support in all aspects of my residency and my other stays there. Likewise, Eileen Markson, Librarian at Bryn Mawr College, was, as usual, generous and helpful with all my queries.

The Biblioteca Apostolica Vaticana was indispensable especially for its manuscript collection, and the German Archaeological Institute in Rome was also useful for holdings not at the American Academy. Other research was conducted at the Biblioteca Nazionale in Naples; the Biblioteca Capitolina in Verona; the Bibliothèque Nationale de France in Paris; the Boston Public Library; the libraries of the National Gallery of Art, the Center for Hellenic Studies in Washington, D.C., Bryn Mawr College in Bryn Mawr, Pennsylvania, and the Institute of Fine Arts, New York University; the New York Public Library; and the Avery and Butler libraries of Columbia University, New York. Finally, because of the interlibrary loan department of the George Washington University, I was able to continue at least some of this research while holding down a full-time teaching schedule.

E-mail and the fax machine proved to be valuable tools in making contact with scholars, all of whom answered my queries and offered advice. Among these I thank Sir John Boardman (Oxford), Bernd Evers (Berlin), Bernd Kulawik (Berlin), and Valery Shevchenko (St. Petersburg), the last three for information regarding a drawing formerly in the Destail-leur collection in Paris, John Herrmann (Museum of Fine Arts, Boston), Mette Moltesen (Ny Carlsberg Glyptotek), Silvia Orlandi (for information on the "Comitato Nazionale per lo studio delle opere di Pirro Ligorio"), William Peck (Detroit Museum of Art), and finally Agnese Pompei (Rome), who contacted me regarding the restoration of the so-called Aula Adrianae (the vestibule).

Ingrid S. Rowland, Magda Ferreti, and John Ziolkowski aided in some difficult translations of Latin and Italian, and, in particular, Dana Burgess translated several difficult Latin passages, as indicated in the notes. Caroline Dexter gave her expertise on several issues concerning inscriptions, as well as influencing the title of this book. John Wilton-Ely answered questions concerning Piranesi and was generous in sending me pertinent photographs. I had fruitful discussions in Rome with Patricia Osmond de Martino concerning Sallust and with Enrico Bruschini, Direttore dei Beni Artistici at the United States Embassy, who is an expert on the old Ludovisi palaces. Daniela Candilio was very kind to discuss with me the pertinent sculptures in the Museo Nazionale delle Terme in Rome, as was Elizabeth Milliker at the Metropolitan Museum in New York. Although they are not responsible for any of the conclusions reached in this study, I am fortunate to be acquainted with Eugenia Salza Prina Ricotti and Wilhelmina Jashemski, both true pioneers in the subject of ancient Roman gardens. I have also been fortunate in having three excellent readers of the manuscript (one anonymous as well as Ingrid S. Rowland and Miranda Marvin), who offered numerous suggestions and gave encouragement for my pursuit of this study. Their comments have been very much appreciated and have made this a better publication.

I am forever in debt to the outstanding group of photographers at the Biomedical Communications Department at the George Washington University that digitized, manipulated, and photographed many of the images. They consistently tolerated with good cheer the many demands I made on them—usually with little time to spare.

Last, but far from least, are the numerous individuals who along the way gave me support and encouragement. In particular, Chrystina Haüber was there at the beginning, encouraging me to pursue garden studies and continuing her support with many conversations and suggestions over the years, especially on how to track down archival material in Rome. Others, perhaps less conspicuous but just as important, include Barbara Barletta, Carl Ibsen, Philip Jacks, Carol Mattusch, Margaret M. Miles, C. Brian Rose, and as usual, Brunilde S. Ridgway. Because of their interest and questions, they all made me think more about the various issues involved and even to recon-

sider my original ideas. Although some of them may not know it, they are very much part of this study.

Finally, at the University of Texas Press, humanities editor Jim Burr, managing editor Carolyn Cates Wylie, and copyeditor Nancy Moore all were extraordinary in the production of this study. I am grateful for their efficiency, good humor, and encouragement throughout the entire process.

I am pleased to acknowledge all the above institutions and people, but the most important is my wife, Maria Ann Conelli, who encouraged my residency at the American Academy and was a guiding force throughout. I know that this study would not have been completed without her.

INTRODUCTION

Readers interested in horticulture will be greatly disappointed because although this study deals with one of the most beautiful of ancient garden estates in Rome, a discussion of the plantings forms only a minor part. This situation is not only because the author is not a horticulturist (in fact, does not even have a "green thumb") but primarily because direct evidence for such plantings in the gardens of Sallust is utterly lacking. Indeed, my interest in these gardens and the resulting present study are completely serendipitous.

Several years ago I began investigating the dramatic lowering in date of presumably "fixed" monuments of the Greek archaic period proposed by E. D. Francis and Michael Vickers.[1] Their arguments included a Greek statue of a Crouching Amazon in the Conservatori Museum (Fig. 3.14) found in 1888 in Rome near the via Boncompagni, about twenty-five meters from the via Quintino Sella in an area known in antiquity as the *horti Sallustiani*. Thinking it important to learn more about the findspot of this statue, I soon became aware that a thorough study of these famous gardens had never been published. Although not being versed in garden history, I abandoned my original project to devote my research to the *horti Sallustiani*.

Since then, several studies by others have been published on the gardens of Sallust, including pertinent essays in the *Lexicon Topographicum Urbis Romae,* two articles by F. Astolfi in issues of *Forma Urbis,* and an important symposium on *Horti Romani* published in 1998 in which, particularly, Emilia Talamo and Mette Moltesen have studies devoted to the *horti Sallustiani*.[2] All these have been enormously important in bringing to light various aspects of the gardens; yet a more complete account, up to now, has been lacking.

Over the years my investigations have led me not only to a better understanding of the importance of garden history in the study of ancient sculpture but also to the necessity of leaping beyond the temporal boundaries of ancient Rome to comprehend better the dynamic quality of antiquity. Indeed, interconnections among space, time, human society, and texts only recently have become priorities in the study of gardens and landscapes. Furthermore, unlike immovable architectural monuments that can be positioned securely, gardens are in constant flux, forever changing and with sometimes unclear boundaries.[3] These insecurities are particularly true with the study of ancient gardens that, as in the case with the *horti Sallustiani*, may be completely destroyed and, therefore, can only be imagined. It is only through such interdisciplinary and post-structuralist perspectives that the meaning and appearance of ancient gardens can be attempted.

It is difficult, therefore, to understand as fully as possible any ancient monument, and in particular an ancient garden, without acknowledging that it has undergone numerous changes and meanings during its lifetime. These transformations are not merely obstructions—things to be discarded or ignored in our evaluation of the "original"—but important aspects to be accepted as part of the natural evolution of ancient monuments. In the case of the *horti Sallustiani*, the substantial changes that occurred in antiquity are in fact overshadowed by their later transformations into the present urban fabric of modern Rome. It is only by including these later changes that the ancient gardens of Sallust can be fairly evaluated and that my original intention—to understand the context of the ancient sculptures found there—can be even remotely realized.

Even when a garden is well preserved, such as that of the sixteenth-century villa Lante at Bagnaia, the original appearance is not always clear, and the meaning of the decorative schemes is sometimes open to interpretation.[4] If this is the case with an almost intact Renaissance garden, then it must be admitted that a complete understanding of the *horti Sallustiani* cannot be a viable goal. Acknowledging the limitations of such a project ought not, however, to discourage an evaluation of what we do know or, at least may reasonably surmise, about these ancient gardens.

The *horti Sallustiani* were among the most important and beautiful of all the imperial *horti* in ancient Rome. Yet, because of the modern expansion of the city after 1871 (when Rome began to be developed as capital of unified Italy), the ancient topography has been irrevocably altered with the filling of the valley between the Pincio and Quirinal hills where these *horti* existed. The study of the gardens is hampered not only by these modern operations but also by the history of this area after A.D. 410, when the Goths, under the leadership of Alaric, invaded Rome, entering the city at the gates of the *horti Sallustiani*. After that time the gardens appear to have been abandoned, and the magnificent sculptural displays and luxury pavilions were pillaged, destroyed, or left to ruin. Vandalism, earthquakes, fires, and the ubiquitous limekilns must also have wrecked havoc on these ancient remains just as they had on other parts of the city. Only in the fifteenth century was the area revitalized with the (re)building of an aqueduct, and by the seventeenth century, it was considered prime real estate. But, even as late as the nineteenth century it is reported that within the walls of Rome the northern and eastern parts were abandoned and that the city was still concentrated along the banks of the Tiber.[5]

Only with the knowledge of the history of this area down to modern times can an attempt be made to understand these ancient gardens. There is, in fact, a considerable body of material that can be collected pertaining to the gardens, including literary, epigraphic, and physical evidence, which all must be evaluated separately as well as collectively. Ancient literary testimony is sparse, and so archaeology has proven to be the best method to employ. Numerous finds were recorded beginning in the fifteenth century and especially during the modern reconfiguration of the area in the nineteenth. Drawings, etchings, and plans of the site before the filling of the valley help in determining topographical markers and at times give a context for the recorded finds.

The history of the site forms the parameters of the first chapter that deals not only with the ancient testimonia but with the later developers of this area. The second chapter is an analysis of the physical remains as they exist today or as they are believed to have existed. This latter aspect is particularly intriguing because it tells us perhaps more about the manner in which scholars debate archaeological issues and less about the gardens themselves. In the third chapter are several "case studies" of sculptures that most likely were decorative elements within these ancient gardens. The discovery of these sculptures and the opinions of scholars concerning their subjects and uses within these gardens are explored. Finally, a short addendum concerns a topographical problem that is intriguing as a vehicle for highlighting a scholarly debate that has yet to be resolved.

By exploring such material my goal is twofold: (1) to determine how these gardens were viewed and interpreted by later scholars—somewhat a "history of scholarship" approach—and the impact that these interpretations have had on our modern perspectives of the subject, and in particular of ancient Roman topography, and (2) to give as complete a picture as possible of these gardens by exploring the architectural remains and sculptural decorations, with an emphasis on the many pieces of statues discovered over the centuries. The arrangement and titles of chapters give the impression of being discrete subjects; however, their contents intertwine my two objectives. The reason for this approach is that it is necessary to have knowledge of a variety of subjects, for example, literary testimonies, ancient and modern topography, medieval and Renaissance guidebooks, archaeological reports, and the nineteenth-century art market, to attempt an understanding of certain topographical markers or of pieces of ancient sculpture or architectural remains.

As a result, this study takes into account the pertinent ancient sources as well as the later reports, conclusions, and identifications that sometimes shed light on the subject and at other times cloud our view. It is not a definitive study but a series of wanderings through the physical and intellectual landscapes of the *horti Sallustiani* that I hope will prompt further explorations into this fascinating subject.

THE GARDENS OF SALLUST

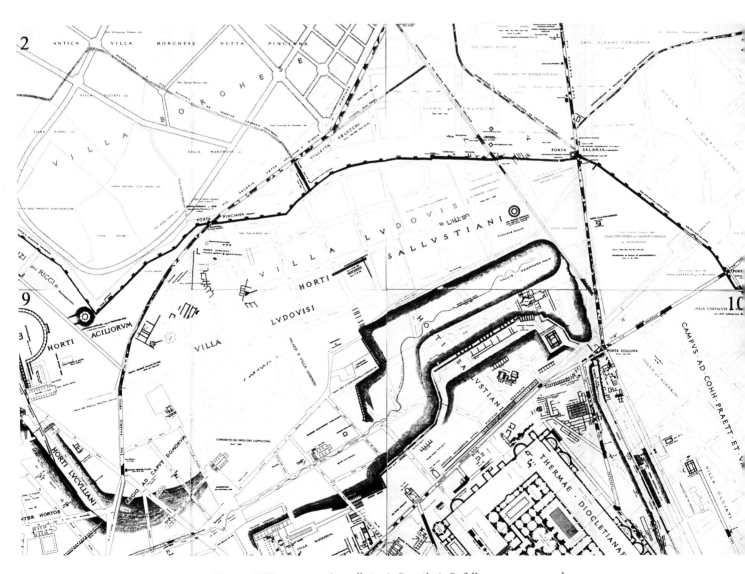

Fig. 1.1: **FUR** *2, 3, 9, 10 (overall view). Details A–D follow on pages 2 and 3.*

PART I

Topography and History

LOCATION AND TOPOGRAPHY

The gardens of Sallust, that were originally laid out at the end of the first century B.C., are known to have included, at least partially, the Pincio and Quirinal hills at the northeast part of the ancient city of Rome (Figs. 1.1–1.2).

In antiquity, a valley, at least twenty-two meters deep, lay between the more gradual slope of the Quirinal at the south, and perhaps the steeper slopes of the Pincio at the north (i.e., Figs. 2.3 [Pincio] and 2.4 [Quirinal]). At the floor of this valley ran a stream, known in modern parlance as the Acqua Sallustiana but whose ancient name is not recorded. Richardson suggested it may be the Spino or Nodinus mentioned by Cicero.[1] Regardless of its ancient name, the stream must not only have played an important role in the overall aesthetic effect of the gardens but also would have made them the envy of less well watered estates. The most prized gardens seem to have had a river or some other natural source of water, as recognized by Pliny the Younger's lament that his Laurentine villa had many amenities but not that of water.[2]

The Acqua Sallustiana began at the eastern head of the valley and continued westward, contributing to the swamplands in the Campus Martius, the *Palus Caprae,* from where Romulus is said to have been carried to heaven.[3] It fed the Euripus (canal) that was in the gardens of Agrippa, and from there it flowed into the Tiber after having received as well the waters called the *Amnis Petronia.* These waters originated from another source on the Quirinal, the *Fons Cati* that lent its name to a secondary hill, the *collis Catialis,* on the Quirinal.[4]

The Quirinal had a very ancient pedigree, as attested by the tradition that Sabines were settled there, and it is from here they exited the city along the ancient via Salaria to obtain salt from the Tyrrhenian coast.[5] Early use of part of the hill for burials confirms a nearby settlement,[6] but these do not speak necessarily to Sabine occupation.[7] The name of the hill could derive from the ancient Sabine city, Cures, and the existence of an ancient cult of Semo Sancus, introduced according to tradition (Pliny records foundation date of 466 B.C.) by Titus Tatius, shows the importance of the hill in early times.[8] More significant perhaps is the report by Varro that Jupiter was venerated first in the *Capitolium Vetus* (the Old Capitol), which was on the Quirinal hill.[9]

The topography of this part of Rome between the late Republican and the end of the Imperial period must have changed continuously through sometimes massive building operations that transformed the landscape and thereby even the routes that must have been determined by the terrain. The principal street traversing the Quirinal hill from east to west was called the *Alta Semita,* whose path is probably represented by the present via XX Settembre (Fig. 1.3: unnamed broad

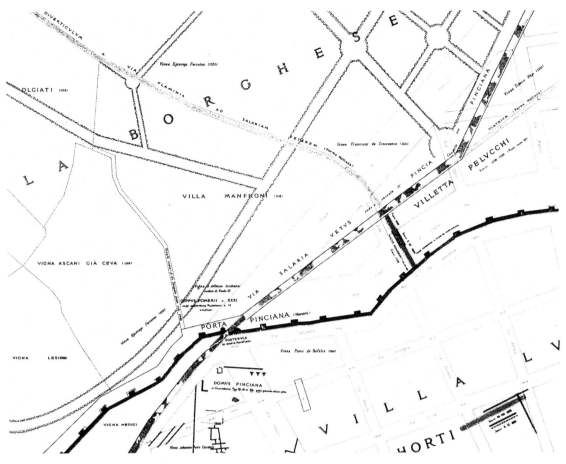

Fig. 1.1A above: **FUR** 2 (detail).

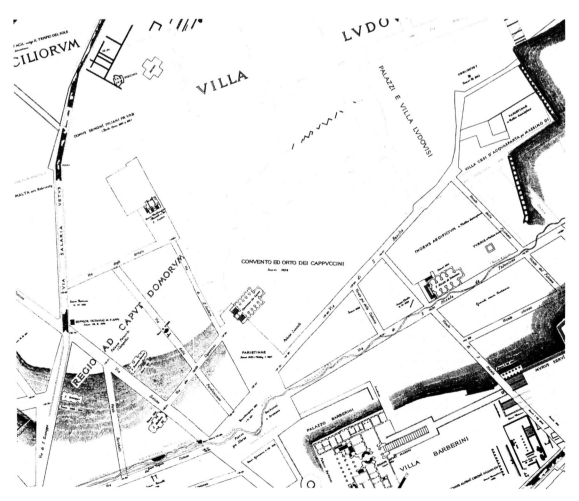

Fig. 1.1C below: **FUR** 9 (detail).

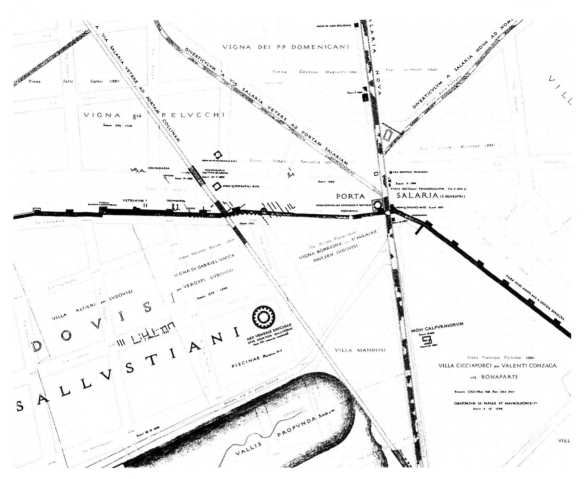

Fig. 1.1B above: FUR 3 (detail).

Fig. 1.1D below: FUR 10 (detail).

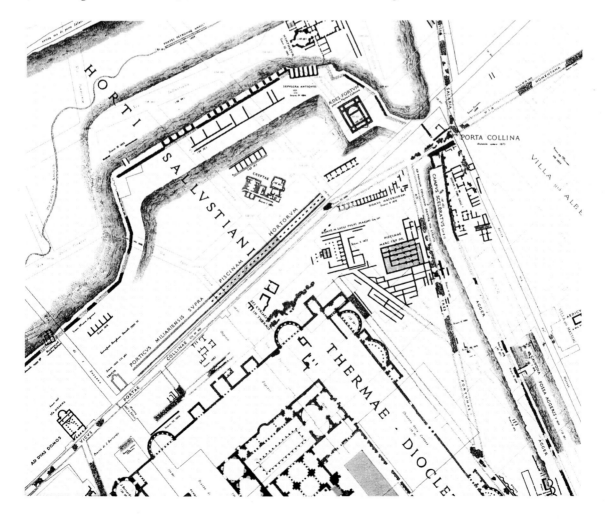

street at lower right running parallel to the via Flavia) and that lends its name to this area, according to early regionaries (fourth-century descriptions of the fourteen regions of Rome; see pp. 61–62) describing Region VI.[10] This street appears to have sloped upward towards the porta Collina (in the old "Servian" city walls).[11] In its final stretch, the *Alta Semita* took the name *vicus portae Collinae,* as attested by an inscription dedicated by the cult of the Lares found near Santa Susanna that records the name and restoration of this street.[12] Near the porta Collina, inside the walls, was the *Campus Sceleratus,* where incestuous vestals were buried alive.[13] The *vicus portae Collinae* was later extended to the more distant porta Nomentana in the third-century Aurelian circuit wall of the city. Elsewhere on the Quirinal, another street carried the name Pomegranate (*Malum Punicum*), where Domitian was born. Martial records the locality *Pila Tiburtina,* where he lived and from where he could see the temple of Flora and the *Capitolium Vetus.*[14]

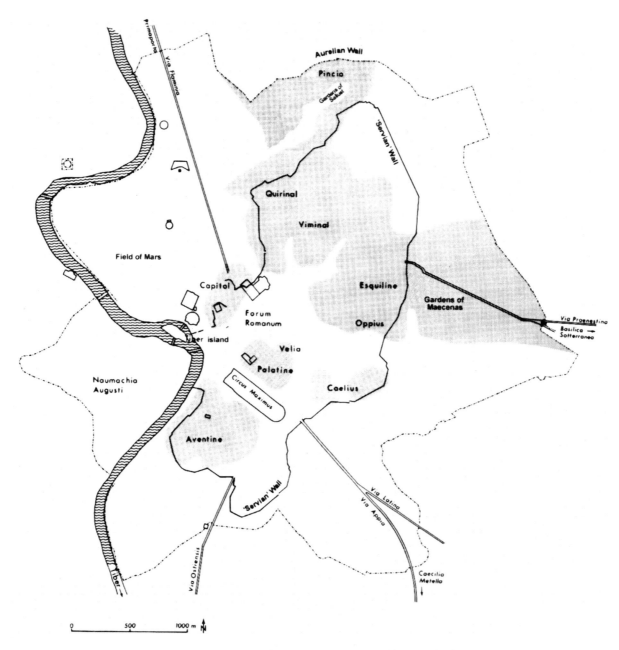

Fig. 1.2: Plan of ancient Rome, by Martin Boss (with additions and subtractions).

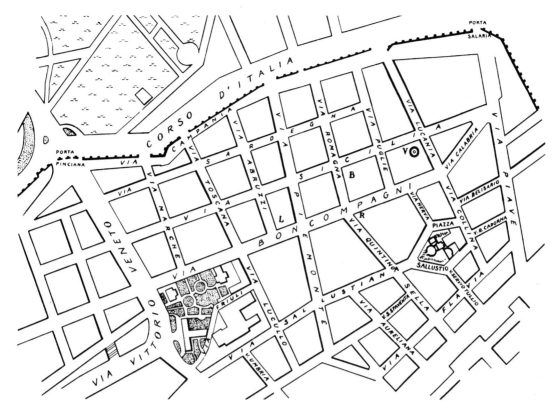

Fig. 1.3: Plan of modern Rome.

The *Alta Semita* ran, within the urban limits of the city, more or less parallel to the ancient city wall built along the crest of the Quirinal. According to several sources, the first construction of a city wall is attributed to Numa Pompilius (seventh century B.C.). Extant remains, however, have been dated later: to the sixth century in the reign of Servius Tullius, to whom other sources give the organization of the city into four regions and the building of its first wall.[15] After the Gallic invasion of 390 B.C., between 378 and 352 B.C., the old city wall was reconstructed, and the *agger et fossa* was built, that is, a bastion consisting of a wall, an interior earth mound (*agger*), and a deep gully (*fossa*) on the exterior.[16] It is this fourth-century *agger,* extending from the porta Collina south to the porta Esquilina, that can be traced near the *Alta Semita,* whose portal (the porta Collina), discovered in 1872, lay at the corner of the present Ministry of Finance between the via XX Settembre and the via Gaeta.[17]

Usually coinciding with the city wall was the *pomerium,* the sacred border marked by *cippi* (stakes or posts), which constituted the confines between *urbs* (city) and *ager* (country) *Romanus.* This line, within which the burial of the dead was not permitted, could not be expanded without the increase of territory of the Roman state,[18] and the *pomerium* on the Quirinal seems to have lasted without change until the time of Sulla.[19] It is not certain that Augustus, to whom is owed a new division of the city into fourteen regions, had extended the *pomerium,* but it was certainly increased by later emperors, such as Claudius, Vespasian, and Aurelian.[20] On the Quirinal outside the porta Salaria (the *ager*), Claudius made a vast zone part of the city, perhaps including portions of the gardens of Sallust, but it appears that later, under Vespasian, this area was excluded from the *urbs.* Under Aurelian, to whom is owed the new (and present) circuit of the city wall, the area of the *horti Sallustiani* fell within the urban limits and the distinction between *urbs* and *ager* became blurred.[21] That is, these gardens immediately outside the ancient "Servian" walls were for almost three centuries technically in the country, but by the third century A.D., they were incorporated into the city proper.

BOUNDARIES

At least by the third century A.D., therefore, these gardens were bounded on the north by the Aurelian wall (present Corso Italia). Numerous graves were found immediately outside, but not inside, this wall, prompting Lanciani to conclude that the position of the third-century city wall between the porta Pinciana and the porta Salaria, in fact, marks the north boundary of the *original* Sallustian gardens.[22] Furthermore, between 1733 and 1736 in the excavations of the Pelucchi and Naro gardens, that is, north of the Aurelian wall, about 150 inscriptions came to light, one of which, found near the outer face of the city wall, mentions a small shrine as "proxime hortos Sa[llustianos]," thus supporting (if the restoration is correct) the proximity of these gardens to the wall.[23] Ruins on the Pincio were identified in the *Mirabilia Urbis Romae* (a medieval description of the city of Rome dating ca. 1150) as "Palatium Salustii," and in the fifteenth century, the site was recorded: "The palace of Sallust was in the place now called the Pincio, and in that place is still the 'sala Salustii.'"[24] Numerous city plans also record ruins on the Pincio, but these are difficult, if not impossible, to identify with any physical remains.[25]

Although the Aurelian wall must have become the northern limit of the gardens, at the east it seems not to have been the boundary, as Richter suggested in 1901,[26] because to the east of the via Salaria, inside the walls between the porta Salaria and the ancient porta Collina (of the "Servian" wall), were found numerous tombs, but none to the west of this road.[27] It seems likely, therefore, that the gardens did not extend across the via Salaria (near the present via Piave), where a graveyard existed. Their limits may have been even farther to the west, defined by an ancient northeast-southwest roadway (near the present via Lucana) identified by Lanciani (Fig. 1.1B: *FUR* 3) as a branch of the ancient via Salaria ("diverticulum a via salaria vetere ad portam collinam").[28]

The southern limits are less secure, although they likely incorporated the ancient slopes of the Quirinal (just south of the present via Sallustiana). It is clear that in the Flavian period (and probably before) the gardens lay close to the porta Collina because it is here that Tacitus explained Vespasian's troops were resisted by the forces of Vitellius from atop the walls of the Sallustian gardens.[29] Indeed, these garden walls may have been those of the "Servian" wall, acting as the original southern boundary of the gardens that must have lain immediately outside the city limits. It is even possible that by the later Republican period this stretch of the fourth-century B.C. defensive circuit carried a branch of the second-century B.C. *Aqua Marcia*, explaining, as Evans argued, the good preservation of the "Servian" wall in this area, in contrast to other parts of the city.[30]

On the other hand, we know that Maecenas (d. 8 B.C.) converted a stretch of the old city wall into a terraced orchard for his gardens.[31] It is possible that something similar happened for that part of the wall near the *horti Sallustiani*. Indeed, Lanciani and others suggested that the southern limit, at least in the third century (after construction of the Aurelian wall), probably extended inside the "Servian" wall and onto the Quirinal as far as the *vicus portae Collinae* (present via XX Settembre).[32] In 1879 a long *piscina* (a fish pond or swimming pool; ca. 200 meters) was discovered running north of and parallel to this ancient roadway (Fig. 1.1D: *FUR* 10).[33] Furthermore, three years before, excavators found three sections of pipe, all carrying the same inscription (ORTORVMSALLUSTIANOR / IMPSEVALEXADRI AVG / NAEVIVSMANESFE-CIT), nearby on the Quirinal in the property of Josef Spithoever, who will be discussed more fully later.[34] According to Lanciani, these pipes represent portions of a very long conduit that ran between the porta Viminale and the Monte della Giustizia and fed the *piscina* along the *vicus portae Collinae*.[35]

Other architectural remains identified on the Quirinal include a series of six vaulted chambers (each 4.10 meters × 4.50 meters) backing onto a large wall found between the via XX Settembre, via Servio Tullio, via Quintino Sella, and via Flavia (Fig. 1.1D: *FUR* 10). These are said to be oriented on axis with the "Venere Sallustiana," that is, the vestibule to the north (to be discussed), and it is tempting to suggest that they represent a portion of this same complex.[36] Finally, the area inside the walls near the porta Collina was referred to as "ad tres Fortunas" because of three temples to this goddess, said to be neighbors of the gardens of Sallust.[37]

On the Quirinal within the so-called Servian wall (where it made almost a right angle near the via Piemonte) were found, after demolition of the villino Spithoever, many traces of concrete walls in *opus reticulatum* (faced with a network of small square stones) and *opus latericium* (faced with brick) as well as a hypocaust room, indicating a modest bath building in this area.[38] Not well constructed and dating perhaps after the second century A.D., this complex could represent a private, nonimperial presence, excluding this area as part of the imperial gardens, at least during the late Roman empire.

These tantalizing and poorly recorded ancient remains on the Quirinal slope near the "Servian" wall point out the complex archaeological record and the uncertainty in determining the southern boundaries of the Sallustian gardens. Of course, this boundary may well have changed over time, and so any definitive statement would be misleading.

Even though the southern limits are vague, the western boundary of the gardens is the most difficult to determine. It is usually proposed that it followed the path of the present via Vittorio Veneto.[39] Richardson, however, suggested that the western limit (at least in the valley) "would probably not have extended beyond Piazza Barberini and very likely not beyond Via Bissolati," and this seems to be the case, at least by the Hadrianic period (A.D. 117–138).[40] On the Pincio, however, the western limit may have been even further to the east because remains of a house, probably of Hadrianic date, were found near the via Toscana.[41] Two sections of an ancient street running north-south, almost parallel with the via Toscana, were also identified, but it was difficult to determine their date. The level of this road was lower than the base of the Aurelian wall at only a short distance to the north. This discrepancy suggested that the road had gone out of use at least by the third century, when the wall was constructed.[42] It seems clear, however, that the ground level had been raised considerably in this area even before the Aurelian wall was built, suggesting either a reworking of the gardens or a possible enlargement of them at that time toward the west. Katterfeld suggested an extension made by Gordian

(A.D. 238–244), but we are told only that there were plans for extensive, porticoed gardens ("viridiaria") in the Campus Martius (which could have included part of the Pincio), but these were never realized.[43]

The *horti Lucullani* as well as perhaps the *horti Aciliorum* are believed to have abutted the western limits of the *horti Sallustiani,* but the exact limits of these gardens (and even their location on the Pincio) are not assured.[44] Lanciani argued that the eastern limit of the *horti Lucullani* was the *via Salaria Vetus* because a tomb of Republican date was found to the east of this road.[45] If the presence of a tomb excludes the extension of the Lucullan gardens further to the east, then likewise it excludes the existence of the *horti Sallustiani* in that area.[46] It is possible, therefore, that these gardens (the Lucullan and Sallustian) were not contiguous but were separated by a road and graveyard. Note, however, that between the ancient via Salaria and the modern via Veneto have been discovered a grotto with five statues,[47] a piscina,[48] and a large cache of amphorae (under the via Veneto),[49] perhaps suggesting a garden environment. But even if this is the case, it cannot be determined to whom this land belonged.[50]

The circuit of the Aurelian wall was primarily determined by defensive strategy, to such an extent that houses, tenements, porticoes, and even tombs were either incorporated into its fabric or cut away if necessary. Noteworthy for our discussion of gardens are remains (found not in the confines of the Sallustian gardens but where the modern porta San Lorenzo cut through part of the ancient city wall) of a garden wall with niches, crowned with a lead-covered cornice and decorated with a limestone encrustation of twigs and stones to create a "rustic" effect. Remarkably, the niches still contained their original sculptures, which were packed round with clay to form the core of the city wall.[51]

In a similar fashion, another wall, identified by Richmond as that of the *horti Sallustiani,* was absorbed into the Aurelian circuit just west of the porta Salaria, and this may be physical evidence that the third-century city wall indeed respected the existing northern boundary of these gardens.[52] The peculiar curving course of the wall as it runs west from the porta Salaria may be the result of attempting to incorporate the gardens as fully as possible into the city limits. If this is indeed the case, then the abrupt obtuse angle made by the wall east of the porta Pinciana could be significant with regard to the western boundaries of the garden. Note that the wall with niches (Fig. 1.1c: *FUR* 9) running northwest-southeast near the via Lucullo (discussed below, pp. 58–61), if extended, would intersect with the angle made by the Aurelian wall to the north. It is possible that this relationship is not simply fortuitous and that in the third century, when the course of the Aurelian wall was determined, the western limit of the *horti Sallustiani* ran just west of the present via Toscana.

Regardless of the exact boundaries of these gardens, it is clear they eventually occupied a significant amount of land. It is also likely they were increased over the centuries from their original, and perhaps even relatively modest, size. Indeed, although the first owner was rich, it is not likely he had a vast estate nor would have even wanted to flaunt his wealth.

THE ORIGINAL OWNER: C. SALLUSTIUS CRISPUS

The first inhabitant and developer of the so-called gardens of Sallust, C. Sallustius Crispus, is a figure well known to modern scholars of ancient Rome because of his histories of events of the late Republican period that have come down to us.[53] Information about the man himself, however, is incomplete, and knowledge about his famous gardens during his lifetime is even less clear.

There is no written physical description of this "foremost of Roman historians," as Martial called him.[54] A marble bust, said to have been discovered in the area of the Sallustian gardens near the porta Salaria, formerly in the Campana collection and now in St. Petersburg, carries an inscription on its base: C. SAL C. The head had been broken from its torso, but it probably belongs to this bust. The inscription, however, seems not to be ancient, and the head has been dated to the time of Trajan (Fig. 1.4).[55]

What had been considered authentic representations of the historian appear on a series of contorniates, each of which carries a profile head with short hair and beard and the inscription SALVSTIVS AVTOR (Fig. 1.5).[56] Because these are related to a series of contorniates, all dating to the fourth century A.D. and bearing images of famous men of letters such as Homer, Demosthenes, Terence, Horace, and Apollonios of Tyana, it has been assumed that the SALVSTIVS AVTOR must refer to Sallustius Crispus. Desnier proposed, however, that this contorniate type does not represent the famous first-century B.C. Roman historian but rather another Sallustius, the author of a fourth-century philosophical treatise entitled Περὶ Θεῶν καὶ Κόσμου.[57] Desnier's arguments are indeed persuasive enough to raise doubts about the usual identification, and so this portrait cannot be related unequivocally to Sallustius Crispus. Regardless of the identification, it is clear that the image is a fictitious portrait and as such cannot be an accurate representation of Sallustius the historian nor of the fourth-century philosopher of the same name.[58]

Details concerning Sallustius' life are equally elusive.[59] According to Jerome,[60] Sallustius died in Rome in 35 B.C., having been born forty-eight years before at Amiternum (modern S. Vittorino in the province of l'Aquila) in the Abruzzi in Sabine land. He was tribune of the plebs in 52 B.C. and was made praetor in 46 B.C.,[61] to recover, according to Dio Cassius, his senatorial rank, which he had lost in 50 B.C. in expulsions carried out by the censor Appius Claudius.[62] From his expulsion to his appointment as praetor there is little information about his life, save for an inglorious incident in the late summer of 47 B.C., when he escaped with his life against mutineers in Campania.[63] He earned employment in the African campaigns under Caesar, but he did not command in battle. Nevertheless, Caesar consigned him three legions, appointing him the first governor of the new Roman province of Africa Novus (Numidia), which, according to Dio, was pillaged by its new governor.[64] Sallust, however, escaped prosecution, likely through the intervention of Caesar himself, who perhaps extorted Sallust or else annexed a share of his Numidian profits.[65] Although he retained his senatorial seat, Sallust's political career was exhausted. His personal coffers were, however,

Fig. 1.4: Portrait bust of Sallust, Hermitage, St. Petersburg, Inv. A 424.

Fig. 1.5: Contorniate. Obverse, portrait of Sallust. Cabinet des Médailles, Bibliothèque Nationale de France, Paris, nr. 17175.

far from empty, and with his remaining wealth he retired to a comfortable private life to devote himself to writing.

His last years were spent at his new estate immediately outside the walls of the city near the porta Collina and adjacent to the via Salaria, which, perhaps not coincidentally, was the very road leading to his hometown of Amiternum.[66] It has been claimed either that Sallust purchased this property from Caesar or that Caesar gave it to him, but the evidence for such a transaction is far from convincing. According to the fourth- or early fifth-century tabulator of Roman prodigies, Julius Obsequens, in 17 B.C. a tower in the gardens of Caesar near the porta Collina was struck by lightning.[67] Modern scholars have connected this lightning strike with an earlier one in 48/47 B.C., reported by Dio as having occurred in the gardens of Caesar where a horse was killed.[68] Dio, however, did not give the location of these gardens, which could well be the famous ones of Julius Caesar along the Tiber rather than any near the porta Collina.[69]

On the other hand, it is possible that Obsequens, writing in the fourth century, refers to the Sallustian gardens as those of Caesar to indicate not the ownership by the dictator but as imperial gardens, which in his day were still property of the imperial family. In other words, Obsequens is probably employing a generic, contemporary identification rather than the name of these gardens when the lightning strike occurred. Indeed, in 17 B.C. the gardens near the Colline gate were likely still those of Sallust's family, as we will see. Furthermore, in the same year as this lightning strike near the porta Collina, Obsequens reported an earthquake in the Apennines at the estate of Livia, wife of Caesar (*uxor Caesaris*), pointing out clearly that the use here of the term Caesar did not refer to Julius Caesar but to the emperor Augustus.

Two inscriptions, indicating that some freedmen were employed in the *horti Sallustiani,* have suggested to scholars that property of Julius Caesar was absorbed into the Sallustian gardens.[70] Nevertheless, the term "Ca[e]seris" as employed in one of these probably indicates, again, *imperial* ownership rather than ownership by Julius Caesar, particularly because this inscription has been dated to the third century A.D.[71] Finally, on the death of Caesar (44 B.C.), his famous gardens and villa in the Trastevere had been willed to the people of Rome, while Sallust, according to Pseudo-Cicero, purchased a garden and a Tiburtine villa of the dead dictator.[72] Many scholars have suggested that the property of "Caesar," where the lightning strike occurred as reported by Obsequens near the porta Collina, must be the same as that purchased by Sallust, as recorded by Pseudo-Cicero, and this formed the nucleus of Sallust's new gardens.[73] Yet the gardens and the villa reported by Pseudo-Cicero both must have been at Tibur, because villa and gardens, in such a context, are always intertwined. Thus, a connection of these Tiburtine properties with presumed holdings of Caesar near the porta Collina is difficult to support. These ancient texts, even if interpreted as suggesting such a sequence of events, may well have been simply rhetori-cal flourish to reveal the devotion held by Sallust for the memory of his dead leader. Syme agreed and even proposed that the purchasing of Caesar's property by Sallust "has no lodgement in history."[74]

On the other hand, others believe that these porta Collina gardens supposedly owned by Caesar, even if they existed, do not coincide with the *horti Sallustiani*.[75] This question of previous ownership is important because modern identifications and theories concerning the gardens of Sallust have been based on the premise that Julius Caesar owned gardens near the porta Collina, which were later absorbed into the Sallustian gardens.[76] This succession of ownership is, to my mind, unproved. What is clear, however, is that these gardens of Sallust eventually became imperial properties.

INHERITORS OF SALLUST'S GARDENS

According to Jerome, in 46 B.C. Sallust married Terentia, who had been divorced from Cicero, perhaps explaining Sallust's silence about her in the Catiline crimes.[77] It is possible, however, that Jerome invented this connection of Cicero's former wife with Sallust, although there is nothing to refute it.[78] Syme, however, believed it was entirely fabricated and that there is no evidence Sallust ever married, referring to this passage by Jerome as "a late fable."[79]

Regardless of his marital status, it seems Sallust did not have male offspring, because a grandson of his sister inherited his estate as well as perhaps his name through testamentary adoption.[80] This second Sallustius Crispus, commemorated in an ode by Horace, figured in the court of Augustus as a counselor of the ruler.[81] Although neither a senator nor a consul, Tacitus furnished him an obituary in A.D. 20, among the earliest in the *Annals*, equating him with Maecenas, for both were ministers and custodians of the "secreta imperatorum," and neither kept the favor of his master to the end—such was the fate of power and influence.[82]

Like his great uncle, Sallustius Crispus II had no male issue, and so he adopted the son of L. Passienus Rufus who, taking the name C. Sallustius Crispus Passienus, likely inherited his estate.[83] This heir was a consul under both Tiberius and Claudius and made two important marriages, the first with Domitia, granddaughter of Marcus Antonius and Octavia, and after divorcing Domitia, with her sister-in-law Agrippina. When Passienus died around A.D. 47, having the honor of a public funeral, Agrippina, along with her son (the future emperor Nero) by her former marriage, must have inherited her husband's wealth.[84] With her later marriage to her great uncle Claudius, and her son's accession to the throne, it is reasonable to assume that these Sallustian estates passed into the imperial family at least by the time of Nero (A.D. 54–68), the first emperor mentioned to have stayed there.[85]

Others, however, believe two inscriptions imply that these gardens came into imperial hands perhaps as early as Tiberian times. A marble plinth for a bronze statue was found in the presumed confines of the *horti Sallustiani* inscribed, LACO • PRAEF • VIG • XIII, which must refer to P. Graecinius Laco, praefect under Tiberius and procurator in Gallia under Claudius.[86] If this statue were indeed erected in the gardens contemporary with its creation, it could be evidence that by the time of Tiberius, the gardens were already imperial property, perhaps having been bequeathed to Tiberius by Crispus rather than to his adopted son Passienus Crispus.[87] There is, however, no reported archaeological context for this inscribed plinth and the size is small (0.23 meters × 0.45 meters), and so it could have been easily transported there from its original location.[88]

A second inscription is dedicated to the deceased *Coetus Herodianus praegustator divi Augusti,* who thereafter became a *vilicus* (manager) in the *horti Sallustiani,* datable usually to 22 but possibly as late as A.D. 42.[89] It seems reasonable that Herodianus, having been in service to the emperor, would find later employment in the imperial household, but this is not assured. Indeed, if this inscription can be dated to A.D. 42, the gardens of Sallust at that time were likely in the hands of L. Passienus Crispus, who was married to the emperor's niece Agrippina and who could have hired Herodianus as a guardian of his property. Regardless of how these inscriptions are to be interpreted to provide evidence of the date that the *horti Sallustiani* came into imperial hands, it is clear these gardens became imperial properties sometime under the Julio-Claudians (likely under Nero) and persisted as luxurious imperial holdings up to at least the early fourth century.[90] Vespasian is said to have preferred them to those of the Palatine, and Nerva reportedly died there in A.D. 98.[91] Like Vespasian, Aurelian (ca. A.D. 270) spent much time in them, and he is believed to have built there a so-called *porticus miliarensis,* where he liked to exercise horses.[92]

What the Sallustian gardens looked like during the original ownership is speculative, although the reported opulence of them during Sallust's time is perhaps exaggerated. Syme, among others, has suggested that the elder Sallust was sympathetic to the precepts of Epicurus, denouncing ease and luxury, but that his adopted son flaunted his wealth, living in monumental splendor in the *horti Sallustiani.*[93] Tacitus explained that the young Crispus approached extravagance not only in his personal refinements but also in his generous lifestyle. It is therefore likely that he, rather than his uncle, made the gardens opulent.[94] Indeed, the only testimony that can be employed to suggest that Sallustius, the historian, lived in luxury is in Pseudo-Cicero (*In Sallustium* 7.19), where it is stated that Sallust "bought the most expensive gardens, the villa of Gaius Caesar at Tiburtum and other possessions." But as Syme pointed out, Sallust's strictures on "domus atque villas . . . would show a singular measure of inadvertence or hypocrisy."[95] It is perhaps safe to say that the fame of these gardens and perhaps even their name are the result of Crispus rather than of his famous uncle, Sallust.

Only after Sallust's death and the eventual passing of the property to the imperial family were the gardens developed into the most beautiful in Rome. It is likely that later authors critical of Sallust's career equated the luxurious imperial gardens, which were still called those of Sallust, with these later gardens, because of his reported avarice and extortion of money from Numidia.[96] As Syme pointed out, Sallust was not on the list of those proscribed under the Triumvirs, and there "is no sign that [he] was molested."[97] Indeed, Sallust spent his final years in his villa and gardens outside the porta Collina until his death only four years before the fateful battle of Actium (31 B.C.), writing his histories and attempting to shield his earlier demagoguery in Numidia.[98] Under these circumstances, it is unlikely that Sallust, even if he were able, would have flaunted his wealth with luxurious gardens.

IMPERIAL PROPERTIES

Sallust's private garden, although later considered one of the most beautiful in Rome, was at first only one among other luxury estates ringing the periphery of the city that came into imperial hands through inheritance, confiscation, or usurpation (Fig. 1.2).[99] For example, the gardens of Pompey, in the Campus Martius and perhaps on the slopes of the Pincio, given by Caesar to Anthony, came into the hands of Augustus after Actium.[100] Caligula received by inheritance the gardens of Agrippina in the area of the Vatican, which later passed to Nero, who was probably buried there.[101] It is reported that before his adoption, Marcus Aurelius lived with his mother in the gardens where he was born and that he had inherited from his father, the *horti Anniani,* perhaps on the Caelian.[102]

Claudius confiscated the old gardens of Lucullus in

A.D. 46 and gained possession of the *horti Tauriani* in A.D. 53, after Agrippina accused their owner of practicing magic.[103] Only four years before, the *horti Lolliani*, laid out in Augustan times by M. Lollius and inherited by his granddaughter Lollia Paullina, were transferred to imperial ownership after her suicide in A.D. 49.[104] Nero confiscated the gardens of Seneca after the latter's murder in A.D. 65[105] and came into possession of the *horti Pallantiani* only after Pallas, who was the owner, was put to death under orders of the emperor.[106] Likewise, Torquatus Silanus was forced to commit suicide in A.D. 64, allowing Nero to make use of his property for construction of a branch of the *Aqua Claudia* that began *ad Spem veterem,* near these gardens.[107] According to Frontinus, a number of aqueducts met *post hortos Pallantianos,* that is, in the vicinity of Spes Vetus (area of the Porta Maggiore); the Arcus Caelimontani, probably a work under Nero, carried this branch of the *Aqua Claudia* to the northwest corner of the hill behind the Temple of the Divine Claudius.[108] These gardens appear to have remained in imperial hands because Elagabulus (A.D. 218–222) occasionally stayed *in hortis Spei veteris.*[109]

These properties therefore, unless perhaps inherited legitimately, appear to have continued as imperial lands rather than passing to members of the former imperial family. For example, it seems to have been assumed Vespasian would inherit all the imperial wealth of the Julio-Claudians.[110] That these were private estates, however, rather than state controlled is clear because they could be dismantled and even sold by the reigning emperor. Under the Flavians and the Antonines the Domus Aurea was destroyed, but the Esquiline gardens beyond the "Servian" wall were kept intact, as were those of Sallust.[111] Pliny reported that Trajan sold off a large portion of his imperial gardens, and it is also likely, as in the case of the gardens of the Domus Aurea, that other imperial *horti* (perhaps Caesar's along the Tiber) were annexed for public construction.[112]

PLANTINGS IN GARDEN ESTATES

It was clearly in the interest of the emperor to obtain private properties and to transform them into luxurious estates. Not only were buildings likely torn down and others reerected, but the plantings themselves must have been likewise changed and continuously rearranged according to individual and contemporary tastes. The natural transformations of the plantings as well as the accumulation and rearrangement of the manmade objects within a garden, therefore, do not permit a single, unique reconstruction. Just as Horace explained that an architectural enthusiast (an *aedificator*) thought nothing of pulling down his house and putting it back up again to change right angles into curves, so the garden was also a flexible backdrop to be reinterpreted and readapted according to taste.[113] Furthermore, trees, plants, and shrubs could be considered extensions of architectural members, which were believed by Vitruvius to have had their origins in such natural materials.[114] For example, in a large garden surrounded by colonnades in the villa of Poppaea at Oplontis, set in the soil in front of each column were planting pots, which may have been for vines.[115] Such pots could have been the norm, at least for most plantings within an architectural setting. As such, these potted plants could have been relatively easily replaced according to taste as well as to seasons. That such devices were employed in the gardens of Sallust seems clear by four small vases with four holes in the sides and one in the bottom. Found in the area of the Ministry of Agriculture near the via delle Finanze (property of the former villino Spithoever), these must be planting jars employed in the gardens of Sallust.[116]

Vitruvius also explained, in essentially his only mention of a country villa, that the luxury parts could be constructed according to rules of symmetry given for urban buildings but in such a way that there was no obstruction to rustic practicalities.[117] It is likely, therefore, that the plans of a luxury villa and gardens took their lead from the urban landscape of formal gardens, right angles, colonnades, and axial views.

The ideas of nature and artifice merged in the garden, where trees or shrubs could become columns and where vines entwined "real" columns that appeared to be trunks of trees—a conceit shown clearly in landscape paintings where single freestanding columns are entwined by trees.[118] Arbor-trellises formed ceilings, and owners raised tapestries (with architectural designs?) between rows of trees that acted like walls.[119] Even statues may have resembled columns, particularly when placed in rows and all the same type. Domitian's villa at Castel Gandolfo provides one example, where four replicas of the "Pouring Satyr" type were all likely displayed together.[120] The repetitive appearance of such statues must have deliberately echoed rows of columns, lending an almost symbiotic relationship between architecture and sculpture.

Yet the marble statues that filled the "natural" environments, with their hard material and frozen positions, were in contrast to the flexible and kinetic vines that surrounded them. It is clear that one of Cicero's brother's villas, for instance, included *horti* that were, at least, partially landscaped, for he praises his gardener who "has so enveloped everything with ivy, not only the foundation wall of the villa, but also the spaces between the columns of the promenade, that I declare the Greek statues seem to be landscape gardeners themselves offering their ivy for sale."[121]

Although these ivy-covered statues may have appeared to be lifelike, many of those discovered in garden settings are under life-size. The distinction of these images from reality would have been obvious (although as images of animate objects, they were too small to be "real") because they stood silent and static amongst living and rustling plantings. Likewise, the herm-form employed for portraits of famous men, particularly philosophers and writers, could not be mistaken as "real" individuals. Yet their "presences," as will be discussed, were most certainly evoked.[122] It is interesting to note in this context that in Georgian England, men would be hired to pose as hermits within the rustic follies of country estates to heighten the realism of garden settings, and it is tempting to imagine that similar activities may have taken place in ancient gardens.[123] Indeed, Tacitus reported the employing of human theatrical props in Nero's gardens as a grotesque scene of Christians dressed in animal skins being butchered by wild dogs.[124] Such

an incident likely took place in a "wild," although completely contrived, landscape planted to evoke the countryside, as known to have been part of the gardens of Nero's Domus Aurea in Rome. It is unlikely, however, that such "natural" environments were part of the formal plantings of most imperial gardens.

For the *horti Sallustiani* there is unfortunately no direct evidence to suggest how these were planted, save for an intriguing boundary stone discovered in the sixteenth century by Angelo Colocci not far from his *vigne* (literally "vineyards," but in this context meaning gardens possessing grape arbors) on the Pincio— likely within the confines of the ancient gardens. The inscription may refer to a circular garden allée (*gestatio,* a driveway for litter-borne outings?) and a garden pavilion (*diaeta*) in these ancient gardens: GESTATIO CIRCINI, EXTERIOR A DIETA. APOLLINIS AD DIETAM EANDEM. IN CIRCVITV. P. CCLXXVII. FFF. VII. M. P. II. ET. P. XVIIII. GESTATIO INTER A DIETA EAND. IN CIRCVITV. P. FFF. V. P. E. LX. M. P. XIII.[125] This *gestatio* appears to have been laid out in two concentric circular paths measuring two hundred and one hundred feet in circumference, presumably different from that at Pliny's Tuscan villa, which was in the shape of a circus bordered by box trees and small hedges.[126]

Apart from the above inscription, which does not mention the *horti Sallustiani*, we must rely primarily on the descriptions of other similar garden estates to obtain any picture of the Sallustian gardens. It is likely that grapevines existed there because the rampart of Servius Tullius (which probably served originally as the southern limits of the garden) was elsewhere considered a good place for vineyards, and the natural slopes of the Pincio and Quirinal may have been ideal for the cultivation of these vines.[127] Indeed, grapevines may have been essential elements in virtually every garden not only for their shade over walkways but perhaps more importantly for their juice. Pliny noted that a single vine in the colonnades of Livia at Rome protected the open walks with its shady trellises and at the same time annually produced twelve amphorae of juice.[128] Offering guests wine from one's own production was a source of pride, even at extravagant parties, and perhaps countered, to a certain extent, Augustus' campaign against the "sterility" of *luxuria*.[129] For example, in the luxury garden of Maecenas on the Esquiline, viticulture played an important part in its fame, as attested by Pliny's remark: In mediterraneo [there is] vero Caesenatia ac Maecenatiana (wines).[130]

Oak trees were associated with vineyards to such an extent that Dionysos, god of the vine, was sometimes called "Phegaleus," from *phegus* (fagus), oak.[131] In *Elegiae in Maecenatem* 1.33 it is stated that Maecenas loved "a shady oak tree" in his *horti* on the Esquiline, which itself was said by Varro to have been named after the plantings of *aesculi* ("oaks") by king Servius Tullius and where existed a "Larum Querquetulanum sacellum" (a shrine of the Oak Grove Lares).[132] Lares and Nymphs were venerated together in Italy to the point that they sometimes inhabit the same sacred location.[133] Nymphs called "Querquetulanae virae" on the Esquiline[134] may have been therefore a part of this shrine of the Lares.[135]

Furthermore, nymphs were believed to protect bees, which were associated with oaks,[136] and so we can imagine beehives as part of the "natural" landscape of the *horti* as well as sources of honey, much as grapevines could both serve as decorative displays and be productive.[137] Indeed, like grapevines and bees, birds on estates could be kept in enclosures and fattened for market, while others could be kept only for pleasure.[138]

Along with the oak tree preferred by Maecenas in his gardens are mentioned *nymphae cadentes* ("falling waters"). The generic term "nymphaeum," deriving from the Greek, is usually applied by modern scholars to such places, even though, as pointed out by Grimal, this probably referred only to sacred places, for it is never used by Frontinus in his *Aqueducts of Rome*.[139] For Maecenas such sacred associations with falling waters perhaps prompted him to recline there to compose verse, where he is called "a jay among birds" ("sederat argutas garrulus inter aves"). The equating of Maecenas with the jay bird, which was known for imitating voices and sounds, was perhaps to allude to Maecenas' imitation of his fellow poets. It is pertinent that the jay feeds predominantly on acorns (Maecenas sits under an oak), which it buries in the ground in great numbers and of which ancient authors were well aware.[140]

Among the sounds of singing birds and rushing streams was an ideal location for not only poetic composition but for intimate conversation, as acknowledged by the Epicurean Atticus, who was relieved that such an environment allowed him not to be overheard by his fellow disciples.[141] Furthermore, the seeking out of shade under a tree is a standard Ciceronian device of introducing a conversation.[142] In *De Re Rustica*, Varro and a friend, the senator Q. Axius, seek shade in the *Villa Publica* in the Campus Martius.[143] There, meeting up with others seated on a bench, Axius asks, "Will you accept us into your aviary?" This was an obvious pun on the augur, Appius Claudius Pulcher, who was present, and on the chattering conversation taking place under the shade of a tree.[144] In this case, it is likely that the trees in the *Villa Publica* were plane trees, which were first brought into Roman gardens from the east, as reported by Pliny. He was astonished by "the fact that a tree has been introduced from an alien world just for its shadow."[145] Statius even composed a birthday poem to Atedius Melior, giving a fanciful reason for the peculiar shape of a plane tree that grew beside a lake on his patron's estate on the Caelian hill.[146] Cicero confirmed that trees in general were valuable. He explained that when Gabinius looted his Tusculan villa, it was not only of its art and furniture but also of its trees.[147]

Districts on the Quirinal were sometimes designated by names such as *Ad malum Punicum* (pomegranate), *Ad nucem* (nut), and *Ad pirum* (pear), which must indicate the presence of such trees, but whether these or the nonindigenous plane tree were in the *horti Sallustiani* is uncertain.[148] The plane tree itself, however, was not the only element introduced from the east. The cultural parvenus in their vast estates attempted to recreate the philosophical gardens of Athens and the erudition of Alexandria by replacing the agoras, palaestras, and gymnasia of the Greeks with evocative names of country pavilions.[149] Beyond a stream and ponds and through an aviary of singing birds enclosed by nets between rows of columns, for example, Varro worked and kept a library in his *Museum,* a name derived from the famous Ptolemaic library in Alexandria. Likewise, at Cicero's Tusculan estate were an *Academia* and a *Lyceum,* which presumably evoked these Athenian institutions even though by his day they had disappeared (the result of the Mithridatic wars and Sulla's sack). At his villa in Arpinum, Cicero was also eager to imitate Atticus' *Amaltheum* in Epirus, probably a grotto shaded with plane trees in imitation perhaps of a sanctuary to the nymphs who nourished Zeus.[150]

This idea in Roman landscape architecture of evoking another place was embedded in the Roman phrase, *ars topiaria* (place art), from which we derive the more limited meaning of carefully trimmed hedges. Among these are the ones at the Younger Pliny's Tuscan estate, where box shrubs were shaped into letters to spell out not only the proprietor's name but that of his gardener.[151] According to Pliny, such *opus topiarium* (ornamental gardenwork) was invented by C. Matius, a friend of Augustus, but such clever trimming of shrubs was only one small part of the works of a Roman *topiarius* (essentially the landscape gardener), who dealt with all kinds of ornamental plants, called *viridia* ("green things").[152]

The location of such green things was known as a *viridiarium* that, at least conceptually, if not physically, ought not to be confused with a *hortus*.[153] *Viridiaria* are identified in the garden stadium of Hadrian's Villa at Tivoli and known at Varro's aviary. A peristyle *viridiarium* has been identified at the villa of Herod the Great near Jericho, which may be one of the balsam groves mentioned in literary sources.[154] In Rome, Gordian (A.D. 238–244) is said to have envisioned building a *viridiarium* in the Campus Martius, planted with laurel, myrtle, and box trees enclosed by parallel porticoes one thousand feet long and with a mosaic of equal length in the middle, flanked by short columns with statuettes.[155]

Clearly, *viridia,* architecture, and decorative displays were not considered separated from each other but equal partners in the creation of an outdoor environment. It is all the more lamentable, therefore, that while at least a portion of the inanimate elements of the ancient gardens of Sallust has survived, we are left with not a single piece of evidence concerning their plantings: neither the more formal and potentially changeable *viridia,* nor the more permanent and rustic trees and wild shrubs and flowers that must have been a part of this extraordinary estate.

There is, however, indirect physical evidence for the plantings in the gardens of Sallust in the form of numerous conduits, cisterns, and reservoirs that supplemented the natural stream in the valley and led Lanciani to declare that these gardens were well supplied with water.[156] Waterpipes, according to Lanciani, have been found bearing the names of Claudius (A.D. 41–54), Trajan (A.D. 98–117), Severus Alexander (A.D. 222–235), and Valentinian (A.D. 364–375), and the periods of their rules must have been when the watering of the gardens was at its height and therefore when the garden plantings were their most spectacular.[157] In particular, the gardens may have reached their peak under Severus Alexander, who reestablished imperial power and massive building campaigns in the city.[158]

Excavators have also identified several reservoirs, including a two-hundred-meter one running parallel with the via XX Settembre,[159] another found in the former riding grounds of the king's guards near the vicolo di S. Nicola da Tolentino,[160] and a third discovered in 1888, according to Lanciani, under the Casino dell'Aurora (*FUR* 9, 10: Fig. 1.1C–D).[161] Two years before was recorded, a short distance from the Casino dell'Aurora (during the demolition of a small building called a "coffeehouse"), an ancient nymphaeum piscina, very well constructed in brick in the form of a semicircle and measuring 14.80 meters in diameter.[162]

Lugli reported a cistern or fountain near S. Nicola da Tolentino, south of the former vicolo del Falcone (present via Barberini), as still visible in his day (1930s) under the Germano-Hungarian College.[163] This ancient building, an impressive structure two stories high, was composed of four parallel corridors, communicating in the middle by arches and covered by vaults. This must be the structure recorded on *FUR* 9 (Fig. 1.1C) directly south of the fountain that Lanciani recorded as east of the vicolo S. Nicola da Tolentino (near the "Servian" wall).[164]

Another cistern consisting of three rooms each 4.45 meters × 4 meters was discovered during the building in 1922 of the Palazzo dell'Istituto Nazionale Assicurazioni, which is located on the former Muti (and the later villa Massimo di Rignano) property between the via Sallustiana and the via Friuli. Although not included on *FUR* 9, it may be identified, at least in part, with the "parietinae a Nollio descriptae" reported by Lanciani.[165]

Finally, three *castella,* probably to be associated with the *Aquae Marcia, Tepula,* and *Julia,* were found during construction of the Ministry of Finance on the Quirinal.[166] On the Pincio are reported other water reservoirs, the remains of which have not been identified.[167] It seems clear that the watering of such a vast garden was critical, requiring the almost continuous laying of pipe and the building of reservoirs and cisterns.

But these garden estates were more than the physical aspects of obtaining water, creating plantings, building villas, and commissioning various forms of decorations; they were manifestations of cultural attitudes towards private tastes and public displays. Such *horti* imply, therefore, a way of thinking about oneself, one's family, and one's position within society.

THE *Hortus* AS SELF-DISPLAY

The precise appearance of these imperial *horti* is difficult to determine, and even the word *horti* can take on different meanings depending on context. *Hortus* originally meant a vegetable garden, but at least during the empire, the term was associated with pleasure gardens, farms, and country houses in the city itself. According to Pliny, they had their origins in "that instructor in leisure activities Epicurus, at Athens: until his time there had not been any custom of living in the country in the town."[168] *Horti,* particularly near the center of Rome, signified then not merely gardens but an estate. To a contemporary Latin speaker, the word would have raised the image of one of the famous pleasure gardens encircling the city, a peri-urban estate, as defined by Purcell.[169] Lying outside the "Servian" wall, these garden estates must be called suburban; yet, in the minds of certain ancient authors, this ring of greenery around Rome was distinguished from the land that lay beyond: the true *suburbium.*[170] Still, that which made the suburb a place where the wealthy could enjoy a respite from the crowded, unhealthy, and busy city for a life of *amoenitas* (visual pleasure), *salubritas* (healthiness), and *otium* (leisure) could be said as well for the nearer *horti.* Indeed, these *horti* just outside the circuit wall offered their owners the added benefit of proximity to the city, a necessity for any good suburban property.[171]

Suburban *horti* clearly served the dual purposes of separation from the city and of gathering places for friends and associates, to such an extent that Pliny the Younger pretended to prefer his Tuscan villa over those of Tibur, Praeneste, and Tusculum because neighbors were not constantly dropping by.[172] Although leisure was a priority of suburban life, it did not mean *quies* (rest from labor), for as Symmachus pointed out,

"I am in the country, but I am not rusticating."[173] In particular, literary society flourished on country estates because *otium* seems to have been a prerequisite for such activity.[174] Furthermore, although the two spheres of *otium* (leisure) and *negotium* (business) are usually distinguished by suburban villa and urban *domus,* politics could not be abandoned while away from the civic center. It even has been claimed that much of the normal business of the empire was conducted from such estates on the outskirts of the city.[175] Horace implied this seemingly schizophrenic aspect of the suburban villa as both a place of retreat and a place of business. He wrote that a Roman did not know whether he wanted to be a town mouse or a country mouse; when in one, he longed to be in the other.[176] Although the suburban retreat was surely quieter than the city *domus,* it was far from private, and the personal *amoenitas*—the art galleries, libraries, and gardens—was not meant only for one's own pleasure but perhaps even more for that of the visitors.

In addition, it was probably in the *horti* and *suburbana* of the late Republic where most of the marble originals as well as other works of art brought to Rome as war booty ended up.[177] According to Varro, people went to Lucullus' villas just to see his picture galleries, and Cicero claimed that one could go to Tusculum to see art treasures.[178] Pliny singled out the *horti Serviliani* (probably by his time a public park on the slopes of the Aventine or perhaps in the area of the Vatican), where one could see marble statues by well-known Greek sculptors such as Praxiteles and Skopas.[179] Yet private ancient Roman gardens seem not to have been places for the display of "museum quality" works of sculpture.[180] That is, the important collections worthy of literary comment were all in public places, either in temple precincts or in porticoes, and it is noteworthy that Pliny never mentioned famous bronze sculptures in gardens. Although Cicero indicated that art treasures could only be seen in the suburban *horti,* he also stated that the true "art museums" were in the *Porticus Metelli,* the *Porticus Catuli,* and the *Aedes Felicitatis,* the last containing the treasures of Mummius.[181] Indeed, there were so many statues and paintings in public places in Rome that Cicero claimed both the rich and the poor could enjoy art treasures.[182] Some of these statues and paintings, borrowed from clients and even sanctuaries, were put on temporary exhibition by aediles attempting to outdo each other in extravagant public displays.[183]

At least in literary references concerning private art collections, large-scale sculptures are not mentioned as much as paintings, toreutic art (probably small bronzes known as *corinthia*), and even glass.[184] In this context it is not surprising that artifacts were held in high esteem and proudly displayed in public and private garden contexts. Typical were the *horti* of Caesar, where, according to Pausanias, in the public Sanctuary of Bacchus was the tusk of the Calydonian boar, brought to Rome by Augustus along with a statue that was set up in the Forum Augustum.[185] Augustus seemed particularly fond of such artifacts, for we hear that at his park on Capri were displayed arms of ancient heroes as well as a collection of "giant's bones" (*gigantum ossa*), the skeletons of extinct animals.[186]

The display of the past in all its forms (oddities such as bones or ancient armor, as well as copies of old sculptures, and sculptural tableaux of ancient myths) rather than "contemporary" images was the aim. A case in point is Pliny's listing of statues (called *monumenta*) in the garden of Asinius Pollio that includes Maenads, Thyiads and Caryatids, Sileni, Centaurs carrying Nymphs by Arkesilaos, Muses by Helikon, Nymphs by Stephanos, double busts of Hermes and Eros, and a Dirke group by Apollonios and Tauriskos, as well as images of gods (Apollo, Neptune, Venus, Jupiter).[187] According to Neudecker, Pollio's assemblage probably was typical and may have "satisfied the emotional longing for a mythological garden landscape of the *aurea aetas.*"[188]

Although commonly on private property, these displays could have been, at least on special occasions,

open to the public. In the *horti Caesaris,* downstream from the city on the right bank of the Tiber (in the district now called Monteverde), a year before Caesar entertained Cleopatra there in 44 B.C., he had held a grand *salutatio* (ceremonial visit) for the plebs; after his death, he willed his gardens to the people of Rome. These gardens, like those of Verres, must have been well stocked with art works, because Marcus Antonius is said to have taken many objects (*ornamenta*) from there and to have divided them between the gardens of Pompey and the villa Scipionis, both of which were in his possession.[189]

How much and how often this material was open to the public is impossible to determine. Clearly, "private" collections of sculptures were sometimes meant to be put on semipublic display, as demonstrated by Pollio's, which was exhibited in perhaps a specially constructed "museum," for he was anxious to attract sightseers.[190] Even private villas at Tusculum and elsewhere could be visited to see art treasures. Cicero pointed out that the famous statues in Heius' chapel at Messana could be seen daily.[191] There may have been a feeling in this period that the public had certain rights of access to works of art, and it was said that Agrippa even wished to nationalize all such works.[192] These collections, therefore, must have carried great influence over public taste, even more than so-called State Art.

As Isager suggested, sculptural friezes, which must have constituted a large portion of State Art, "did not belong in any of the traditional categories, for by sculpture is only understood [by Pliny as] free-standing, three-dimensional sculpture."[193] Such public collections were deemed so important that in A.D. 74 the emperor Vespasian, interrupting "normal" procedures, took the office of censor, whose duty was the safekeeping of these public treasures. Among these treasures, freestanding sculpture was probably preeminent because, as Strong pointed out, the only new official to come out of the reforms of the fourth century A.D. was the *curator statuarum.*[194]

Indeed, according to Roman law, *ornamenta* were protected primarily to ensure the preservation of state monuments, but this protection also extended to the private sector. Certain works of art, therefore, were defined by law as being integral parts of the house proper. For example, *sigilla* (little figures or images) and *statuae adfixae* (attached or fixed statues or images) were considered part of the *ornamenta* of the house, as were statues in niches (those *inhaerent parietibus*).[195] A practical result of such laws was that houses were sometimes purchased to gain the *ornamenta* they contained.[196] In this way, new villa owners could obtain sculptural collections for their newly formed *horti*, including even some pieces that were not always suitable for the new owner, such as certain imperial or private portraits.[197] For example, the gardens of Regulus near the Tiber were filled with statues of himself, which likely would not have been valued by a new owner.[198]

After the death of a villa owner, it was not unusual that with the division of inheritance, at least some property was auctioned, including sculptures and other works of art not considered by law to be *ornamenta*.[199] When Domitius Tullus died, his widow inherited the villa. The collection of sculptures, however, was auctioned, and the emperor Tiberius purchased paintings as well as an Egyptian statue.[200] According to Neudecker, such auctions may have been one means by which owners of newly formed *horti* obtained the apparently vast number of sculptures necessary for their decoration.[201] Other means of obtaining private sculptures could be as gifts, particularly during the Saturnalia, or through lawsuits, looting during fires, and theft.[202] Furthermore, Nero cast lots for paintings and, according to Pliny, L. Seius Strabo, who was praefect of Egypt, willed to Tiberius an obsidian statue of Menelaos, which Tiberius later returned to Heliopolis.[203] Even emperors such as Titus and Marcus Aurelius are known to have had auctions of art works (lasting as long as two months and including robes, goblets, jewels, as well as statues and paintings) from their personal storerooms to obtain ready-cash in emergencies.[204]

Regardless of how such sculptural collections were assembled, the adornment with statues of a private garden was a personal act reflecting the character of its owner more than could any public collection, even one assembled by an individual such as Mummius or Pollio. Tastefully displayed sculptures were a necessity, reflecting the social status of their owners. We are informed that Damasippus, who was perhaps from the Junius family, owned substantial gardens along the Tiber, and he seems to have been a specialist in designing such gardens for others.[205]

Although one may have employed a Damasippus, a man's house and gardens, like his manner of speech, was an extension of his personality. Seneca expressed this thought, as did Cicero in his remarks on Caesar's sculptural collection, which revealed not only the taste of the dictator but his fate.[206] Cicero himself, who revered Plato above all others, had a statue of this philosopher (probably a copy after a statue of Plato sculpted by Silanion and commissioned by the Persian Mithridates for the Mouseion of the Academy) in his gardens, where his friends would gather.[207] Similarly, in the gardens of Atticus stood a portrait of Aristotle beside which he would have philosophical conversations with his friend Cicero.[208]

These sculptures served dual purposes: as reflections of the philosophical leanings of their owners and as physical "participants" in philosophical conversations that would take place near them. Seneca indicated such statues were used "to kindle enthusiasm" for these great men.[209] They were, like most images in villas, both private statements and public displays. But such statues of Greek philosophers in suburban settings also reflected the general pursuit of Greek culture that at least in the late Republican period, could take place perhaps only outside the city.[210]

A garden estate was clearly not only a physical manifestation of the owner's social and political standings, or philosophical leanings but a potential source of his immortality. The *domus* could publicly advertise the owner's glory as effectively as or even more effectively than an inscribed name on the architrave of a temple. After one's death, a grand estate could retain the name of its former owner, just as temples sometimes were referred to after their founders rather than for the divinity to which they were dedicated.[211] In the case of the gardens of Sallust, these seem never to have lost the name of the original owner. Even in the Middle Ages, the district was called "Sallustricum," and in the sixteenth century, it was known in common parlance as "Salustrico."[212] Perhaps accounting for the interest in his gardens during these times was the importance of Sallust's historical writings in the medieval and Renaissance periods.[213]

It is not surprising, therefore, that the Roman garden, reflecting one's life and anticipating the preservation of one's memory, could serve as the final resting place after death and that monumental tombs on villa properties were characteristic features already by the second century B.C.[214] Such burials, at least in the Republican period, however, did not have to be in suburban gardens. Tombs in the city on private property were an ancient custom reserved for patrician families until imperial times, when this right was reserved for only the emperor and the vestals.[215] Indeed, when Lucullus died in 56 B.C. not only was he honored with a public ceremony, but the people requested he have a tomb in the Campus Martius. His family, however, declined this offer, opting to bury their relative at Tusculum in a tomb perhaps already constructed.[216]

The impulse to bury in private gardens may relate to the Greek world that conflated the Hesperides with the concept of Elysion as super-terrestrial paradises, where dead heroes, such as Herakles, blissfully existed in gardens.[217] Such tombs could have been erected during one's lifetime, as advised by the Younger Pliny after his visit to the monument, still incomplete after nine years, of Verginius Rufus on his estate at Alsium.[218]

It may have been common to visit a country estate to see the tomb of a well-known individual that ensured the preservation of his name for later generations. Seneca visited the tomb of Scipio Africanus, which may have been in the gardens of Scipio's country estate. Cicero was determined to preserve the memory of his daughter Tullia with the addition of a cenotaph in his private gardens.[219] Emperors, particularly those who were unpopular at their deaths and not given public honors, were sometimes buried in private gardens. Caligula's tomb was in the *horti Lamiani,* probably on the Esquiline, and Galba, who was murdered in the Roman forum, was buried in private gardens.[220] Likewise, Nero owned the gardens of the Domitii, and it is likely where the nurses Egloge and Alexandria buried him.[221] On the other hand, it is possible that Vespasian, who was honored at his death, was buried in, or at least near, the *horti Sallustiani.* According to Suetonius, Domitian converted his father's house on the Quirinal into the Temple of the Flavians with the intention of it serving as a family mausoleum.[222] Vespasian likely considered the Sallustian gardens a part

of his family home, which may account for his spending considerable time there and perhaps even being buried nearby. These monumental burials on country estates were common until the second century, when after a plague, Marcus Aurelius forbade the building of such tombs: a regulation that remained in effect until the fourth century.[223]

Although any mention has been lost, it is likely that Sallust, like Maecenas, was buried on his own estate and that his heirs were expected to maintain his tomb.[224] The only recorded human burials in the *horti Sallustiani,* however, are curious ones during Augustan times: the corpses of two very tall individuals, Pusio and Secundilla, kept amazingly well preserved in the *conditorium Sallustianorum hortorum.* Two hundred years later, Solinus said they were still on view in this same *conditorium*—probably a display casket of some sort.[225] In the 1550s in the presumed confines of these ancient gardens was found the skull of a man of very large size who was argued to be one of these very "giants" mentioned by Pliny.[226] Such identification is not surprising because the discovery of oversized human burials commonly led to the identification of superhumans even in antiquity. Among these were two chests of unusual size discovered at the foot of the Janiculum, one supposedly containing the body of King Numa.[227] In a similar fashion, over a millennium later, in 1191, abbots at Glastonbury discovered the remains of a very large man and a woman, whom they named "King Arthur and Guinevere."[228]

A burial in the Sallustian gardens even more unusual than those of Pusio and Secundilla was that of a lightning bolt. A now-lost inscription, reported by Visconti as found around 1883 in the gardens of Sallust, reads FVLGVR CONDITV, physical evidence of a ritual called *fulgur condere* or *fulgur sacrum condere* (to establish a lightning strike [as sacred]), in which the ground struck by lightning is enclosed by four low walls and made sacred usually with the sacrificing of a lamb (*bidens*). Such a structure is usually called, therefore, a *bidental* but also a *puteal* because of its similarity to a parapet wall surrounding the opening of a well.[229] If this lightning burial was indeed in the gardens of Sallust, it is likely to have been on one of its two hills (the Pincio or the Quirinal) that were most vulnerable to lightning strikes. Indeed, as already discussed, according to the fourth-century historian Julius Obsequens, in 17 B.C. a tower near the porta Collina *was* struck by lightning.[230]

This tower may well have been part of the Sallustian gardens because from a similar tower in the gardens of Maecenas, Nero watched the fire of A.D. 64, and another tower is known at Tiberius' Villa Iovis on Capri.[231] Such structures were likely on the highest levels of these estates to take advantage of their strategic and aesthetic possibilities.[232] Indeed, Horace described the view of the Alban hills from the gardens of Maecenas on the Esquiline, presumably from a

tower, comparing it to a kind of "skyscraper."[233] Visible from considerable distances, these towers were probably markers of important estates, but their great heights also made them susceptible to lightning strikes.

It is indeed unfortunate that such towers have crumbled and that virtually all the other buildings and most of the sculptures of the gardens of Sallust have disappeared. The post-antique period proved to be devastating for the preservation of the ancient remains, and the centuries have not been kind to the physical memory of this important garden estate.

POST-ANTIQUE PERIOD

Late antique Rome, like other cities in Italy, was composed of numerous islands of habitation surrounded by areas less settled or even abandoned, a phenomenon termed the "regionalisation of urban experience."[234] The Roman Forum became the "Cow Pasture" (Campo Vaccino); the Capitoline Hill was known as "Goat Hill" (Monte Caprino); even the Palatine became deserted ("disabitato") during the later Middle Ages. There is evidence to suggest that many of the buildings on the Palatine had been despoiled or partially buried as early as the fifth century.[235] It is not surprising that the area of the gardens of Sallust was likewise abandoned, although the *Acta martyrum* (official and nonofficial documents relating to the early Christian martyrs) note the existence of a *palatium Sallustii*, a *forum Sallustii*, baths, a tribunal, and a *palatium Constantini* or *Constantii*. Such names, however, cannot be considered reliable, and it is difficult to associate them specifically with any extant physical remains.[236]

Although many ancient remains were most certainly still visible throughout the medieval and early Renaissance periods, the habitation in the area of the former gardens of Sallust was reduced to only several ecclesiastical enclaves. The abandonment of the site was at least partially because the abundant sources of water from the ancient aqueducts, particularly for our discussion that of the *Aqua Alexandrina,* were interrupted by the sixth century. By the second half of the sixteenth century, however, there were numerous

owners of property there, as recorded by Ligorio: "In the Gardens of Sallust are today many *vigne,* among which are those of the reverend fathers of Santo Salvatore del Lauro, of Bishop Muti, of the Bishop of Pavia, of Bishop Colocci, and of Francesco Sibylla, as well as of twenty other owners."[237] These *vigne* (sing. *vigna*) were not merely cultivated vineyards, as the word might first suggest, but properties containing usually a house or other buildings, sometimes used as residences and/or for entertaining guests in a garden setting away from the center of the city.

One of these *vigne* mentioned by Ligorio, that of Angelo Colocci (1474–1549: discoverer of the "gestatio" boundary stone already discussed), is known to have been high up on the Pincio between the porte Collina, Pinciana, and Salaria. Ubaldini, Colocci's biographer in the seventeenth century, writes that Colocci purchased in 1513 property on the Pincio, and there, having built such beautiful houses and gardens, he renewed the magnificence of the ancient gardens of Sallust.[238] Furthermore, as Kultzen and Aldrovandi showed, adjoining the Colocci gardens were those of Stefano del Bufalo all'Acqua Vergine in whose property was an ancient obelisk that will be discussed later.[239] These two contiguous sixteenth-century *vigne,* as well as others on the Pincio, had notable gardens that were likely watered by subterranean streams, but such means of irrigation were to change dramatically with the papal election of Sixtus V (Felice Peretti).[240]

Only eleven days after his inauguration, Sixtus V

Fig. 1.6: Acqua Felice, engraving by G. B. Falda.

signed, on May 5, 1585, a decree to begin the rebuilding of the ancient *Aqua Alexandrina* (constructed by Alexander Severus between A.D. 222 and 225), the source of which was near Palestrina on Colonna property that the pope purchased.[241] Constructed under the guidance of Domenico Fontana, water began to enter the villa Montalto on the Esquiline by October 1586. By March of the following year, a public basin was temporarily erected in front of Santa Susanna. On June 15, 1587, a permanent fountain was inaugurated, and a portion of these waters was used to feed the Medici palace on the Pincio (Fig. 1.6).[242] The aqueduct was renamed Acqua Felice after the pope who created it, and a straight street was laid out from the porta Pia running beside the new fountain and bearing the name Felice (later called the via della Porta Pia and presently the via XX Settembre). Water to the Pincio and to the Quirinal revitalized the entire area. The former ancient gardens again became lush, allowing Torquato Tasso, a contemporary poet (1544–1595), to

declare that these waters restored Rome to its former grandeur under Augustus.[243]

THE LUDOVISI

In 1621, thirty-five years after the building of the Acqua Felice, Alessandro Ludovisi, a Bolognese, became Pope Gregory XV, and his nephew Ludovico (an energetic and intelligent young man of 27) was raised immediately to the status of papal nephew. Gregory, an interim pope between Paul V and the influential and powerful Urban VIII, is regarded perhaps more for the success of this nephew than for his own achievements. Within the two short years of his uncle's papacy, Ludovico increased by leaps and bounds the fortunes of his family, accumulating vast estates in and around Rome and patronizing particularly Bolognese artists such as Domenichino, Guercino, and others.[244]

Within five months of his uncle's election, Ludovico began negotiations for the purchasing of several par-

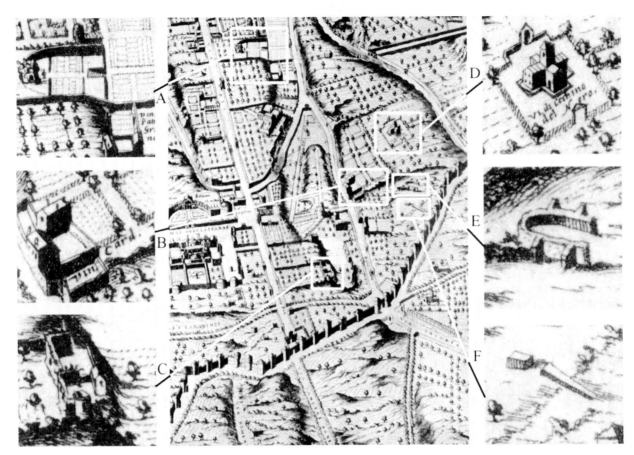

Fig. 1.7: Perspective plan of Rome, by Stefano du Pérac, edited by Antonio Lafréry, 1577. Details:
A: Boccacio **vigna** containing a stadium-shaped garden imbedded into the slopes of the Quirinal hill.
B: "Vin. Card. Ursini."
C: Remains of the so-called vestibule.
D: "Vi. Di Cechino del Nero."
E: U-Shaped building on the Pincio.
F: Broken obelisk on the Pincio.

cels of land on the Pincio. By June 3, 1621, Ludovico had purchased from Cardinal Franceso Maria Bourbon del Monte, for ten thousand *scudi,* a *vigna* and a cruciform-planned casino. This casino is attested on the 1577 Rome plan by Stefano du Pérac (Fig. 1.7D) as having been owned by "Cechino del Nero" (Francesco del Nero), an apostolic secretary.[245]

A month later Cardinal Ludovisi bought from Leonora Cavalcanti, wife of Agostino Maffei, her *vigna* that bordered that of del Nero's to the northeast, and on February 5, 1622, he doubled his land holdings with the addition of the adjacent large *vigna* to the east, owned by Duke Giovanni Antonio Orsini

(Fig. 1.8). The Orsini property also contained, along the via di porta Salaria, a palazzo Grande, which was refurbished by the cardinal and aggrandized by Carlo Maderno with the addition of a large frontispiece in the center of the façade.

In the following year, another *vigna,* adjacent to the east, became available. After the establishment of ownership, it too was purchased by Cardinal Ludovisi from the Carmelite monks of Santa Maria in Traspontina. The extent of the cardinal's property, as depicted by a later engraving by Falda (Fig. 1.9), was about forty-seven acres, extending from the via di porta Pinciana to the via di porta Salaria.

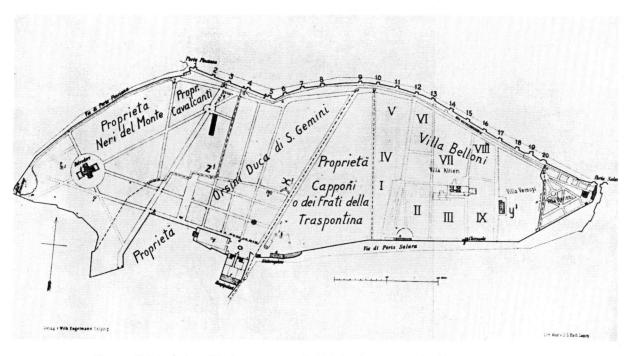

Fig. 1.8: Original plots of Ludovisi property, by T. Schreiber 1880, with additions by Felici 1952.

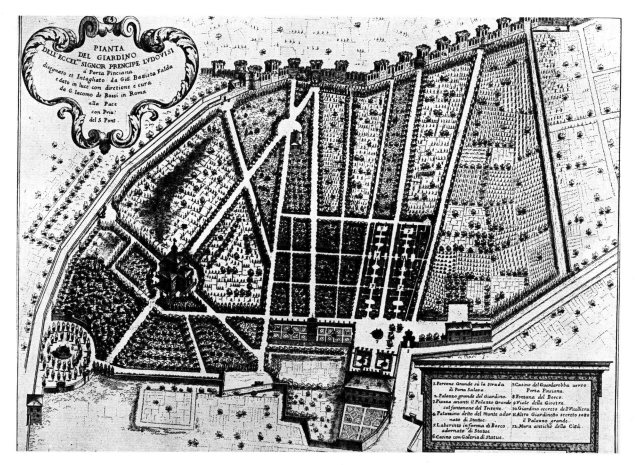

Fig. 1.9: Plan of the gardens of the Ludovisi, by G. B. Falda.

Although it is true that papal nobles, as pointed out by Haskell, "thought of themselves far more as Florentines, Bolognese, or Venetians than as Romans," it is equally true that the newcomer was also interested in integrating himself into Roman society.[246] In particular, one could add to the splendor of Rome and at the same time raise the prestige of the family by completing a new church, but personal expression was embedded in the building of one's villa and its gardens. Ludovico pursued both of these prestigious architectural projects, financing a new church next to the Collegio Romano, the Jesuit College in the heart of the city, and buying nineteen hectares of land on the outskirts of town for the construction of an impressive family villa. It is perhaps not by chance that Ludovico chose land that was known to have been imperial property (that is, the *horti Sallustiani*) and at the same time began assembling possibly the finest collection of antique sculptures ever seen in the city. Following in the footsteps of previous inheritors of papal power from as early as the fifteenth century, this Bolognese family understood that control of antiquities could be an instrument of power.[247]

The collection of antiquities was of course an established prerogative for the aristocratic and learned society of the seventeenth century. By this time, however, the majority of ancient sculptures in Rome had been already uncovered and assembled into family collections like that of the early sixteenth-century Giuliano Cesi, whose "Antiquario" became famous as the oldest assemblage of ancient sculptures to be created especially as a museum space.[248] By the seventeenth century the Cesi family fortune was greatly depleted, and a papal brief of July 16, 1622, allowed Federico, grandson of Giuliano, to sell to Ludovico many of these antiquities—a summary inventory lists over one hundred pieces.

Ludovico was clearly interested in acquiring the Cesi collection not only because of its fame but because of the realization that a proper Roman family needed to have antiquities, particularly sculptures, to adorn its villa. Furthermore, the siting of the new Ludovisi villa on grounds that were known to have been important ancient gardens connected this Bolognese family physically to Rome's imperial past

and permitted the prospect of discovering new works of antiquity literally in one's back yard. For example, *The Dying Gaul* (Fig. 3.15) and *The Suicidal Gaul and 'Wife'* (Fig. 3.16) are two of the well-known statues that are not listed among the inventories of works purchased by the Ludovisi. A logical conclusion from this omission is that these were found on the property by chance in the course of the building of the villa, or in deliberate excavations undertaken to obtain antiquities for the enlargement of the already impressive collection of purchased material. That the area of the villa Ludovisia[249] still contained potential for valuable discoveries is suggested by a clause contained in a rent contract of March 14, 1744, in which the renter, Domenico Marini, promises and is obligated to give to the owner any objects that might be discovered on the property.[250]

The Ludovisi inheritors (who with the marriage of Ippolita Ludovisi to Gregorio Boncompagni in 1681 were now called Boncompagni Ludovisi) did not stop increasing their collections after the seventeenth century. Indeed, they continued to purchase adjoining properties (such as those of the Verospi and the Altieri) and their collections up through the nineteenth century, until they owned ultimately the entire Pincio area of the ancient gardens of Sallust, some twenty-five hectares in total (Fig. 1.8).[251] Presumably, at least some of the material from these smaller collections of adjacent properties came directly from the general area. It is sometimes impossible, however, to separate purchased pieces from those that were actually excavated there.

Many of the Ludovisi sculptures were placed out of doors, and over the years they suffered greatly from weather as well as from deliberate damage (Fig. 1.10).[252] Only after Winckelmann (1717–1763) was the collection as a whole seen as noteworthy, and a gallery in the form of a true museum was established in the former stables, which had housed earlier the library and archives. Permission to visit this museum was not easily granted, and it is not surprising that very few outsiders ever saw the works of art it contained.

Of great importance for the sculptures scattered still in the gardens was the decision made around 1840 to replace the original plan with an English garden.

Fig. 1.10: Casino di Villa Lodovisi presso Porta Pinciana, engraving by G. Vasi.

The labyrinth was removed and along with it numerous sculptures that were placed in the Palazzo Grande or in the Casino dell'Aurora or mostly in the basement under the gallery.[253]

JOSEF SPITHOEVER

The Ludovisi property was entirely on the Pincio, while the valley and the Quirinal slopes were owned by others. In the eighteenth century the valley as well as perhaps part of the slopes of the Quirinal were owned by the Mandosi, as shown on an anonymous city plan of 1775–1777. A later plan dated 1846 by Enrico Salandri (Fig. 1.11) reveals the Mandosi still in the valley (recorded as number 24 on this plan), while the Pincio, between the valley and the later via XX Settembre, was occupied by the "Villa Barberini."[254]

Indeed, an earlier plan of 1668 by Matteo Gregorio de Rossi (Fig. 1.12) records the "Giardino di Barberini," divided into four parterres, on the Quirinal slopes, and this family later owned at least part of the valley where they pastured horses.

Both these properties, the Mandosi and Barberini, were purchased in the nineteenth century by Josef Spithoever (1813–1891), who in 1845 opened the first German bookstore in Rome and began as early as 1859 to purchase property on the Quirinal.[255]

For two decades Spithoever continued to expand his land holdings, buying adjoining properties from the Barberini and the Mandosi, until he owned the entire southern portion of the ancient *horti Sallustiani,* including the valley (Fig. 1.13: detail of plan published by Spithoever). The Spithoever villa and gardens, therefore, occupied the former properties of the Barberini (on the northern slopes of the Quirinal overlooking the valley) and the Mandosi (who had owned the valley itself).[256] Lanciani recorded excavations as early as 1872 undertaken by Spithoever, adding that the "orti Sallustiani, già Mandosi e Barberini" now belonged to him.[257] Clearly, Spithoever not only wished to live in one of the most exclusive and healthiest areas of Rome but was desirous of owning property with important ancient monuments that were considered perhaps more valuable than his own villino

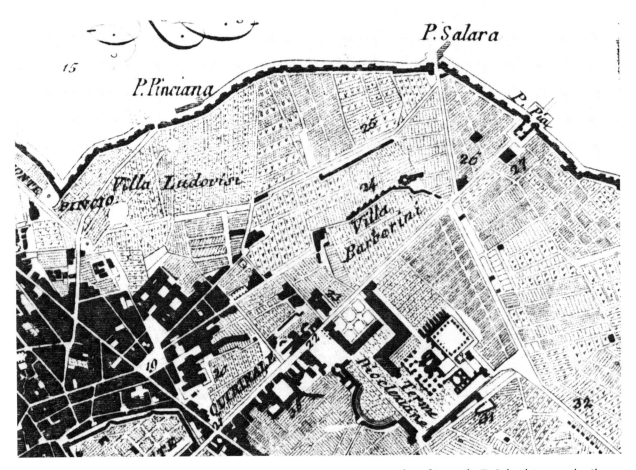

Fig. 1.11: Plan of Rome, by E. Salandri, 1846: detail.

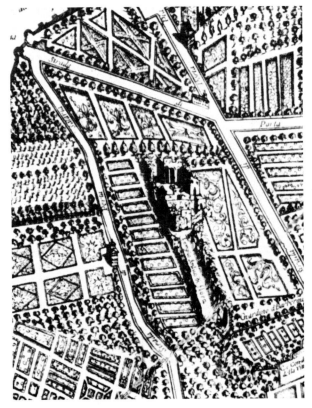

Fig. 1.12: Plan of Rome, by M. Gregorio de Rossi: detail.

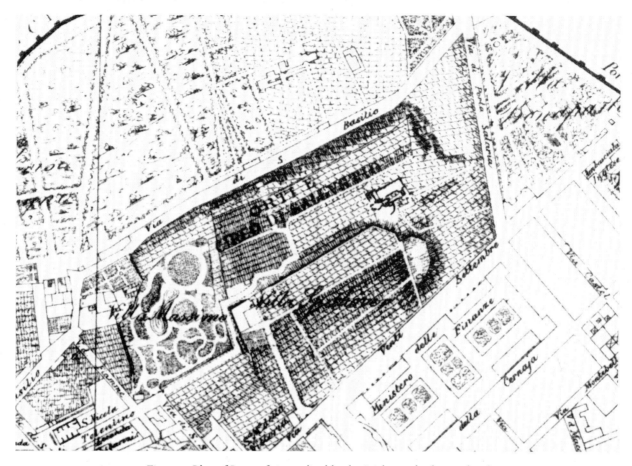

Fig. 1.13: Plan of Rome of 1878, edited by the Spithoever bookstore: detail.

on the Quirinal overlooking the valley and facing the Ludovisi villa further to the north.[258]

In the years 1881–1882 Spithoever began operations to fill up the valley "with the materials of the Servian embankment which crowned the cliffs, and turned one of the most picturesque corners of the city into flat building lots."[259] On June 2, 1883, Spithoever

and Leopoldo Torlonia (mayor of the city) signed an agreement to turn the villa Spithoever into building sites for a new town quarter, with the stipulation that all artifacts found during construction (except for the building of streets and sewers) would be Spithoever's property.[260]

THE 1880'S "BUILDING FEVER" AND ITS AFTERMATH

Spithoever was merely taking advantage of a remarkable building boom that was occurring at the time as the result of the planning for a new Rome, as capital of unified Italy. Vittorio Emanuele II, from the Savoy house of Piedmont, was proclaimed first sovereign of Italy in 1861. Rome, however, was not part of this unification, for it was still under the influence of the papacy, which had the support of France. Only

after Napoleon III was taken prisoner and a republic was declared in France did Italian troops enter Rome (through the porta Pia [present porta Nomentana]) on September 20, 1870, proclaiming it immediately as the new capital of a truly unified Italy.[261]

An unprecedented building fever began as a result of inflated prices for land and houses. Laws were passed in 1881 stipulating substantial public funds for the aggrandizement of Rome, and a new plan of the city (the Piano Regolatore—one of several to follow) was drawn up in 1883 establishing straight boulevards (such as the corso Vittorio Emanuele II, the via Arenula, and the Lungotevere) and public spaces, all of which further increased land speculation.[262] In particular, the areas outside the designated archaeological zones—the Palatine, Celio, a large part of the Aventine, and a small portion of the Esquiline—increased in value as potential building sites.[263] Entrepreneurs made fortunes, and construction was at a frantic pace. Property was held primarily by a handful of bankers who had a virtual monopoly over prices, which in some cases rose an extraordinary one thousand percent between 1873 and 1887.[264]

It is important to understand these events, for it is within this period that large parts of the city of Rome were being turned, literally, upside down. Excavations for apartments, luxury villas, public buildings and commercial establishments—all of which needed roads, sewers, and water—tore through layers of archaeological history that could barely be recorded (if at all) before its covering by modern constructions.[265]

In this heady atmosphere, the Prince of Piombino, Don Antonio III, inheritor of the Ludovisi fortune, died (on July 10, 1883), leaving his estate to his two sons and three daughters. The division of property resulted in numerous negotiations between the inheritors and the Ministry of the Interior, which wished to annex the property for a new residential quarter of the city.[266] Terms were not finalized until April 1885, and two relatively new financial players, the Banca di Roma and the Società Generale Immobiliare, obtained the right of financing for the rebuilding. Within a month work began in removing statues, pedestals, columns, vases, and other decorations from the gardens, demolishing the monumental gateway into the villa, opening tracts of new streets, and cutting down admired groves of trees and a famous street of cypresses.[267] The villa Massimo (where the Palazzo delle Assicurazioni now stands, at the corner of the present vie Sallustio and Lucullo), which stood just south of the entrance to the Ludovisi villa, was also sold by its owners in 1886. Lanciani, writing in 1897 about the new Ludovisi quarter, declared that "those who sold and those who bought the grounds have failed alike in their speculations, and the new quarter remains still unfinished."[268] Indeed, extreme prices and the speculative atmosphere overextended the market, and a collapse began in 1885, resulting in the bankruptcy of the Banca di Roma and the paralyzing of the Immobiliare and other institutions whose loans could not be paid.[269]

The Ludovisi, however, gained from their sale, allowing the head of the family, Don Rodolfo, to build for himself a new luxury residence, the so-called palazzo

Fig. 1.14: Palazzo Piombino (later villa Margherita), elevation by G. Koch.

Piombino, with its façade on the new via Veneto (Fig. 1.14). At the back was the Palazzo Grande, the original Orsini residence still existing on the property of the Ludovisi, which was intended for the primogenitor, Don Ugo and his family. They were being displaced from their palazzo (also called Piombino) in the piazza Colonna, which was being torn down by the state to widen the street in anticipation of the announced visit (October 11, 1888) by the German emperor William II.[270]

The new palace on the via Veneto was still unfinished in the autumn of 1890 when the family occupied it. In less than two years the Boncompagni/Ludovisi found themselves in grave financial difficulty, the result of the general building crisis and the failure of two banks in France and England, in which the family had invested 11,000,000 lire. The family had to abandon its new residence only eighteen months after they moved in, and the entire area between the vie Veneto, Boncompagni, Lucullo, and Friuli (including the new residence as well as the old palazzo Grande) came into the possession of the Banca d'Italia. The new Ludovisi palace, designed by Gaetano Koch (builder of the Banca d'Italia and the exedrae of the piazza della Repubblica), had to be sold, becoming the residence of Queen Margherita (d. 1926) after the assassination of her husband, Umberto I, in 1900.[271]

The famous sculptural collection, however, remained unsold in the palazzo. A reason for this was a law of June 28, 1871, stating that "art galleries, libraries, and other collections of art and antiquities will remain undivided and inalienable among those involved in the resolution of the deed of trust, their inheritors, or the rightful parties," which tied the hands of the Ludovisi in the piecemeal selling of their art collection.[272] The family decided in 1890 to open the collection to the public, who could visit it on Tuesdays, Thursdays, and Saturdays from 9 a.m. to noon, and from 2 p.m. to 5 p.m.[273] Eventually, on December 21, 1900, the collection was sold to the state for the reasonable price of 1,400,000 lire, to be paid over ten years and without interest.[274]

By 1921 this new quarter, which had been called rione Colonna (Rione III) created in 1748 by Pope Benedict XIV Lambertini (1748–1758), was reduced almost by half to create a new Rione XVI: Ludovisi. Another region was also created (Rione XVII), which

Fig. 1.15: Stemma of Rione XVII: Sallustiano.

had comprised part of the earlier rione Trevi (Rione II), and this was designated Sallustio.

These two new, contiguous regions correspond, more or less, to the extent of the ancient *horti Sallustiani,* although it is rione Sallustio that is most closely identified with the ancient gardens and, as such, employs the mirror of Venus Erycina (a sanctuary believed to have been somewhere in these gardens, see pp. 68–82) as its insignia (Fig. 1.15).[275]

The gridded plan (Fig. 1.3) introduced into rione Sallustio in the nineteenth and twentieth centuries regularized not only the streets but their very names—Sardegna, Sicilia, Toscana, Piemonte, etc.—commemorate the unity of the Italian peninsula. Even the large straight street on the Quirinal leading to the porta Nomentana was eventually renamed XX Settembre: the day of unification. Finally, the via Boncompagni recognizes the former Ludovisi owners, and the via Sallustiana, which runs into the piazza Sallustio, recalls the original inhabitant, who made this area famous with his garden estate.

PART II

The Architecture of the Gardens

THE DESTAILLEUR PLAN AND PERTINENT ANCIENT REMAINS

Because of the massive building operations in the nineteenth and twentieth centuries, there is little remaining of ancient structures or monuments that once were part of the gardens of Sallust. The scarcity of such remains, of course, makes those still visible, or securely recorded, all the more valuable as topographical reference points, and it is to these that we will now turn our attention.

There are a variety of sources from which we can draw some sense of the topography of this area as well as the type of buildings and other architectural modifications that were in these gardens. For example, old topographical plans of the city show clearly the deep valley separating the Quirinal and Pincio hills (Fig. 2.1) and, in particular, the massive retaining wall at the south with its series of arched niches (Fig. 2.2).

Furthermore, seventeenth-, eighteenth-, and nineteenth-century *vedute* (views of the city) by, for example, Overbeke (Fig. 2.3), Piranesi (Figs. 2.4–2.5), and Rossini (Fig. 2.6), and late nineteenth-century photographs from the collection of J. H. Parker (Figs. 2.7, 2.12, 2.27, 2.36), all of which will be discussed later, reveal the topographical configuration and the ancient remains as they existed in the more recent past.

Particularly intriguing is a sixteenth-century drawing/plan (probably by Aristotile da Sangallo) formerly owned in the nineteenth century by Hippolyte Destailleur, from whom its modern name derives—the

Destailleur plan (Fig. 2.8). It is labeled "Horti Salustij," and Lanciani interpreted it convincingly as depicting the ruins of the gardens from the slopes of the Quirinal at the south (top) to the Pincio at the north (bottom).[1] Labels identify some recognizable topographical features such as an overlook on the Quirinal, at the top of the page ("a cavalliero a tutti" = level "A"), and the valley beyond ("valle" = level "C"), shown as a stadium surrounded by high walls and a portico. The blind-arched retaining wall along the Quirinal as seen on topographical city plans (Fig. 2.2) and on a Piranesi engraving (Fig. 2.4), among others, is shown on the Destailleur plan as supporting on level "A" a row of double rooms that is otherwise unattested and, according to Lanciani, seems to be completely arbitrary.[2] Level "B" is interpreted as the location of the vestibule that is here represented by its second-story plan rather than its round ground plan (cf. Figs. 2.19, 2.25). A series of stairs flank this building (cf. Figs. 2.16, 2.23) and rise to an apparently upper terrace behind, indicated as level "B cavalliero alla B."

According to Lanciani, the most important parts of the plan are those at the bottom of the page, referring to the area between the street (via di San Basilio = the later via Boncompagni; see Fig. 1.3) and the Aurelian wall (which is not shown on this plan): the area, until 1887, that was the villa Ludovisia. The depiction of a large staircase (near the bottom right corner) and the

Fig. 2.1: Plan of Rome, by B. Marliano, 1544: detail.

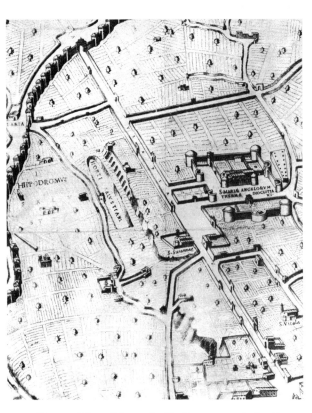

Fig. 2.2: Plan of Rome, by M. Cartaro, 1576: detail.

Fig. 2.3: Valley of the Sallustian gardens showing slopes of the Pincio
("Le Marché de Salluste," engraving by B. van Overbeke, 1709).

Fig. 2.4: Valley of the Sallustian gardens, engraving by J. B. Piranesi, 1762.

Fig. 2.5: Valley of the Sallustian gardens, engraving by J. B. Piranesi, 1756.

Fig. 2.6: Valley of the Sallustian gardens, engraving by L. Rossini, 1828.

Fig. 2.7: Primitive fortifications, Quirinal, Parker nr. 153.

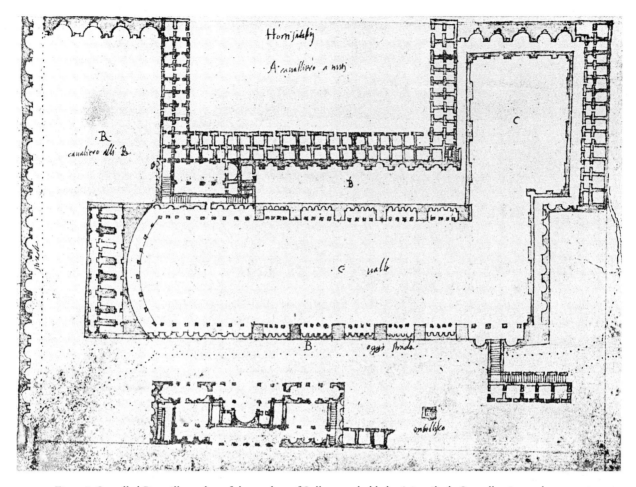

Fig. 2.8: So-called Destailleur plan of the gardens of Sallust, probably by Aristotile da Sangallo, sixteenth century.

indication by dotted lines of a modern path ("oggi strada" = level B; perhaps following an ancient road leading to the porta Salaria) suggest that the buildings and monuments are on the slopes of the Pincio and include an intriguing, unidentified U-shaped structure, with a central apsidal complex opening onto a colonnade and facing the valley.[3] According to Lanciani, no physical traces of this building were able to be identified on the Pincio during excavations carried out in the nineteenth century for construction of sewers for the new urban quarter.[4] Riemann, however, suggested that this U-shaped building ought to be associated with discoveries reported in the eighteenth century in the villa Altieri, in the villa Verospi, and under the via Sicilia.[5] Ruins were reportedly found near the entrance to the villa Altieri of a series of rooms with barrel vaults and painted wall decoration

(marble imitation and fields with figures: seated female playing a lyre; a man in a mantel). Intriguing is the mention of the depiction, in the middle of the painted composition, of a domed oval or round building with four entrances that perhaps merely coincidentally resembles a description of an actual oval or round building with four entrances found apparently within the confines of these gardens (see pp. 68–82). Also reported is a corridor, two hundred paces long, and a room with a travertine portal positioned opposite the garden house of the villa Maffeo Barberini on the Quirinal.[6] Another room was reached by a descending flight of stairs to a cellar.[7]

Piranesi shows ruins to the northeast near the villa Verospi, probably those identified as *hypogea Villae Belloniae* (Fig. 2.9: nr. 115 [near the "P" of "P. Salara"]).[8] He also depicted a Doric, a basket-weave,

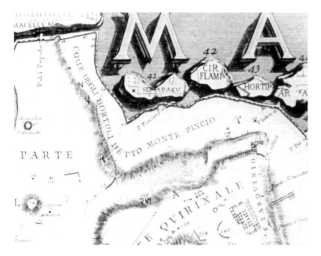

Fig. 2.9: Plan of Rome, by G. B. Piranesi, 1756: detail.

Fig. 2.10: Various capitals, by G. B. Piranesi, 1761.

and a composite capital, which were found in the villa Altieri (Fig. 2.10).[9] The excavations under the via Sicilia were never published, although numerous black-and-white mosaics were identified as well as a water basin, suggesting a bathing complex.[10]

On the Destailleur plan behind the apsidal complex (near the bottom of the drawing) is another colonnade, which Talamo suggested may have faced north onto a large, enclosed area surrounded by walls and a colonnade, found in 1969 and perhaps appearing in earlier plans and excavations (Fig. 2.11, nr. 32).[11] If these excavated remains are indeed correctly identified as being pertinent to the U-shaped building, it would securely position it within the gardens and perhaps indirectly increase the reliability of this anonymous plan. On the other hand, such an identification would run counter to the usual association of this building with Egyptian statues found in the early eighteenth century by Bianchini, whose discoveries were made in the confines of the Verospi/Vitelleschi properties situated further to the east (see pp. 130–138). It has been assumed that these Egyptian statues were displayed in this unusual building, and consequently this structure is sometimes identified as a *casino egizio*.[12] Perhaps supporting such an identification is the appearance on the Destailleur plan to the right (west) of this building of an obelisk ("onbellisco"), which is still extant and whose foundations were found in the twentieth century, establishing not only the precise location of it but the relative location on the Pincio of the U-shaped building (see pp. 52–58 and Fig. 1.7F).

The Destailleur plan is obviously a valuable early document, but it must be used with caution as a true record. The artist contrived at least some of the plan to reconstruct the entire area by completing the presumably enormous lacunae among the actual physical remains. Furthermore, the buildings and their physical distances from each other clearly have been compressed and regularized into a strict rectangular format, dictated no doubt by the edges of the page. It is, therefore, the identification of physical remains with structures on this plan that increases its value as an archaeological document. One such building depicted on this drawing as an apsidal plan with a single side aisle can be securely identified, as alluded to above, with the still-visible remains on the Quirinal.

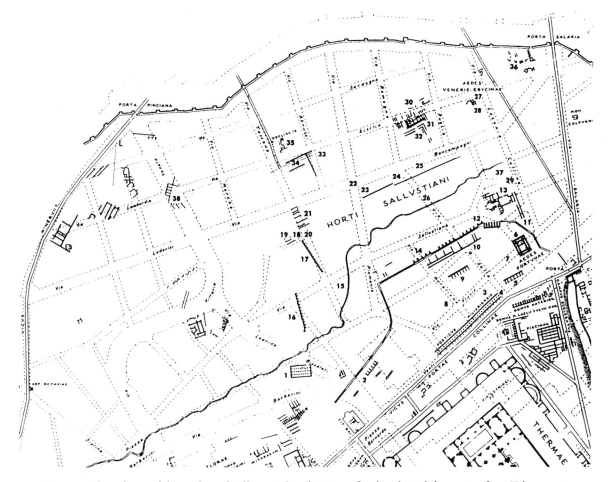

Fig. 2.11: Plan of area of the gardens of Sallust, with indications of archaeological discoveries, from Talamo 1998.

THE "VESTIBULE" IN THE PIAZZA SALLUSTIO

The deep valley that had separated the Quirinal and the Pincio, as already discussed, was partially filled in 1883, creating, eventually, more-or-less-level ground between the two hills. A substantial ancient complex at its eastern end was left visible, however, now some fourteen meters below the present ground surface of the modern piazza Sallustio, which surrounds it (Figs. 2.12–2.14; depicted also in Figs. 2.4–2.6, 2.8).

This structure was never lost to sight, as shown on numerous city plans beginning as early as Bufalini's in 1551 (Fig. 2.15D), in drawings and engravings of the seventeenth century, and in discussions of these gardens in the eighteenth and nineteenth centuries. It was identified sometimes as the villa of Sallust himself, as a nymphaeum[13] or garden pavilion, or even as a temple to Venus (i.e., Fig. 2.5–6) or Diana.[14]

The identification by Ligorio of this brick structure as a temple to Diana was the result of an inscription found in the vicinity and reported, mistakenly, by Fulvio in 1527 as dedicated to Diana, while a report of the finding nearby of a statue of Venus prompted an association to this goddess.[15] In the eighteenth century, Venuti, however, went even farther than others in identifying this building not merely as the temple of Venus in the gardens of Sallust (known in inscriptions as Venus hortorum Sallustianorum) but as the temple to Venus Erycina (believed to be somewhere in these gardens; see pp. 68–82 for a complete discussion).[16] Nibby asserted that this identification must be incorrect because these two Venus temples were not the same. He commented that this "edificio ottagono" was admirable for its beautiful brick construction,

Fig. 2.12: House of Sallust(?), Parker nr. 1020.

which he believed dated to the time of Sallust.[17] It is clear that this "octagonal" brick building is, in fact, the round structure in the piazza Sallustio, which because of its pedimental entrance lends from the outside the appearance of an octagon.[18] It will be argued below that this round structure is likely to be a vestibule, and this will be the term used for these discussions.

The vestibule was never lost to sight, and the remains were substantial enough to be worthy of drawings and measurements by Pirro Ligorio in the sixteenth century (Figs. 2.16–2.21).

It was not fully published until 1935 (Figs. 2.22–2.25), and in the late 1980s, on the occasion of restoration and of paving the upper surfaces, several exploratory trenches were opened.[19] Most recently, in April 1998, Tecno Holding S.p.A. united with the Unione Italiana delle Camere di Commercio and others to form the Horti Sallustiani Expò S.p.A. The

Horti Sallustiani Expò saw to the partial restoration of the ancient structure (including glazed windows and air conditioning) and transformed it into a convention center (inaugurated 23 May 2000).[20]

The ancient remains are still impressive, consisting of a large rotunda 13.28 meters high and 11.21 meters in diameter, resting on rectangular foundations,[21] and a dome segmented into alternating flat and bowed sections, which were once decorated by mosaic (Fig. 2.28).[22] Numerous brick stamps dating to the Hadrianic period show that it was built after A.D. 126, contemporary with the second phase of the villa of Hadrian in Tivoli.[23]

Access into the rotunda (originally from a staircase)[24] is directly through an arched foyer at the west, rectangular in plan and covered by a barrel vault. This entrance was flanked by pilasters (in large part restored in the nineteenth century) and crowned by

Fig. 2.13: So-called Nymphaeum (vestibule), Piazza Sallustiana.

Fig. 2.14: Ruins of the vestibule, Piazza Sallustiana.

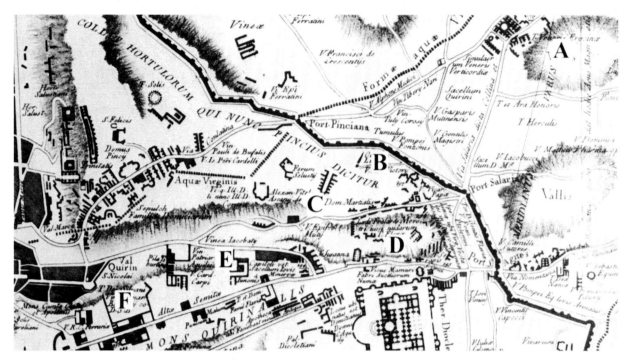

Fig. 2.15: Plan of Rome, by L. Bufalini, 1551. Details:

A. *"T. Veneris Erycina."*

B. *"Obolisc. Lunae; V. Vinc. Victorij."*

C. *U-Shaped building near "V. Episco. Mutij."*

D. *"Ludi Florales Meretricum nudarum; T. Florae."*

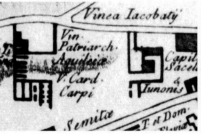

E. *"Vinea Iacobatij."*

F. *"Vin. Leonar. Boccacij co. D.S.B."*

a pediment, completely destroyed (Fig. 2.17 perhaps shows it still preserved in the sixteenth century).[25] Opposite the door is a room (Fig. 2.23: "B"), also rectangular in plan and barrel vaulted, which mirrors the entrance vestibule, even to having had pilasters originally flanking its doorway. Inside the rotunda, the wall surface is divided horizontally into two areas. On opposite sides of the central axis at the lower, ground level were side-by-side round and quadrilateral niches that were later closed off, and doorways leading to narrow, and low, barrel-vaulted rooms. On the second level (about 4 meters above the ground) are two semicircular and two quadrilateral niches (with small travertine consoles projecting under them) and large round-headed windows flanking the entrance (Figs. 2.16, 2.20, 2.24).[26] On this level as well are semicir-

cular niches at the short sides of the entrance foyer and its matching room opposite. Beyond, and on axis with the entrance, is another large rectangular room (about 5.60 by 8.00 meters) that was partially open to the sky (Fig. 2.23: "C") but later was closed by a coffered barrel vault that considerably reduced its height. This large room was flanked by narrow, enclosed corridors that perhaps originally served as nymphaea. At the north, on ground level, is a large rectangular room, groin vaulted and with a half-arched doorway facing west (Fig. 2.23: "F"). Access to this room could also be made by an exceptional enclosed staircase that rose to an upper story and descended to lower ones (Fig. 2.23: "G"). Finally, at the southeast is a large unit, two stories in height (Fig. 2.24), consisting of two rooms (Fig. 2.23: "μ," "ν" and a staircase (Fig. 2.23: "o"). Above this

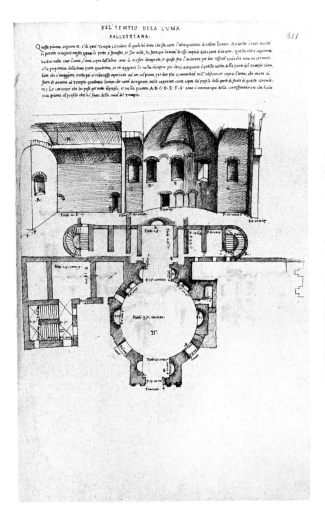

Fig. 2.16: "Del Tempio dela Luna Sallustiana" (plan and cross-section), **Cod. Paris. ital.** *1129 (formerly St. Germaine 86), fol. 311r.*

Fig. 2.17: "Del Tempio dela Luna Sallustiana" (three-dimensional elevation), **Cod. Paris. ital.** *1129 (formerly St. Germaine 86), fol. 312.*

ground-level complex was an upper level of at least two stories, but this is no longer well preserved (Fig. 2.25). It is clear, however, that this level had a cantilevered balcony supported by arches springing from travertine consoles that ran around the entire western perimeter of the complex (Figs. 2.17, 2.21–2.22), an architectural motif of particular interest because it made this façade seem like that of an *insula*.[27]

The principal space, still somewhat recognizable, of the upper story measures about 24 meters in length and 11.50 meters in width and is on the same east-west axis as the rotunda below (Fig. 2.25: "a"). This room apparently was entered from the east, although thresholds or doorways can no longer be identified.

The back wall and a short trace of the right wall had been visible not long ago, and two nineteenth-century photographs from the Parker collection show a reticulate wall (Parker, nr. 2110: Fig. 2.26), corresponding to the north wall of this space, and other reticulate walls employed for a later, modern building (Parker, nr. 1018: Fig. 2.27). This photograph, taken from the southwest, is of the same building in shadow at the left of Fig. 2.26, corresponding to room "c" on Figure 2.25. It is possible that this is also the same structure shown on the du Pérac plan of 1577 (Fig. 1.7c) as standing on these ruins.

This upper story, at the modern ground level, was explored in 1988 on the occasion of creating a paved parking lot on top of it for the Societé Unioncamere, which then owned the property.[28] Eventually, test trenches were extended in an attempt to uncover the entire floor. A wall 1.25 meters wide running southeast-

Fig. 2.18: "Del Tempio dela Luna Sallustiana" (Ionic capital), **Cod. Paris. ital.** *1129 (formerly St. Germaine 86), fol. 313.*

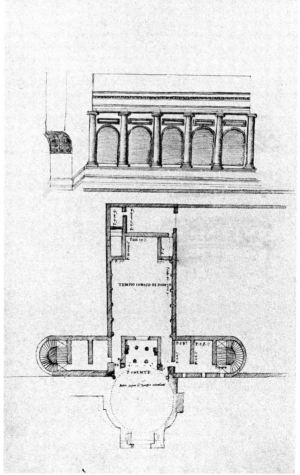

Fig. 2.19: "Del Tempio dela Luna Sallustiana" (plan and cross-section: "Tempio Ionico di Diana"), **Cod. Paris. ital.** *1129 (formerly St. Germaine 86), fol. 314.*

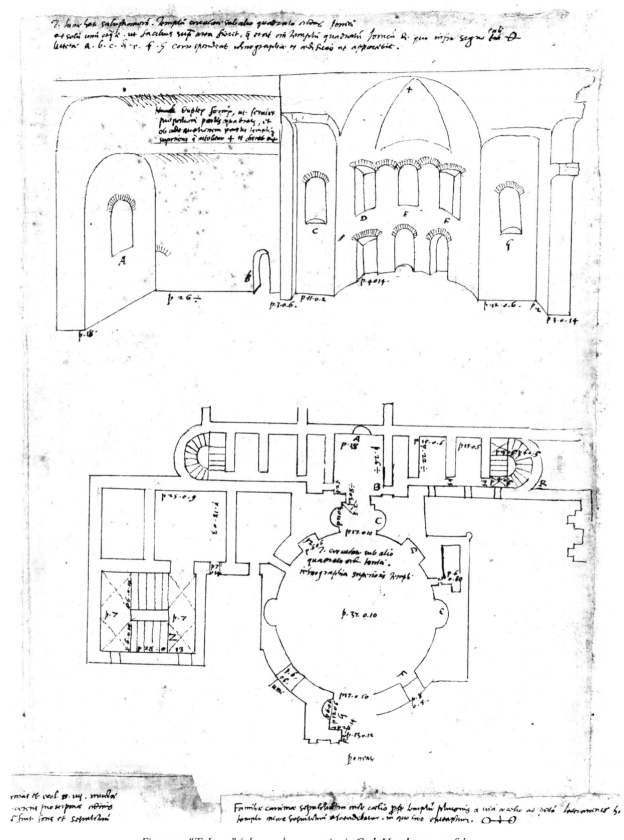

Fig. 2.20: *"T. Luna" (plan and cross-section),* **Cod. Vat. lat. 3439, fol. 27r.**

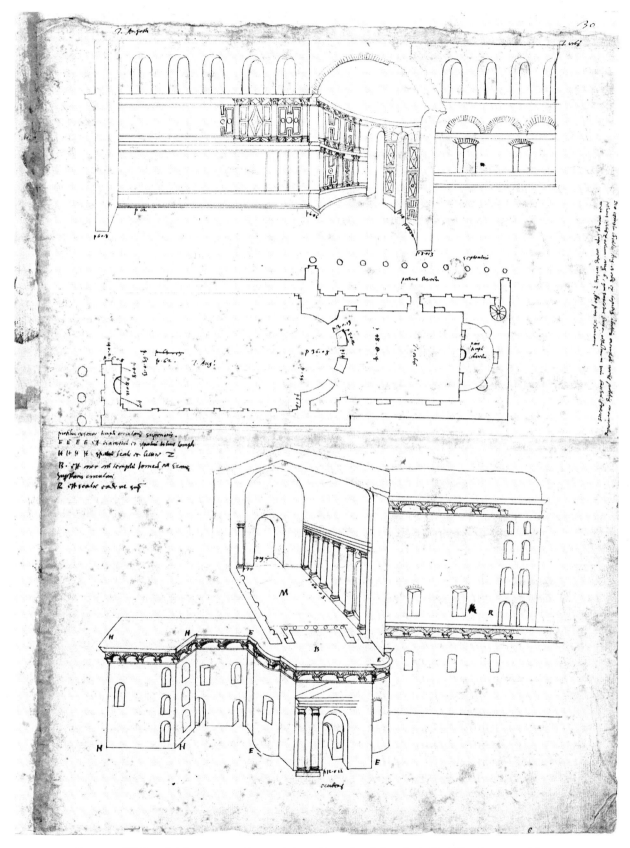

Fig. 2.21: "T. Luna" (plan, cross-section, and three-dimensional elevation), **Cod. Vat. lat.** *3439, fol. 30r.*

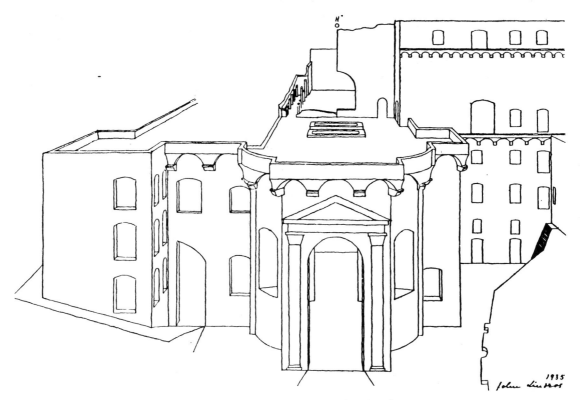

Fig. 2.22: Vestibule: reconstruction, by J. Lindros.

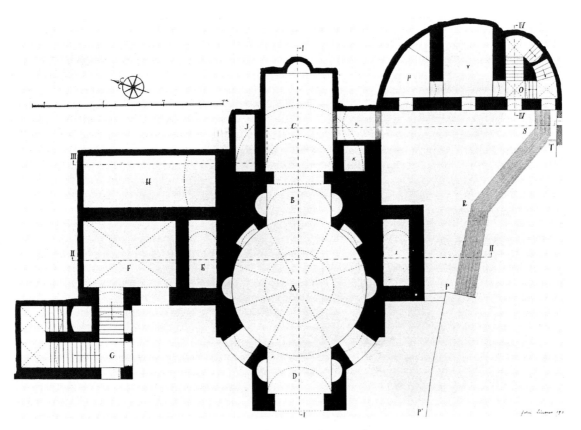

Fig. 2.23: Vestibule: plan, by J. Lindros.

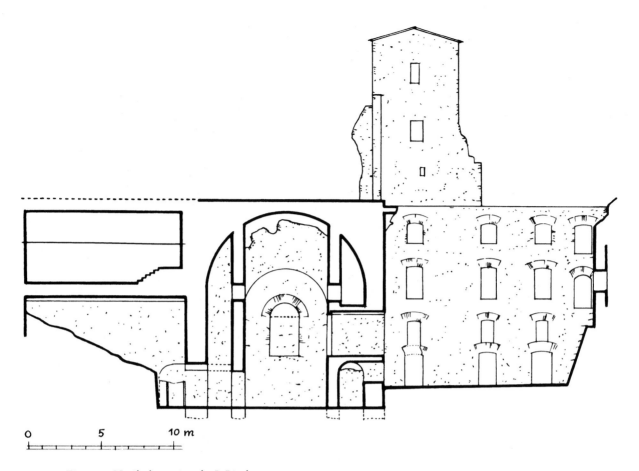

Fig. 2.24: Vestibule: section, by J. Lindros.

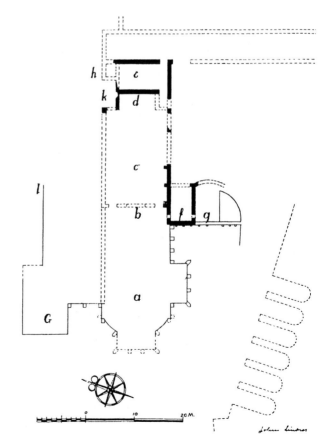

Fig. 2.25: Vestibule: plan of upper story, by J. Lindros.

Fig. 2.26: House of Sallust, Parker nr. 2110.

northwest (that is, perpendicular to the lateral walls of the hall) has been recently identified. This lateral wall of mixed brick and reticulate facing is preserved for a length of 7.60 meters and a maximum height of 1.26 meters. Still *in situ* are fragments of marble slabs that represent the socle revetment and imprints of other slabs. A second dividing wall running parallel to the first has also been identified (although not excavated) about 8.50 meters southwest of the first, which Lehmann-Hartleben noted previously (wall "b" on Fig. 2.25). This space, therefore, appears to have consisted of at least two almost equal-sized rooms, which are indicated on sixteenth-century drawings by Pirro Ligorio (Figs. 2.17: "м" and "в", 2.19). There are in fact several drawings of this building—those in the Vatican and others in Paris—that are virtually identical in the information conveyed and that are likely copies after original drawings (no longer extant) by Ligorio (Figs. 2.16–2.21).[29] These plans and elevations are indeed invaluable documents; however, they must be used with caution in determining what was still vis-

ible when they were made and what may have been interpreted or added by the artist. In this context it is indeed important that remains of a collapsed vault in the form of yellow clay slabs and pumice were found at the southwest, and Parker, nr. 1018 (Fig. 2.27) shows a massive concrete pier at the northeast with the remains of the springing for a vault. It is likely therefore that both rooms were covered by a barrel vault, as depicted in the elevations of the Vatican and Paris drawings (Figs. 2.17, 2.21).

Other trenches opened in these 1988 excavations yielded decorative items: polychrome marble, mosaics recovered in fragments of various sizes, small slabs of marble and porphyry for borders, plaster in various colors, paintings in a very good state of preservation, and decorative stucco. Furthermore, pavements consisting of pieces of cipollino and another in limestone and pozzolana are in the course of restoration and probably represent different phases of construction. No architectural pieces were recovered; however, one drawing in Paris shows an Ionic capital and architrave

Fig. 2.27: House and gardens of Sallust, Parker nr. 1018.

(Fig. 2.18) that apparently was still surviving. Another drawing (Fig. 2.19) suggests that the interior walls had half-columns, decorating what was thought to have been the so-called Tempio Ionico di Diana, as named on this plan. Indeed, Ligorio's small plan of 1553 identified the building at the head of the "For. Sallusti" as "T. Diana" (Fig. 2.39).

Several years before 1988, trenches had been opened, principally outside the vestibule, where a beaten reddish-colored floor consisting of ground pozzolana, tufa, and stone pieces of various kinds was found.[30] Under this beaten floor was discovered, resting on a wall of *opus reticulatum* (having a northeast-southwest direction), a base of Parian marble preserving the paws of an animal. This wall was followed for the entire length of the trench and showed clearly that it had faced south with fine reticulate facing. The north face was without any revetment. Another similar wall parallel to this one and some 30 centimeters from it was reported, but it was impossible to follow because of the scaffolding being used for the restoration. Another

trench inside the rectangular room behind the rotunda revealed traces of a wall in *opus reticulatum* running in an east-west direction. It was not possible to continue to follow this, but it appeared to curve slightly to the west, to be late Republican in date, and to have been partially removed for the construction of this building.

In June 1906 Enrico Maraini[31] discovered, parallel to the via Collina at a depth of 11 meters, a subterranean gallery or corridor that must be part of this complex in the piazza Sallustio. No longer visible, we must rely on Lanciani's report and his plan on *FUR* 10 (Fig. 1.1D) for our evaluation of these remains.[32] The corridor runs north-south and is almost parallel to the south wing of the vestibule complex. It should be noted that Lehmann-Hartleben reported a small window above the stepped retaining wall of the Quirinal (near the southwest corner of the south wing of the vestibule complex). He proposed that this could indicate a cryptoporticus, perhaps running northeast-southwest under the Quirinal (Fig. 2.22: the window drawn in perspective at the extreme right, and Fig. 2.23, nr. II). If this were the case, then this east-west cryptoporticus would intersect at almost a right angle with the north-south corridor found in 1906.

At the south along the slopes of the Quirinal hill is a large, angled retaining wall of small brick steps on cement foundations (Fig. 2.23: "p"–"s"). Lehmann-Hartleben suggested that this retaining wall represented a second building phase sometime after the building of the rotunda, and he proposed an Aurelian date.[33] According, however, to the 1986 excavation report, a number of brick stamps are still visible, all dating to the Hadrianic period.[34]

Contiguous to the west of this stepped retaining wall is another wall consisting of alternating rectangular and semicircular niches, of which three are still vis-

ible (Fig. 2.22: lower right corner; Fig. 2.23: "p"–"p'"). This wall is not straight, presumably to allow it to run parallel to the "Servian" wall above. Lehmann-Hartleben believed that this wall was constructed after the stepped brick retaining wall, and he therefore suggested a Diocletianic date (A.D. 284–305), attempting to associate it with a discovery made in the nineteenth century and reported by Lanciani in 1906.

According to Lanciani, Spithoever found on his property in the bottom of the valley an ancient drain running towards the west (that is, between the slopes of the Pincio and Quirinal), which he was able to trace sporadically for a length of one hundred meters.[35] Lanciani described this drain as covered like a hut (that is, with two slabs forming a pitched roof) and with reticulate walls repaired in brick. It ran under a

Fig. 2.28: Vestibule: interior, engraving, by L. Rossini, 1828/1829.

pavement of white marble, perhaps forming a basin or canal, and at the northern part, this pavement terminated in a wall of niches revetted in marble.[36] Because this wall was not well constructed, Lanciani dated it to the third century.[37] There were discovered two sections of this wall, one 6 meters and the other 45 meters "dal muro divisorio con la villa del duca Massimo," that is, a wall that had divided the Spithoever property from the property of the Massimi.[38] The slabs of pavement sloped towards the face of the wall representing the natural inclination of the tufa bedrock.

Lehmann-Hartleben and Lindros reported a similarly constructed canal to the southwest of the vestibule and further to the southwest the wall of three niches that the authors equated with the canal and wall of niches reported by Lanciani.[39] It is difficult, however, to reconcile Lanciani's report with these features near the vestibule because Lanciani is clear in indicating that Spithoever found the canal at the bottom of the valley running parallel to it and that the wall of niches was to the north. The vestibule is such a prominent topographical feature that Lanciani would certainly have mentioned it as a point of reference, if these walls of niches lay near it, rather than the wall dividing the properties of the Spithoever and Massimo villas.[40] It seems clear that the two sections of walls found by Spithoever must be somewhere at the west of the valley (near his villa) for them to be only 6 meters and 45 meters from the Massimo property, as reported by Lanciani.

It is indeed possible that the canal reported by Lehmann-Hartleben and Lindros near the vestibule fed into the one at the bottom of the valley, and these together represent only a small portion of an extensive system of water flow from the top of the Quirinal down to the valley. As already discussed, it is possible that a branch of the second-century B.C. *Aqua Marcia* existed on the Quirinal and that this was employed to water the slopes as well as the valley.[41]

For all the indication of a well-watered area, it is perhaps surprising that the vestibule reveals no trace of ever having water within it, save for a water channel found in room "K" and another reported under the window of room "L"—both subsidiary rooms that later were closed off or whose access was greatly

reduced (Fig. 2.23). Lehmann-Hartleben's comparison of the architecture of the vestibule with that of the "Egyptian" Canopus at Hadrian's Villa in Tivoli is not as compelling as it had been when he was writing because it was only later seen that the Canopus pavilion is a half-circle.[42] Also, Lehmann-Hartleben used the term "diaeta egiziana" to describe the vestibule because he thought that Egyptian statues had been found nearby. These statues were found not "on the slopes of the Pincio," but rather, according to Nash, on top of the Pincio some 110 meters north of the north wall of the valley (see pp. 130–138).[43] Finally, the placement of the vestibule is not on axis with the valley, so that, as Nash stated, one cannot speak of this building as being analogous to the Canopus of Hadrian's Villa.[44]

Rakob has made more compelling comparisons of the vestibule to the apsidal vestibule in the Casa dei Dioscuri at Ostia and to the *frigidarium* in the imperial baths at Trier, both of which partially project from a larger complex into which each is imbedded.[45] Rakob pointed out that rooms (apsidal or rectangular) projecting into gardens or taking advantage of panoramic views were particularly popular for domestic architecture. Yet none of Rakob's examples have the monumental entrance distinguished by pilasters and a pediment, and a rectangular entry room like that of the vestibule of the *horti Sallustiani,* which he related to the domed structures of the so-called Venus, Diana, and Apollo Temples in Baiae.

The *horti Sallustiani* building is remarkable because from the outside it served as a monumental entrance into a series of rooms, and from within as an architectural setting through which the landscape was visible (Fig. 2.28). It drew one inside and at the same time took advantage of its natural setting within a garden landscape. From the remains it appears there was access to the rooms above by a large, enclosed staircase, but this cannot have been the main entrance into these upper rooms. It is likely, therefore, that this rotunda served as an elaborate entrance for the gardens below (which could be reached by a staircase) and for the collection of rooms behind and above. Hence, it may be best described as a vestibule.[46]

AN OBELISK

The sixteenth-century Destailleur plan records an obelisk on the Pincio that, in fact, has been discovered and, as will be discussed, reerected above the Spanish Steps in Rome (Fig. 2.29). It is an actual Egyptian obelisk, but with hieroglyphic inscriptions added in the Roman period. Apparently, it is the very one mentioned in the first half of the fourth century A.D. by Ammianus Marcellinus, who gave its location as in the gardens of Sallust and its date as post-Augustan.[47] In the eighth century an anonymous writer, perhaps a pilgrim who visited Rome during the time of Charlemagne, listed among a series of important monuments in the city, a "pyramidem" near the "thermae Sallustianae." It is likely, although not universally accepted, that this "pyramidem" was the still-standing obelisk mentioned earlier by Marcellinus and later indicated on the Destailleur drawing and on plans of Rome (Figs. 2.8, 1.7E, 2.15B).[48]

The anonymous Carolingian text is known as the Itinerary of Einsiedeln after the name of the Benedictine monastery in Switzerland where it is preserved.[49] The itinerary is divided into various "walks," indicated by titles in red ink designating the beginning and termination points, and the landmarks between are listed by "left" and "right" (also in red ink) of presumably the most direct street(s) from each point of departure. The two pertinent itineraries are the following:

A PORTA SANCTI PETRI USQUE AD PORTAM SALARIAM
PER ARCUM.

IN SINISTRA. Sancti Apollinaris.	IN D. Circus Flamineus; ibi Sancta Agnes. Thermae Alexandrianae et Sancti Eustachii.
Sancti Laurtentii in Lucina.	Rotunda et thermae Commodianae.
Oboliscum. FORMA VIRGINIS.	Columna Antonini.
Sancti Silvestri; ibi balneum.	Sancta Susanna et aqua de forma Lateranense.
Sancti Felicis in Pincis.	Thermae Sallustianae et piramidem.

A PORTA NUMENTANA USQUE FORUM ROMANUM

IN S. Thermae Diocletianae.	IN D. Thermae Sallustianae.
Sancti Cyriaci. Sancti Vitalis.	Sancta Susanna et cavalli marmorei.
Sanctae Agathae in diaconia.	Sancti Marcelli.
Monasterium Sanctae Agathae.	Ad Apostolos.
Thermae Constantini.	Forum Traiani.
	Sancti Hadriani.

The area of the *horti Sallustiani* is mentioned twice: at the end of the itinerary "a Porta Sancti Petri usque ad Portam Salariam," and at the beginning of the other entitled "a Porta Numentana usque Forum Romanum." These two contiguous itineraries have in common the landmarks of the "Thermae Sallustianae" (perhaps the remains of the vestibule in the piazza Sallustio) and the church of "Sancta Susanna," and at least the church is designated correctly on each itinerary as standing to the right of the path. The assumption, however, that each itinerary follows a single, continuous route leads to difficulties in interpreting other less defined markers such as the elusive "pyramidem" and its possible pertinence to the obelisk on the Pincio.

According to the Einsiedeln itinerary, the "pyramidem" stood on the right side of what has been presumed to be an east-west street (the name of which is not recorded) as one approached the porta Salaria.[50] Indeed, a portion of an ancient road was found in 1888 south of the via Sicilia, between the vie Toscana and Abruzzi, running in the direction of the porta Salaria, and it is possible that this is the street taken by the anonymous eighth-century pilgrim (*FUR* 2: Fig. 1.1).[51] If, however, this is the case, then the obelisk, as we will see, was to the left and not to the right of this road as one headed east.[52] This discrepancy prompted Lanciani to doubt that the "pyramidem" is the obelisk and to suggest that it identified a now lost pyramidal tomb (like that of Cestus) that stood somewhere between the porta Salaria and the porta Collina.[53] Palmer agreed but believed there was a pyramid on the opposite side of the road from the obelisk.[54]

Fig. 2.29: Sallustian obelisk above Spanish Steps, Rome.

The assumption that the itineraries follow a single road from beginning to end seems difficult to support. If we begin with the premise that the writer of these itineraries composed them on site and intended for pilgrims not only to follow his route but to visit each monument, then a single, continuous path is impossible, given the sometimes distant physical separations of monuments listed together. Indeed, it is almost universally accepted that these lists were meant to accompany a map of the city, and so each itinerary would be much more explicit than it now appears.[55] Furthermore, the listing of the monuments is under a single heading, but in two columns designated by right and left. It is clear that one must jump back and forth from one column to the next for each itinerary to identify the monuments in a logical, topographically progressive manner. If this is indeed the intent and purpose of these itineraries, either the right and left designations are a simple way to position the monuments between two points or they, in fact, designate the right or left position in relationship to each as one was expected to visit them.[56] For example, one could visit San Silvestro in the Campus Martius, then Santa Susanna on the Quirinal, after which one could see San Felice on the Pincio, having looked on the way at the "aqua de forma Lateranense"—perhaps the mistaken identity for portions of the *Aqua Vergine*.[57] How these monuments were positioned with respect to the viewer's right and left would depend, obviously, on one's viewpoint at any given moment.

A point in favor of seeing the "pyramidem" as separate from the obelisk is the indication in the Einsiedeln itinerary of another obelisk (in the Campus Martius) as "Oboliscum," yet the two terms, "oboliscum" and "pyramidem" in this period probably are equivalent.[58] It is possible, of course, that the writer of the Einsiedeln itinerary made a mistake in locating the "pyramidem" with respect to left and right and that it indeed refers to the obelisk.[59] Otherwise, it is peculiar he did not report an obelisk nearby that seems always to have been a prominent landmark, and it is noteworthy that no other writer mentions nor do any cartographers depict a pyramid in this location.

If one believes that the Einsiedeln itinerary indeed lists the Sallustian obelisk as the "pyramidem," then it is likely to have been still standing in the post-antique period. By the early fifteenth century, however, the Anonymous Magliabecchianus reported that it lay in two pieces in a thicket of reeds near its base (Fig. 2.30).[60]

All early topographers had a clear idea where the obelisk lay.[61] On a map of 1544 by Bartolomeo Marliano (Fig. 2.1), where it is given the name "ob(eliscus) lunae," its position is placed on the Pincio at "about one stadium from the P. Collatina (porta Pinciana) and 4½ stadia from the P. Collina (porta Salaria)."[62] It was also designated according to the contemporary owner of the property, which changed hands several times from the Bufalini, the Orsini, and Vergilio Crescentio to Messer Patella.[63] Fulvio wrote in 1527 that in his day the place of the obelisk was called Girlo, an abbreviation of Girulus, and the valley itself was called Sallustrico.[64] It is only on several nineteenth-century plans of Rome that the obelisk is located mistakenly on the Quirinal.[65]

The hieroglyphic inscriptions were seen first by Athanasius Kircher (a German Jesuit scholar appointed professor of mathematics, physics, and oriental languages at the Collegio Romano in 1633) to be closely related to those on the Augustan obelisk from the Circus Maximus (now in the piazza del Popolo), and he proposed that the Pincian obelisk had been brought to Rome under Claudius.[66] Because Pliny did not mention it, however, a Claudian date seems unlikely, as does a suggestion in the mid eighteenth century that it was brought to the gardens by Sallust himself.[67] The poor carving of the inscription suggested to Zoega, in the late eighteenth century, that the hieroglyphs were copied in Rome between the periods of Commodus (d. A.D. 192) and Gallienus (A.D. 268).[68] In 1989 Grenier suggested an even later date of A.D. 272 under Aurelian, who may have erected this as a victory monument over Egypt and as a dedication to the solar cult of Sol Invictus.[69] Grenier equated the copying of the hieroglyphs from the obelisk of the Circus Maximus to Aurelian's reported passion for exercising his horses in the *horti Sallustiani*.

Sixtus V (1585–1590) planned to reerect the obelisk in the piazza he had opened in front of Santa Maria degli Angeli, but this was never realized. Maps of the

Fig. 2.30: Obelisk in the gardens of Sallust, engraving, by B. van Overbeke, 1709.

late seventeenth and early eighteenth centuries do not record the obelisk, and this omission suggested to Iversen that it might have been buried.[70] Indeed, a drawing of 1706 by Carlo Fontana reports that it was made "when the obelisk was rediscovered," and this may have been the case for in this same year Fontana urged Clement XI to erect it in the niche of the fountain of Trevi.[71] Another plan, to set it up in the piazza in front of the church of the Madonna dei Monti, was proposed as well, but again this project never was undertaken. It lay broken in its original location until 1733, when Clement XII, as a gift from one of the Ludovisi princesses, had it brought to the Lateran in anticipation of erecting it there, but it was rightly considered too small, particularly in relationship to the obelisk already set up under Sixtus V.[72] The pieces remained abandoned beside the wall of the villa Giustiniani, which faced the Lateran, until 1788, when Pius VI had them finally erected in the piazza in front of Santa Maria della Trinita above the Spanish Steps (Fig. 2.29).[73]

The original red granite base (2.50 × 2.55 m.) had not been removed in 1733, and its whereabouts were unknown until it appeared unexpectedly in 1843 during the removal of the roots of a large, dead tree that stood on the property of the villa Ludovisia.[74] Schreiber[75] indicated the location as behind the "colossal statue of the reclining Silenus," that is, in the area where the obelisk is reported to have been seen (Fig. 1.8c: the Silenus indicated by a rectangle in the northeast *parterre* that had been a labyrinth), yet Lanciani placed this excavation near the entrance to the villa some two hundred meters to the south (*FUR* 9: Fig. 1.1).[76]

The correct location of the obelisk, however, was already given on a seventeenth-century plan of the villa Ludovisia by Maderno (Fig. 2.31: "E," a meadow north of a labyrinth ["D"]). Given no knowledge that the base had been moved from its original location before 1843, it seems most probable that it was discovered still *in situ,* even though the foundations for it were not reported at the time. These foundations

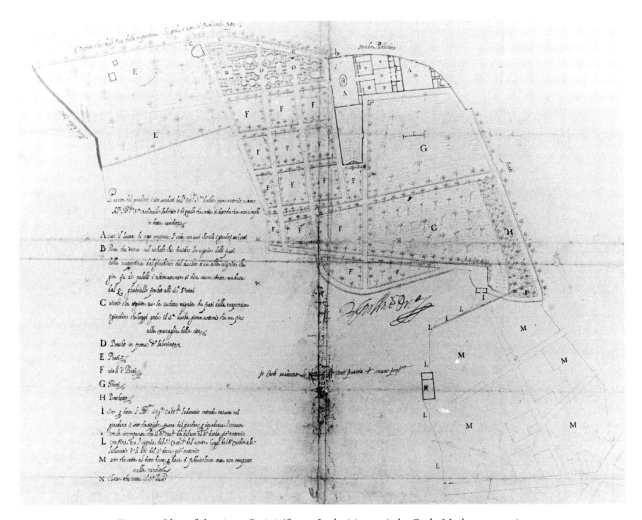

*Fig. 2.31: Plan of the **vigna** Orsini (future Ludovisi estate), by Carlo Maderno, ca. 1622.*

were identified only later in 1912, still in their original position between the modern vie Sardegna, Sicilia, Toscana, and Abruzzi (Fig. 1.3).[77]

The base could not be reunited with its original obelisk, already mounted atop the Spanish Steps, so the Ludovisi family offered it as a gift to the city to use for another, smaller obelisk that was found on July 5, 1883, near the Collegio Romano. It was not until 1887, however, that a decision was reached concerning the appropriate use for this smaller obelisk. In that year Italian troops in East Africa had moved inland and were destroyed by a large Abyssinian force at Dogali, and this obelisk (without the Ludovisi base) was erected near the Termini in dedication to these victims of war.

The base had not been removed from the Ludovisi gardens, and so by the end of the century, when the property of the villa Ludovisia was in the process of redevelopment for a new quarter of the city, the base was now in the way of progress. It was transported in 1890 to a storeroom of the *Aqua Marcia* at the crossroads of vie Gaeta and Volturno (in the garden of the piazza del Macao), and there it remained for the next thirty-six years.[78]

In 1926 it was taken to the small garden southwest of Santa Maria in Aracoeli on the Capitoline, and with the addition of a base and crowning of white marble, it became a monument to the fallen of the Fascist regime (Fig. 2.32). It remained with these additions until 1954, when they were removed and the base was positioned

Fig. 2.32: Obelisk base as monument to the fallen Fascists, 1928.

Fig. 2.33: Obelisk base on the Capitoline, 2002.

a short distance away against the Republican wall (Fig. 2.33). The top shows perhaps the setting for the obelisk (four shallow holes are near the corners), and the surface facing the wall still has (now upside down) the Fascist inscription. This enormous granite block, although abandoned and forgotten, is nonetheless a striking testimony to the power of the ancient Roman Empire to absorb foreign Mediterranean cultures into its own Latin world and the later abortive attempt in the twentieth century by the Italian state to recreate such dominance over its neighbors.

WALL(S) OF NICHES

Several substantial stretches of walls have been recorded, perhaps within the environs of the gardens of Sallust, and one of these is still visible on the west side of the via Lucullo between vie Friuli and Sallustiana (Figs. 2.34–2.35; *FUR* 9: Fig. 1.1).[79] Running almost parallel to the via Lucullo (it is displaced only about 2° towards the southwest) it has seven niches that, according to Neuerburg, contain conduits, perhaps for a fountain or for drainage.[80]

It is unclear, however, whether these are water conduits, because their placements off-center speak against being used for fountain works. Nash, who consulted even the unpublished nineteenth-century records of Lanciani and Gatti, stated that this wall is not mentioned in any topographical literature, although in 1947 Blake dated it to the time of "Julius Caesar or more probably (to) Sallust in the early years of his possession" (of the gardens).[81] It is unlikely this wall is as early as the time of Sallust, but regardless of its date, it could indicate the western limits of the gardens as late as the third century A.D.

A photograph in the German Archaeological Institute in Rome (Fig. 2.36) is enticing because it shows an impressive two-story wall of niches (of *opus reticulatum*) that must have been a retaining wall for a large platform. The photograph is identified as part of the Sallustian circus (that is, the valley between the Quirinal and Pincio). It is tempting, however, to suggest that this is the same as the wall of niches still visible along the via Lucullo. It is possible that what exists today above ground is either the upper story, if the roadway was substantially raised, or else the lower story, in which case the upper niches were removed to build the present palazzo delle Assicurazioni.

As previously discussed, the Aurelian wall makes an abrupt obtuse angle east of the porta Pinciana (*FUR* 2: Fig. 1.1A). This wall of niches along the via Lucullo, if extended north, would meet the Aurelian wall at or near this angle, and therefore, it could represent the limits of these gardens. If Figure 2.36 is the wall of niches along the via Lucullo, this wall would have created a substantial physical and visual barrier at the west of the valley, suggesting that after its construction it was, indeed, the western boundary of the gardens.

Another wall with niches was mentioned by Lanciani as near the corner of via d. S. Nicola da Tolentino and vicolo delle Fiamme (no longer a street, but it ran west of and parallel to the via Umbria on the grounds of the then villa Massimo). Lanciani wrote that "about two years or so ago" (that is, ca. 1889) he measured what was left of this wall, which was preserved only in its foundations, and located it where in his day rose the second house on the via Susanna (present via Lucullo) near the corner of the via Sallustiana. But these statements are inconsistent with each other as well as with *FUR* 9, which shows a wall running across via Umbria and not the vicolo delle Fiamme, as Lanciani reported (Fig. 1.1C).[82]

Some fifty years before Lanciani's recording of this wall of niches, Bunsen mentioned a wall of brick and *opus reticulatum* with colored marble revetment formed by at least seventeen niches partially buried but some 18 feet deep and 14 feet wide.[83] He suggested that this series of niches could have been for repose or even as living quarters and that at a later time, each niche had badly constructed pillars in front that could have carried a terrace. It is possible this is the wall of niches that ran across via Umbria, and which by Lanciani's day was preserved only to its foundations. On the other hand, it is possible that this impressive

Fig. 2.35: So-called wall of niches along via Lucullo.

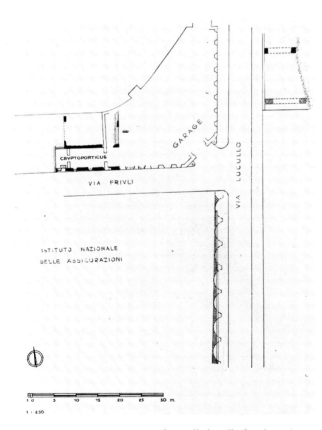

Fig. 2.34: Cryptoporticus and so-called wall of niches: plan.

Fig. 2.36: So-called wall of niches along via Lucullo(?).

wall of niches with marble revetment was a retaining wall built along the northern edge of the Quirinal and recorded in several early engravings (Figs. 2.4–2.6) as well as in a Parker photograph (Fig. 2.7), and now completely buried. Regardless of where this particular wall stood, it is clear that all these enormous walls of niches were used for retaining the embankments surrounding the valley between the Quirinal and Pincio hills and may have been, in at least some parts, used as fountains, grottos, and backdrops for sculptural displays (see, in particular, the Artemis-Iphigenia statue group, pp. 89–93).

A CRYPTOPORTICUS

Not far from the wall of niches along the via Lucullo a short stretch of a presumably much longer cryptoporticus was found in the winter of 1949–1950 during construction of a parking garage at the corner of the vie Lucullo and Friuli on the property of the American Embassy, formerly the garden of the villa Boncompagni-Ludovisi (Figs. 2.34, 2.37).[84]

It was partially restored (in particular, the barrel vaults and the walls were completed in cement) and incorporated into the new building, allowing entrance to it from a subterranean room of the garage. The portion preserved is oriented northeast-southwest and measures 10.90 meters in length and 4.20 meters in width. Along the preserved parts of the barrel vault at the south are three splayed windows that open onto the present via Friuli. A wall erected in the nineteenth

Fig. 2.37: Cryptoporticus along via Friuli.

century closes it to the west, and another to the east with a door (built in the twentieth century) separates it from the modern garage. The *opus testaceum,* visible where frescoes have come loose, reveals the remains of a marble surface that was later removed and covered by plaster and paintings. The need to restore these paintings nearly half a century after their discovery prompted a recent archaeological investigation that has yielded new details and conclusions.[85]

Based on architectural elements, the date of building is now believed to fall between A.D. 50 and 125 rather than ca. 190 (as originally proposed), which is the probable date of the later paintings covering the sides of the corridor. Two small chambers, on either side of the main corridor, may have been for repose, as suggested by a possible bench along the east wall. A secondary wall running parallel to the east wall of the corridor was likely built to prevent moisture from entering the central gallery. The cryptoporticus was open during the early Christian period, as graffiti attest, and was at least still partially entered as late as the fifteenth century, if the drainage systems running along the two sides of the corridor are correctly dated.[86] At least some of the Christian graffiti (a cross and the words "martyr" and "Adraste") may be as early

as the third century and could suggest that this passage was used as a martyrium.

Although it is clear that this was an important passageway perhaps for centuries, it is difficult to determine whether this cryptoporticus was indeed under the *horti Sallustiani,* because its location, just west of the via Lucullo, could lie outside the western confines of the gardens, as previously discussed (pp. 7–8). On the other hand, in 1902 to the south of the via Boncompagni (between the via Quintino Sella and the via Nerva) was found a section of a cryptoporticus measuring 8 meters in length and 4.20 meters in width and running in a northeast-southwest direction.[87] The width and the direction of this cryptoporticus are the same as those found near the via Lucullo. It is tempting to suggest that these are two sections of a long underground passage that ran along the south slope of the Pincio. Likewise, Lehmann-Hartleben proposed a cryptoporticus along the northern slope of the Quirinal, but without actual remains, this is impossible to confirm (pp. 49–50). On the other hand, it would not be surprising that a network of underground passages would have linked different parts of the grounds of the gardens of Sallust.

THE SO-CALLED CIRCUS OF FLORA

Beginning in the fifteenth century, a circus of Flora was believed to have been in the gardens of Sallust, but it is now clear that this circus never existed. A discussion of how and why this erroneous identification developed is enlightening because it underlines the diverse elements of "evidence" concerning the appearance of these gardens and the manner in which such evidence may be interpreted.

To Augustus is owed in 7 B.C. a new division of the city into fourteen regions.[88] These were designated officially by numbers. The residents, however, must have soon adopted names to facilitate recognition and to distinguish each region.[89] At least some of these names seem to have become "official," for they appear along with their number on several inscriptions.[90]

An important catalogue of monuments in each of these fourteen regions was compiled sometime in the

fourth century[91] and is preserved in two later editions: one without a title but called usually *Notitia urbis Romae regionum XIIII;*[92] the other entitled *Curiosum urbis Romae regionum XIIII*[93] (in a corruption of these, one finds also *Regiones urbis Romae*).[94] The *Notitia* cannot be earlier than A.D. 334 (because it records the equestrian statue of Constantine dedicated in that year) and not later than A.D. 357 (because it does not mention the sixth obelisk erected in the Circus Maximus at that time).[95] The pertinent texts of each include:

Curiosum:[96]
Regio VI. Alta Semita[97]
Continet:
    Templum Salutis et Serapis.[98]
    Floram.[99]

Capitolium Antiquum.[100]
Thermas Constantinianas.[101]
Statuam Mamuri.[102]
Templum dei Quirini.[103]
Hortos Salustianos.[104]
Gentem Flabiam.[105]
Thermas Diocletianas.[106]

. . .

Notitia:[107]
Regio VI. Alta Semita
   Templum Salutis et Serapis.
   Templum Florae.
   Capitolium Antiquum.
   Statuam Mamuri.
   Templum dei Quirini.
   Malum Punicum.[108]
   Hortos Salustianos.
   Gentem Flaviam.
   Thermas Diocletianas et Constantinianas.[109]

. . .

For our purposes, however, these are not the most significant listings because Giulio Sanseverino (1427/28–1497), who went by the Latinate name Julius Pomponius Laetus (more commonly known in Italian as Pomponio Leto), added to the *Notitia* and the *Curiosum* with topographical remarks gleaned from various ancient authors. It is his fifteenth-century elaboration (probably completed between 1476 and 1488) that became the basis for later editions and further elaborations.[110] Because of the importance of this later listing of monuments, it is necessary to include it in our discussion. Leto begins his itinerary of Region VI from the *vicus Bellonae,* near his home:[111]

Vicus Mamuri
Vicus portae Querquetulanae
Vicus Menapii
Templum Salutis [in colle Quirinali]
Templum Serapeum
Templum Apollinis et Clatrae[112]
Templum Florae [et circus][113]
Floralia[114]
Capitolium Vetus
[Fortuna publica in col[le]][115]

[Divus Fidius in col[le]]
Forum Sallusti[116]
Statua Mamuri plumbea
Templum Quirini
Domus Attici
Malum Punicum [ad quod Domitianus .DD.]
Templum gentis Flaviae [quod erat domus sua]
Horti Sallustiani
Senatulum Mulierum[117]
Thermae Diocletianae
Thermae Costantinianae

. . .

A comparison of Leto's listing and those of the *Curiosum* and *Notitia* makes clear the fifteenth-century additions and elaborations. Particularly significant is that of "et circus" after Templum Florae, on which Leto elaborated in a guide to Rome that introduced a visitor to the monuments of the city. Known as the *Excerpta,* this itinerary seems to have been established by 1479 and certainly fixed by 1484 (the death of Sixtus IV).[118] In this Leto explained that there was a valley between the Quirinal and the Hortulorum (Pincio) and that near here was the house of Martial.[119] It is apparent that Leto himself lived nearby, for he began his description of the north slope of the Quirinal from his house, pointing out two marble equestrian statues and three other Constantinian statues as well as a statue of Cybele seated on two lions.[120]

Leto continued: "Eundo a sinistris est vallis inclusa parietibus: ibi fiebant floralia et mons a sinistris[121] habet domum cardinalis Neapolitani et est pars Quirinalis montis: et vocatur mons Clatiae et Apollinis" (To one proceeding to the left there is a valley enclosed by walls: there were celebrated the Floralia and on the hill to the left was the home of the Neapolitan cardinal, part of the Quirinal hill; and this is called the Clat[r]a and Apollo hill).[122] The itinerary proceeds with the old Capitolium on the Quirinal to the right, further on the church of Santa Susanna near the vicus Mamuri and soon thereafter the church of San Gabinus and the forum of Sallust.

Important is the "vallis inclusa parietibus" mentioned as near the home of the Neapolitan cardinal (Oliviero Caraffa), for it was believed to have been the place where the Floralia were celebrated. This small valley has now disappeared, but it was clearly visible in the sixteenth century, as shown on a perspective plan by Cartaro in 1576 (Fig. 2.2: near bottom right) that gives an idea of its depth and depicts three large arched niches, presumably remains of an ancient retaining wall. This valley was long and deep enough to distinguish a separation of the Quirinal into two parts, the western identified as "mons Apollinis" and the eastern area called the "Capitolium Vetus" by Marliano, who identified this saddle as the Circus of Flora on his 1544 plan (Fig. 2.1).[123] Marliano's plan gives visual substance to Andrea Fulvio's remarks of 1513 that identified this saddle and the flanking hills in much the same way, although he called it not a "circus" but a "theater."[124]

The idea for a circus in which the Floralia were celebrated was given credence by the repeated reprintings, beginning sometime between 1503 and 1505 of Leto's regionary, falsely attributed to a Publius Victor, who was identified as a civil servant under Augustus but who in fact never existed.[125] As already discussed, Leto's regionary added "et Circus" after "Florae," so that in 1527, Fulvio was confident enough to list "circus floralia" after "templum florae" and even explained that the oblong saddle in the environs of the vineyards of Cardinal Jacovacci (that is, the home of Oliviero Caraffa on the Quirinal) took the form of a circus.[126]

This small saddle later enclosed by walls and mentioned by early topographers was not, however, the only location identified as the Circus of Flora because by 1527 the obelisk on the Pincio was pressed into service as a marker for the location of this circus. In that year Fabio Calvo published the first schematic reconstruction of ancient Rome, and in Region VI is mentioned the only circus, that of Flora, located on the Pincio where an obelisk was still preserved in the vineyard of Antonio de Bufalo.[127] This placing of the Circus of Flora on the Pincio did not influence later topographers because it did not correspond to the early regionaries that put it always on the Quirinal; however, the obelisk would indeed play an important role later in the identification of another circus as well as of a hippodrome on the Pincio.

Certainly a more influential plan was that created in 1551 by Bufalini,[128] who shows the area of the small saddle beside the old Capitoline defined by walls and designated as the vineyard of Leonardo Boccaccio (Fig.

2.15F), whose property had been owned by Orsini and rented to Caraffa, the Neapolitan cardinal mentioned by Leto in his *Excerpta*. A circus of Flora is not specifically labeled, but the large valley to the east between the Pincio and Quirinal hills is given the title "T. Florae." Above this is written: "Ludi Florales Meretricum nudarum"—a clear reference to the place of the games of Flora. Surprisingly, Bufalini did not identify this area as the gardens of Sallust but instead located these in the Campus Martius below the southern slopes of the Pincio near the present Spanish Steps (Fig. 2.15: far left).

Pirro Ligorio's plan of 1552,[129] however, retains the usual designation of the large valley as the "Hort. Salustiani" but identifies not only a circus of Flora (in the usual location in the saddle of the Quirinal) but also a "Hippodromus" on the Pincio in the area of the obelisk (Fig. 2.38).

Ligorio's plan of 1553 reconstructs a hippodrome on the Pincio with the obelisk in its center, the large valley is identified as "For. Sallusti." (rather than "Hort. Salustiani"), and the slopes of the Quirinal are called the *horti* (Fig. 2.39). The "Circus Flora" is still identified with the small saddle in the Quirinal. It is, however, mistakenly placed east of the "Capitolium" rather than to the west between it and the mons Clatrae et Apollinis. In the same year that Ligorio published his small plan, he published a short text in which he stated clearly his opinion that there had existed *two* circuses in this area: one on the Pincio, as he had indicated on his two plans, near the obelisk in which he believed the games of Apollo had been played; the other, a circus on the Quirinal for the games of Flora, he located, agreeing with the common opinion, on the properties of Ippolito d'Este, Cardinal of Ferrara (formerly the property of the Caraffa) and of Boccaccio.[130]

Ligorio elaborated on the Circus of Flora in his great "Encyclopedia of the Ancient World,"[131] known in manuscript only, in which he reported remains of a temple, of brick construction and marble revetment, at the head of this circus. All these ruins, according to Ligorio, were completely destroyed or covered by Ippolito d'Este in the extension of his gardens.[132] Precisely when these building operations occurred is uncertain, but they cannot be earlier than 1560, the year of the purchasing of the adjacent Boccaccio prop-

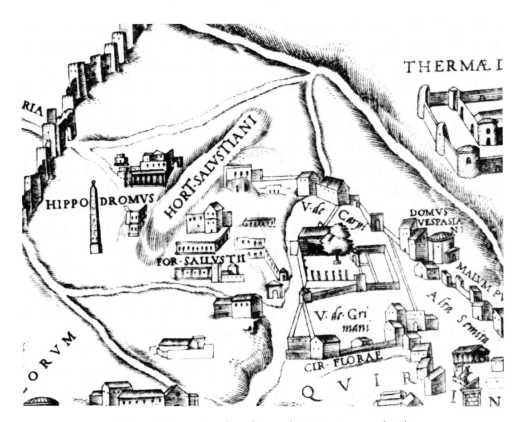

Fig. 2.38: Perspective plan of Rome, by P. Ligorio, 1552: detail.

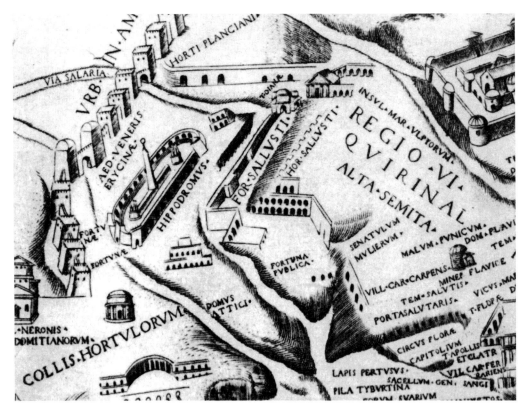

Fig. 2.39: Perspective plan of Rome (piccola), by P. Ligorio, 1553: detail.

erty by Ippolito. The saddle seems not to have been filled in at this time, but built over. The perspective plan by du Pérac of 1577 (Fig. 1.7A) shows clearly the Boccacio *vigna* as containing an impressive stadium-shaped garden imbedded into the slopes of the Quirinal hill and giving access to the valley below by a large, straight staircase. According to Hülsen, this sixteenth-century stadium garden may have used ancient substructures of the so-called Circus Florae.[133] But it is also possible that the presumed "Circus Florae," which was believed to be there, inspired the creation of this garden without any ancient remains being necessary to dictate its shape as a circus.

Another notice by Ligorio of the destruction of the Circus Florae by building operations is problematic, for it does not correspond with the above-mentioned report. He remarked that the circus had a *round* temple at its head, and the valley in which it stood was filled by earth excavated from the building of the via Nomentana in such a manner that any memory of its ancient form had disappeared. According to Lanciani, this report related to Pius IV's building activities of 1561 for the porta Pia, which included considerable moving of earth.[134] The land outside was piled up near the tombs of the Nomentana (outside the Aurelian wall), and this formed the small hill on which later was built the Casino Patrizi (Fig. 1.7: bottom left). The earth excavated inside the wall was dumped into the Sallustian valley.

It is likely that Ligorio is discussing here the large valley between the Quirinal and Pincio and is conflating this with the saddle of the Quirinal because his 1561 reconstruction of ancient Rome (Fig. 2.40) identifies this saddle as the Circus Florae (with its own obelisk[135] and with a *rectangular* temple at its head). The large valley contains another circus shape (albeit without an obelisk and identified as the "Forum Sallustii") and near its curved end a *round* temple identified as the "T. Veneris Hortor. Sallustianorum."[136]

It is possible that by the end of the sixteenth century, some alteration of the small saddle had occurred, for in 1597 Boissard argued that the Circus of Flora was located elsewhere.[137] He described in detail the substructures in the garden of Cardinal Carpi, which served later as the foundations of the Sforza and Barberini palaces, and he identified these as the remains of

the Circus Florae.[138] It is certain that the small saddle of the Quirinal was filled by the future Urban VIII (1623–1644) in 1617, as reported by an account published in 1638 by Donati, who agreed with Boissard's identification of the remains in the Barberini palace as those of the Circus of Flora.[139] With the filling of the saddle and the new placement of the Circus of Flora, it is not surprising that by 1665 Nardini stated with confidence that under the piazza Grimani (which was to the south of the present piazza Barberini) were the remains of the "vallis inclusa parietibus" reported by Fulvio in the sixteenth century and identified with the Circus of Flora.[140]

Nardini also promoted another important (and erroneous) identification: locating a second circus in the large valley separating the Pincio and Quirinal—a place that had been seen earlier to take the *shape* of a circus but was identified usually as the forum or gardens of Sallust. The retaining walls of this valley, according to Nardini, were for seats, and the obelisk on the Pincio (according to Nardini, apparently moved there at some unspecified time) had been originally part of this circus, identified as that of Apollo or of Sallust.[141]

The assessment of the topography of this area was not clarified in the following century and, in fact, was somewhat obscured by Overbeke's placement of the Circus of Flora in the Campo dei Fiori.[142] Only in the nineteenth century was the existence of a circus of Flora questioned, although the large valley continued to be identified, through the middle of the twentieth century, as a generic circus of Sallust or as the more specific Circus Apollinaris, and sometimes the Pincio obelisk was shown, mistakenly, within it.

The persistence of a circus in the valley was in spite of comments by Becker[143] and Hülsen,[144] who questioned the identification of the valley as the Circus Sallustii or Circus Florae.[145]

Ironically, in spite of Hülsen's misgivings, the Kiepert and Hülsen "Formae Urbis Romae Antiquae" of 1912 outlined the shape of a circus in the valley (Fig. 2.41). Scholars continued to indicate such a circus up to 1949, when Lugli and Gismondi still indicated the outline of its shape in the environs of the valley, although without a specific identification (Fig. 2.42).[146] The western limit of this "circus" is shown on the Lugli/Gismondi plan

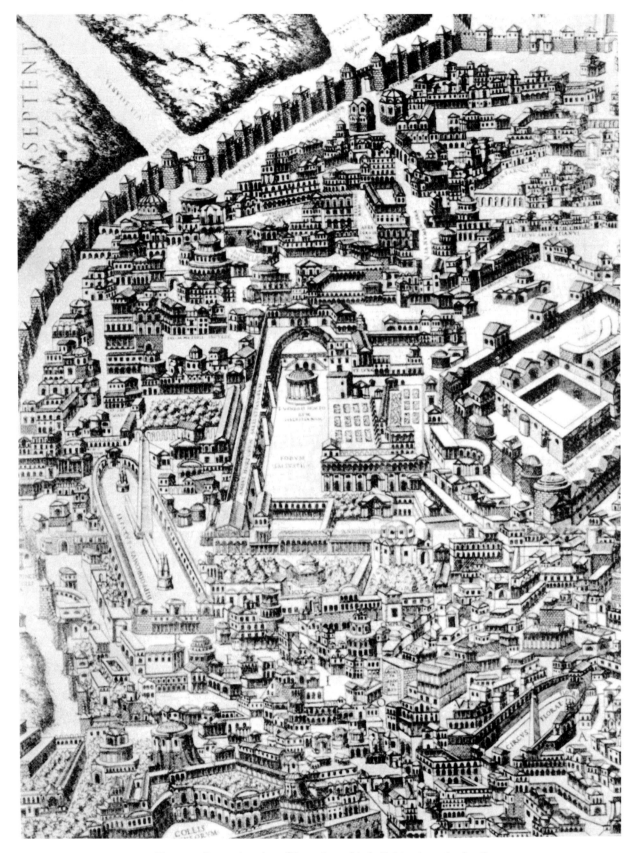

Fig. 2.40: Perspective plan of Rome (grande), by P. Ligorio, 1561: detail.

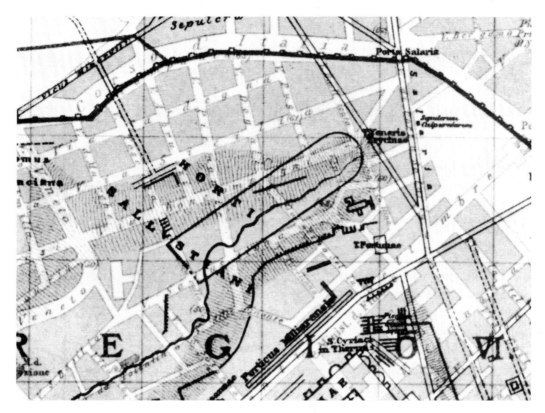

Fig. 2.41: Plan of Rome, by H. Kiepert and C. Hülsens, 1912: detail.

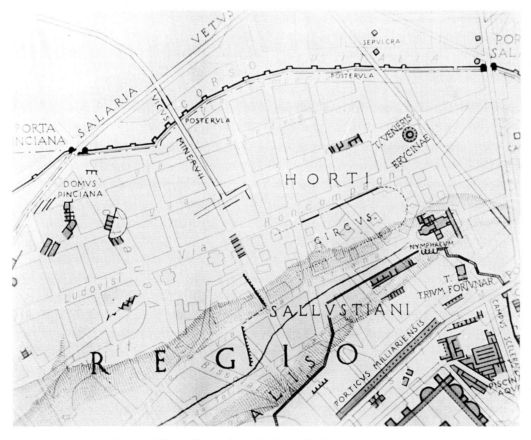

Fig. 2.42: Plan of Rome, by G. Lugli and I. Gismondi, 1949: detail.

as the wall of niches still visible on the west side of the via Lucullo between vie Friuli and Sallustiana (see Fig. 2.35 and pp. 58–60).[147] It is unlikely, however, that this wall has anything to do with a circus, for it lies some 18 meters lower than the valley floor at the east—an impossible slope for a circus.[148]

The very existence of a circus of Flora must be abandoned. Furthermore, the circus shape of the valley does not indicate a real circus but instead perhaps a stadium-shaped garden like that on the Palatine.[149] The obelisk with hieroglyphs copied after those found in the Circus Maximus could indicate a real circus on the Pincio. Yet there is no physical evidence of such a structure, and it is prudent at this time to suggest that no circus existed on the Pincio or anywhere else in the gardens of Sallust.

TEMPLES OF VENUS

Flaminio Vacca, a noted Roman sculptor, wrote a series of short reports on archaeological discoveries and ancient remains that he had observed in Rome from his childhood to his fifty-sixth year in 1594. He presented these to Simonetto Anastasi of Perugia, who was compiling a work on Roman antiquities.[150] Among Vacca's observations are these:

in the vineyard of Gabriel Vacca, my father, near the porta Salaria within the city walls ("accanto Porta Salara dentro le mura"), in a valley that is called the Sallustian gardens; digging there he found a large oval structure ("una gran fabbrica di forma ovata"), with a portico about it, adorned with fluted columns of yellow marble, eighteen palms high, with capitals and bases of the Corinthian order; this oval structure ("detto ovato") had four entrances with steps that descended into it to a pavement of *opus sectile;* and at each of the entrances there were two columns of transparent oriental alabaster. Under this oval structure we found some large conduits all lined with slabs of Greek marble, and so high that a man could walk upright in them; as well as two lead pipes, one of which was ten palms in length, and with a diameter more than a palm, inscribed with the name NERO-NIS CLAUDIUS. There were also found many coins of bronze and silver the size of a "quattrino" of the emperor Gordian; and a quantity of mosaics. The Cardinal of Montepulciano purchased the yellow columns and had them made into the balustrade for his chapel in San Pietro Montorio; he also purchased the alabaster columns, one of which being whole he had polished, and the other broken ones he had made into slabs, and with other antiquities he sent these as a gift to the king of Portugal; but when they were in the open sea, impetuous Fortune, finding them in her domain, made them a gift to the sea.[151]

Gabriele Vacca's vineyard was within the confines of the *horti Sallustiani,* as Flaminio indicated, and his description of an ancient building—oval in plan, a portico of yellow marble columns of the Corinthian order, four entrances flanked by columns of alabaster, and steps inside descending to a pavement (of *opus sectile?*)—gives a relatively clear idea of its appearance. In addition, large conduits (drains?) were found under the building, and several lead pipes were also reported, one bearing the letters NERONIS CLAUDIUS.[152]

Connected by modern scholars (first by Lanciani) with Vacca's description is a plan, presumably by Pirro Ligorio, in *Cod. Vat. lat.* 3439, fol. 28r[153] of a round building, on the exterior articulated by alternating hemicircular and rectangular niches and surrounded by columns (Fig. 2.43). Around the perimeter of the interior is shown a series of rectangular niches flanked by small columns. Several measurements are recorded, including the intercolumniation of the outer colonnade and the diameters of the interior space ("p[iedi] 20") as well as the whole diameter including the outer colonnade ("piedi 52").

A crucial aspect of all later interpretations of this Ligorian plan is Lanciani's own drawing after it, which is faithful except for one detail (Fig. 2.44). In the middle of the cella wall where a rectangular niche is shown on the Ligorio drawing, Lanciani indicated, without comment, that this niche was originally an opening that had been later blocked.[154] A separation is clearly shown, and even the diagonal hatching lines

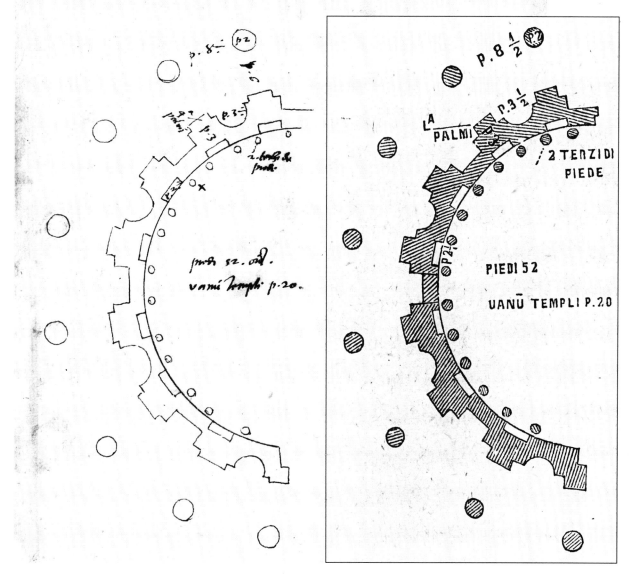

*Fig. 2.43: "T[emplum] veneris salustianae in capite fori salustii," **Cod. Vat. lat.** 3439, fol. 28r.*

*Fig. 2.44: Drawing of 1888 by R. Lanciani after "T[emplum] veneris salustianae in capite fori salustii," **Cod. Vat. lat.** 3439, fol. 28.*

DEL TEMPIO DI VENERE SALLVSTIANA   309

In una Testa della pia Via, ò uogliamo dire. Foro Sallustiano fu un Tempio di cinquanta dui pie
di diametro contitto il peristero o circuitioni di colonne le quali erano didui piedi grosse del marmo
Caristio giallo. suename di alcune macchie rosse, erano striate il portico era di uani sei piedi. i mu
ri dentro del tempio era grosso tre piedi senza le paraste a encontor delle colonne che sportauano
rifuori un quarto di palma. Le base delle colonne ciò è basi, non haueano il plinto o uogliamo dire
Zocco. erano alte un piede senza intagli, dell'ordine composito esse a icapitelli i quali erano alti
dui piedi a un quarto, i fusi delle colonne piedi deciotto manco un quarto di piede. i nicchi di fuori
erano larghi tre piedi a mezo, quelli didentro al tempio piedi dui a mezo questi erano ornati di
colonnette picciole dui auer 2¼ di piede del marmo o alabastro, che posauano sopra à certi modelletti
o ornauano essi nicchi de quali non hauemo damostrata stella alcuna. per esser stati già ro
uinati. per li tempi passati a quel che u'era remasto sotto delle rouine ci ha insegnato la forma
di quanto ho scritto a damostrato inquesta pianta circolare, era didentro o difuori incrostato di
tauole sottili di alebastro di porphidi, serpentini o d'altri marmi come anche era fatto il suo piano
del panimento suo di fuori o didentro del Tempio in cui s'ascendeua per tre gradi che atorno tutto
il circuiuano. certamente opera picciola ma di grandissima spesa o di uaghezza mirabile. di cui
fano inuentione nei buoni testi scritti a penna Publio Vitore a sesto rufo. L'architraui a
le cornici sue tutte per altri tempi furono portati uia. fu trouata una inscrittione che diceua
VENERI HORTORVM SALLVSTANORVM. C. SALLVSTIVS DVRIDVS AEDITVVS D D. Furo
no gli horti prima fatti da sallustio che scrisse le cose di catelina, o dopo dalla fameglia ma nessun
o nobilitati dall'imperatori

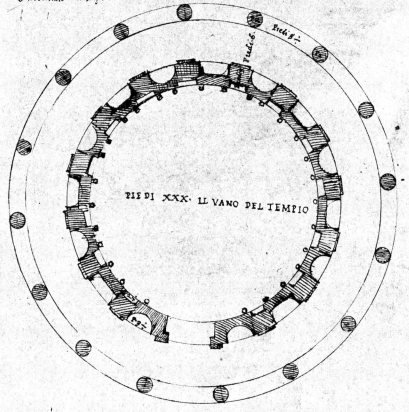

Fig. 2.45: "Del Tempio di Venere Sallustiana," **Cod. Paris. ital.** 1129 *(formerly St. Germaine 86), fol. 309.*

do not line up with those of the rest of the cella wall. It appears that Lanciani's drawing is an edited creation used to support his view that the Ligorian plan is a contemporary drawing of the building described by Vacca as having had four entrances.

Most important of all is the information written above the Ligorian plan. It gives not only the name of the building, and the height and marble (yellow with red veins, and alabaster) of the columns, but perhaps steps in the interior (not depicted on the drawing), interpreted by Lanciani as *descending* to a porphyry and serpentine pavement:

T[emplum] veneris salustianae in capite fori salustii columnae e marmore caristio gialo/suenate[155] di

alcune machie rosse striate: spire[156] basium sine plinto nel[157] zocolo alte p[es] 1 sine intalio ordo compositus. capitula alta p[edes] 2 et in 4[to]—columnae p[edes] 18 minus 4[to] pedis. +[158] columellae e marmore alabastrico incrustata tabullis alabastrinis porphyreticis serpentinis[159] unum solum a pavimentum ascensus tribus gradibus circumcirca. (Temple of Venus Sallustiana at the head of the Forum of Sallust. Fluted columns of yellow Carystian marble with red veins; moulded bases without plinths, 1 piede in height; composite order, capital 2¼ piedi in height—columns 17¾ piedi in height. Little columns of alabaster. (The walls were) incrusted with slabs of alabaster, porphyry, and serpentine. Three steps ascended all around to a paved floor.

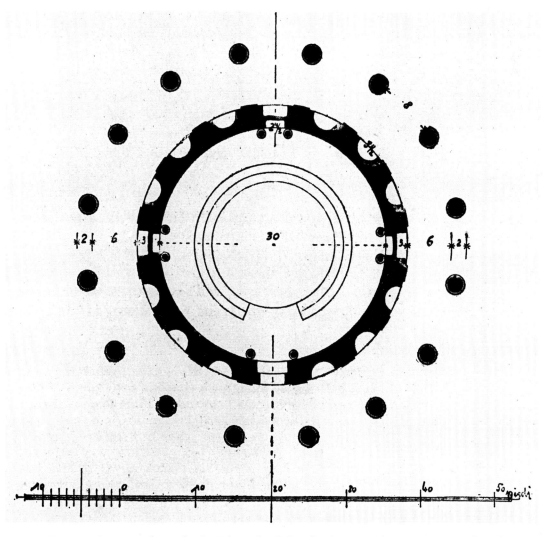

Fig. 2.46: Drawing of 1889, by C. Hülsen after "T[emplum] veneris salustianae in capite fori salustii," **Cod. Vat. lat. 3439, fol. 28.**

This written description and Vacca's report are believed to be related, yet the relationship of this information and the presumed Ligorian plan is unclear because the description, according to Lanciani (following De Rossi), was added by Onofrio Panvinio.[160] Hülsen agreed but believed the plan was also by the hand of Panvinio; yet it has been proposed by Vagenheim that *Cod. Vat. lat.* 3439 is almost entirely in the hand of Pighius.[161] Regardless of who composed *Cod. Vat. lat.* 3439, the description as well as the plan of the round building on folio 28 clearly derived from *Cod. Paris. ital.* 1129 (formerly St. Germaine 86) folio 309 in the Bibliothèque Nationale in Paris (Fig. 2.45). It is surprising in all the discussions of the plan in the Vatican that this page in the Parisian codex is mentioned only in passing (and had not been published), since it contains a more detailed written description and a more complete plan of this round building.[162] The Parisian description indicates that the building found at the head of the piazza called the Foro Sallustiano was 52 piedi in diameter, with a peristyle of yellow columns with red veins 6 piedi from the cella wall. These columns (17¾ piedi) stood on a base 1 piede in height and carried composite capitals 2¼ piedi in height (for a total height of 21 piedi). The outside niches of the cella wall were 3½ piedi wide, while those of the interior were smaller by 1 piede and were flanked by small alabaster columns (⅔ piedi in diameter?). The building was encrusted with thin slabs of alabaster, porphyry, and serpentine, and these same stones were used for the pavements both inside and outside the building, which was surrounded by three steps *ascending* into the temple.[163]

The measurements given in both the Vatican and Parisian versions are identical, save for the interior diameter that is recorded as 30 piedi in the Paris drawing but 20 piedi in the Vatican one. It is clear that the Parisian measurement is correct, because the total diameter of 52 piedi (given in both versions) must allow for an interior diameter of 30 piedi. Hülsen's assumption that the written comments in the Vatican codex were influenced by the Parisian description is supported by this error in the recording of the interior diameter as 20 piedi. Lanciani was clearly misled by this mistake, because he believed the Vatican plan represented a small building with an actual diameter

a little larger than seven meters. This would mean, however, the ancient diameter would be about 24 piedi, a measurement nowhere recorded on the drawing. Hülsen gave the correct inner diameter of 30 feet (likely drawn from his own calculations extrapolated from the Vatican version rather than from the Parisian drawing, which, it appears, he did not see), but he did not translate this into modern measurements.[164] According to my calculations, the interior diameter is 8.9 meters (30 × .297), and the whole diameter including peristyle is 15.44 meters (52 × .297), a substantial structure, although the Parisian manuscript calls it "a small but costly work" ("opera picciola ma di grandissima spesa").

If we look only at the two plans, without the aid of Vacca's descriptions, the connection between these and Vacca's report becomes less meaningful. The most glaring difference is Vacca's statement that the building found on his father's property was oval, while these plans are round.[165] That Vacca's statement "di forma ovata" ought *not* to be translated as "round" is clear from Vacca himself, who distinguished between round and oval when attempting to describe a building found near the via Pia: "non sovvenendomi se detto tempio fosse di pianta rotunda ovvero ovata."[166] Secondly, Vacca did not identify the building in his father's vineyard as a temple or tempietto, but as "una gran fabbrica" or "detto ovato." Finally, and most importantly, the two round plans indicate neither four entrances nor steps in the interior. Indeed, the idea that steps descended into the interior is the result of the misreading of the Vatican description. The more detailed Parisian codex indicates (in the written description) that three steps *ascended* into the temple presumably from the exterior; otherwise, a more unusual interior staircase would have been stressed.

The implications are clear: the oval building having four entrances and descending interior stairs reported by Vacca should not be identified with the round plans in the Vatican and Parisian codices. The vague "Pighius" description was perhaps meant to make a connection with the Vacca building, even though the round plan was incompatible.[167] Lanciani's acceptance of this erroneous connection appears to have established it as fact, forming a house of cards of speculations and assumptions supported on insubstantial or nonexistent foundations.

Finally, at the upper left corner of the Vatican drawing appears the transcription: "VENERI HORTORUM SALLUSTIANORUM C. SALLUSTIUS DRUDUS AEDITUUS D. D." This inscription is also recorded on the Parisian description. It is clear that on the Vatican version, it was added last (and perhaps by a different hand from the "Pighius" description) because the last three letters of "SALLUSTIANORUM" are written above to accommodate the seven lines of text to the right. Unclear is whether this is a legitimate transcription or a fabrication, so that it is classified among the so-called falsi ligoriani.[168] It does, however, relate to an annotation by Ligorio in *Cod. Ottob. lat.*, 3364, fol. 262:

TEMPLE OF VENUS IN THE GARDENS OF SALLUST. There was also this temple, small but quite ornate, entirely of Parian marble with brilliant white fluted columns of the Corinthian order in a circular peripteros all around, that is, surrounded by a portico, as we indicated in the drawing of the horti Sallustiani [that is, Ligorio's 1561 plan of Rome (Fig. 2.40)], which was on a rise overlooking the forum of Sallust at the ridge of the valley towards the east, precisely from where we saw excavated some very precious ruins, worked with great skill. And nearby was found this dedication that Monsignor Angelo Colocci [1474–1549; president of the Roman Academy] had [displayed] on a marble base among those dedicated to Diana, who had another temple in the same gardens, [and] there was that of the Nymphs, which is still visible in a corner fragment of brick constructions [that is, the vestibule in the piazza Sallustio].[169]

The "dedication" refers to *CIL* VI.1, 122, discovered by Fulvio in 1527 and transcribed as:

M. AVRELIUS PACORVS

M. COCCEIVS STRATOCLES

AEDITVI. VENERIS. HORTORVM

SALLUSTIANORUM. BASEM. CVM

PAV[I]MENTO. MARMORATO

DEANAE

D(ono). D(ederunt).[170]

Ligorio mistakenly recorded the name in the second to the last line as DIANAE rather than DEANAE (from

the Greek δέανα, meaning "goddess"), believing it to be dedicated to Diana and associating it with the vestibule near where the inscription apparently was discovered.[171] Indeed on Ligorio's 1553 small plan of Rome (Fig. 2.39), a building is identified as "T. DIANAE," and it appears to be this brick vestibule that, however, is in the valley rather than on the slopes of the Quirinal.

Two other inscriptions mentioning a temple of a "Venus of the Gardens of Sallust" have been identified: "D(is) M(anibus) / [M.] Ulpio Aéthrio / [U]ranius Caésaris n(ostri) servus / aedituus Veneris hortorum / Sallustianorum fecit s[ibi] / et suis posterisq(ue) eorum" (Discovered in Piazza di Pietra in 1880 in a dump),[172] and "Ti. Claudius / Apollinaris minister al[mae] / Veneris ex ho[rtis] / Sallustian[is], / testameno fi[eri] / iussit et / [I]u[l]iae Thyadi / [contu]bernali" (stele discovered in 1885 in the Villa Patrizi).[173]

There is another inscription, however, found in Rome in the gardens of the French cardinal, Jean Du Bellay:[174] a marble block bearing a relief and an inscription, indicating a dedication of an altar and its pavement to the goddess Hope (Spes) after a dream of Marcus Aurelius Pacorus, "aeditus sanctae Veneris in Salust.hortis," the same individual recorded in *CIL* VI.1, 122 above (Fig. 2.47).[175]

These inscriptions are not dedicated to Venus. Rather, each dedicant recorded himself as a custodian (*aedituus*) of a temple of this goddess in the gardens of Sallust.[176] It is tempting to equate this Venus Sallustiana temple with a temple to Venus Erycina recorded by Ovid and Livy as standing outside the porta Collina, which is perhaps within the area of the *horti Sallustiani* that was later incorporated into the city by the Aurelian wall.[177] Livy reports elsewhere that a temple to Venus Erycina "ad portam Collinam" was vowed by the consul L. Porcius Licinius on the occasion of the war against the Liguri in the year 574 of Rome (184 B.C.), and his son dedicated it when he was duumvir in 182/81 B.C.[178] But this Erycinion in or near these gardens was not the earliest in Rome to this particular manifestation of Venus, for another had been vowed by Q. Fabius Maximus in 217 B.C., in response to the Sibylline oracle, and he dedicated it himself when he was duumvir in 215 B.C.[179] According to Livy, this ear-

M. AVR. PACORVS AEDI
TVVS SANTAE VENE
RIS IN SALVST HORTIS
SPEI

ARAM CVM PAEMENTO
SOMNIO MONITVS SVM
TV SVO DD.

Romæ ad Bellaianis hortos.

Fig. 2.47: *Spes relief and inscription from the gardens of Jean du Bellay, Rome, engraving in J. J. Boissard,* **Antiqq** *IV 130.*

lier temple of Venus was in the same enclosure with the temple of the goddess Mens, such that it was separated from it by an embankment or a moat.[180] It is probably to be equated with the name *Aedes Capitolina Veneris* in the imperial period.[181]

These Venus temples in Rome were certainly imports from the ancient Sicilian city of Eryx (modern Erice), where Venus was one of the major cults of the island. Numerous dedications record the restoration of the Sicilian sanctuary in the Roman period. Consuls and senators visited it and supported its rites, not surprising because Aeneas was said to have visited Eryx, and Vergil later made him founder of the temple.[182] A senate decree established that the seventeen cities most faithful to Sicily were to offer to Eryx an annual gift and to furnish a military guard at the temple.[183] At the time of Strabo the sanctuary was in decline, but a little later Tiberius, after a request from some Segestians, ordered its restoration, although the work seems to have been carried out only under Claudius.[184]

The cult arrived in Sicily from the east, and therefore Venus Erycina carried eastern attributes and symbols such as the dog, the wheel, and the swastika.[185] The cult on the mainland appears first in Campania as recorded by an inscription found at Pozzuoli, while another (Oscan) shows the cult at Herculaneum.[186] The temple dedicated to Venus Erycina outside the porta Collina thus stood in a long migration and transformation of the cult from the east, to Sicily, through Campania, and finally into Rome.

According to Ovid, the *dies natalis* of the Roman temple was April 23, the festival of the Vinalia,[187] and this day is indicated in an inscription as the *festus meretricum*.[188] The *meretrici* were the sacred prostitutes who may have lived in the temple following a custom established by the Sicilian cult at Erice. Other non-Roman aspects of the cult at Erice were the flight of doves from the temple to the Libyan coast, and altars in the open sky—all practices going back to the Semites and, in particular, to the Phoenicians.[189] The Erice temple on the Capitoline, however, was completely romanized, unlike its Sallustian counterpart, which appears to have retained much of its Sicilian character. The use of sacred prostitution would likely have been met with some resistance, particularly since the Sallustian temple was voted in the year of the conservative

censor Cato, a strenuous defender of religious orthodoxy.[190] The extra-pomerial location perhaps allowed for leniency, and Castelli suggested that it was meant for more humble clientele as opposed to the Capitoline Venus, who was worshipped by the leading class.[191]

The Sallustian cult retained perhaps more than just the practices of its Sicilian progenitor because Ovid alluded to the transferring of a statue from Erice to Rome on the occasion of the founding of the temple outside the porta Collina.[192]

It is tempting, indeed, to see the *Ludovisi Acrolith* (Fig. 2.48), bearing perhaps a Magna Grecian character, as the very image of Venus imported from Sicily to Rome at its founding in 181 B.C. or at a later time, after the middle years of the first century A.D., when the worship of Venus at Erice may have ceased.[193] Furthermore, a passage in Strabo describes the close relationship between the Erycinian and Roman cults and may indicate that the Sallustian temple copied the architecture itself.[194] Because neither the Roman nor the Sicilian temple has been identified in any physical remains, it is impossible to make firm conclusions; however, it is clear from Strabo that the porta Collina temple was surrounded by a portico.[195]

There is only one inscription found in Rome (from the imperial period) in which Venus Erycina is cited: a funerary dedication to a fortune teller who, according to Wiseman, "gives his address as the nearby temple of Venus Erycina."[196] The only nonliterary evidence of the Republican period for the cult of Venus Erycina is a silver coin (*denarius*) of Considius Nonianus, datable from 63 to 57 B.C. (Fig. 2.49).[197]

A head of Venus on the obverse with earrings and a diadem could be related to the so-called Ludovisi acrolith, perhaps found on Ludovisi property; however, the connection is tenuous at best. In fact, the obverse, with the head of the goddess, is not consistent with the Ludovisi acrolith. Furthermore, this same head type is found on a contemporary coin series, issued by Faustus Cornelius Sulla, son of the dictator, which probably has nothing to do with the Erycinian Venus.[198] Speaking against the Ludovisi acrolith as the cult image of the temple is Ovid's report of the annual celebration of the dedication of the temple in which the statue may have been carried in a procession amidst a sea of roses, an unlikely scenario for a colossal acrolithic statue.[199]

Fig. 2.48: So-called Ludovisi Acrolith, Museo Nazionale delle Terme, Rome:
Palazzo Altemps, Inv. 8598.

Fig. 2.49: Silver coin from mint of Rome, ca. 57 B.C.
A: obverse—bust of Venus; B: reverse—Temple of Eryx.

On the reverse of the Considian coin is a temple with four columns standing on top of a tall mountain that is surrounded by a wall with a gate, over which is inscribed "ERUC." It is likely, because of the inscription indicating the city of Eryx, that this image represents the sanctuary in Sicily rather than that in Rome, but the plan of the temple as round or rectangular is impossible to determine.[200]

It is difficult, therefore, to reconcile all the evidence. Is the temple mentioned in several inscriptions as "Venus in the Gardens of Sallust" the same as that of the Erycinian Venus outside the porta Collina, as Lanciani first proposed, or are they separate structures?[201] A funerary inscription found in 1924 near the via Salaria outside the Aurelian wall could suggest that these two temples are indeed the same.[202] It reads: Iulia Aug(usti) l(iberata) / Helena, / Veneria ex hort(is) Sallustianis, / sibi et suis / In fro(nte) p(edes) XII, in agr(o) p(edes) XII.[203] According to Mancini, this indicates that Julia Helena, an imperial freedwoman (perhaps of Agrippina or of Caligula), was an attendant ("veneria") in the temple of Venus in the *horti Sallustiani*.[204] Furthermore, slaves attached to the temple of Venus Erycina in Sicily were called "Venerius" and "Veneria," and so it is indeed tempting to believe that Julia Helena served the same function in the Roman temple as her Sicilian counterparts.[205] If this is the case, then the temple of Venus Erycina may well be equated with the temple of Venus in the Gardens of Sallust in the inscriptions discussed above, and they could permit a definite location of this famous temple in these gardens. Yet these conclusions may be premature because "veneria" as recorded in this inscription, as well as others, may not mean "an attendant of Venus" but merely a name of the deceased.[206]

G. Pugliese Carratelli suggested that a replica of the famous Knidian temple to Aphrodite was in the gardens of Caesar near the porta Collina and that this temple was called "Templum Veneris hortorum Sallustianorum," in which case, any connection of this "Temple of Venus in the Gardens of Sallust" to the Temple of Venus Erycina, as Lanciani would have it, is denied.[207] According to Carratelli, the Venus to which Caesar traced the origins of his *gens* goes back to the Aphrodisian-Dionysian religious sphere at Knidos.

Caesar's connection with Knidos is exemplified by an honorary inscription to Theopompos, son of Artemidoros, and to his two sons, who having gone as ambassadors of Knidos to Caesar, had obtained for their city the assurances of freedom and the exemption from tribute, concluded in November 45 B.C. Although no ancient text confirms a replica of the Knidian temple, Carratelli hypothesized that with such a close connection of Julius Caesar to the cult in Knidos, it is possible a replica of the Knidian temple stood in the gardens of Caesar. These gardens, according to Carratelli, became the gardens of Sallust.

Vacca's reporting of the Corinthian building found on his father's property and the Ligorian plans of a monopteros are pressed into service as supporting evidence for such a structure near the porta Collina, where we have seen it is believed, perhaps mistakenly, Julius Caesar had property. Furthermore, according to Carratelli, the Knidian temple of Aphrodite Εὔπλοια was a Corinthian monopteros, as demonstrated by the original at Knidos and the replica built by Hadrian in his villa at Tivoli.[208] But the Hadrianic monopteros is Doric, and Iris Love, the excavator of the Knidian one, believed the original was also Doric.[209] Fragments of Corinthian column drums were found in the foundations of the Knidian Doric building, and Love suggested that these could represent the original monopteros for the Aphrodite, but she reached no definitive answer.[210]

Bankel's recent reevaluation of this round structure at Knidos shows that it is datable to the second century B.C. (with later Roman remodeling) and was not a Doric monopteros but a Corinthian tholos with cella. Furthermore, Bankel suggested that this tholos likely was dedicated to Athena, not to Aphrodite, who instead may have been housed in a rectangular rather than a round temple.[211] It is perhaps pertinent that a rectangular enclosure on the Pincio (at least 60 meters × 42 meters) is tentatively identified by Talamo as the sanctuary of Venus Erycina (Fig. 2.11, nr. 32). This suggestion is perhaps supported by a large rectangular area uncovered at Knidos, which Bankel proposed as the famous temple of the Knidian Aphrodite (Fig. 2.50, nr. 10).[212]

La Rocca suggested that the temple complex of

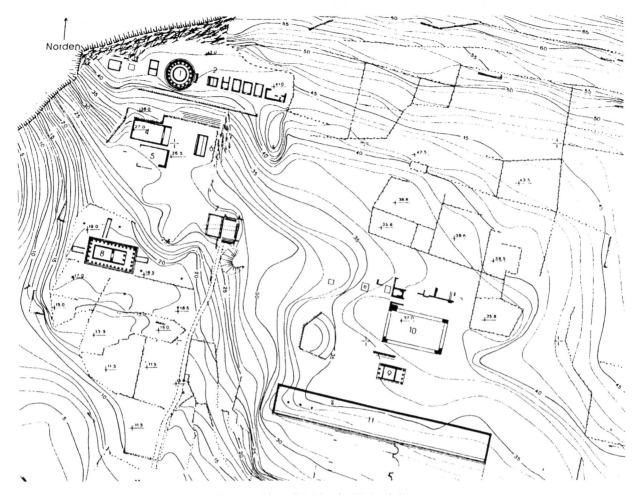

Fig. 2.50: Plan of Knidos, by H. Bankel, 1997.

Venus had been constructed on the slopes of the Pincio in a series of terraces similar to those of Fortuna Primigenia at Palestrina.[213] Indeed, as early as 1850, Canina's plan of Rome (Fig. 2.51) depicted on the slopes of the Pincio a large rectangular terrace on which is placed a temple.

It is intriguing to compare Canina's plan with the Destailleur drawing, which also shows a monumental building on the Pincio (Fig. 2.8; see pp. 31–36). Yet Canina could not have known the Destailleur drawing, which was not published until forty years later. Is this rectangular temple complex depicted in 1850 a complete fantasy, or did Canina base his reconstruction on physical remains? It is unfortunate that the 1969 excavations on the Pincio that brought to light a monumental rectangular structure have been neither published nor continued. The tantalizing identification of these remains as the sanctuary of Venus Ery-

cina, if correct, would have profound repercussions on the topography of this area, and on the cult itself, both in Rome and on Sicily.

In spite of the difficulties in accepting Carratelli's conclusions that a replica of a round Knidian Aphrodite temple was in the gardens of Sallust, Coarelli agreed that such a structure was likely by equating the tempietto-like form of Ligorio's "round" plan to other garden structures, in particular with the *aviarium* of Varro, which had four axial entrances and a circle of concentric steps. Coarelli added that this Knidian replica may have served also as a *coenatio*—not necessarily incompatible because such garden buildings could have both a public-sacred character as well as a private function.[214] Only Vacca reported the four entrances and the concentric steps inside the building of the *horti Sallustiani* but these are not shown on the drawings in Paris and the Vatican. Lanciani,

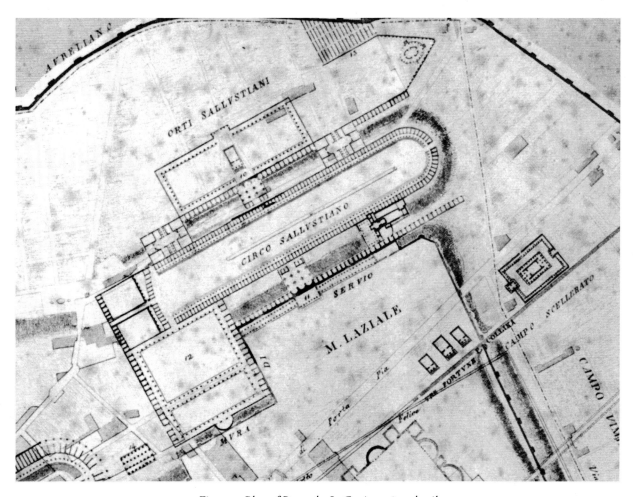

Fig. 2.51: Plan of Rome, by L. Canina, 1850: detail.

as already discussed, had attempted to interpret the Ligorian drawing as having at least one entrance that had been blocked, and he even hints there may have been another entrance (at the top of the drawing) that the original Ligorian drawing does not show.

Hülsen revised Lanciani's plan by continuing the half-circle into a fully round structure showing four entrances flanked by columns in the interior (Fig. 2.46). Furthermore, the interior rectangular niches have disappeared and along with them their flanking columns, but three concentric steps have been added. We are a long way from the original Ligorian plan. Although Coarelli reproduced Lanciani's more accurate plan, he interpreted it incorrectly as showing four entrances.[215] The evidence has been mixed together and pulled apart without regard to the facts. Interpretations and revisions of the sixteenth-century plans have been considered factual "originals," and

these form the shaky foundations on which more interpretations and theories are constructed.[216]

Besides the difficulty in interpreting the original Ligorian plan, the association of such a structure with a possible Knidian temple in the gardens of Sallust is, to my mind, even more speculative. In particular, if Julius Caesar never owned property near the porta Collina (as previously discussed, pp. 9–10), then attempts to connect architectural finds in the gardens of Sallust with a temple believed to be in the gardens of Caesar are moot.

Regardless of how the physical, literary, and inscriptional evidence is interpreted today, it must be recognized that references to either of these temples—the "Temple of Venus in the Gardens of Sallust" or the "Temple of Venus Erycina outside the Porta Collina"—were lost to memory until the sixteenth century. After this time they were considered always independent until Lanciani proposed, in the nineteenth century, they were the same. Bufalini's 1551 ichnographic plan of Rome is the earliest to include the temple of Venus Erycina, which he depicted as a round plan (Fig. 2.15A). He confused, as others before and after him, the gates of the "Servian" wall with those of the Aurelian, mistaking the porta Collina (which had disappeared since antiquity) for the later porta Salaria.[217] Consequently, the temple of Venus Erycina, known from ancient texts to be beyond the porta Collina, was placed by Bufalini outside, rather than inside, the Aurelian wall. Pirro Ligorio's 1561 plan (Fig. 2.40), which is confined within the Aurelian walls, therefore, does not depict the temple of Venus Erycina but indicates for the first time the *templum Veneris Hortorum Sallustianorum*.[218] Ligorio showed it as a domed, round building with a colonnade and placed it in the valley between the Pincio and Quirinal hills.

Ligorio must have learned of the existence of a temple of Venus in the *horti Sallustiani* from the inscription cited previously, which had been transcribed by Fulvio and published thirty-four years earlier. It is possible that the depiction of this temple as round on Ligorio's 1561 plan was the result of Ligorio's earlier 1553 plan that shows, mistakenly, the round vestibule in the valley, where it is identified as a temple to Diana (Fig. 2.39). On the other hand, according to Castelli, the depiction by Ligorio of a round temple in the valley was the direct result of the excavation of such a building on the Vacca property.[219] Consequently, Castelli believed that Ligorio's placement of this structure is not one of the famous distortions of this Neapolitan humanist but is a true recording of the location of an ancient building in the valley discovered only a short time before.

Castelli's interpretation is in sharp contrast to the usual placement of the Vacca building on the Pincio (rather than in the valley) near the porta Salaria and to the common interpretation of Vacca's report that his father's vineyard was "accanto Porta Salara dentro le mura, vi è un fondo, dove si dice gli Orti Salustiani." Lanciani interpreted this passage to mean that the Vacca vineyard was immediately beside the porta Salaria, while Castelli believed it indicated that the gardens of Sallust lay against the porta Salaria and

that the Vacca land was somewhere unspecified within these gardens. If this is the case, Ligorio's placement of a round structure in the valley, rather than on the Pincio, could show, according to Castelli, the true location of the building found on the Vacca property.

Lanciani's interpretation of the Vacca report convinced him that the Vacca vineyard, whose location is otherwise not known, passed later to the Verospi family, whose seventeenth-century villa lay near the porta Salaria (*FUR* 3: Fig. 1.1B).[220] As Castelli pointed out, these assertions are not supported by any documents recording the purchasing of the Verospi property but are based on Lanciani's interpretation of Vacca's report and on the examination of various city plans of Rome. On the other hand, Vacca did mention elsewhere that his father's vineyard was "accanto della porta Salaria" (although the *vigna* Borioni was stated to be also "beside" this gate).[221] The term "accanto," as used here by Vacca, cannot, however, indicate "beside," but perhaps "nearby" or even "in the vicinity of." Indeed, "accanto" may be even more general, similar to the Latin term "iuxta" as used in the *Liber Pontificalis*, which can have a variety of meanings, including the indication of merely the same *regio*.[222]

What seems to have gone unnoticed in this context is Vacca's statement that follows immediately after the passage recording the discovery of the oval-shaped building on his father's property:

> I remember that Carlo Muti, in his *vigna* a short distance from the gardens of Sallust, found an over-life-sized Faun holding a small boy in his arms, and a large vase with Fauns and Baccantes, dancing with cymbals in their hands—these are now in his gardens. Many other statues were found that were very much scattered about, and these could have been part of that building found in my father's *vigna;* there were also visible high walls with niches, and the statues were transported to the *vigna* of Carlo Muti.[223]

The Muti property appears from this statement to have been adjacent to the Vacca property for Vacca to suggest that the finds there could belong to the building found on his father's property mentioned just before. Lanciani emended Vacca's text to read "nella sua vigna poco lontano dagli (*dal ninféo degli*) Orti

Sallustiani," suggesting that the Muti *vigna* lay near the vestibule (called a nymphaeum by Lanciani), just south of the Verospi property. Hence, according to Lanciani, the Verospi must have purchased this land from the Vacca family.[224] Earlier, in 1897, however, Lanciani explained that these sculptures found on the Muti property were from the area of the casino Massimo, just south of the main entrance to the villa Ludovisia on the via Friuli and immediately west of the western limits of the Sallustian valley, that is, far from the brick vestibule and the Verospi property (this is the area designated on *FUR* 9 [Fig. 1.1C] as "Villa Cesi d'Acquasparta poi Massimo di Rignano").[225] Indeed, Bufalini (1551) shows the location of the "V. Episco. Mutii" in just this location (Fig. 2.15C), and the "high walls with niches" reported above must be the still-visible wall with niches along the via Lucullo on the former Muti property (see Figs. 2.35–2.36 and pp. 58–60). Furthermore, Venuti reported that Piranesi believed to have found ruins of the *Porticus Migliarensis* in the Villa Cesi, and he immediately followed this statement with the Vacca report of the discovery of the oval building in his father's *vigna,* concluding that the oval building was perhaps part of this portico.[226] Venuti clearly believed that the Vacca building was found in or near the grounds of the Cesi villa, which had been former Muti property.

The ramifications of the Vacca *vigna* not being against the Aurelian wall on the Pincio, but adjacent to the Muti property to the west of the valley are, of course, significant for the placement of the oval building reportedly found in it. Ligorio's depiction of a round building in the valley is difficult to support, and Lanciani's placement of a round building on the Pincio north of the vestibule (*FUR* 3: Fig. 1.1B) must be viewed with skepticism.

What seems clear is that the building excavated on the Vacca property was destroyed shortly after its discovery. The columns were sold and recut for other uses, and it certainly did not survive beyond the seventeenth century, when much earth moving and leveling of land for villa construction took place.[227] Bartoli's mention in the seventeenth century of remains of another temple, however, has been thought pertinent to this discussion: "Più avanti verso porta Pia, non mi ricordo in quale vigna . . . l'e-mo Massimi vidde cavare le vestigie di un bellissimo tempio, le metà del quale era sopra terra, e nel suo tempo fu disfatto, ove furono trovate colonne e marmi nobilissimi" (Further ahead [from the church of the Vittoria = Santa Maria della Vittoria, east of Santa Susanna] towards the porta Pia, I don't remember in which *vigna* . . . His Eminence [Cardinal] Massimi had seen excavated the remains of a most beautiful temple, half of which was above ground, and in his day it was scavenged because there were found first-rate columns and marbles).[228] Although Lanciani thought these remains to be those of the oval building found on the Vacca property,[229] this is unlikely, given the location as towards the porta Pia.[230] It is enticing to equate this temple with one of the three temples of Fortuna reported by Vitruvius as near the porta Collina or with the temple of Venus Erycina, which could have stood just outside the old city wall near the *agger*.[231]

Besides our inability to pin down the location of the Vacca building, we must confess that the identification of this structure as a temple is not assured. The conduits reportedly found under it convinced Nibby and others that the building must have been part of a bath.[232] Hülsen identified it as a luxury pavilion, a sort of small nymphaeum.[233] Conduits, however, do not rule out a temple, which could have a water supply, as indicated by Ovid, if it is not simply literary flourish, who advises taking cool waters from the temple of Venus to quench the heat of love.[234] Also, the date of this oval structure is unclear. Vacca reported that many coins of Gordian were found under this building, perhaps suggesting that it had been constructed as late as the fourth century A.D. Indeed, it is recorded in an ancient text that Gordian projected a massive garden project for the Campus Martius, perhaps near the slopes of the Quirinal, and so a fourth-century date for the oval building must be considered a distinct possibility.[235]

Pertinent to this discussion is a large building depicted on the Bufalini plan of 1551, located near the area designated as the Muti *vigna* (Fig. 2.15C). It is shown as a long, apsidal building with a series of parallel walls on the exterior running perpendicular to the long walls. The open short side appears to have a square forecourt or porch whose roof is supported by perhaps four large piers. The apsidal end is separated from the main hall by small spur walls. Twenty-six years later, du Pérac depicted this same building on his perspective plan of Rome (Fig. 1.7: E), locating it in the general area of the Bufalini plan. Although it appears to be an impressive building, it is not shown definitively on plans earlier than Bufalini's and surprisingly not later than du Pérac's.

The limited chronology suggests that this building may have appeared only in the mid 1500s and was completely destroyed and lost from sight before the end of the century. In other words, it is possible *this* is the building that Flaminio Vacca remembered as having been discovered in 1551 (when he was about thirteen years old) in his father's *vigna,* which was contiguous to the Muti property. In 1594 when he recorded his thoughts about this event, the building had been completely destroyed probably decades before. Although Vacca remembered well the architectural details, he was cautious in identifying the building, calling it "di forma ovata," a term Vacca's contemporaries used for the shape of a circus.[236] The long, apsidal building depicted by Bufalini and du Pérac may well have

suggested to Vacca a circus-like shape, and hence he designated it a "forma ovata."

It is tempting to believe that Vacca's large oval building was indeed a circus-shape structure that in antiquity served as a garden-stadium. The large conduits lined with Greek marble, reported by Vacca, could have been remains of open basins, and the three steps (used as planting beds?) in the interior could have evoked the seating of an actual stadium.

Regardless of how we interpret the apsidal building on the Pincio or the fragmentary and disparate evidence for identifying Ligorio's drawing as a temple of Venus in the *horti Sallustiani,* the physical reality of the Vacca building has been lost to memory. The only other substantial remains visible in the gardens of Sallust were those of a large brick construction on the slopes of the Quirinal: the vestibule. It is not surprising, therefore, that Piranesi in 1748 identified *this* brick building as the temple of Venus (see Fig. 2.5 [dated 1756]). Although he corrected his error in 1762, it persisted under later scholars such as Venuti and Nibby.[237]

PART III

Sculptural Finds

Numerous pieces of sculpture are reported to have been discovered in the confines of the gardens of Sallust. It would be difficult, therefore, to give a full report on each of these; however, there are a number of sculptures that deserve special attention as works of art because of issues surrounding their findspots. Many of these could have (and some have had) their own book or at least extensive article. For all these reasons, it is impossible to discuss every issue and to pursue every scholarly argument that may be of interest to the reader. Thus these discussions are personal selections and as such are not meant to be definitive.

Because of the importance bestowed on them by modern scholars, several statues or groups deserve a second look, particularly with regard to their discoveries and their possible association with the gardens of Sallust. Indeed, several statues, like the Copenhagen Niobids, which have been thought to come from the gardens of Sallust, perhaps do not come from there at all. Furthermore, the Artemis, Iphigenia, and hind group, also in Copenhagen, although certainly from the area of the gardens, likely does not derive from where it is believed to have been found. Egyptian and Egyptianizing works, Gauls, and Dionysiac sculptures are discussed as possible groupings and in the context

of their potential meaning in a garden setting. The well-known Boston and Ludovisi "Thrones" continue to be controversial, but an attempt is made below to legitimize both as ancient works and to define their findspots in the gardens. Several other sculptures came to light in 1888, but it is difficult to determine whether their mutual findspot has any significance. In other words, in this case, a "cache" of sculptures may be merely serendipitous, and the common findspot of the sculptures irrelevant in determining a common use in the ancient gardens. Finally, the group of Orestes and Electra, considered by some scholars to derive from the gardens, is an example of how sculptures are sometimes arbitrarily assigned to these gardens.

The comments and discussions do not claim to be exhaustive. For example, stylistic analysis is deliberately minimized, because the focus is primarily on the findspots, early reports and theories, and the ultimate pertinence to the gardens of Sallust. Finally, the ordering of the discussion of these sculptures is not meant to indicate the relative importance of each but is merely the result of the kind of information included. This section, therefore, although having distinct headings, is conceived of as a whole.

Fig. 3.1: ***Artemis, Iphigenia, and a Hind,*** *Ny Carlsberg Glyptotek, Copenhagen, Kat. 83, I.N. 481–482a.*

ARTEMIS, IPHIGENIA, AND A HIND

Marble fragments, discovered in July of 1886 during the sinking of pylons for the construction of a new house for Cesare Bai near the piazza Sallustio, have been joined to recreate partially a statuary group of *Artemis, Iphigenia, and a Hind,* now in the Ny Carlsberg Glyptotek in Copenhagen (Fig. 3.1). The property in which these fragments were found had been owned by Josef Spithoever, who, however, still retained the rights to all archaeological material that would come to light during this building operation. The location of the discovery of this impressive sculpture, and its possible position in the ancient gardens, have been believed secure, but the precise findspot may not be as definite as the reports suggest.

According to the original notices of 1886 by Visconti and Lanciani in the *Bullettino Comunale* and in the *Notizie degli Scavi,* both monthly journals devoted to the immediate reporting of archaeological material,[1] an area near the piazza Sallustio had revealed subterranean chambers (apparently all originally vaulted; see Fig. 2.25: lower right). These chambers were mostly destroyed, but one contained an elaborately inlaid marble floor, mosaic walls of glass, and/or marble tesserae as well as of shells, and paintings of landscapes and figures.[2]

Of even greater importance were fragments of sculptures that included a torso of the goddess Artemis, a smaller torso of another female figure, published by Visconti as a "Running Girl"[3] (later mistakenly identified by Lanciani as a "Niobide"; see pp. 95–96) (Fig. 3.2),[4] fragments of a hind, and numerous other pieces, some of which were seen to have been part of these three larger fragments.[5]

The Artemis and the hind were recognized by Vis-

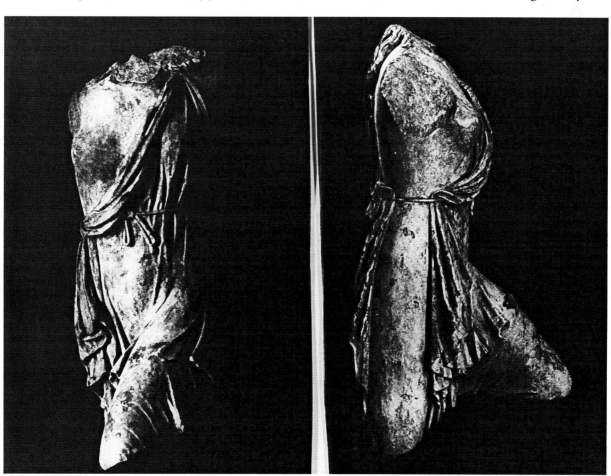

Fig. 3.2: So-called Running Girl, from Visconti 1886.

*Fig. 3.3: Plaster reconstruction of **Artemis, Iphigenia,** and a **Hind.***

conti as belonging together to form a group similar to a better-preserved example in the Louvre that shows the goddess in the hunt.[6] Carl Jacobsen soon purchased these pieces and the smaller female torso in 1888 for the Glyptotek in Denmark. Jacobsen displayed the two torsos side by side, believing they belonged together as a group because of their similar workmanship and style.[7] Furtwängler, however, believed the Artemis was stylistically close to the work of Praxiteles (fourth century B.C.), while the other torso was seen as "entirely Pergamene" (Hellenistic).[8]

In spite of Furtwängler's reservations of the pertinence of the female torso and Artemis, in 1898 Studniczka concluded that the figure preserved only by its torso, the so-called Running Girl (Fig. 3.2), was in fact falling, and he identified it as Iphigenia collapsing at the feet of Artemis. A place where the figures touched was identified on the left leg of Artemis, and the two were joined and restored (Fig. 3.1).[9]

Jacobsen decided to have Studniczka reinvestigate the area where this statuary group was discovered to obtain more fragments and information concerning their possible display. By this time, it seems, the house of Cesare Bai had been replaced by a multistory apartment house at via Sallustiana IA, on the southwest corner of the piazza Sallustio, near the vestibule.[10] The owner of the property, the Banca d'Italia, granted permission to excavate, and the digging of a deep shaft was begun within the basement, whose floor was some 3.50 to 3.60 meters below the modern ground level.[11]

For one week in April 1901 and for one month the following year, Studniczka conducted archaeological investigations at a site that had been uncovered fifteen years earlier.[12] After 7 meters of excavation, a chamber, ca. 4.10 meters wide and at least 11 meters long, was reached. It contained the foundation piers for the modern building above, and was half-filled by the partially collapsed barrel vault, which originally rose 6.6 meters above the pavement. Below this chamber and running in the same northwest-southeast direction was discovered an impressive drain about 3 meters deep and perhaps as wide as 3.20 meters—larger than the Cloaca Maxima in the Roman Forum.[13]

Over three hundred fragments of marble were collected from this chamber and inside the drain, and some of these could be joined to the existing pieces in

*Fig. 3.4: Fragments of the **Artemis, Iphigenia, and a Hind** group and a round altar, from Studniczka 1926.*

Copenhagen. Among the most important identifications were those of a piece of a strut at the neck of the hind that joined to a strut on Artemis, and the thumb of Artemis on the left antler.[14]

The animal's position in relation to Artemis was thus assured, convincing Carl Jacobsen, director of the Glyptotek Museum, to support a complete recreation of the original group (Fig. 3.3).[15]

Furthermore, several of the "numerous fragments" of sculptures mentioned by Lanciani as having been discovered in 1886 in this area were able to be identified from a photograph in the possession of Josef Haass, a nephew and heir to Spithoever. Studniczka's publication of this photograph (Fig. 3.4) shows a round marble altar,[16] fragments of a hind (hoof, part of the snout, a portion of the body), the right foot of Artemis, and part of the left hand of Iphigenia. Studniczka discovered these in the basement of a Florentine art dealer, Stefano Bardini, with other fragments, including part of the right thigh of this same figure as well as the right lower arm of Artemis.[17]

In 1911 the three figures (Artemis, Iphigenia, and hind) were restored, and their positions in relation to each other were well enough established that a complete plaster replica could be made in Leipzig and sent to Copenhagen (Fig. 3.3). In the 1902 excavations a square brick base, about 1.5 meters on each side and 0.955 meters high, was found (but not removed by Studniczka) against the middle of the short southern wall of the chamber. The presumed marble facing was missing, but the brick top still retained a recess at the front right corner into which Studniczka thought must have been set a small altar over which Iphigenia leaned (not, however, shown on Fig. 3.3).

Besides the impressive restoration of an important marble group, the 1902 excavations returned valuable information about the chamber itself and its physical relationship to the gardens. It is certain that the short southern wall, in front of which the Artemis, Iphigenia, and hind group was believed to have stood, was completely closed. The opposite northern area was unable to be excavated entirely, for it continued under the modern highway, and the vault had collapsed there onto the floor. A long marble slab was found face down across the width of this side. Studniczka believed it to be the vertical edge of a water basin.

A piece of white marble wall revetment was preserved *in situ* only at the south end of the chamber near the statue base. Holes for the attachment of other marble plaques were observed on the other walls but only for about two meters from the pavement, suggesting a marble dado with perhaps a wall painting or mosaic above. Likewise, the floor was paved in *opus sectile,* possible fragments of which were found (not *in situ*) and identified as pavonazzetto, alabaster, and green "porphyry."[18] Also, fragments of mosaic decoration made of square or wedge-shaped pieces of colored glass were perhaps for the upper walls and/or the vault.

Finally, a single broken, marble plaque with horizontal "steps" was identified as a "ladder" meant to be applied to a wall for the cascading of water over its surface, and thus the chamber appears to have been a nymphaeum. Fragments of similar water ladders came from a "nymphaeum" of a private house of the late

Antonine period (brickstamps have been dated to A.D. 150 and A.D. 164) found in the former garden Rospigliosi on the Quirinal (whose remains were housed in the "Magazzini Piatti" of the via Nazionale), but Studniczka was unable to find them there.[19] From the excavation report and Lanciani's *FUR* 16, the Rospigliosi remains were part of a long corridor, with its back wall against the slopes of the hill and from which water descended into pools below. Visconti believed, probably rightly, that these fountains served as a retaining wall as well as foundations for structures above. The *horti Sallustiani* nymphaeum, and its likely neighboring series of rooms, probably functioned similarly. Indeed, Evans suggested that the so-called Servian wall along the Quirinal may have continued in use not for defensive purposes but to carry a branch of the *Aqua Marcia* built in 144 B.C.[20] If this were the case, then the possible series of nymphaea on the northern slopes of the Quirinal would have had a ready water supply.

It seems likely, therefore, that this vaulted chamber found in 1901/1902 ought to be identified as a nymphaeum, even though water conduits were not readily visible. Yet it is still unclear how one would have entered this room, for no thresholds were found. The southern end seems most certainly to have been closed, and the acceptance of a basin of water spanning the width at the north allows for no apparent entrance there. It may have been conceived for viewing rather than entry, but this is not the only possibility. Openings on the long sides could have allowed passage between the water basin and the statue group, as well as a view northward down the valley and beyond to the Pincian hill. Studniczka did not rule these out, accepting the possibility that the large modern pylons could be hiding side doorways from sight.[21] Other rooms, in very poor preservation, were reported, and these may have been of similar shape and use, with a lateral corridor permitting passage from one to the other.[22]

Also unclear is the physical relationship of this chamber to the vestibule at the east and to the valley at the north. The plotting of the location is made difficult because Lanciani's recording of 48 meters above sea level (a.s.l.) for the floor of the vestibule appears to be erroneous. According to Lehmann-Hartleben's detailed study, it is, in fact, 45 meters a.s.l. or 14 meters below the modern level of the piazza Sallustio.[23] Likewise, for the 1901/1902 excavations, Studniczka did not record absolute levels; rather, he measured the various depths in relationship to the contemporary ground level of the piazza Sallustio, which is 59 meters a.s.l. Starting from these measurements, one can determine that the floor of the presumed Artemis nymphaeum was 41.80 meters a.s.l. or, if Lanciani's measurements of 41 meters a.s.l. for the valley floor are correct, a mere 0.80 meters above the valley floor. The large drain under this chamber lay about 3 meters lower and, therefore, could have extended easily under the valley. Furthermore, the top of Studniczka's chamber is approximately 48.4 meters a.s.l., and so it rose above the ground level of the vestibule by as much as 3.4 meters. It would not have obstructed, however, the view from the inside of the vestibule because this nymphaeum was not on axis of its door (see Fig. 2.28).

Although the location of Studniczka's chamber is relatively certain, it is unlikely, however, that this is where the torsos of Artemis and Iphigenia came to light. There are important discrepancies between the physical remains as recorded by Studniczka in 1901/1902 and those of the original, earlier, reports of the finding of the torsos. In particular, in 1886 Visconti described in detail a partially vaulted room measuring at least 7 meters (the full extent was not uncovered) by 3.94 meters and decorated as a nymphaeum with mosaics of marble and shells, and wall paintings of landscapes, animals, and flowers. He located it 17 meters below the ground, and at the same level as the vestibule and some 80 meters from it. This is not, however, where Visconti reported the discovery of what he identified as the Diana (Artemis) and Running Girl (Iphigenia), for he continued that "in the hollows of the piers for the new building were observed *other parts of the same structure* [my italics], but in a very sorry state and badly preserved. And in the middle of these ruins on the pavement of a large room were discovered the two beautiful torsos."[24] Studniczka addressed this discrepancy of the findspot and concluded that Visconti was mistaken because Lanciani reported the sculptures to have been found in a nymphaeum. Josef Haass, a nephew of Spithoever, remembered the finding of the Iphigenia torso in such a place, lying upside down in a drain.[25]

There are indeed other differences between Visconti's description of his nymphaeum and that found by Studniczka in 1902. Studniczka washed some of the walls, but he was unsuccessful in finding any of the paintings that Visconti reported. Furthermore, some colors of the marble mosaic Visconti mentioned in his 1886 report, such as violet and yellow, were not discovered in Studniczka's chamber. Nevertheless, Studniczka believed that his chamber was the same as that reported in 1886, and he even claimed Visconti's description of marble mosaics was a mistake because Studniczka's mosaics were of glass paste, "as Lanciani had correctly seen."[26]

Not addressed by Studniczka is Visconti's locating of his nymphaeum some 80 meters to the west of the vestibule. The chamber excavated by Studniczka lies, at most, 25 meters from the vestibule, so there is a 55-meter discrepancy that is difficult to explain. It is likely, as discussed above, there was a series of nymphaea along the slope of the Quirinal and that Visconti described a more elaborate version of one of these than that discovered by Studniczka. Indeed, Visconti believed that a series of niches (reported lying between the Bai property and the newly created retaining wall around the vestibule) belonged to the same complex as his nymphaeum.[27] It is conceivable that one of these niches could be Studniczka's chamber, that is, only about 15 meters from the present retaining wall for the piazza Sallustio (see Fig. 2.25, lower right).

Further arguments can be raised to suggest that Studniczka's chamber was not the place of discovery of the torsos. The 1886 building campaign exposed a considerable area at the same moment, and the refilling must have moved pieces, particularly small ones, from their former locations. It is possible, therefore, that the small fragments pertinent to the Artemis, Iphigenia, and hind group identified by Studniczka were not originally part of the chamber in which they were discovered. Studniczka admitted that even larger "foreign" elements intruded into the chamber such as a Corinthian marble capital (H: 0.52 meter; D: 0.40 meter) and other architectural pieces that were later used as decoration in the gardens of villa Flaminia, the residence of Commander Marchiori, general director of the Banca d'Italia.[28] Other pieces in the vaulted chamber may have been deposited from a considerable distance, as suggested by a statuette, found in 1886, of Silvanus, inscribed with the names of two pretorian guards, that may have come from the Castrum.[29]

Many other pieces, besides those pertinent to the Artemis, Iphigenia, and hind group, were recovered by Studniczka, including a considerable number of fragments of Campana reliefs as well as terracotta ornaments that perhaps came from upper stories, neighboring rooms, or later intrusions.[30] Small remains of potsherds, mostly *terra sigillata* (some with stamps), amphora handles, and lamps were inventoried, the latest pieces dating to the fifth century A.D. Also recorded were a bronze coin of Flavian date (with a head of either Vespasian or Titus) and three joining fragments of the foot of a marble candelabrum (see pp. 116–119), carved with a delicate leaf-pattern on three sides, which Studniczka dated to the Hadrianic period.[31]

Studniczka noted that the pavement bricks were in large part stamped, but he did not copy these, although he recorded them as Hadrianic. He took this brick pavement, however, for a possible redecorating of the room rather than part of the first building phase, which he believed was represented by large slabs of peperino. On the other hand, the slabs could have been the covers for two large, square openings into the drain.[32] As Block pointed out, Studniczka was content with the earlier report by Gatti of stamps that were recovered from a nearby dump and assumed these were representative of his room. Of these, two are late Trajanic, and three are Hadrianic.[33] The evidence, therefore, points to a Hadrianic date for the presumed series of nymphaea along the Quirinal slopes, contemporary with the large vestibule nearby. Although the layout of the distribution of water is unclear, as we have already discussed, all these nymphaea most likely had a connecting series of water pipes that linked them together.

The dating of the sculptural grouping is not as secure as the architecture in which it was discovered. Studniczka dated it to the fourth century B.C., the period just after Lysippos, while Kjellberg believed it to be an original of the middle of the following century.[34] Lippold saw the sculptures as even later, perhaps at the close of the second century, and Poulsen opted for an early imperial date in the time of Augustus.[35]

More recently, Ridgway considered an imperial date, perhaps as late as Hadrianic, rather than the more usually accepted late Hellenistic.[36] Ridgway noted that Artemis' sandals were "of undoubted Roman date," and she accepted a suggestion by Simon that the hind is not to be substituted for Iphigenia but used to transport her to the land of the Taurians, a version of the story attested in Pompeian paintings.[37] Most scholars, however, date this group earlier than the architecture in which it was found. Its Hadrianic use, therefore, would be at minimum a secondary manifestation from its original "life." Indeed, Studniczka identified several small areas of Luna (Carrara) marble as indications of later repairs to the statue, but these would have gone unnoticed in the darkness of the nymphaeum.[38]

Although all scholars accept the general reconstruction of the three figures, the small altar Studniczka restored at the viewer's right is not. Bieber believed it should be at the left, while Simon has queried whether it was even necessary.[39] Studniczka restored an altar, as discussed, because of a depression in the square brick base he found in 1902. Moving the altar or believing it may never have existed implies that the physical evidence of the base is being ignored or interpreted differently from Studniczka's reconstruction. To my mind, the connection of the sculptural group to this square base depends exclusively on the pertinence of the depression as an indication of an altar; otherwise, there is no other physical evidence to link them.

It is likely, regardless of the dating, that the *Artemis, Iphigenia, and a Hind* had been displayed elsewhere before ending up in the gardens of Sallust because replicas have been found in contexts other than gardens.[40]

For example, in the course of three excavation campaigns in the early 1970s on the island of Samos, excavators found seven fragments of a torso. Three other fragments already in the storerooms of the archaeological museum in Pythagoreion (Samos) were seen to belong together with these seven. The pieces could be partially assembled as an over-life-sized female figure dressed in a long, high-belted peplos of dark gray marble, with the right shoulder and breast exposed, and made of white marble (Fig. 3.5).[41] Freyer-Schauenburg identified this as a replica of the Copenhagen Iphigenia and, therefore, assumed a similar arrangement of figures.[42] This Iphigenia was discovered in a Roman bath dating, in four building phases, from the Hadrianic period through the late third century (A.D. 270–280), ending by the middle of the fourth century.[43] The fragments come from a rectangular room at the west of the complex (Room N0-N1) whose pavement covers ceramic sherds of the first to early second centuries, and whose walls are believed to be Antonine in date.[44] Consequently, because of its findspot as well as the dry, stiff folds of the drapery, the figure is dated to the early Antonine period.[45] An Asia Minor workshop for the Samian Iphigenia appears likely. Not only were the exposed parts of the body pieced together in white marble, this being a technique in Asia Minor, but the dark-marble drapery was also composed of joining pieces, a technique attested also by the Dancing Girl from Perge.[46]

According to Freyer-Schauenberg, the finding of this statue type on Samos could indicate that the prototype was in Ephesos, a source Studniczka suggested previously for the marble of the Copenhagen figures.[47] Furthermore, she suggested that the cults of Cybele and Artemis show close connections between Samos and Ephesos, as a shrine on Samos to Artemis and votives to Cybele reveal.[48] Yet this Samian Artemis cult flourished only in the sixth century B.C., and similar votives to Cybele of the Greek classical period have been found not only at Ephesos and Samos but also at Magnesia, Miletus, Tyre, Notion, and Priene.[49] These cult practices were not significant in the time of the Artemis, Iphigenia, and hind group and would have disappeared as early as the first century B.C., which Freyer-Schauenberg considered the period of the prototype.[50]

Another statue group similar to that of the Copenhagen *Artemis, Iphigenia, and a Hind* was discovered in 1935 on the Aventine in a second- and third-century sanctuary of Jupiter Dolichenus (Fig. 3.6).[51] It was the largest statue (H: 1.88 meters) found there and depicts a striding female holding a torch in the left hand and the horns of a rearing hind in the right. Reclining at her feet, and at greatly reduced scale, is a long-haired female, dressed in a flowing garment but with the right breast bared. This grouping is indeed a variant that not only reduces the role of "Iphigenia" to

*Fig. 3.5: Torso of **Iphigenia**, Archaeological Collection of Pythagoreion, Samos.*

*Fig. 3.6: **Artemis, Iphigenia, and a Hind** from the Sanctuary of Jupiter Dolichenus on the Aventine, Museo Capitolino, Rome, Inv. 9778.*

almost a mere attribute of the goddess, but the torch and the wind-blown arc of drapery behind the head of the larger figure perhaps identify it as Diana/Luna. The head has been recognized as a portrait of Faustina Major, and the sculpture is dated accordingly to the middle of the second century A.D.[52] Indeed, a Diana/Luna was common in the Antonine period for the apotheosis of women of the imperial house as well as for private individuals.[53]

Apart from its significance to the cult of Jupiter Dolichenus, this grouping shows how far a sculpture can be from its prototype and still be recognizable as a variant. If Simon is correct in explaining the small, reclining "Iphigenia" as an identifying marker for the Taurian Diana, then a conscious effort was made to evoke the "original" subject, however remote it may first appear.

It seems clear that a grouping of Artemis, Iphigenia, and a hind is more than a generic evocation of the huntress of wild animals and is not a subject necessarily associated with garden settings. On the other hand, this episode of the Trojan epic would have been not only well known but an appropriate one for a Roman audience, reflecting the initial mythological/historical stage in the long process of the founding of the city of Rome itself. Furthermore, such a Greek subject within a strictly Roman context could have raised the issue of Rome's dependency on the Greek world as well as its domination over it. It would not be surprising, therefore, that such a sculptural grouping would have been given a special place of honor in an imperial garden, even perhaps with its own architectural space. In this way a viewer would be required to pause in admiration both of its aesthetic qualities as a work of art and of its significance as a visual manifestation of the past.

A garden setting would be an ideal location, allowing the time and inclination for reflection and perhaps even discussion that would be prompted by such an image. Like the portraits of philosophers that could have been assembled in chronological or even alphabetical order along garden paths, so sculptural groupings such as the *Artemis, Iphigenia, and a Hind* from the gardens of Sallust could have been juxtaposed with other subjects dealing with the Trojan War or even with Artemis herself. Given the difficulties in establishing the precise location of this grouping within the larger context of the gardens of Sallust, we cannot be sure how it was displayed. We can be secure in accepting, however, that it played a significant role in the sculptural ensemble overlooking the valley from the slopes of the Quirinal.

In the vicinity of this sculpture was believed to have been another group representing the slaughter of the children (Niobids) of Niobe, a nymph who boasted to have borne more children than Leto, mother of Apollo and Artemis. The appropriateness of displaying together a sculpture representing the sacrificing of Iphigenia, and a group representing the slaying by Artemis (and perhaps by Apollo, her brother) of the children of Niobe, is apparent and enticing. Yet the misidentification of sculptures as Niobids (as hinted above with Lanciani's identification of the "Running Girl" as a Niobid), and the confusion of findspots of at least some of these sculptures must be explored before any pertinence to the gardens of Sallust can be drawn.

NIOBIDS[54]

Two statues identified as Niobids (a *Fleeing Maiden* and a *Dying Youth*: Figs. 3.7 and 3.8 respectively) were purchased in 1888 by Carl Jacobsen through his new Roman agent, Wolfgang Helbig, who acquired them from the German bookseller Josef Spithoever.[55]

Lanciani admitted that the reports did not shed much light on the findspots of these statues; however, according to him, it is certain that one was found in August 1886 15 meters under the Casa Bai on the cor-

ner of the piazza Sallustio, and the other in "ottobre seguente" under the same house.[56] These dates (August 1886 and October 1886/1887?), and findspots (near the piazza Sallustio) derive, however, from apparent misunderstandings.

In 1906 Lanciani quoted Visconti's 1886 description of a "Running Girl," discussed in the previous section (Fig. 3.2), said to have been found in "the hole made for a corner pylon of the Bai house, almost opposite

*Fig. 3.7: **Fleeing Maiden**, Ny Carlsberg Glyptotek, Copenhagen, Kat. 398.*

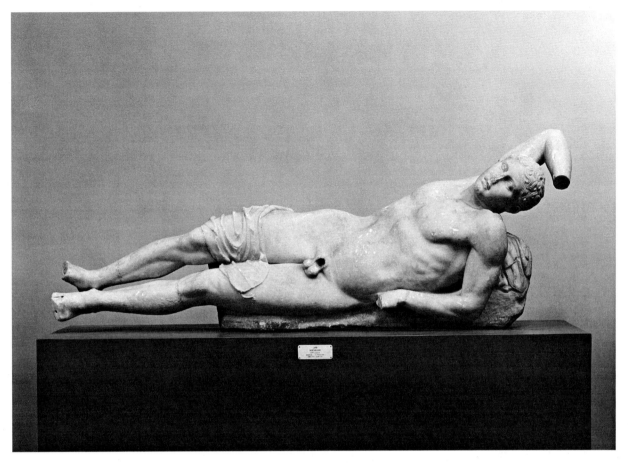

Fig. 3.8: **Dying Youth,** *Ny Carlsberg Glyptotek, Copenhagen, Kat. 399.*

the front of the Nymphaeum (the 'vestibule') at a depth of 15 meters" in August of that year. He mistakenly suggested that this figure was a "Niobide," in spite of Studniczka's previous identification in 1898 of the figure as Iphigenia, demonstrating, as discussed above (pp. 85–87), its pertinence to a statue group with Artemis and a hind.[57] Lanciani's claim that one of the Copenhagen Niobids was discovered in August 1886 15 meters under the casa Bai must be the result of his misidentification of the Iphigenia as a Niobid. His mistaken identity of Studniczka's statue is significant with respect to the date and findspot not only of the *Fleeing Maiden* (Fig. 3.7) but probably, as we will see, of the *Dying Youth* (Fig. 3.8).

Furthermore, in 1906 Lanciani quoted his own 1886 report of the discovery in October of that year (during the building of the home of Cesare Bai) of a torso of Diana (the Artemis of the Artemis, Iphigenia, and hind group, later identified by Studniczka), as well as

of "another similar one with fluttering drapery (a Niobid)." This must be, once again, the mistaken identification of the Iphigenia of the Artemis, Iphigenia, and hind group as a Niobid.[58] The October 1886 find date implied by Lanciani in his 1906 report is intriguing because both the Artemis and Iphigenia statues were published as having been found in August of that year.[59] It is probable, therefore, Lanciani's claim that one of the Copenhagen statues was found "nel ottobre sequente" (following an August 1886 discovery) was based on the false October 1886 date for the finding of the Iphigenia (Lanciani's Niobid). The usual interpretation of "nel ottobre sequente" as October of the following year, 1887, is unlikely because by that time, the house of Cesare Bai was already completed.[60] In other words, Lanciani's conclusions that these discoveries (the Artemis and Iphigenia of "August and October 1886") represent the figures of Niobids now in the Ny Carlsberg Glyptotek were based on the *double* misidentification of the single statue of Iphigenia as *both* Niobids in Copenhagen, even though neither of Lanciani's so-called Niobids (represented by female torsos) could be the male *Dying Youth*.

Furthermore, Josef Spithoever reported a(nother?) figure of a Niobid to Lanciani. Spithoever had this statue, along with other sculptures (Leda, Endymion, a replica of a Praxitelean faun, and a ram in rosso antico), on the ground floor of his home on the Quirinal.[61] Lanciani and Visconti were able to see *some of these* in the spring of 1888, but Lanciani did not state which pieces were available for examination.[62] It is possible, therefore, that the Niobid reported by Spithoever is, in fact, the figure of Iphigenia that was purchased from him for the Glyptotek in 1888, perhaps before Lanciani's and Visconti's spring visit. If this were the case, then Lanciani never saw this "Niobid," accounting for his confusion and the subsequent misunderstandings about findspots, dates of discoveries, and even numbers of Niobids. In other words, there is no direct evidence that these so-called Niobids mentioned by Lanciani (which are likely the misidentifications of the torsos of Artemis and Iphigenia) have anything whatsoever to do with the two statues of the *Fleeing Maiden* and the *Dying Youth* in Copenhagen.

Lanciani wrote an intriguing letter to the Ministry, which I have been unable to see, preserved in the Archivio Vittoriano (P 875) that could support, however, at least one Niobid identified by Lanciani. According to Talamo, the letter, dated June 21, 1882, spoke of Lanciani's and Visconti's visit to the villa Spithoever, where they saw statues of Endymion, Leda, a Niobid, a Praxitelean faun, and a ram in rosso antico—precisely the statues reported as having been seen there in 1888.[63] Were there *two* visits by Lanciani and Visconti to Spithoever's villa, six years apart, or is this another example of confusion in the reporting of dates?

The 1882 date given by Talamo for the visit by Lanciani negates the identification of the Niobid mentioned in this letter as one of the two figures in Copenhagen that are believed to have been found only later in 1886 and/or 1887. Lanciani did report, however, the discovery in April 1882 in the *vigna* Spithoever (during operations of the building of the via Flavia) of a youth, partially clothed, and missing only the left arm.[64] This statue has been equated by Talamo with the *Dying Youth* in Copenhagen (Fig. 3.8), but this identification seems unlikely because the Copenhagen youth has the left arm preserved and is missing both hands and the toes of both feet.[65] The statue reportedly found in April 1882 is, therefore, unlikely to be this sculpture in Copenhagen.

In fact, a figure of a satyr now in Copenhagen (*Resting Satyr* in the Ny Carlsberg Glyptotek; Fig. 3.9), possibly from the gardens of Sallust, is virtually intact save for the missing left arm. Such a satyr type was reportedly found in 1882 near the vestibule, and it matches the vague description of the statue found in April 1882 during the building of the via Flavia in the vicinity of the vestibule. As we have discussed, Lanciani and Visconti saw a Praxitelean "faun" in Spithoever's collection possibly as early as 1882, but most certainly by 1888, and it seems to have been still there in 1897 when Ludwig Pollak and Matthew Stewart Prichard reported seeing it on January 22, 1897. The *Resting Satyr* in the Ny Carlsberg Glyptotek was, according to Poulsen, acquired in 1897 from the palazzo Piombino-Boncompagni (Ludovisi) in Rome, but it reportedly was found in the grounds of the villa Spithoever.[66] According to Moltesen, however, this Copenhagen satyr was offered to Jacobsen by Helbig, who was told that it had been discovered in August 1897 during building operations for the stables of the American ambassador, in the new palazzo Piombino (Ludovisi), the present palazzo Margherita.[67] It is of course possible, as Moltesen speculated, that there could have been several statues of this same type in the Sallustian gardens, and so the *Resting Satyr* in Copenhagen may not be the one Spithoever once owned.

Indeed, according to Piranesi, in 1745 during the clearing away of some remains of an ancient building in the villa Verospi there were found "some statues, reliefs, and pieces of columns and many capitals of various sorts as well as other rarities."[68] From such a vague description it is impossible to identify any of these finds, but intriguing is the report by Venuti of these 1745 discoveries, which he described as "many statues that are in the Villa Ludovisi, *particularly the Faun,* [my italics] were found in these gardens, as (were) those (statues) of the Palazzo Verospi."[69] According to Schreiber, the only statue of a "faun"

known to him in the Ludovisi collection is his number
71 (satyr statue), but this cannot be the one mentioned
by Venuti: number 71 was already reported in the
Ludovisi inventory of 1633, and there are no reports
earlier than the eighteenth century of discoveries made
in the area of the palazzo Verospi.[70] Thus, it is possible
that the *Resting Satyr* in Copenhagen, purchased from
the Piombino-Boncompagni (Ludovisi), is, in fact, the
"faun" found in 1745 on the Verospi property.

Given the difficulties in pinning down the findspots
of many of these statues, an intriguing statement by
Arndt reported that the so-called *Fleeing Maiden* in
Copenhagen (Fig. 3.7) was found in 1873 on a high
terrace on the Esquiline Hill.[71] Only later was it mentioned to have come from the villa Spithoever.[72] Rizzo,
who published this statue six years before Arndt's
catalogue of the Ny Carlsberg Glyptotek, was already
aware of this discrepancy and concerned enough to
suggest that the provenance of this statue be reex-
amined.[73] Lanciani's report of 1906 (the same year as
Rizzo's) concluded mistakenly, however, as we have
seen, that this statue was found in 1886 near the piazza
Sallustio. Since Lanciani's publication, the findspot
until now has never been questioned. It is possible,
therefore, that the Copenhagen *Fleeing Maiden* is not
from the gardens of Sallust or at least was not discovered within the presumed confines of these gardens.

The *Dying Youth* in Copenhagen (Fig. 3.8) was purchased at the same time as the *Fleeing Maiden.* Both,
as we have seen, were believed (mistakenly) to have
been discovered more or less at the same time and in
the same place.[74] Arndt, who did not recognize the
hole in the back as one for an arrow and therefore did
not recognize this figure as wounded, did not believe
that it should be paired with the *Fleeing Maiden.*[75]
In fact, according to Arndt, the *Fleeing Maiden* was
seen as a Roman work, while that of the *Dying Youth*
was believed to be a genuine Greek creation. In keeping with his skepticism concerning their association,
Arndt identified the marble of the *Dying Youth* to be
Greek, while that of the *Fleeing Maiden* was identified
merely as "white marble."[76] More recently, Moltesen
claimed that the marble for both figures is in fact the
same (Parian lychnite) and that both are most certainly original Greek works "of good quality."[77] The
determination that the youth was once pierced by an

*Fig. 3.9: **Resting Satyr**, Ny Carlsberg Glyptotek,
Copenhagen, Inv. 474.*

Fig. 3.10: **Wounded Niobid,** *Museo Nazionale delle Terme, Rome, Inv. 72274.*

arrow is considered further evidence that both figures belong together, and they likely are Niobids.

Although the two Niobids in Copenhagen cannot with certainty be assigned to the environs of the gardens of Sallust, another Niobid, now in the Palazzo Massimo delle Terme (Museo Nazionale) in Rome, was most assuredly found within the confines of these gardens (Fig. 3.10).[78]

A corridor or underground gallery within the city block defined by the vie Collina, Flavia, and Servio Tullio was uncovered on June 13, 1906. Three days later was discovered an almost kneeling female figure (of Parian marble) with a wound in the back, identifiable as a Niobid. The property was owned by the Banca Commerciale Italiana, which took possession, and the statue was transported to the main office of the bank in Milan. It was later given to the Italian State, becoming the property of the National Archaeological Museum. Moltesen concluded that "in style, dimensions and material, this figure corresponds to the two pieces in Copenhagen" and, therefore, according to her, speaks for the findspots of the Copenhagen Niobids as nearby.[79]

Furthermore, Lanciani reported that another "Niobid" was discovered on September 28, 1888, at the corner of the vie Boncompagni and Quintino Sella. This fragment was taken to the Antiquario Comunale del Celio, a "magazzino archeologico" that Lanciani opened to the public beginning in 1894 and that by 1900 was called the "Antiquarium."[80] When these numerous uncatalogued sculptural fragments were dispersed, the identifications of many of them were lost.[81] It is, therefore, perhaps not surprising that even in 1906 Rizzo was unable to identify this "other Niobid" mentioned by Lanciani that same year.[82] On the other hand, Riemann, without explanation, identified the figure "im Antiquarium comunale" with the Chiaramonti Niobid type in the Vatican.[83] Moltesen later suggested that it was perhaps the nude male figure acquired in 1956 by the Berlin Museum that had been remounted as a wounded man sinking to one knee. According to Moltesen, "This triangular motif again suggests that it was a pedimental figure and a Niobid," and she would link it to the others reportedly found in the vicinity.[84] But these identifications are futile because this "other Niobid" is, in fact, a figure of Apollo.

In an unpublished notebook of Lanciani in the Vatican is a photograph identified as a "Frammento di Niobide del Celio," which must be the "other Niobid" (Fig. 3.11). It is clear that this figure is, in fact, that of a known fragment of a colossal, draped leg identified as the striding Apollo Kitharoidos type (Fig. 3.12).[85] This large "fragment of a draped leg" was reportedly found in 1888 during the digging for a drain on the via Boncompagni near the via Nerva,[86] and it is likely to be the same as a "fragment of a colossal draped figure" reported elsewhere as having been found on the via Boncompagni some 25 meters east of the via Q. Sella—that is, near the via Nerva.[87] In other words, the reporting of a "colossal draped leg" and of a "colossal draped figure" are in fact for the same fragment, and this is now identified as a striding Apollo, not a fleeing Niobid, as Lanciani believed. Thus, another "Niobid" from the gardens of Sallust must be eliminated as the result of a misidentification. The only statue of a Niobid that without question was discovered in the gardens of Sallust is the one now in the Palazzo Massimo delle Terme in Rome (Fig. 3.10).

Yet another fragment of a statue that can be associated with Niobids was found during restoration work in 1840 near the vestibule in the gardens of Sallust.[88] It was at that time put on top of the restored pilaster at the left of the entrance to the vestibule, as seen in a photograph of the early twentieth century (Fig. 2.13). Apparently because of its inaccessibility, it was misidentified as a man on horseback.[89] Only recently has Candilio shown that this statue, now in the National Archaeological Museum (Palazzo Massimo delle Terme), is in fact a second-century (Hadrianic?) replica of a type known from examples in the Uffizi,[90] the Louvre,[91] and the Ny Carlsberg Glyptotek,[92] identified as the "pedagogue" of the children of Niobe (Fig. 3.13).

The remains of the Palazzo Massimo *Pedagogue* correspond well with a replica in the Uffizi that is part of a group of thirteen Niobids. This figure is restored with a raised right hand shielding one of the children of Niobe, in a futile attempt to protect him/her from the arrows of Apollo and Artemis.[93] Candilio, there-

fore, concluded that there must have been a group of Niobids displayed in the gardens of Sallust, similar to the Niobids now in the Uffizi.

The group in Florence was discovered in the sixteenth century in Rome, in the *vigna* of Tommasini on the slopes of the Esquiline, a site probably comprising the area of the ancient *horti Lamiani* (or *Maiani*).[94] Following their acquisition by Ferdinando de'Medici, these statues were taken to the villa Medici in Rome. At the end of the eighteenth century they were transferred to the Galleria degli Uffizi.[95] As we have seen, the *Fleeing Maiden* in Copenhagen (Fig. 3.7) was believed to have come originally from the Esquiline, and so it is possible that it once belonged, in spite of its fifth-century date, to the Hellenistic Niobid group in Florence rather than a possible grouping in the gardens of Sallust. Indeed, in a letter dated June 24, 1583, Stefano Pernigoni, writing of the statues found in the *vigna* Tommasini, mentioned fifteen rather than the present fourteen statues now in the Uffizi.[96]

Also, the *Pedagogue* in Copenhagen, although not purchased by the Ny Carlsberg Glyptotek until 1893, was known before the middle of the sixteenth century, as recorded by a Renaissance drawing (dated 1560–1572) of it.[97] Unfortunately, the provenance of the Copenhagen *Pedagogue* is not known, although a Roman findspot is likely because it was purchased from the Salviati family in Rome, which also sold the *Kneeling Barbarian,* found in the confines of the gardens of Sallust (p. 127, and Fig. 3.32), to Jacobsen for the Ny Carlsberg Glyptotek.

The identification of the *Pedagogue* (Fig. 3.13) is intriguing particularly in relationship to the possible grouping of the figures of Niobids thought to have been found likewise in the gardens of Sallust. As early as 1899 Furtwängler proposed that the *Dying Niobid* and *Fleeing Maiden* in Copenhagen must have formed part of a pedimental composition for the temple of Apollo Patroos in Athens, created, he believed, by the fifth-century school of Kresilas.[98] The discovery of a "third" *Niobid* (in the Palazzo Massimo delle Terme: Fig. 3.10) in 1906 was thought to contradict Furtwängler's identification and attribution but not the belief that these figures formed part of a pedimental grouping.[99] In fact, the Terme *Niobid* was brought

*Fig. 3.11: "Frammento di Niobide del Celio," from unpublished notebook of Rudolpho Lanciani, **Cod. Vat. lat.** 13035, fol. 110r.*

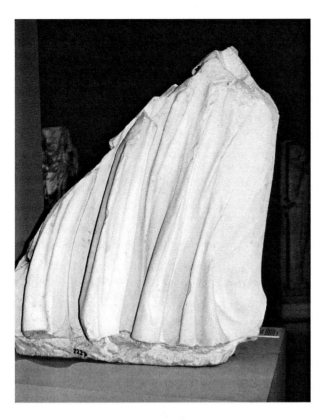

Fig. 3.12A (top left)–B (bottom left):
Striding **Apollo Kitharoidos:** *fragment of draped leg,
Museo Capitolino, Rome.*

Fig. 3.13 (below right): **Pedagogue** *of the children of Niobe,
Museo Nazionale delle Terme, Rome: Palazzo Massimo.*

into the equation in 1960, when Schefold associated it with the two Copenhagen statues and a figure of Apollo/Theseus, believing that they all belonged to the pedimental sculptural decoration of the temple of Apollo Sosianus (Apollo Medico) in Rome.[100] La Rocca, however, recognized a group of sculptures in Parian marble found between 1932 and 1937 as the decoration for the pediments of this temple, identifying them as a battle between Greeks and Amazons and thus excluding the Copenhagen Niobid figures in this reconstruction. Nonetheless, they were considered in La Rocca's discussion because the pedimental statues for the Apollo Medico are actual Greek works of the fifth century, and they are stylistically close to the two Niobids in Copenhagen.[101]

Stylistic parallels with sculpture carved in south Italy suggest that both Niobid figures in Copenhagen were carved there as well.[102] Especially close to the *Fleeing Maiden* is a head of Athena from Tarentum, which, according to Moltesen, is "possibly by the same master as the Niobids (in Copenhagen)."[103] Some scholars have even speculated that the Tarentine Athena head is from a temple pediment, and they have thought that the Copenhagen Niobids also derive from pedimental decoration. Others have seen the hand of a Peloponnesian master,[104] or a connection with sculptures from the Temple of Zeus at Olympia, which demonstrate both Doric and Ionic,[105] or only Ionic,[106] or possibly Attic styles.[107] Alkamenes has been offered as a possible sculptor for the Copenhagen Niobids, and La Rocca, seeing an eclectic character, at least tentatively supported such an attribution.[108]

The Terme *Niobid* (Fig. 3.10) seems stylistically different from the two figures in Copenhagen. La Rocca even suggested that all three were created by different sculptors, although for the same project: to decorate a Greek pediment perhaps only a few years after that of the Amazonomachy grouping on the temple of Apollo Sosianus.[109] It is even possible that such pedimental sculptures decorated the same fifth-century Greek temple; that is, an Amazonomachy grouping was made for one pediment to be followed shortly thereafter by a group of Niobids for the other pediment. When transported to Rome, these sculptures were eventually separated, one grouping (Amazonomachy) employed for the temple of Apollo Sosianus, and the

other (Niobids) perhaps originally set up nearby. Pliny (*HN* 36.28) suggested as much when he wrote that sculptures of dying Niobids, made by Skopas or Praxiteles, were part of the temple of Apollo Sosianus.[110] It cannot be determined if any of the Niobids discussed above were once part of the sculptural decoration of the sanctuary of Apollo Sosianus. What we can say is that at least some Niobids ended up in the confines of the gardens of Sallust, and they likely had been transported there from some earlier grouping(s) which had been displayed elsewhere, such as at the temple of Apollo Sosianus.

Even if the above scenario could be proved, it would still be impossible to determine the context in which such sculptures were displayed in their final grouping. The presumably different dates and even different places of manufacture for the Copenhagen statues, and the Terme *Niobid*, speak for their possible later association as a makeshift grouping. Ridgway even suggested that the two Niobids in Copenhagen were reworked (in the Roman period?). La Rocca agreed that in particular the head of the *Fleeing Maiden* could have been partially recut.[111] Furthermore, the recently recognized Hadrianic *Pedagogue* from the gardens of Sallust suggests that a Roman statue was created to enhance the narrative, and it is possible that some recutting of the earlier statues took place at that time.

If all four statues (two Copenhagen *Niobids,* Terme *Niobid,* and *Pedagogue*) indeed were brought together to form a narrative tableau (which is far from certain), it is not perhaps too speculative to add another statue to this group.

A *Crouching Amazon* in the Conservatori Museum (Fig. 3.14) was found in 1888 near the via Boncompagni about 25 meters from the via Quintino Sella.[112] It was soon identified as an Amazon in "lo stile arcaico," kneeling to pull a bow. A large cutting in the back allowed it to be recognized as having been once attached to the wall of a pediment.[113] Due to subject matter and style, this Amazon statue appears likely to have come from a sixth-century pedimental group for the temple of Apollo Daphnephoros in Eretria.[114] In other words, it seems likely that this statue was discovered in Eretria sometime during the Roman period and that it was taken for display in some unknown context.

The circumstances surrounding its ancient discov-

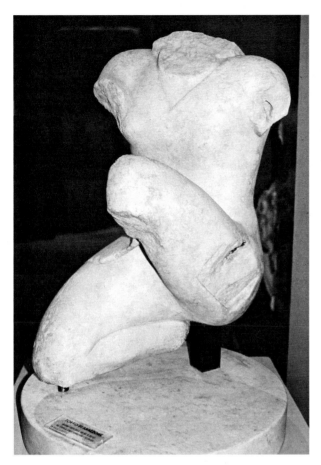
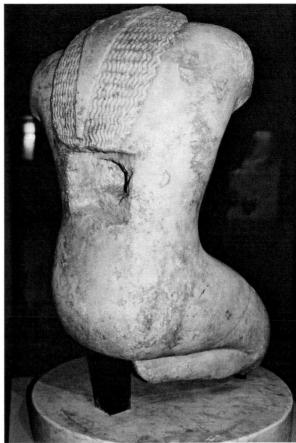

*Fig. 3.14A–B: **Crouching Amazon**, Conservatori Museum, Rome, Inv. 840.*

ery are unclear; however, other sculptures from the sixth-century pediment appear to have been deliberately buried after the destruction by the Persians of the Apollo temple in 490 B.C.[115] The temple was rebuilt or restored, and La Rocca suggested, probably rightly, that the sculptures from the temple of Apollo Sosianus in Rome were originally decoration for this fifth-century building. Eretria was destroyed in 198 B.C. by Lucius Quinctius Flamininus, and later by Sulla in 87 B.C., and so the pedimental statues, as well as the entire temple, were probably removed at least by the first century B.C.[116] The archaeological finds and their interpretation suggest that the *Crouching Amazon* was an unexpected discovery made in the first century B.C., perhaps during the operations for the removal of the Apollo Daphnephoros temple, and that it was, by chance, removed along with this fifth-century building. Therefore, this Amazon was, at least to the Romans, not part of a larger narrative, but an inde-

pendent statue that could be presumably employed for any purpose considered appropriate.

The large cutting in the back makes it likely that this figure was displayed against some backdrop so that it was viewed from the front only.[117] That it was apparently separated from the other original pedimental figures to which it belonged, and displayed independently, possibly in the gardens of Sallust, speaks for its value in spite of the disfiguring cutting, possible damage, or weathering.

Because the slaying of the children of Niobe may have been composed of disparate figures, assembled together to form a visual narrative, it is possible that the Amazon archer was displayed as an acceptable substitute for Artemis. She should, along with her brother, Apollo, be present. Indeed, Rolley made the suggestion that the so-called Theseus of the Apollo Sosianus temple pediment was originally the Apollo for the Niobid pediment.[118] In this case, the mixing of

Greek sculptures from two distinct groupings to create a single composition (presumably desirable for a Roman audience) should allow for an open and fluid interpretation of such assemblages. These observations cannot be proved, of course, but the strict, formal presentation of narratives, as they appear for example on coins and public monuments, may not always be the case when serendipity comes into play. The assembly of garden sculptures, in particular, must have been more haphazard and less formal than similar narrative displays made to order for public consumption.[119]

Of course, in spite of the potential for a laissez-faire attitude in some garden displays, their very assemblage together gives them value as possible "moral lessons" or "parables" beyond their inherent narrative content. For example, the sculptural representation of the myth of the children of Niobe expressed in visual form the idea of "hybris," and this "moral lesson" could be associated as well with the Gauls, for both were found guilty of impiety towards Apollo.[120] It is therefore of interest to recognize that Gauls may have been set up somewhere in the gardens of Sallust. It would not be difficult to imagine that such a display could have been visually near a grouping of Niobids.

GAULS

Two important statues of Gauls are believed to have been found in the seventeenth century within the confines of the *horti Sallustiani*. Both belonged to the Ludovisi collection, and silence concerning their purchase has led scholars to assume that they were found on the property of the Ludovisi villa.

The *Dying Gaul,* formerly identified as a dying gladiator (Musei Capitolini; Fig. 3.15), is probably the statue mentioned in one of the earliest Ludovisi inventories dated November 2, 1623: "A Gladiator of marble measuring some 10 palms with a painted and gilded wooden pedestal containing the carved and gilded coat of arms of the Cardinal [Ludovisi]."[121] It is most certainly mentioned in the 1633 inventory of the villa (soon after the death of Ludovico): "an ancient statue of a wounded gladiator larger than life, on a marble base with a horn and shield lying nearby; a wooden pedestal covered with stone, and framed in gold with the gilded coat of arms of the Cardinal [Ludovisi]."[122]

Sometime after 1696 it was transferred to Prince Livio Odescalchi, nephew of Innocent XI, as a guarantee for the borrowing of 1,650 scudi. It was back in the Ludovisi possession certainly before 1733, even though it is not included in the inventory of that year.[123] The reason for its absence in this listing is that the statue may never have returned to the Pincian villa. Ippolita Ludovisi Boncompagni, duchess of Sora, inherited it in 1715. According to Mattei, perhaps she had it taken to the palazzo Boncompagni in the piazza di Sora (al Parione).[124] According to Franceschini, after Ippolita's death on December 29, 1733, the inheritors (her six daughters) decided to sell some of the sculptural works, and the *Dying Gladiator/Gaul* was at that time moved to Parione. If this were the case, however, it ought to have been included in the 1733 inventory.[125] Regardless of where the statue stood in 1733, it did not remain long in the possession of the Ludovisi/Boncompagni, who, after considerable negotiation, sold it to Clement XII for the Musei Capitolini in 1737. Napoleon took it to Paris in 1797, but it was returned to Rome in 1816.[126]

Knowledge about the findspot of the statue was made even more difficult by early reports that have it coming into the hands of the Ludovisi from the Cesi Collection. According to Aldrovandi, "in the porticoes of the courtyard [in the house of Cesi near St. Peter's] is a torso of a gladiator lying on the ground ["gittato à terra"], a sleeping putto, an ancient sarcophagus with two carved heads, and other fragments; near every column of the portico of the palace is a piece of ancient marble with quite beautiful ancient inscriptions."[127] Maffei[128] interpreted the words "gittato à terra" as part of the composition, and Heyne[129] reported falsely that the Capitoline Gaul was preserved only as a torso, and so a connection between Aldrovandi's report and the Capitoline statue was made. Indeed, Fea[130] reported that Michelangelo had restored the Capitoline Gaul, and this led to Friederichs' belief that it had been found in the sixteenth century.[131] Schreiber rightly questioned Maffei's interpretation of the Cesi

Fig. 3.15: **Dying Gaul,** *Musei Capitolini, Rome.*

statue as a reclining figure and dispelled the assumption that the Capitoline Gaul was preserved only as a torso. Although the date of discovery and the findspot are nowhere reported, the sudden appearance of the statue, without comment in a Ludovisi inventory of 1633, led Schreiber to propose reasonably that it had been found on the Ludovisi property sometime after 1622.[132]

Likewise, the celebrated statue of the so-called *Suicidal Gaul and "Wife"* (Fig. 3.16) from the Ludovisi collection was not reported as having been purchased, and it appeared first in the villa's inventory of 1623. It too, therefore, probably was discovered on the Ludovisi property during the initial redevelopment of the land under Ludovico in 1622.

Although the provenance of this statue had always seemed clear, the identities of the pair were opened to various interpretations. They were believed in the seventeenth century to represent Marius and his daughter, or Pyramus and Thisbe, but in the following century were identified as Arria and Paetus, or Macareus and Canace.[133] In 1831 Visconti associated this statue group

with an episode from the war against the Gauls, and since then scholars have accepted the identification as Gauls.[134]

Brunn later connected the *Suicidal Gaul and "Wife"* with the *Dying Gaul,* suggesting they were images sculpted by a Pergamene artist.[135] The two sculptures indeed appear to belong together: both are created from the same marble, the dimensions are similar, the form of the bases and the details of the shields are virtually identical, and their findspots seem to be the same. Brunn's attribution to a Pergamene sculptor gained acceptance after the discovery in Pergamon of statue bases commemorating the Pergamene victory over the Gauls between 240 and 230 B.C. Attempts were made by Schober and Künzl to show that these statues originally stood either on a large circular base in the center of the sanctuary of Athena Nikephoros or on a long base to the south.[136] Neither suggestion can be supported with any physical evidence, and even the attribution to a Pergamene school has been questioned.[137]

More important for the present study is not so much the attribution but the probable employment of

Fig. 3.16: **Suicidal Gaul and "Wife,"** *Museo Nazionale delle Terme, Rome: Palazzo Altemps, Inv. 8608.*

these in the *horti Sallustiani*. Although it is impossible to determine when they ended up in these gardens, Coarelli hypothesized that Caesar set them up to commemorate his victories in Gaul.[138] This enticing scenario relies, however, on the assumption that Julius Caesar owned gardens on the Pincio, which, as discussed above, is questionable at best. Indeed, it is significant that Neudecker did not mention a single statue of a Gaul in a private garden or villa setting, suggesting perhaps that these subjects were more appropriate for a public venue.[139]

Furthermore, the head of the *Dying Gaul* is broken at the neck, and it seems to have been repaired sometime in the Roman period. The evidence for this repair is a pour channel of ancient shape, preserved at the back near a much larger, U-shaped hole that represents the repairs made in the seventeenth century. The head is attached to the neck precisely below the torque—the fracture is too regular to be a natural break and too irregular to be a joining surface worked *ad hoc*. Therefore, Mattei and others proposed that the break is natural and either regularized in a Roman restoration or more probably in the seventeenth-century repairs. Thus, the present attachment and positioning of the head must be slightly changed from the original.[140] Likewise, the proportions of the restored right arm are different from those of the left, but Stuart-Jones believed that this restoration may be antique.[141]

It is also possible, given this physical evidence, that the head is a Roman addition to a headless statue or at the very least that the original head had been damaged and repaired. Note that the hair on the proper right does not react naturally to the tilting of the head; instead, the locks are horizontal to the ground. These Roman repairs and the possibility of a more extensive later ancient restoration indicate that this statue must have been employed for different uses long before its discovery in the seventeenth century. It is impossible to determine, therefore, whether these statues were created for a garden setting or whether they were reemployed as garden decoration at a later time.

In addition, a statue of perhaps another Gaul is reported in the Ludovisi collection and may have been found on the property of the villa Ludovisia.[142] Mentioned in an inventory of 1641 (Reg. 611, n. 56),

it cannot be the famous *Dying Gaul* (Fig. 3.15) that is also listed in this same inventory as an "over-life-sized statue of a dying gladiator, of the elegant and classical style, seated on a base." This "other" Gaul was described later by Visconti as a "Resting Warrior. A seated statue. A young warrior of robust form seated on the ground with his legs bent, with the arms resting on the legs, and with his back somewhat arched, holding a sword: an edge of his chlamys extends onto the ground, and wraps around his left thigh."[143] Thus, it seems that the Ludovisi may have possessed three sculptures of Gauls, all of which could have been excavated from their property.

Although it is reasonable to assume that these sculptures were found in the Ludovisi estate in Rome, it is not assured that they have anything to do with the gardens of Sallust. The property of the Ludovisi likely extended beyond the limits of these ancient gardens, as previously discussed. It is therefore possible these statues of Gauls may well have been associated in antiquity either with another garden estate or else with some unknown public structure or monument in this area. The assumption that these come from the confines of the Ludovisi property ought not to determine their ancient location as in the gardens of Sallust.

On the other hand, such images would not necessarily be inappropriate for an imperial garden. As Marvin suggested, these Gauls, heroic even in the throes of defeat, are distinctively different from the usual Roman treatment of the subjugation of the barbarian.[144] Yet this deviation from the norm does not have to speak for direct copies but rather a particularly Roman response to Greek images of the defeated. In other words, sculptures that carry Greek style do not necessarily have to go back to particular Greek originals. Such style, when created by and employed for a Roman, must have conveyed a series of complicated and reciprocal meanings that expressed admiration for the Greek past while asserting Roman domination over it. If these Gauls were in fact such emulation, then an imperial garden would be a place where the viewers, presumably sophisticated and well read, would have recognized such dichotomies. Public sculptural decoration, by definition, had to convey messages understood by the masses. The sculptural decoration in imperial *horti,* on the other hand, could have expressed more complicated meanings to be discovered and discussed in the leisure and quiet of a garden setting.

A garden setting, however, was not only for deep reflection and perhaps philosophical discussion but also for leisure and amusement. It is not surprising, therefore, that within a garden context could be displayed figures that conveyed a sense of the outdoors and of abandonment. This is nowhere more apparent than in the context of Dionysos and his entourage of woodland creatures.

THE WORLD OF DIONYSOS

Numerous fragments of sculptures were found in the *vigna* of Carlo Muti, as reported by Flaminio Vacca, "a short distance from the *horti Sallustiani.*" Two of these can be identified as an over-life-sized faun with a little boy in his arms (Fig. 3.17) and a large vase with fauns and baccantes who dance with cymbals in their hands (Fig. 3.18).[145]

Lanciani believed these were discovered in 1575, but Palma suggested an earlier date of 1566.[146] Regardless of the precise year of discovery, they were certainly known as early as 1594 (the year of Vacca's report), when at least the faun was already restored and displayed in the Muti gardens.[147] In 1897 Lanciani added to evidence of the findspot with the statement that these works were found in the area of the then-standing Casino Massimo, which was just south of the main entrance to the villa Ludovisia on the present via Friuli and immediately west of the western limits of the Sallustian valley (*FUR* 9: Fig. 1.1C).[148] Indeed, Bufalini (ca. 1550) showed the "V. Episco. Mutii" in just this location (Fig. 2.15C).[149] Yet in 1906 Lanciani emended Vacca's text to read that these statues were found a short distance "from the nymphaeum" of the *horti Sallustiani.*[150] This led to the placement of these finds in the valley at its *eastern* limits near the still-extant brick vestibule in the piazza Sallustio, mistakenly called a nymphaeum.[151] As argued above (pp. 80–81), the Muti property lay near the via Friuli and was probably contiguous with the Vacca *vigna,* where an oval building was reported. Any connection, therefore, of this sculpture or vase with the vestibule in the piazza Sallustio must be abandoned.

The "Faun" (Fig. 3.17) entered the Borghese collection by 1613 (in the Borgo palace of Cardinal Scipione), when it was identified by Francucci as "Saturn with a boy in his arms."[152] Before 1628 it was transported to the Borghese villa on the Pincio and eventually was installed by 1644 in a room in the northern apartments of the casino, where it remained until its removal in 1808 to the Louvre.[153] There is no definitive publication of this Louvre group, now identified as *Silenus with the Baby Dionysos,* and so it is impossible to render a complete description of the repairs, replacements and restorations of this statue. Yet from simple observation it is clear that this statue is composed of numerous ancient, broken pieces as well as extensive restorations in marble and plaster.

The original was made from a fine white marble, while much (all?) of the marble restorations are grey veined. This grey-veined marble is used for most of the tree trunk support, the entire edge of the base, and the right buttock, left hand, and left shoulder of Silenus. The proper right back of the head and the right side of the face of the baby Dionysos are restored, as well as his left arm, left leg, and lower right leg. The legs of Silenus are restored with numerous ancient and modern pieces of marble bound by plaster. The head of Silenus appears to be relatively intact, save for the missing nose, and although it was broken from the neck and reattached, there is little doubt of its pertinence to this statue. The head of Dionysos is also partially preserved (the nose and chin are restored), although it may have been entirely reworked.[154] The statue had been considered a work of the Flavian period, but this dating has been questioned.[155]

The type is known in at least three heavily restored statues with preserved heads (in the Louvre, the Vatican, and Munich [antiquity or pertinence of head not assured]), two torsos, and perhaps as many as seven disembodied heads.[156] None of these has any firm

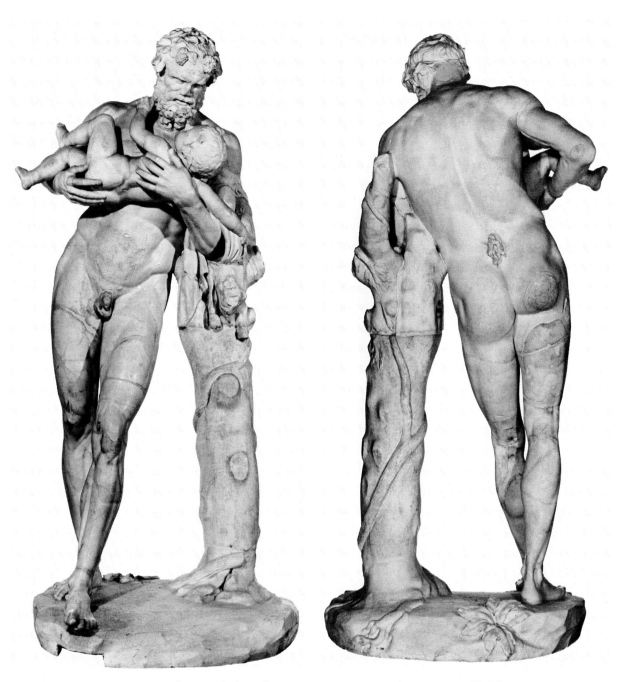

Fig. 3.17A–B: ***Silenus with the Baby Dionysos,*** *Louvre, Paris, Inv. 9880212 AGR: Ma 922.*

*Fig. 3.18A–B: **Borghese Krater,** Louvre, Paris, Inv. 985-N 275: MA 86.*

findspot, and so they are not helpful in determining the possible display of the statue from the gardens of Sallust.

The vase with reliefs of satyrs and baccantes (Fig. 3.18) was reported by Vacca to have been discovered at the same time as the statue of *Silenus with the Baby Dionysos.* It too became part of the Borghese collection (in 1645), and the French government purchased it in 1811, displaying it that year to great public admiration in the Musée Napoléon.

Commonly referred to as the *Borghese Krater* after the seventeenth-century owners, this vase, of Pentelic marble, is in the shape of a calyx krater.[157] It now stands 1.715 meters, including a modern base that is 0.50 meters high, and is elaborately carved in relief with figures of Dionysos, Ariadne, and eight baccantes (satyrs and maenads).

Two marble vases that are remarkably similar to the *Borghese Krater* were discovered in fragments in the so-called Mahdia cargo. The sinking of this ship probably occurred between 120 and 100 B.C.,[158] and the homogeneity of its contents—large-scale statuary in bronze and marble, architectural members (columns and capitals), items of furniture, statuettes—speaks for a contemporary cargo. Although the places of origin for individual items cannot be determined, Truszkowski stated that the Mahdia vases must have been sculpted in an Athenian workshop.[159] The preserved fragments show that the carving of the figures on the Mahdia vases is of better quality than that on the *Borghese Krater,* suggesting a possible later date of manufacture for the Louvre example, if, indeed, quality is a diagnostic marker for relative chronology. Historical considerations led Truszkowski to believe that the *Borghese Krater* dates to the years 40 to 30 B.C., or perhaps fifty years earlier, before the outbreak of the Mithridatic wars with Rome in 90 B.C.[160] On the other hand, Fuchs, on stylistic grounds, believed that the *Borghese Krater* dates to the imperial period under Tiberius.[161] Without a firm archaeological context, it is impossible to determine an accurate date for the *Borghese Krater*; however, it is not impossible that it belongs to the imperial age.

According to Grassinger, marble kraters began to be produced by the late second century B.C. in Athens. By the middle of the first century B.C. (at the latest in the early Augustan period), local Roman-Italian workshops were producing these as well.[162] It is possible that the Borghese type was in fact being produced by a Roman rather than by an Athenian workshop because like the marble candelabra found in wealthy villas and gardens, large marble kraters of the Roman period derive from the Greek world of ritual and funerary contexts as well as the symposium.[163] These kraters could have been set up between columns or inside rooms, but unlike the candelabra, they are also found out of doors in garden settings. These kraters also could have been paired, like candelabra, to flank, for example, a doorway; however, no pairs have been identified. Although they were clearly seen as part of the furnishings of a wealthy abode, their functions are unclear. From depictions in Roman wall paintings, they appear usually as decorative devices; yet sometimes they are shown as planters and even fountains. These garden paintings were intended to evoke a land of paradise in which kraters and basins, marble trellis-fences, and birds were as appropriate as mythological scenes.[164]

Because the *Borghese Krater* with its Dionysiac Thiasos reliefs was found with the over-life-sized statue of a *Silenus with the Baby Dionysos,* it is tempting to believe that these two sculptures had been displayed together. Indeed, a marble krater in the villa at Oplontis was associated with a satyr-maenad group.[165] Of the numerous examples of satyrs in gardens, however, Silenus as the protector of the baby Dionysos is not frequent.[166] Nonetheless, a garden setting, with its trees and fountains, would have been ideal for such Dionysiac subjects. It is possible that other types, such as nymphs, maenads, Pans, and even theatrical masks,[167] could have created bucolic/idyllic tableaux in imitation of a "locus amoenus" (charming place) as recorded in ancient literature.[168]

*Fig. 3.19: **Resting Satyr,** Ny Carlsberg Glyptotek, Copenhagen, Inv. 2237.*

Fig. 3.20: **Papposilenus,**
Museo Nazionale delle Terme, Rome: Palazzo Massimo.

It is not surprising, therefore, that other statues associated with the Dionysiac world are recorded as having been found within the gardens of Sallust. In fact, it is possible that two replicas of the Praxitelean *Resting Satyr* were discovered in the confines of these gardens. One, reportedly found near the vestibule (as discussed above, pp. 96–97),[169] could be the statue now in the Ny Carlsberg Glyptotek (Inv. nr. 474; Fig. 3.9). Acquired in 1897 from the palazzo Piombino-Boncompagni in Rome, this satyr was said by Poulsen to have been found in the grounds of the villa Spithoever.[170] Indeed, Ludwig Pollak and Matthew Stewart Prichard saw such a statue at the villa Spithoever on January 22, 1897. According to Pollak's diary, among the many fragments of sculptures were the torso of a bearded pugilist,[171] a Praxitelean resting satyr, a slim Athena with aigis, a badly preserved statue of Leda, a torso in rosso antico (a copy of the centaur by Aristeas and Papias), inscriptions and terracotta reliefs. Yet it seems unlikely that the satyr, still in the Spithoever collection in 1897, was the statue purchased in this same year by the Glyptotek from the Piombino-Boncompagni. Moltesen speculated, therefore, there could have been several of this same type in the Sallustian gardens.

In fact, another *Resting Satyr* type (mistakenly restored as Dionysos) in Copenhagen (Fig. 3.19) came from the villa Borghese, which is known to have possessed sculptures from the villa Verospi on the Pincio—a location near the vestibule and therefore perhaps a better candidate for the one reportedly found there.

Regardless of the difficulties in pinning down the Copenhagen satyrs to specific reports of their findspots, it is clear that both likely were found in the gardens of Sallust. Their presence in garden settings would not have been unusual because this statue type is known from the villa of the Quintilii on the via Appia, as well as from the villa of Cassio in Tivoli.[172] Also, the probability of two identical statues in the same gardens speaks for their display together as perhaps pendants to an architectural or even to a planted setting.

Smaller, less distinguished sculptures were also displayed to contribute to a Dionysiac environment. For example, a *Papposilenus* (Fig. 3.20) was found in 1908

*Fig. 3.21: Double-sided **Marble Slab Sculptured in Relief** with A: heads of a maenad and a silenus, and B: dancing fauns, Inv. 5668.*

Fig. 3.22: **Faun Seated on a Wineskin**, Museo Nazionale, Rome, Inv. nr. 72 from EA 5004.

Fig. 3.23: Statuette of **Faun on a Large Goat**.

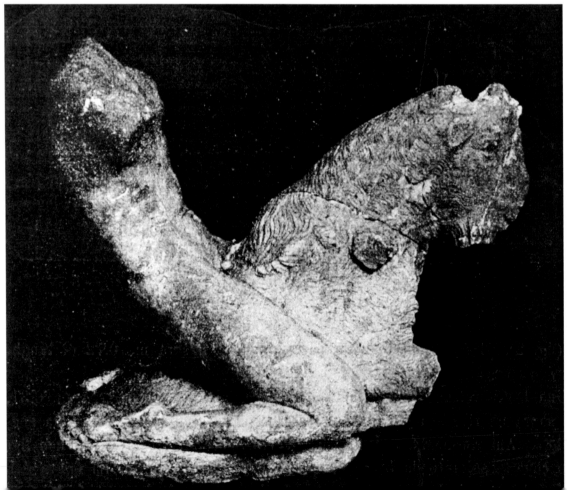

*Fig. 3.24: **Goat Tied by Its Hooves**, Metropolitan Museum of Art, New York, Acc. No. 10.151.*

during building operations between the vie Flavia, M. Pagano, and Aureliana (formerly Spithoever, then Boggio property).[173] Although small, it must have been admired because it was found in a cavity that appears to have been made to save it from harm. The back is unfinished and rather flat, suggesting it stood in a niche or against a wall.[174]

In this same cavity was discovered a fragment of a rectangular *Marble Slab Sculptured in Relief* on one side with dancing fauns, and on the other with heads of a maenad and Silenus (Fig. 3.21).[175] It must have been displayed on a pillar within a garden setting as similarly sculptured slabs, for example, from the Casa degli Amorini dorati in Pompeii.[176]

Two other fauns are known, both found near the via

delle Finanze. One is a small *Faun Seated on a Wineskin* (Fig. 3.22),[177] and the other is a marble statuette of a *Faun on a Large Goat* (Fig. 3.23).[178] Found in the general location as these, and perhaps belonging with them as a group, is a *Goat Tied by Its Hooves* (Fig. 3.24), an image in keeping with a possible Dionysiac environment.[179]

These relatively small sculptures must represent only a minor portion of similar images that would have enhanced the other-worldliness of these gardens in which such playful creatures existed. It seems clear that the natural environment of the garden must have encouraged, if not demanded, images of Dionysos and his entourage and that these statues represented not only the god himself, but even more the "wild" creatures of satyrs and fauns.

"NYMPHS" AND CANDELABRA

Related to other-worldly creatures, like satyrs and fauns, are those that inhabited watery realms: the nymphs. As we have seen, the brick vestibule was believed to be dedicated to the nymphs because of discoveries reported by Ligorio of three statues of the nurses of Zeus, including Amalthea with a goat and the infant god, and two others pouring water.[180] Lanciani was dubious about this report, but in 1935 near the vestibule was found a fragment of a marble statue identified as a nymph, supporting Ligorio's recording of nymphs in this area.[181]

It is noteworthy, therefore, that in 1765 two statues were discovered in the *vigna* Verospi (just north of the vestibule), which Winckelmann reported as representing "two girls playing a game with astragals" (knuckle bones); however, these can perhaps best be described as *Nymphs*.[182] One of these was in the Wallmoden Collection now in Göttingen (Fig. 3.25); the other is in the British Museum (Fig. 3.26).[183]

Cavaceppi, who restored the statue in Göttingen, identified it as a nymph, giving, however, a false year of discovery as 1766 and indicating, apparently without proof, that the findspot was "near an ancient fountain."[184] Cavaceppi's findspot must have influenced an 1812 report that indicated these sculptures were found in a crescent-shaped basin, composed of rich marbles and mosaics, suggesting these figures formed part of the decorations of a fountain.[185] It appears likely, however, that Cavaceppi simply "interpreted" the findspot to conform to a conception of his restored figure and that the later published comments are embellishments of this false reporting of a fountain.

Cavaceppi's identification of both figures as nymphs, however, is perhaps more appropriate than Winckelmann's "astragal players" because the exposed breast and clinging drapery are more appropriate for nymphs than for girls at play. On the other hand, in both cases, a small bow (terminating in heads of griffins) is carved on the plinth near the left hands, which may relate these to Artemis, goddess of the hunt, or even to bow-carrying Amazons, particularly in light of the exposed breast. Furthermore, under the right hand of the Göttingen figure the concave molding is slightly

flattened, perhaps an indication this hand once held an object that projected over the plinth. Regardless of the uncertainty of identification, it seems safe to eliminate Winckelmann's identification as astragal players and to put them into a more appropriate garden context as probably nymphs and/or figures associated in some way with Artemis or even Amazons. The tentative identification, made by Smith in 1904, of the British Museum figure as a "nymph of Artemis," is, therefore, very much appropriate.[186]

It is impossible to determine where they originally stood, although their mutual findspots and their similarities must indicate they were displayed together, perhaps as pendants (although not mirror images). On the other hand, they are not identical. In particular, the plinth of the Göttingen figure is decorated with half-rosettes under the feet, while the figure in London is not. Such decoration implies that the Göttingen figure was meant to be viewed from the side rather than from the front, but this is not to say that the London figure could not have been also displayed in a similar way. It is, of course, possible that the two preserved examples are only a part of the original ensemble that could have included more of the same.

In fact, three more apparent replicas are known, two of which were presumably found in Rome (a third example came from Tyndaris). One was in the villa Borghese, now in the Louvre; the other, in Berlin, was reported to have been found on the Caelian Hill in 1730.[187] Their poor states of preservation are not helpful in interpreting the original meaning of these sculptures; however, their similarities to the two sculptures excavated in the Verospi gardens on the Pincio (certainly within the confines of the gardens of Sallust) could speak to an original display together in antiquity.

It is intriguing that with the two nymphs from the Verospi property, a *Candelabrum* (Fig. 3.27), now in the Vatican, was also found.[188] It has been heavily restored as a tall acanthus shaft composed of four, two-tiered acanthus drums, each supporting large *phialai*. This shaft rests on a tall, triangular base, surmounted by rams' heads at the corners, supported by crouching sphinxes at the bottom, and decorated on each face by a single figure in relief. The entire base is a modern restoration, save for two small relief fragments: one representing the head, chest, and right arm of Herakles; the other, the upper body of Zeus. The thickness of the marble on which these reliefs are carved cannot be determined. It is, therefore, not possible to know whether these reliefs were once part of an ancient base. On the other hand, according to Cain, the style of the reliefs and the form of the acanthus leaves (in spite of the apparently different marbles: base perhaps Pentelic, the shaft probably Italian) speak for a similar dating in the middle of the first century B.C. and could support their original decoration of a single candelabrum.

Other candelabra have also come to light within the presumed confines of the gardens of Sallust. In 1885 a "historiated" candelabrum, broken and destroyed, was found near the vestibule at a depth of 12 meters.[189] At the beginning of the twentieth century, lion's feet of a candelabrum were found along the via Lucullo, near the corner of the via Sallustiana.[190] Seven years later a monopode in the form of a sphinx and a fragment of a candelabrum with oak leaves and acorns came to light near the via delle Finanze (present via G. Carducci), which is near the via Lucullo.[191] The similarity in findspots of the last two suggests that these fragments could belong together. Finally, in his 1901 excavations near the vestibule, Studniczka found the foot of a marble candelabrum carved with delicate leaf patterns on three sides. It is tempting to suggest that the "historiated" candelabrum found earlier may once have belonged with it.[192]

According to Cain, marble candelabra are found almost exclusively in the west and are a particularly Italian phenomenon, like marble relief masks, oscilla, and so-called Hellenistic reliefs.[193] Furthermore, that such candelabra could be used in private gardens is

Fig. 3.25: **Nymph,** *Wallmoden Collection, Archäologisches Institut, Göttingen.*

Fig. 3.26: **Nymph,** *British Museum, London, Inv. 145689.*

*Fig. 3.27: **Candelabrum**, Galleria dei Candelabri, Vatican, Inv. 2667.*

indicated by finds in Hadrian's Villa in Tivoli and elsewhere, where they perhaps were merely elaborate sculptural displays rather than votive light-stands as employed in sacred precincts or funerary complexes. Indeed, as Cain pointed out, it is difficult, given the sparse information on the findspots at Hadrian's Villa, to determine the use of most of these.

That they were luxury items is clear, for when findspots are recorded, they appear in association with temples, funerary complexes, occasionally in basilicas, theaters and baths, and wealthy villas, but never in the houses of Pompeii or Herculaneum. They are also always associated with architectural settings (perhaps to be displayed between columns, flanking doors, or inside niches) and are not believed to have been meant for outdoor display. If this is indeed the case, then the candelabrum found with the two nymphs may be helpful in defining their setting. Because it seems clear that candelabra were always associated with

architectural settings, it is likely that the two nymphs were not, therefore, displayed outdoors but within some kind of architectural backdrop or even within an enclosed room, as Winckelmann originally reported.

Candelabra and nymphs seem, to our minds, perhaps not to be associated; yet their reported discovery in the same place ought to at least pique our interest. Were they originally displayed in the same context, or is their final burial together merely coincidental? It is true that the archaeological discovery of sculptures in the same location may not always be significant as to their original display, but it ought to be taken into account to see where it may lead. On the other hand, objects found in apparently different locations can sometimes be associated because of stylistic or technical qualities that relate them to each other. Perhaps the best-known case of such association, for objects in the gardens of Sallust, is the Ludovisi and Boston "Thrones."

THE LUDOVISI AND BOSTON "THRONES"

LUDOVISI "THRONE": DISCOVERY AND EARLY THEORIES (FIG. 3.28)

In 1887 Visconti, without giving precise information concerning where and when it was discovered, published a description and a photograph of an unusual three-sided sculptural relief "recently unearthed in the villa Ludovisi."[194] Five years later Petersen reported (from two workmen: one who had been present at the discovery, the other during the rescue operation) that the work came to light some 1.20 to 1.50 meters below the ground surface in the area limited by the vie Boncompagni, Abruzzi, and Piemonte. Because the via Sicilia (the street enclosing this block to the north) was not mentioned by Petersen, Lanciani believed in 1897 that the discovery must have been "near the junction of the vie Boncompagni and Abruzzi."[195] In 1906, however, Lanciani reported information given to him by the Polish Count Michel Tyszkiewicz, to whom this relief had been offered for 300,000 lire. According to Tyszkiewicz, the relief was found protruding one-third into a trench opened for a sewer that ran under the sidewalk of the via Sicilia, which was partially on

municipal property.[196] Tyszkiewicz added that being a Sunday (in the summer), there were no inspectors, and thus it would have been easy for the discoverers to take possession of this sculpture unmolested.[197]

The reported change from the via Boncompagni to the via Sicilia is significant because, according to an agreement of January 29, 1886, the state could claim antiquities excavated under the via Vittorio Veneto and the present via Boncompagni but not under the other streets that composed the network of roads through the former villa Ludovisia.[198] That the state never attempted to claim ownership of the relief suggests that the findspot was believed not to have been near or under the via Boncompagni.

According to Lanciani, this state of affairs is useful in explaining the secrecy that the builders-proprietors successfully maintained for such a long time on the discovery of this relief and why Visconti, the first illustrator of the monument, had ignored its findspot.[199] Lanciani concluded that the details offered by Tyszkiewicz and the question of ownership accounted for the mystery of the findspot and the truth of the reports.

By 1950 Riemann defined the findspot even more

Figs. 3.28: **Ludovisi "Throne."** *A: front; B: left side; C: right side. Museo Nazionale delle Terme, Rome: Palazzo Altemps.*

precisely, reporting that the three-sided relief came to light under the southern sidewalk of the via Sicilia, 325 meters from the palazzo Grande (Margherita) of the villa Ludovisia. The following year, Langlotz supported this report of the findspot.[200] Nash concluded, however, that the find was near the via Boncompagni, where now stands the church of Saint Patrick of the Irish Augustinians.[201]

Regardless of the difficulty in isolating a precise findspot, it seems certain that the relief appeared from the ground within the confines of the *horti Sallustiani*. Supporting this supposition are not only the numerous reports (even though not always compatible) of its discovery, but the apparently accepted legal ownership by the Ludovisi/Boncompagni family, which seemed, however, unaware of its importance. According to Ludwig Pollak, a contemporary to the discovery of this "throne," Reinhard von Kekulé, then director of the State Museum of Berlin, did not accept an offer from the Boncompagni/Ludovisi family to purchase the relief, believing that it was an unimportant archaistic work. Indeed, even the owners treated the relief with little respect, employing it as a place to store empty wine bottles.[202]

Petersen, who was the first to attempt an identification of the subject as the birth of Venus, considered the odd shape to be a throne of this goddess.[203] Moreover, because this "throne" was believed to have come to light near a temple to Venus Erycina, the Sicilian city of Erice had been believed to be a possible original location for it.[204] Benndorf accepted Petersen's identification and added to it by associating this "throne" with the so-called Ludovisi head (Fig. 2.48) as part of a seated figure believed to be from the sanctuary of Venus Erycina.[205] In this case, their removal would be perhaps a ritual act to establish this cult in Rome. Thus, these two early publications established the identification and use of this three-sided relief as well as the Ludovisi head, and the term "throne" continues to be applied in spite of its difficulties and probable inaccuracy. Furthermore, Benndorf's association of this relief with a sanctuary to Venus Erycina, believed to have been somewhere within the confines of the gardens of Sallust, continues to be an accepted theory.[206]

BOSTON "THRONE": DISCOVERY AND EARLY REPORTS (FIG. 3.29)

Ludwig Pollak, who was in Athens in the summer of 1894, reported that he was informed of the discovery of a second "throne" in a letter by his friend, Paul Hartwig, who apparently told him that it came to light behind the palazzo Piombino during construction for a new building.[207] Some believed it was discovered during the construction of the Hotel Excelsior near the via Marche, but others suggested it was found in the courtyard of the frati Cappuccini at the crossing of the via Sicilia and the via Romagna (formerly Dogali).[208]

According to Pollak, this "throne," believed at that time to be part of an ancient sarcophagus, was refused immediately by Eliseo Borghi, a self-made antiquarian and dealer. Antonio and Alessandro Jandolo, however, did purchase it. From them it was soon acquired, according to Pollak, in 1894, by Edward Perry Warren, through Paul Hartwig and his then good friend Friedrich Hauser (the two later became the bitterest of enemies). Having been taken by February 1896 to Warren's house (Lewes House in Sussex) in England, it is there where Pollak finally saw it in 1906. Pollak's reporting about the date of its purchase is different from that of John Marshall, who claimed that Warren first heard of the Boston relief in January 1895 and only purchased it a year later, on January 27, 1896.[209] Marshall's report appears the most likely scenario, allowing (after its purchase) the almost immediate removal (on February 1, 1896) of the "throne" from Italy to England.

Not surprisingly, this issue of the findspot, and the apparent discrepancies in the date of discovery and purchase, raised doubts among some about the authenticity of this work as ancient. In the 1960s Jucker, Ashmole, and Young attempted to put doubts to rest, but in the 1980s and 1990s others again questioned seriously the antiquity of the piece, suggesting that it was a deliberate forgery.[210] The unconfirmed discovery in the confines of the *horti Sallustiani* surfaced as evidence of a hoax.

Ludwig Pollak, according to Guarducci, at first defended the authenticity of this second "throne," but later, under the influence of his friend, Pico Cellini,

Figs. 3.29: **Boston "Throne."** *A: front; B: left side; C: right side. Museum of Fine Arts, Boston, Inv. 08.205.*

Pollak changed his opinion.[211] But Pollak's *Memorie* (written between 1940 and 1943) of the antiquarian activities in late nineteenth- and early twentieth-century Rome do not document this revision of opinion.[212] In fact, E. A. Gardner and even Wilhelm Klein (Pollak's teacher) questioned its authenticity, but Pollak persisted in attempting to change their opinions, believing the work to be one of the most important and beautiful Greek sculptures of the Archaic period. He continued to refine his views up to his deportation in 1943, and if Pollak had changed his opinion, as Guarducci claimed, there should be some written record.[213]

In 1909 this "throne" finally was put on permanent public display in the new Museum of Fine Arts in Boston. Two years later Studniczka published it together with the *Ludovisi "Throne."*[214] No evidence, however, was presented concerning the definite findspot of the Boston relief, unlike the *Ludovisi "Throne,"* which Petersen had published only five years after its discovery.[215] Soon after Studniczka's publication, doubts were raised concerning the authenticity of the *Boston "Throne."*[216] These doubts were concerned with perceived technical, stylistic, and iconographic ambiguities, suggesting the possible or likely falsehood of the *Boston "Throne"* as an ancient work.[217]

Only in 1955 was the findspot recorded by Pico Cellini.[218] According to this information, the relief was found near a wall surrounding the gardens of the monastery of San Isidoro in what had been the environs of the villa Ludovisia, embedded into a watering trough for cattle. Nash reported that Cellini's informant was none other than Ugo Jandolo, son of Antonio, who together with his brother, Alessandro, had the *Boston "Throne"* in their antiquarian shop on the via Margutta. Jandolo claimed, however, that he never mentioned to Cellini the convent of San Isidoro but rather the courtyard of the Cappuccini, whose monastery had been torn down by 1887 to make room for the square of the via Veneto. In a letter to Nash dated December 10, 1957, Jandolo confirmed these statements, writing that "this sarcophagus [i.e., the *Boston "Throne"*] came from the courtyard of the Capuchin monks at the via Sicilia and the via Romagna, where it was embedded into a wall."[219] According to Nash,

Jandolo's remarks must be taken as confirmation that the *Boston "Throne"* was found probably no more than 160 to 180 meters from the *Ludovisi "Throne."*[220] On the other hand, Guarducci employed Jandolo's observations as well as those of others to conclude that the *Boston "Throne"* was a deliberate forgery commissioned by the Jandolo brothers and supported by Wolfgang Helbig and his Russian princess wife, Nadina Shakowsky.

Technical analyses have not produced any results to claim that the thrones are modern creations, and the identification of the marble in both cases as Thasian, from the area of Capo Vathy, could be evidence for their authenticity.[221]

With respect to the marble employed for these altars, it is of interest that a *Nike* (Fig. 3.30), found in 1886 (the same year as the discovery of the *Ludovisi "Throne,"* although in a different location) in front of the vestibule near the via Sallustio, is also made of Thasian marble. This under-life-sized statue is universally accepted as a genuine fifth-century B.C. work, and it is considered to have been made perhaps in south Italy—in the same area, as we will see, the "thrones" are believed to have been originally used.[222] It is possible that the similarities in marble, place of manufacture, and even dates among the two "thrones" and this *Nike* are not merely coincidental but indicative of a common past.

In further support of the antiquity of the "thrones" is the difficulty in believing that a modern forger could have found two blocks of Thasian marble in Rome or in the west of sufficient size to create these three-sided reliefs. Ancient sarcophagi of Thasian marble have been proposed as a possible source; however, the lengths of the front reliefs do not correspond to any known dimensions of ancient sarcophagi: they are too short for the long sides, and too long for the short sides of any extant marble sarcophagus found in Rome. Reused architectural blocks are possible, yet nothing about the marbles as they exist today points to such a source.

If the identification of the marble as Thasian suggests the antiquity of both "thrones," it does not assure they were made at the same time. In fact, in 1946 Colin proposed that the *Boston "Throne"* (measure-

Fig. 3.30: **Nike,** *Museo Capitolino, Rome: ACEA, Montemartini.*

ments correspond to Roman units) had been sculpted in Rome in the imperial period, probably during the time of Tiberius, under the inspiration of the *Ludovisi "Throne"* (measurements correspond to Lokrian units), and that both were in the sanctuary of Venus Erycina near the porta Collina.[223] Such a proposal would account for the apparent stylistic differences between the two "thrones" and perhaps also for the unusual subject matter of the Boston reliefs.

USE AND REUSE

Petersen was the first to propose, as we have seen, that the odd three-sided shape suggested a throne. This identification has been attached to these reliefs ever since, despite the absence of thrones with dimensions similar to these.[224] As a result, scholars are in agreement that these are most certainly not thrones, and thus alternative uses have been proposed. Among the most recent arguments is that at least the *Ludovisi "Throne"* (and perhaps the Boston one) may have come from the sanctuary of Marasà in Lokroi Epizephyrioi in south Italy, as Mertens-Horn most cogently argued.[225] Because of the correspondence in measurements of existing foundations with the *Ludovisi* and *Boston "Thrones,"* Mertens-Horn suggested that both came originally from inside the temple of Aphrodite in Contrada Marasà, where these reliefs may have been employed as a balustrade or *prostomion* for the large square opening in the floor of the cella.[226] Mertens-Horn suggested further that there may have been a wooden lifting device whereby a woman would rise from the square pit in the middle of the cella as a *deus ex machina.* The scene on the front of the *Ludovisi "Throne"* would not, therefore, represent a mythological event but a cultic ritual.[227] In this case, the absence of the depiction of water on the *Ludovisi "Throne"* would be a deliberate omission to relate it to the proposed ritual, which would not have employed, according to Mertens-Horn, a water bath.[228] On the other hand, the pebble ground on which the attendants to Aphrodite stand allude to the shore where the landing of Aphrodite took place either at Cape Zephyrion on Cyprus or at Lokroi Epizephyrioi. The physical evidence of corresponding measurements, the unusual square pit inside the temple of Aphrodite at Marasà, and the appropriateness of the reliefs are indeed enticing arguments for the original location of both the Boston and Ludovisi "Thrones" in Lokri.

La Rocca, however, rightly did not see any stylistic affinities with Lokrian artistic production, and he questioned the proposed use of these reliefs as enclosures for a bothros or for a ritual area. According to him, the volutes of the Boston "Throne" and the odd positioning of certain anatomical features (e.g., the crossed legs of the flautist, the bent toes of the nude youth) speak for the placement not directly on the ground (as Mertens-Horn suggested) but higher up, supported on a wall or some other surface.[229] La Rocca's views were in sympathy with those of Rodenwaldt, who observed that some of the figures are carved so that the optimum viewpoint is from below, suggesting an original position well above ground level.[230] As a result, Rodenwaldt believed they were originally decorative crowning acroteria for naiskoi, accounting for the trapezoidal shapes, the carving of the figures, and the unfinished interior surfaces. Although La Rocca accepted Rodenwald's proposal as having "una logica incontrovertibile," the comparisons to such crowning members are, to my mind, not entirely convincing. In particular, the trapezoidal shapes of the side panels do not correspond to known examples of volute acroteria, and the elaborate subject matter on the reliefs is not comparable to crowning members that depict usually only palmettes or single heraldic figures.

Likewise, other proposals that these "thrones" represent the wind screens for an altar or that they originally decorated the short ends of a rectangular altar above a sacrificial pit are also unlikely because the unfinished interior surfaces and the trapezoidal side panels are incompatible for such identifications.[231] Indeed, Curtius, who proposed their use as the short ends of an altar, believed the odd sloping upper surfaces to be the result of later recuttings.[232] Nevertheless, as La Rocca pointed out, these sloping surfaces must have been original because the relief figures are designed to accommodate the existing trapezoidal shapes.[233]

An intriguing proposal by P. Irdi Coretti is that both works are parts of stone chariots used to display images of Aeneas (Boston "Throne," dated post-Augustan) and Venus (Ludovisi "Throne," originally from Eryx [modern Erice]).[234] Unfortunately, this theory has been published only in abstract form; yet it seems as plausible a use for these reliefs as crowning members for naiskoi or the wind screens for an altar. The diversity of opinions for which we can find supporters shows clearly that we do not know enough about the various uses of sculptural relief in antiquity.

The question of original use is related to when and where these "thrones" could have been made. The volutes on the Boston "Throne" have been compared to a reconstruction of an acroterial volute from Macedonia, and as a result, the Ionic area of northeast Greece could be a possible location of the creation of at least this "throne."[235] Furthermore, a relief from Kirki on the Aegean island of Evros, now in the museum of Komotini, shows the hands of a musician that supports a lyre on his knees, touching the strings with the left hand and holding a plectrum in the right. The form of the lyre and the large plectrum are almost identical to those depicted on the Boston "Throne."[236]

The source of the "throne" reliefs may have been even further east, as suggested by stylistic similarities that exist between the Boston "Throne" and a late Archaic marble Sarcophagus, ca. 520–500 B.C. found in 1994 near the ancient battlefield of Granicus, in Asia Minor.[237] On the short right side is a mourning Hecuba (Fig. 3.31) that recalls the old woman on the Boston "Throne" (Fig. 3.29B).[238] This visual connection does not necessarily speak for an Asia Minor provenance for the Boston "Throne," but it does support the antiquity of the work as well as a possible original location in Sicily, which was very much influenced by Ionic elements in its monumental art of the Archaic period.[239] Finally, that both reliefs are carved of Thasian marble does not speak against a provenance in south Italy or Sicily because this marble was widely exported in antiquity throughout the Mediterranean.[240]

Regardless where these two relief sculptures originated, they ended up in Rome, presumably employed in the gardens of Sallust. The findspots and their somewhat checkered history do not aid in deciphering the location within these gardens, and their incomparable shapes hinder a definitive determination as to their original or secondary use(s).

In this context it is of interest to note that these reliefs are never discussed in relationship to the

*Fig. 3.31: Archaic marble **Sarcophagus**, detail: mourning woman [Hecuba].*

*Fig. 3.32: **Kneeling Barbarian,** Ny Carlsberg Glyptotek, Copenhagen, Inv. 1177.*

Fig. 3.33: **Kneeling Barbarian**, *Museo Nazionale,
Naples, Inv. 6117.*

Fig. 3.34: **Kneeling Barbarian**, *Museo Nazionale,
Naples, Inv. 6115.*

reported discovery at the same time and in the same place of a larger-than-life figure of a barbarian, on his knees and head bent, in a servile attitude to support some heavy object.[241] This could be the statue of pavonazzetto stone of a *Kneeling Barbarian* now in the Ny Carlsberg Glyptotek (Fig. 3.32),[242] although two others, virtually identical to this Copenhagen statue, are in the Museo Nazionale di Napoli (Figs. 3.33–34).[243] The Neapolitan ones are from the Farnese collection and, according to Talamo, were discovered in the del Bufalo *vigna* on the Pincio; that is, in perhaps the same location as the Copenhagen *Kneeling*

Barbarian and the *Ludovisi "Throne."*[244] On the other hand, Castelli reported in 1988 that the "re barbaro genuflesso" found in 1887 was still *in situ* but in poor condition and therefore was awaiting transfer to the Museo Nazionale Romano, presumably for restoration.[245] It appears, therefore, there may have been at least *four* identical statues (the two in Naples are mirror images) found within the confines of the gardens of Sallust, and perhaps all near the *Ludovisi "Throne."* That these (four?) statues formed a group (regardless of their findspots) seems likely not only because of the use of pavonazzetto stone but because of common sty-

*Fig. 3.35: **Trophy**, Museo Capitolino, Rome.*

listic and technical features. They had been believed to be Trajanic; Schneider, however, has presented persuasive stylistic arguments for an Augustan date.[246] If such an early date is accepted, and an "archaeological context" with the *Ludovisi "Throne"* is possible, are these relationships merely serendipitous?

Equally intriguing is a large *Trophy* (H: 2.10 meters) carved from Parian marble that was discovered in 1888 near the intersection of the via Boncompagni and the via Piemonte (Fig. 3.35); that is, within the same block as the *Kneeling Barbarian* and the *Ludovisi "Throne."*[247] According to Picard, it may date to the Augustan period, making it contemporary with the four *Kneeling Barbarians,* and it is tempting to believe that they were displayed together within the gardens of Sallust.[248] A trophy may seem out of place in a garden setting, but military displays are known in private houses beginning around 300 B.C., when victorious generals were permitted to adorn their vestibules with enemy spoils.[249] The latest occurrence in the literary record of *spolia* displayed in a private context is that at the door of Augustus.[250] It is unlikely, therefore, if the trophy and barbarians date to the Augustan period, they were created for these gardens, which did not pass into imperial hands until Nero.

It is not surprising, given the confusing archaeological record and the apparently disparate discoveries, that most scholars ignore or do not give much weight to the findspots of the "thrones" but instead are concerned with the subject matter of the reliefs. Yet even this approach, although producing enticing theories, finds no consensus. In fact, the identification of subjects relies at times on the determination of whether both reliefs are original fifth-century B.C. creations, if the *Boston "Throne"* is a Roman work, or if it even is a forgery. To my mind, perhaps the most intriguing scenario is the consideration of the *Boston "Throne"* as a Roman pendant to the Ludovisi relief. In this case, the subject could be Roman as suggested, for example, by Colin, who identified the scene on the front of the *Boston "Throne"* as the fates of Aeneas and Turno weighed in the presence of Juno and Venus.[251] Such a juxtaposition of original early works with contemporary images was perhaps perfectly acceptable and even at times desirable. In this way, the ancient Romans could have paid homage to, and at the same time

*Fig. 3.36: **Head of a Horse**, fifth-century B.C. Greek, Detroit Institute of Arts, Acc. nr. 39.602.*

dominated, the Greek world by removing a work of art from its original Greek context and placing it into a truly Roman one. Indeed, the copying of an Egyptian work, as will be discussed in the next section, presumably to create a pendant for display in the environs of the gardens of Sallust, was a similar situation of the assimilation and manipulation of imported, foreign works of art geared to a Roman spectator. This seeming contradiction—the affirmed superiority of what is foreign, and the affirmation of national excellence—is, perhaps, the very heart of acculturation.[252]

With this in mind, it is worthwhile to note a badly weathered marble *Head of a Horse* (Fig. 3.36) now in the Detroit Institute of Art that reportedly was found in the confines of the gardens of Sallust.[253] A precise findspot was not recorded; however, a letter in the museum archives from Otto Brendel states that he saw the piece when it was in the collection of Giacomo Nuñez in Rome (from whom the Detroit Institute purchased it). He remembered being told that it had been found "near the place of the Ludovisi Throne."[254] According to Robinson, who first published the head in 1940, it is probably from a pediment of the fifth century B.C., comparable to, but smaller than, the horses of Helios from the east pediment of the Parthenon. A large hole was later bored through, presumably to allow a waterpipe to exit the mouth, thus transforming it into a fountain. Brommer agreed, but he suggested that it is a Roman copy, at one-third scale, of the horses of Helios.[255] If this head is indeed pedimental (Brommer suggested that it could be part of a statue support), then regardless of its date there may have been a pedimental grouping that copied either entirely or partially the east pediment of the Parthenon. If fifth-century Greek, then we could expect possibly an Attic temple, approximately one-third the size of the Parthenon, on which this head belonged; if Roman, a temple in Rome that perhaps in some manner reflected the famous Greek temple. How, why, and even whether this head belonged to the gardens of Sallust in its reincarnation as a fountain are impossible to determine with any assurance. Yet the possible findspot near the *Ludovisi* (and *Boston?*) *"Throne(s)"* could be significant for the use of the "throne(s)" as decoration for an elaborately decorated fountain, a form perfectly in keeping with a garden setting.

The bringing together of apparently disparate pieces to form an ensemble is indeed speculative, given the information that has come down to us. It is all the more welcomed, therefore, that another group of sculptures is known to have been found in the same place. Furthermore, they are all of Egyptian or Egyptianizing style, and so their association as an ensemble is difficult to refute.

EGYPTIAN SCULPTURES

In the gardens of the Verospi on the Pincio, Monsignor Francesco Bianchini, who had been appointed "Presidente delle antichità di Roma" in 1703,[256] discovered statues in Egyptian style that are now in the Vatican collection.[257] These over-life-sized granite figures include one of the nineteenth dynasty (*Touya, Queen of Seti I,* and mother of Ramses II; Fig. 3.37), two of Ptolemaic date (*Ptolemy II* and *Arsinoe;* Figs. 3.38–3.39), and an almost exact Roman copy of the Egyptian statue of *Arsinoe* (Fig. 3.40).[258] A fifth statue without head and feet, male, of black stone and life-size is reported to have been found, but it is either lost or has not been identified among extant fragments.[259] A listing by Schreiber of six statues is incorrect, although one of these, an under-life-sized male in basalt, could belong.[260]

Not only is there a discrepancy in the number of statues but also in the year of their discovery.[261] Montfaucon and Braschi[262] reported a date of 1710, Posterla[263] a date of 1711, while Ficoroni[264] reported they were discovered three years later in 1714. Lanciani indicated mistakenly that two were found in 1714 and two in 1720.[265] Bianchini, the excavator, reported the date as 1710, and there is little evidence to suggest a different one.[266] Perhaps not coincidentally, in this same year, according to Lanciani, "Cardinal G. B. Spinola granted permission to Mr. Leone Vitelleschi to excavate in his gardens in Rome just before the porta Salaria next to his own borders, stones, palettes, marbles, statues, columns, peperini, travertini, gold, and silver" under the supervision of Francesco Bartoli.[267] Although nothing links directly Bianchini's campaigns with Vitelleschi's, it is possible that the excavations granted by Spinola prompted those in the Verospi vineyard, which was also near the porta Salaria and presumably immediately adjacent to the Vitelleschi property. Pietrangeli combined these properties as if they were the same, by declaring that Bianchini's excavations were in the gardens of Leone Verospi-Vitelleschi.[268] Indeed, Bianchini gave all five statues to Pope Clement XI in exchange for water from the Trevi for the Vitelleschi palazzo on the via del Corso, and a payment of 150 scudi, and so it is clear the Vitelleschi/ Verospi were the owners.[269]

These are not the only Egyptian or Egyptianizing statues found in the area. Winckelmann reported statues in the villa Altieri (adjacent to the Verospi), half of which were of Egyptian style: fragments of a figure in basalt, other heads in the same material, among which is a female with a very similar hairstyle to one of the

Fig. 3.37: **Touya, Queen of Seti I**, *Musei Vaticani, Inv. 22678.*

Fig. 3.38: **Ptolemy II**, *Musei Vaticani, Inv. 22682.*

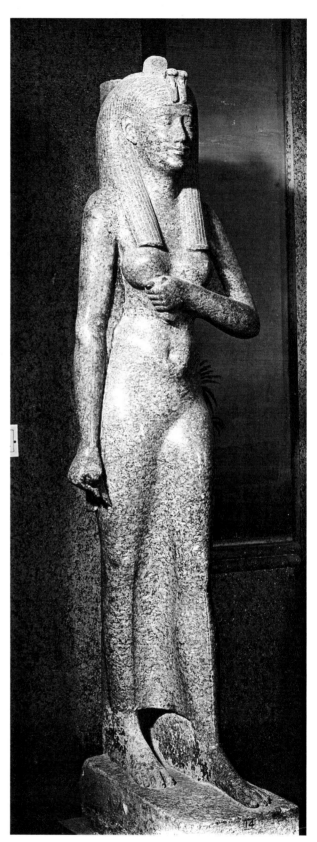

Fig. 3.39: **Arsinoe,** *Musei Vaticani, Inv. 22681.*

Fig. 3.40: Roman copy of statue of **Arsinoe,** *Musei Vaticani, Inv. 22683.*

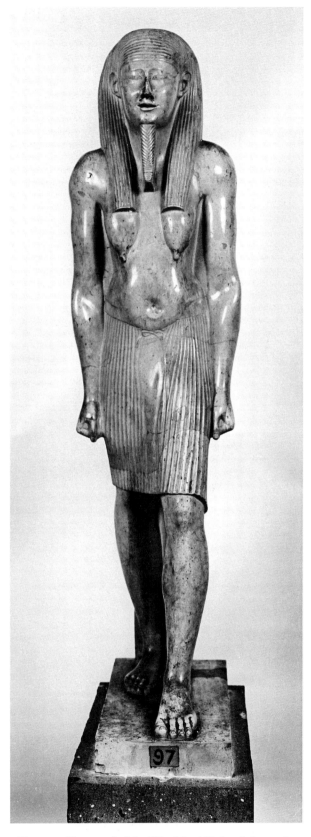

Fig. 3.41: Hieroglyphic inscription on back of Fig. 3.40, Musei Vaticani.

Fig. 3.42: **Hapy,** *god of the Nile, Musei Vaticani, Inv. 22809.*

*Fig. 3.43: Statue of **Macrinus**, Musei Vaticani.*

statues coming from the villa Verospi.[270] Adjacent to the Verospi and the Vitelleschi properties to the east was that of Borioni from whose collection was reported a late first-century B.C. or early first-century A.D. statue of *Hapy*, god of the Nile, now in the Museo Gregoriano Egizio, Vatican (Fig. 3.42).

It is possible that it was found on the Borioni property and could belong with the group reported by Bianchini.[271] Also reportedly from the villa Borioni is a canopic jar in grey basalt, now in the villa Albani collection, and a statue of *Macrinus* (A.D. 217–218), now in the Vatican (Fig. 3.43).[272]

Finally, a herm statue of Pan in red marble may also have been found on the Borioni property.[273]

Excavations took place at the end of the nineteenth century on the property of Josef Spithoever (apparently in a narrow, deep passageway [a cryptoporticus?]

on the Quirinal slopes and therefore not to be associated with the excavations by Bianchini, which were on the Pincio). During these excavations was found, according to Lanciani, a "montone [ram] in rosso antico," which Moltesen suggested may have been a mistaken identification for a *Hippopotamus* allegedly found in the *horti Sallustiani* and now in the Ny Carlsberg Glyptotek (Fig. 3.44).[274]

Although it is true that large animal sculptures in rosso antico are rare, it is difficult to believe that Lanciani mistook a hippopotamus for a ram. Lanciani's 1906 reporting of this ram was, in fact, a recollection of an 1888 visit to Spithoever's villa, where he and Visconti apparently saw sculptures that had been found in a narrow and deep passage, among which, as previously discussed, were a Leda, an Endymion, a Niobid, a replica of a Praxitelean faun, and a ram

Fig. 3.44: **Hippopotamus** *in rosso antico, Ny Carlsberg Glyptotek, Copenhagen.*

Fig. 3.45: **Leda and the Swan,** *Ny Carlsberg Glyptotek, Copenhagen Kat. 336, Inv. 1834.*

in rosso antico.[275] But Lanciani had recorded already in 1897 "many works of art . . . collected by Spithoever (including) . . . a statue . . . , life-size and of good workmanship, representing Endymion asleep on the rocks of mount Latmos.[276] A few steps farther a statue of *Leda and the Swan* [Fig. 3.45][277] came to light, a good copy of a better original, and also the figure of a dog finely cut in rosso antico."[278]

It is possible that the ram reported in 1906 is this dog recorded earlier, although it seems unlikely that Lanciani would have confused a ram for a dog. Nine years after Lanciani and Visconti made their visit to Spithoever's villa, Ludwig Pollak and Matthew Stewart Prichard were there on January 22, 1897. According to Pollak's diary, among the many fragments of sculptures, as mentioned above, were the torso of a bearded pugilist, a Praxitelean resting satyr, a slim Athena with aigis, a badly preserved Leda-statue, a torso in rosso antico (a copy of the centaur by Aristeas and Papias), inscriptions and terracotta reliefs.[279] Of particular interest is the torso in rosso antico identified as a centaur, which may well be the same work identified by Lanciani as a dog. Regardless of the correct identification of these animals in rosso antico (ram, dog, and centaur), it is possible all or some belonged originally with the group of Egyptian statues from the Pincio, in spite of their findspots (presumably on Spithoever's property on the Quirinal). Furthermore, the *Hippopotamus* in Copenhagen could well have been part of this ensemble of rosso antico sculptures.

According to Bianchini, his Egyptian statues were found "in circum videlicet Sallustii," which by 1665 had been identified by Nardini as *in the large valley* between the Quirinal and Pincio hills.[280] Only later did Lanciani first indicate they had been discovered in the ruins of a small building *on the Pincio,* which was given the label "casino di stile egizio" or "diaeta egiziana" and a precise location some 110 meters north of the north wall of the valley opposite the vestibule (at that time, as discussed above, identified as a nymphaeum).[281]

In his detailed handwritten report (including drawings) preserved in Verona (*Cod. Veron.* 347, fols. 152–154 [repaginated in graphite as 137–139]), Bianchini did not mention a building, although brickstamps were transcribed (Fig. 3.46).[282] It is likely that because of these brickstamps as well as the so-called Destail-

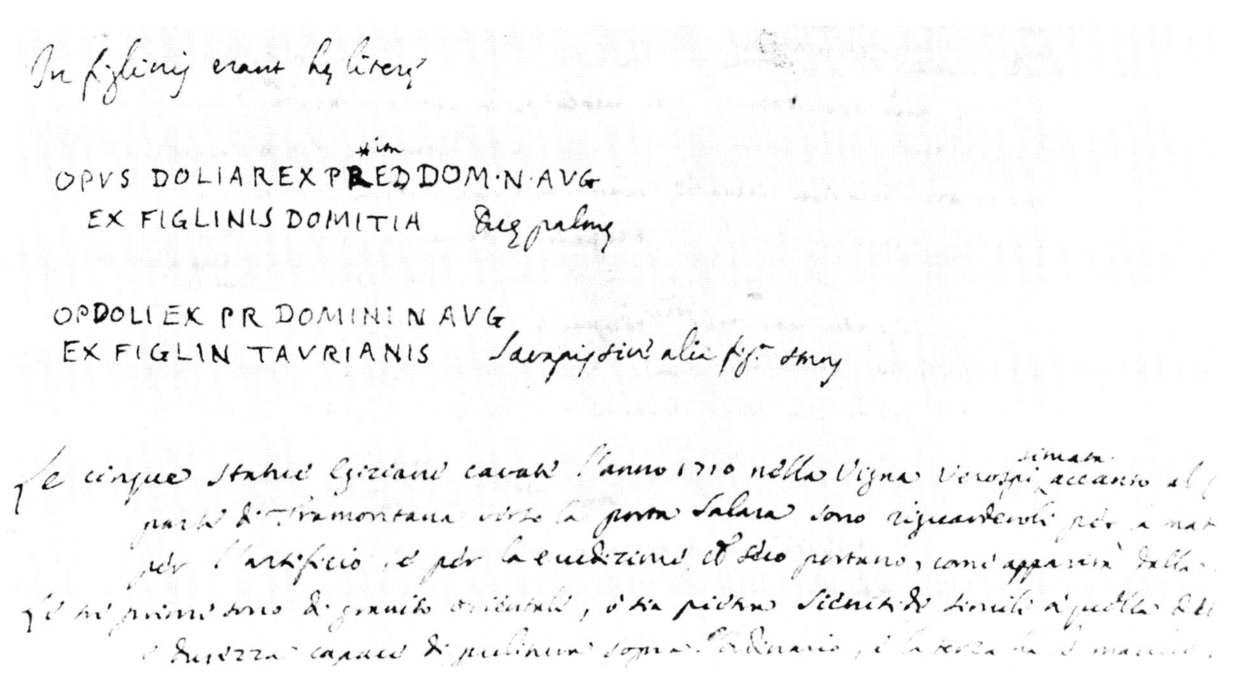

In figlinis erant hæ literæ

```
OPVS DOLIAREXPREDDOM·N·AVG
    EX FIGLINIS DOMITIA
```

```
OP·DOLI·EX·PR·DOMINI·N·AVG
    EX·FIGLIN·TAVRIANIS
```

Fig. 3.46: Cod. Veron. 347, fol. 152v [137v]: brickstamps transcribed.

leur plan showing a building on the Pincio near where Bianchini presumably excavated (see pp. 31–36, and Fig. 2.8), Lanciani was convinced of the existence of such a building. Whether or not an identifiable building can be associated with these statues, it is clear they were all found at approximately the same location, and therefore they must be seen as a deliberate ensemble.

The statues of Ptolemy II Philadelphos and his wife Arsinoe (Figs. 3.38–3.39) probably came to Rome as a pair from Heliopolis, as the inscriptions connect each with Heliopolitan divinities.[283] These two statues may well have proclaimed the union of Ptolemy with his sister-wife, and her divinization because her inscription evokes her as daughter, sister, and wife of the king, as well as having a rapport with the gods. Grenier equated this coupling with Caligula's marriage to his sister Drusilla and his revival of pharaonic traditions of sister-wife queens, and saw in the twin statue of *Arsinoe* (Fig. 3.40) a portrait of Drusilla. The statue of *Touya* (Fig. 3.37), mother of Ramses II, who had received exceptional honors at her death, therefore, could be seen as a reflection of Caligula's own mother to whom he gave special funerary honors.[284] The figures, according to Grenier, may have been assembled after the death of Drusilla in 38 and before Caligula's

assassination in 41. But Caligula was not the only Julio-Claudian emperor to be intrigued by Egypt: one of Nero's tutors was the Egyptian priest Chaeremon, and according to Suetonius (*Nero* 56), Nero worshipped Dea Syria exclusively.

Nevertheless, Grenier's theory and even a Neronian connection disregard the usual assumption that these Egyptian statues belong with a structure on the Pincio designated as "Egyptian." It appears, according to reported brickstamps, that this building is to be dated to the reign of Commodus. Palmer made an intriguing suggestion that it lay in an area called, by the Severan period, Memphis.[285] According to an inscription mentioning Septimius Severus and Julia Domna, a place called Memphis sat above "the Nymphs." According to Palmer, "the Nymphs" refers to an ancient street that ran northwest from the via Salaria (near the porta Collina) and near where Lanciani sited, I believe mistakenly, a round temple of Venus (*FUR* 3: Fig. 1.1B).[286] The place called Memphis then would be to the west of this road, in an area where Egyptian statues were found as well as where Palmer would place the "pyramis" of the anonymous Einsiedeln.

Regardless of how one may interpret the specific meaning of these statues to a Roman audience, the group is indeed intriguing. It indicates that on the Pincio, within the confines of the *horti Sallustiani,* existed an area in which the decorative schemes (and perhaps even the architecture) were influenced strongly by Egyptian and Egyptianizing themes. The Egyptian obelisk found further to the west on the same

hill could suggest that in the later Roman empire, this part of the Pincio was substantially focused on Egyptian elements and possibly on Egyptian rites. On the other hand, a sculptural grouping may be decorative only and not indicative of cult.[287]

SCULPTURES FOUND IN 1888 NEAR THE VIA BONCOMPAGNI

Unlike the cache of Egyptian and Egyptianizing sculptures found on the Pincio, a group of sculptures uncovered in 1888 near the via Boncompagni probably were not displayed together in antiquity despite their mutual findspot. Among this group was reported a "colossal draped leg" and a "colossal draped figure," which were believed to be two distinct pieces (see p. 99). It is more likely, however, these refer to the same sculpture, because both were found, apparently, not only at the same time but in the same place—near the via Boncompagni, between the via Quintino Sella and the no-longer-preserved via Nerva. The confusion in the reporting of this single fragment as two may have contributed to Lanciani's identification of it as a fleeing Niobid, as we have seen, and the futile search by modern scholars for a "lost" Niobid. The "colossal draped leg/figure" seems clearly to be the fragment of a colossal striding *Apollo Kitharoidos* (Fig. 3.12), which is preserved in the Museo Capitolino. Furthermore, found with this sculpture of Apollo was a *Crouching Amazon* (Fig. 3.14), dated by style to a fifth-century B.C. Greek workshop, and, as discussed above, this Amazon could have played a role in a possible ensemble of Niobids.

Other sculptures also came to light at about the same time and in the same location. These include an over-life-sized eagle[288] and perhaps most important and intriguing of all, fragments of three large (restored lengths: 4.10 meters) *Sculptural Friezes* (Figs. 3.47, 3.48), each carved with an elaborate vegetal design terminating at both ends in almost three-dimensional crouching sphinxes.[289]

Viscogliosi, the only scholar to have made a serious study of these reliefs, believed the design and motifs were adapted from large altar reliefs, such as those of

the Ara Pacis. They may not have been used originally, however, as altar reliefs but as the sides of tribunes. This conclusion arose from observing the unfinished back and no surrounding edge, indicating they were encased in a wall.[290] Of the four remaining sections, Viscogliosi identified two types of marble and two different workshops.

The largest preserved section is of microasian marble, perhaps Dokimeion, and is the work of a master of sinuous modeling (Viscogliosi's Type A). The other smaller three fragments are of Luna marble, with some bluish-gray striations. Viscogliosi related the carving of these to the capitals of the interior order of the Apollo Sosianus temple, and it was clearly executed in a drier style than the largest fragment (Viscogliosi's Type B). Viscogliosi proposed that these three fragments, therefore, are copies after the "original," better Type A.

If this is the case, at least two scenarios are possible: (1) the reliefs in Luna marble were created as pendants to a relief already existing but used in a new context, or (2) the Master of Type A, a contemporary of the sculptors of the Luna marbles, worked in Rome or somewhere else in material of higher quality. A difficulty with an earlier prototype is that an elaborate and well-established tradition of such friezes is not attested in Asia Minor in the first century B.C. Nonetheless, Viscogliosi suggested that these could be considered "Neo-Attic," the result of the romanization of Greek art around the time of Augustus. The date of their manufacture would indeed be of interest; however, a precise dating would not necessarily indicate how they were employed in the gardens or when they arrived there. Whether or not originally displayed in the gardens of Sallust, it is clear they must have been

*Fig. 3.47: **Sculptural Frieze,** Palazzo dei Conservatori, Rome.*   *Fig. 3.48: **Sculptural Frieze,** Palazzo dei Conservatori, Rome: drawing of fragments.*

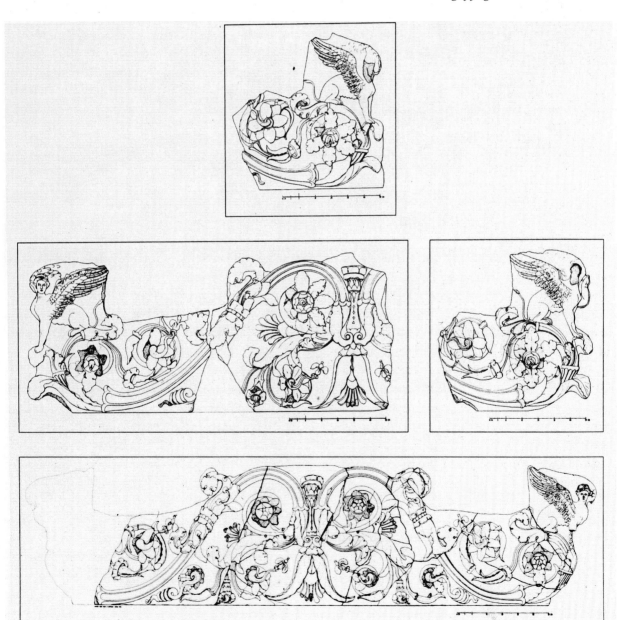

once part of a significant structure. It is not known, however, if they were created for the gardens or if they arrived there at a later date.

Scholars ignore, or at least do not discuss, the systematic cutting down of all the preserved pieces. Irregular rectangular cuttings were made from the wings of each of the sphinxes to the tendril stalk behind, carefully following the tips of the wings and the down-turned leaves. Likewise, the leaves under the sphinxes were carefully left when marble was removed from the original ends of the reliefs. Each relief, from sphinx to sphinx, was cut down in the identical manner for some unknown but clearly specific reason. It is impossible to know whether such recutting was accomplished in antiquity or at a much later time, but it may well have been done when these were adapted to a garden setting. Whether the other sculptures found with them—the *Crouching Amazon*, the *Eagle*,

and the colossal *Apollo*—have anything to do with these reliefs, or with each other, is difficult to determine.

The superior quality of the reliefs and their impressive size speak, I believe, against their original use as garden sculptures. When first discovered, they were believed to have decorated a nymphaeum, and it is indeed tempting to consider the later careful recuttings for such an adaptation into a typical garden setting in the late imperial period. On the other hand, it must be admitted that a much later time ought to be considered for the cutting down of these reliefs, perhaps in the Early Christian or Medieval periods when this area was beginning to be taken over by ecclesiastical complexes. The subject matter would not have offended Christian sensibilities, and the beauty of the carving and the size of the reliefs must have played a role in their likely preservation into the post-antique period.

ORESTES AND ELECTRA

Finally, scholars have sometimes argued that a sculptural group identified usually as *Orestes and Electra* was found in the gardens of Sallust. Unlike much of the preceding material, however, there is little to warrant such a conclusion, and even the identification and meaning of the group are open to interpretation.

Schreiber suggested that the so-called group of *Orestes and Electra* (Fig. 3.49), which is mentioned in the 1623 Ludovisi inventory as "un'Amicizia di due statue di marmo," was found in the property of the villa Ludovisia.[291] In the eighteenth century it was identified as two Romans, Lucius Papirius and his mother.[292] Winckelmann proposed the Greek identifications of Electra recognizing her brother, Orestes, and although this may not be correct, most scholars have accepted it.[293]

Palma observed that the short hair of the female figure could be an indication of mourning and that the support by the right leg of the young man takes the shape of an Attic stele.[294] These aspects of the group would then be compatible for the identifications as Orestes and Electra, who greet each other at the grave of their father, Agamemnon. Furthermore, these funerary connotations are perhaps supported by the

discovery, in the necropolis of Porto, of a replica of the Electra figure (now in the Museo Torlonia).[295] Indeed, Furtwängler believed that the group goes back to a grave monument of the fourth century as indicated by the body of "Orestes," which is comparable to figures on gravestones dating from the end of the fifth to the beginning of the fourth centuries B.C.[296] The head of this figure, however, finds its closest stylistic parallels with works around 100 B.C., and so it is clearly a pastiche and not a direct copy of a Greek original. Likewise, the figure of Electra has been judged by scholars to be Praxitelean or post-Praxitelean and thus stylistically incompatible with Orestes.

On the stele support is an inscription in Greek: Μενέλαος Στεφάνου μαθητης—"Menelaos, pupil of Stephanos (made this)." Furthermore, a statue in the villa Albani in Rome (Inv. nr. 906) is signed: Στεφανος Πασιτελους μαθητης εποει—"Stephanos, student of Pasiteles made this." It is possible from these two inscriptions to recognize a "school" of Pasiteles, with at least two generations of successful sculptors: Stephanos and Menelaos. Although such a Pasitelean "school" seems apparent, the precise chronological markers of it are not.

Fig. 3.49: **Orestes and Electra,** *Museo Nazionale delle Terme, Rome.*

According to Pliny (*HN* 36.40), Pasiteles was born in 89 B.C. and was certainly an adult during the time of Pompey (*HN* 33.156: circa Pompei Magni aetatem Pasiteles) and Varro (*HN* 33.130, 156). Furthermore, a Stephanos is known from Pliny (*HN* 36.33), who explained that a sculptor by this name had made a statuary group of nymphs that were set up with other sculptures in the estate of Asinius Pollio. It is not obvious, however, whether these nymphs were made for Asinius Pollio because at least another group in his collection—*Centauri Nymphas gerentes* by Arkesilaos—may have come from the estate of Lucullus.[297] It is tempting to suggest that Stephanos' nymphs also came from Lucullus' estate and that he is the same man who is mentioned in the inscription on the ephebe in the villa Albani. In this case, Stephanos most likely was active before the death of Lucullus who retired in 59 B.C. to live a life of luxury. Yet opinions vary widely as to the date of this sculptor.

The sculptures, as already discussed, are stylistic pastiches and therefore are difficult to date. Curtius believed that the *Orestes and Electra* by Menelaos must be Flavian because of similarities to hairstyles of portraits from that period. In this case, he dated Menelaos' teacher, Stephanos, to the period of Nero, and Pasiteles to the early first century A.D. According to Curtius, the Pasiteles mentioned by Pliny as born in 89 B.C. must therefore be a different man than the teacher of Stephanos.[298] Zanker, as well, dated Menelaos' group to after the middle of the first century A.D., but he believed that his "teacher," Stephanos, in all likelihood must have been active in the middle of the first century B.C.[299] Zanker reconciled this seemingly irreconcilable chronology by suggesting that the indication of "pupil" in the inscriptions may be understood as "working in the manner of" or being in sympathy with the workshop practices (the making of pastiches) of Pasiteles and his "school."[300] Thus, Menelaos may have seen himself as a successor of Stephanos without being contemporary with him. Lippold dated the *Orestes and Electra* to the Augustan or Tiberian periods. Moretti agreed that the form of the letters of the inscription could be early Augustan in date.[301] Most recently, Fuchs suggested a date, on stylistic grounds, between 50 and 30 B.C. for the *Orestes and Electra,* thereby compressing the Pasitelean "school" to perhaps fewer than thirty years—from ca. 60 B.C. to 30 B.C.

Regardless of the correct dating of the creation of this sculpture and its relationship to a Pasitelean "school," the meaning of the sculpture is far from secure, making the appropriateness of this group for a possible garden estate difficult to determine. Without a specific context or accompanying inscription, the identification of these ambiguous images had changed since the seventeenth century. Even in antiquity, such diverse opinions could also have been expressed depending on context and viewer. Furthermore, the rarity of this group and the lack of any firm evidence concerning its discovery exacerbate an already difficult situation of interpretation, and so no definitive conclusions can be reached. It is, therefore, proper to suggest only the *possibility* of this sculptural group as a part of the ancient gardens of Sallust. Indeed, if a funerary connotation is accepted, it is possible that it could have been erected in a cemetery context. It should be remembered that although the western limits of the gardens of Sallust (the location of the original Ludovisi property in the seventeenth century) are vague, they were likely bordered by a cemetery at the west. It is, therefore, possible that this statuary group, apparently found on Ludovisi property, may be related more to the western neighbor rather than being a part of the decorative program in the gardens of Sallust.

ADDENDUM

The Templum Gentis Flaviae and the Three Temples of Fortune

According to Suetonius (*Dom.* I): Domitianus natus est VIIII Kal. Novemb. . . . regione urbis sexta ad Malum Punicum, domo quam postea in templum gentis Flaviae convertit. Thus, the future emperor Domitian was born on 24 October (A.D. 51) in the sixth region of Rome, in an area known as the "Pomegranate," in a house which he later transformed into a temple dedicated to his family.

This temple was not only for the Flavian imperial cult but for the tomb of this dynastic family.[1] It must have been constructed by A.D. 94/95, when Martial first mentioned it, and it was still standing in the third century, even having been enlarged by Claudius the Goth (286–270).[2] The specific location is not recorded; however, according to the *Curiosum* and the *Notitia,* it was *after* the "Hortos Salustianos" and *before* the "Thermas Diocletianas." According to Paris, the *Curiosum* and the *Notitia* are not necessarily listing monuments in a linear topographical order. Thus the *horti Sallustiani* could be seen on the left and the Baths of Diocletian on the right as one proceeded towards the Colline gate.[3] In that case, the Flavian temple would be between these, near the present church of Santa Susanna, completed in 1603, standing in the same location as its original Early Christian predecessor, and over ruins of a late first- or early second-century *domus.*[4]

According to an early fifth-century version of the *Martyrologium Hieronymianum,* August 11 was a festival day of Santa Susanna "*ad duas domus iuxta duo clecinas*" (*duo clecinas* probably being a misreading for *diocletianas*). The *duas domus* likely refer to the house of Susanna's father, Gabinius, and the adjoining house of Pope Caius (283–296), brother of Gabinius, and the place where mass was celebrated in Susanna's honor.[5] The location is further distinguished as "*in regione sexta iuxta vicum Mammurtini ante forum Sallusti.*"[6] According to Paris, this literary evidence defines the location of the Flavian temple as between the corners of the via XX Settembre and the via Quattro Fontane and the largo di Santa Susanna, rather than at the southwest corner of these two roads, as Lanciani proposed.[7]

Furthermore, archaeological evidence, according to Paris, supports a location near the Baths of Diocletian.[8] This evidence (not in the order presented by Paris) includes two inscriptions. A travertine cippus found in the *vigna* Sadoleto in the sixteenth century reads: *Inter duos parietes ambitus privat(us) Flavi Sabini.*[9] According to Tacitus (*Hist.* 3.69), during the tumult of A.D. 69 the most influential Romans took refuge in the house of T. Flavius Sabinus, who likely lived near the house of his younger brother, the emperor Vespasian. Thus, where this cippus was discovered could pin down the location of this house and by extension the placement of the Flavian temple.

Unfortunately, the precise location of the *vigna* Sadoleto is not known. Marliano indicated that it was near the church of Santa Susanna, but Nibby later believed it was near the churches of Santa Teresa and San Caio, that is, near the present crossing of vicolo San Nicola da Tolentino and the via XX Settembre.[10] Lanciani placed it immediately southwest of the intersection of the via XX Settembre and the via Quattro Fontane.[11] It was in the gardens of Sadoleto that Ligorio (*Ottobon.* 3374, 263. *Taur.* XV) identified a circular building with a hexastyle pronaos as the Templum Minervae Flaviae, and where a marble image of this goddess was uncovered.[12] According to Lanciani, this is the same building reported by Flaminio Vacca (*Mem.* 37, 38) as a round or oval tempietto on the via Pia near San Vitale. Thus, Lanciani reconstructed (*FUR* 16) a round building surrounded by a square colonnade and positioned it where he believed the Sadoleto gardens were—west of where Paris believed them to have been.[13]

A second piece of "evidence" was uncovered at the end of the nineteenth century, during excavations for the building of the Methodist church between the via Firenze and via XX Settembre (on the opposite side from Santa Susanna), where part of a lead pipe was discovered with the inscription *T. Flavi Sabini.*[14] It is uncertain, however, whether this pipe was *in situ,* and so its findspot does not necessarily indicate the precise location of the Flavian house.[15]

An impressive glass-paste mosaic decorating a fountain exedra was found more than thirty years ago under the refectory for the caserma dei Corazzieri (who are an elite corps of guards for the president of the Republic), which was located on the via XX Settembre only a few meters to the southwest of the church of Santa Susanna.[16] Representing a rich architectural fantasy with niches occupied by statues, this mosaic is in the tradition of wall painting during the so-called fourth style and therefore has been dated to ca. A.D. 50, or to the Flavian period. This dating, the above-mentioned inscriptions, and the literary testimony have prompted the identification of these remains with the house of the Flavians. This identification has led to the proposal that a large cement wall (found during the uncovering of the mosaic walls) with a canal running along side it, probably an aqueduct, is part of the foundation of the Flavian temple, known to have been adjacent to the house.[17]

Finally, sculptural fragments of Pentelic marble, datable to the Flavian period, were found at the beginning of the twentieth century north of the north arm of the exedra of the Baths of Diocletian.[18] Within this hastily excavated area ancient architecture was revealed, and Paris suggested that the sculptures need not have belonged originally to the building represented by these walls but may have been reused.[19] Regardless, it is clear that these walls and the sculptures were covered by the northwest wing of the Diocletianic bath complex.

The reliefs represent large scenes of sacrifice (a flamen stands before the temple of Quirinus) and an *adventus* (Vespasian crowned by Victory). Two freestanding figures served as columns for the building of which only several pieces of the entablature and of Ionic or Composite capitals are preserved. A proposed reconstruction of this monument is based on the form and proportions of the Ara Pacis Augustae, with the under-life-sized male Caryatids serving as decorative elements on the exterior. The relief panels are not incorporated into this reconstruction.

It is clear that this Ara-Pacis-like building, if identified correctly as the Templum Gentis Flaviae, can be only a small part of what must have been a much larger structure. Indeed, Torelli suggested that all these sculptural fragments might have decorated a large arched entrance to the Flavian sanctuary as perhaps depicted on a Domitianic sestertius.[20]

These disparate pieces of evidence—the literary testimonia that the Flavian temple and villa were on the Quirinal, the inscriptions found there carrying the Flavian family name, the elaborate mosaics suggesting a wealthy *domus,* and the fragments of sculptures of Flavian date—have been assembled to suggest the location and even the possible form of the Templum Gentis Flaviae. Collectively, they are indeed enticing, yet when seen separately, nothing speaks for the location and for the form of this famous temple.

The findspot of the cippus and the pertinence of the lead pipe to its findspot are unclear, and the mosaic fountain, although indicating a wealthy abode, need not have belonged to the Flavian family. Finally, the sculptures seem not to have been found in their original location, although they are *assumed* to have not traveled far from it. But because they are so fragmented, one could suggest just the opposite: that they had migrated to their findspot from a considerable distance, possibly as part of the massive earth moving that must have preceded the building of the Baths of Diocletian. Furthermore, that the baths seem to have buried these sculptures speaks against their pertinence to the Flavian temple, which had been only several years before restored and enlarged by Claudius the Goth. These sculptures, therefore, ought not to be used, in circular argumentation, as "evidence" for the location of the Flavian temple, however enticing this may be.[21]

Finally, if the present church of Santa Susanna stands on or near the houses of her father and uncle, who was pope between 283 and 296, and where it is recorded he said mass, then we cannot believe that the Flavian temple stood on the same spot. It must be acknowledged that the location of the Templum Gentis Flaviae is still unknown.

Manca di Mores, reinterpreting the literary evidence, and employing terracotta architectural fragments discovered near the largo di Santa Susanna, and archaic votives from under the stairs of Santa Maria della Vittoria, located the temple of Quirinus near this church.[22] Her arguments concerning the location of the Quirinus temple are indeed enticing, but her acceptance of the Templum Gentis Flaviae as near Santa Susanna does not follow the *Curiosum* and the *Notitia,* both of which have the *Gentem Flaviam* coming *after* the Quirinus temple (that is, east of this temple).

Massive foundations to the east of Santa Maria della Vittoria are recorded on *FUR* 10 as *Aedes Fortunae,* but these are too large for such an identification (see below).[23] Thus, the large size of these foundations and the fact that no others were found nearby speak against the identification as one of the three temples of Fortune. Furthermore, a series of contiguous rooms at the south of these foundations running parallel with the ancient roadway may well be the remains of a precinct wall for this sanctuary. It is perhaps possible, therefore, to reconstruct the Flavian temple here: the penultimate monument listed in Region VI by the *Curiosum* and the *Notitia.*[24]

The nineteenth-century excavations that uncovered these foundations do not lend any evidence for or against such an identification. According to Lanciani, "many works of art were collected by Spithoever on this occasion. Twenty meters below the platform of the temple, at the bottom of the moat which protected the Servian embankment from the outside, a statue was found, life-size and of good workmanship, representing Endymion asleep on the rocks of mount Latmos. A few steps farther a statue of Leda and the swan came to light, a good copy of a better original, and also the figure of a dog finely cut in rosso antico."[25]

These excavations by Spithoever were never published,[26] although on *FUR* 10, the platform of the temple is recorded as 68 meters a.s.l. The sculptures listed above by Lanciani were found, therefore, at 48 meters a.s.l. (that is, 20 meters below the presumably upper surface of this platform). It also appears that most of these foundations must have been removed during the nineteenth-century building operations because the present ground level—at the intersection of via Flavia and via S. Tullio—recorded by Lanciani (*FUR* 10: Fig. 1.1D) is 60 meters a.s.l., some 8 meters below the recorded height of the ancient temple foundations, which were some 12 meters deep (according to *CAR* II-F, 65a). There may be, therefore, at least 4 meters of foundations still remaining immediately under the present street level.[27]

These recordings of levels also suggest that the sculptures found in the moat *outside* the "Servian" wall and many meters below the temple foundations cannot be associated with the building once standing on this platform. With no evidence other than the existence of these foundations, the identification of this building is impossible. As suggested above, the regionaries *could* indicate that this is where the Templum Gentis Flaviae stood, but it is clear that these do not list every building, not even the three temples to Fortuna that apparently were in the vicinity.

Vitruvius indicated that these Fortuna temples were close to the porta Collina, and he described one of these as *in antis*—apparently a small temple like that of the temple of Themis at Rhamnous—and it is assumed that all three temples were equally small.[28] That Vitruvius defined the location as "in Colle" is probably significant, suggesting that it stood inside the walls; otherwise, he would have used the phrase "ad" or "extra portam Collinam" as he did for Venus

Erycina. Furthermore, Krinagoras mentioned three temples of Tyche near the house of Sallust, which must be the same three temples reported by Vitruvius as near the Colline gate.[29]

The most important of the three temples seems to have been the *Fortuna primigenia in colle,* which was voted in 204 by the consul P. Sempronius Tuditanus and dedicated ten years later, perhaps by Q. Marcius Ralla.[30] Another temple called *Fortunae p(ublicae) p(opuli) R(omani) Q(uiritium) in colle Quirin(ali)* had been believed to be the same as that of *Fortuna publica populi Romani primigenia* because both were recorded as having the same *dies natalis.* But Ziolkowski and Coarelli have shown that these must be different and, therefore, this represents the second of the three

temples dedicated to Fortuna on the Quirinal.[31] Finally, a temple of *Fortuna primigenia* recorded in a partially preserved inscription on the Arval calendar as dedicated on November 13 had been thought to be the third temple. Coarelli suggested, however, that the inscription reads *Fortun(ae) Prim(igeniae) in C(apitolio)* rather than the usual assumption of *in C(olle).*[32]

Regardless of the specific identifications of these three temples, it is clear that they were on the Quirinal near the Colline gate, and it is enticing to speculate that an even earlier temple to Fortune existed in this location because this goddess was the guardian of Servius Tullius, who had built the Colline gate.[33]

AFTERWORD

The present study can be only a preliminary work because it is clear that not all questions have been answered. Yet I believe my initial desire to put at least some of the sculptures discovered in the *horti Sallustiani* into their proper context has been fulfilled.

Although the gardens lasted until ca. A.D. 410, the sculpture that can be identified from this area is in fact, on the whole, much earlier. It is possible that at least some of it was original to these gardens or that it had been transported there at a later date. It must be recognized that these kinds of archaeological discoveries, unstratified and with little or no context, are difficult to interpret. These finds show us, however obscurely, the kinds of decorative material that were displayed in these gardens when they were finally abandoned. Thus, they do not allow us to determine the development of the gardens over the centuries of their existence. It is, therefore, only a single, hazy snapshot of the end of a long process of development, rearrangement, expansion (or even contraction), and eventual abandonment. But even this scenario may be too optimistic because the course of events that followed the desolation of these gardens played a profound role in our knowledge and opinion of the ancient remains. Not only was ancient material constantly coming to light, but the architectural remains also were being scavenged for building material or being incorporated into later constructions. The most serious physical changes did not occur until the nineteenth century with the filling of the valley and the laying out of the modern quarter of the rione Sallustio, which has essentially sealed this area from any serious archaeological exploration.

Although the physical changes to the ancient landscape have been profound, the intellectual interventions are perhaps equally noteworthy. The almost continual interest in the physical remains of these ancient gardens since their abandonment has played a significant role in how we interpret them today. It is only by investigating the history of the scholarship on these gardens that a picture can emerge. It is not perhaps an image of clarity, but it is at least one of fairness to the subject.

In the introduction I acknowledged that this study would be a series of serendipitous wanderings through the landscape of the *horti Sallustiani*. The journey, however, has not been only a physical one but perhaps more importantly an intellectual one. Indeed, the physical and intellectual in this case are inseparable because of the irrevocable loss of the reality of these gardens. They can be judged, as we have seen, only by the disparate physical remains that can be identified and by the evolutionary processes that have created the present obfuscation of the ancient past. This evolutionary process of the transmission of the past from one generation to the next must be acknowledged as having a profound effect on our present views. Modern scholars are obviously a part of this chain, linking the present not only to the past but to the future. We must attempt to recognize our intellectual heritage, learn from it, and, when possible, to interpret it for ourselves and for those to follow.

We must also attempt to separate fact from fiction (not always an easy task in the best of circumstances). Indeed, Darwin had it at least partially right when he stated that "false facts are highly injurious to the progress of science, for they often endure long; but false views, if supported by some evidence, do little harm, for every one takes a salutary pleasure in proving their falseness" (*The Descent of Man,* Ch. 21). It is not so much salutary pleasure in disproving false views but the evolutionary process itself (a nod to Darwin here) of intellectual development that is the real pleasure. For a "humanistic archaeologist" with an interest in the history of how scholars have studied and interpreted ancient material culture, the gardens of Sallust have provided a landscape filled with twisting paths, dark recesses and sometimes dead ends, and enough challenges for all who dare to enter.

NOTES

INTRODUCTION

1. E. D. Francis and M. Vickers, "*Signa priscae artis:* Eretria and Siphnos," *JHS* 103 (1983) 49–67 (Amazon statue mentioned on page 51): the date of 525 B.C. for the Siphnian Treasury is lowered to the 470s B.C. For one of several doubters, see R. M. Cook, "The Francis-Vickers Chronology," *JHS* 109 (1989) 164–170.

2. Astolfi 1998(a); Astolfi 1998(b); Talamo 1998; Moltesen 1998.

3. See D. Fairchild Ruggles's reviews of J. Wescoat, Jr. and J. Wolschke-Bulmahn, eds., *Mughal Gardens: Sources, Places, Representations, and Prospects* (Dumbarton Colloquium on the History of Landscape Architecture 16; Washington, DC 1996) and M. Hussain, A. Rehman, and J. L. Wescoat, Jr., eds., *The Mughal Garden: Interpretation, Conservation and Implications* (Karachi 1996) in *JSAH* 57:3 (1998) 339–341.

4. C. Lazzaro, *The Italian Renaissance Garden* (New Haven 1990) 243–269 for the Villa Lante, and 270–286 for "The Garden in Time."

5. See Ridley 1992, 53.

I. TOPOGRAPHY AND HISTORY

1. Richardson 1992, 203; Cicero (*Nat.D.* 3.20.52). According to *FUR* 3, 10 (Fig. 1.1B, D), the valley floor lay twenty-two meters from the modern ground level, which in part reflects the upper portions of the ancient hills.

2. See Grimal 1969, 295–296, and Pliny, *Ep.* 2.17.25.

3. See Platner and Ashby 1929, 98. The via Sallustiana runs more or less parallel to the ancient course of the Acqua Sallustiana. See also discussion of water conduits found in the valley, pp. 50–51.

4. Pietrangeli 1977, 13. See *CAR* II-F 49(I), and Lanciani 1990, I, 83: In ca. 1484 are recorded "cunicoli" that distributed water from the Amnis Petronia to the valley. For the location of the Amnis Petronia, see F. Coarelli, *Il Campo Marzio* (Rome 1997) 148–155, and Tambroni 1936, 435, who discussed the finding of these waters underground during the building of the church of San Camillo. The name *collis Catialis* is known only from Placidus, *Glossae:* Catialis collis, ubi nunc lacus funditur, est dictus a Cati cuiusdam loco.

5. Pliny, *HN* 31.89, Festus, *Gloss. Lat.* 318L, made reference to three gates, one of which he called the Sabines'.

6. Two archaic sarcophagi containing the skeletal remains of two women were found in 1884 (Fiorelli, *NSc* 1884, 154) in the former villa Spithoever (via Quintino Sella) at a depth of 8.50 meters and at a distance of 46.70 meters from the "Servian" wall (almost directly opposite the center of the Palazzo delle Finanze) and 2.50 meters apart. Both sarcophagi are made from two joining half cylinders of terracotta closed at both ends and with large bosses running the length of each half cylinder, perhaps used for binding the two together and for lifting the sarcophagus into place. Pietrangeli 1977, 62, n. 4, characterizes them as tree trunks. See *FUR* 10 ("Sepulcra Antiquiss, Scavi IV 1884") and *CAR* II-F, 64 (note that the location differs from that of *FUR* 10: Fig. 1.1D). For drawings of one sarcophagus and of items discovered inside, see G. Pinza, "I sepolcreti alla estremità Nord del Quirinale e sul Campidoglio," *MonAnt* 15 (1905) cols. 248–252. There was also a tomb that had been cut by a wall found in 1907 under the Ministry of Agriculture in the area of the old villa Spithoever: *NSc* 1907, 505–517. This wall is positioned inside the "Servian" wall, and it could represent the existence of a special necropolis in the area between the former villa Spithoever and the Baths of Diocletian. Just north of this wall, numerous vases were found as well as other small finds, indicating the presence of a necropolis. The furnishings of these tombs are similar to those from the necropolis of the Roman Forum that are dated in the eighth century: Pietrangeli 1977, 62, n. 4. Note that a single bucchero jug was discovered, datable to the fourth century B.C.: see *NSc* 1907, 517, fig. 32. According to *CAR* II-F 96a, a part of the "Servian" wall near the via A. Salandra (formerly via delle Finanze) is composed of diverse material, including fragments of terracotta similar to those used for these tombs. For a general discussion of the tombs of the Quirinal, see J. Gjerstad, *Early Rome* (*SkrRom* 17.2 [Lund 1956]) 265–279, and Santangelo 1941, 84–88.

7. See M. Pallottino, "La Prima Roma," *StRom* 5 (1957) 256–268; M. Pallottino, "Le origini di Roma," *ArchCl* 12 (1960) 1–36; M. Pallottino, "Fatti e leggende (moderne) sulla più antica storia di Roma," *StEtr* 31 (1963) 3–37; J. Poucet, *Recherches sur la légende sabine des origines de Rome* (Louvain 1967); D. Musti, "Tendenze nella storiografia romana e greca su Roma arcaica, Studî su Livio e Dionigi d'Alicarnasso," *Quaderni Urbinati di cultura classica* 10 (1970) 5–158; J. Poucet, "Les Sabines aux origines de Rome: Orientationes et problème," in *ANRW* I.1 (1972) 48–135; M. Pallottino, "Le origini di Roma: considerazioni critiche sulle

scoperte e sulle discussioni più recenti" in *ANRW* I.1 (1972) 22–47.

8. For alternative sources of the name Quirinus, see *RE* 24 (Stuttgart 1963) s.v. Quirinalis collis, cols. 1299–1301 (G. Radke); *RE* 24 (Stuttgart 1963) s.v. Quirinus, cols. 1310–1312 (C. Koch); and Santangelo 1941, 88–90.

9. Varro, *Ling.* 5.158; Santangelo 1941, 93–95.

10. Traces of paving have been found near the via Quattro Fontane (*BullCom* 25 [1897] 152, 156); in front of the Scottish church (*BullCom* 12 [1885] 22); in front of the Ministry of Defense (*NSc* [1910] 546). For the suggestion that the Republican *Alta Semita* was in a different location from the later ancient street so designated, see Rodríguez-Almeida 1980–1981, 75–82 and Rodríguez-Almeida, *LTUR* I, s.v. Alta Semita, 30.

11. See Di Manano 1989–1990, 100.

12. *CIL* VI, 450 (dated A.D. 98–99). As early as the eighth century, the area of Santa Susanna was called "ad duas domus": see A. Bonanni, s.v. Duae Domus in *LTUR* II, 217, who suggested that the two homes may refer to those of the Ceionii and the Nummii, which were located in this region. See Addendum.

13. See Festus, s.v. Sceleratus Campus: Scel(er)atus campus appellatur proxime portam Collinam, in quo virgines Vestales, quae incestum fecerunt, defosse sunt (J. W. Pirie, W. M. Lindsay, eds., *Glossaria Latina* IV [Paris 1930] 424 [448]), and Livy, 8.15.8: "(Minucia Vestalis) viva sub terram ad portam Collinam extra viam stratam defossa Scelerato campo."

14. Mart., *Epig.* 5.22.2–4: Sed Tiburtinae sum proximus accola pilae, / qua videt anticum rustica Flora Iovem. Lugli 1930–1940, III, 134, wrote of a "vicus Pilae Tiburtinae," but this seems not to be attested in the ancient sources: see Hackens 1961, 75, n. 5. Rodríguez-Almeida 1980–1981, 87, suggested the location of Martial's house at the northwestern corner of the Quirinal. See also Rodríguez-Almeida 1986, 49–60.

15. Livy, 1.43.13 (four regions); 1.44.3 (building of wall). See also Dion. Hal. *Ant. Rom.* 4.13.3. The most ancient walls have been recognized as those constructed of small blocks of "cappellaccio," while the blocks of Grotta Oscura are dated to the fourth century after the conquest of Veii in whose territory lay the quarries. See Coarelli 1984, 149, and Pietrangeli 1977, 16.

16. Säflund 1932, 44–75; Lugli 1930–1940, II, 99–105; Santangelo 1941, 99–116; Gjerstad 1954, 50–65; Nash 1968, II, s.v. Murus Servii Tullii, 104–116.

17. Säflund 1932, 74–75. See also Wiseman 1998, 13, who calculates the size of the *agger* as 1,344 meters long and 16 meters wide.

18. Frézouls 1987, 373–392.

19. Sen., *De brev. vit.* 13.8: Sullam ultimum Romanorum protulisse pomerium; Tac., *Ann.* 12.23: Nec tamen duces Romani . . . usurpaverant (ius proferendi pomerii) nisi L. Sulla et divus Augustus. See Frézouls 1987, 378.

20. It is possible that the pomerium was not expanded under Augustus: see A. DeGrassi, *Doxa* II (1949) 85; Frézouls 1987, 379–380 (with pertinent ancient references); and M. T. Boatwright, "The Pomerial Extension of Augustus," *Historia* 35 (1986) 13–27. Of the fourteen Augustan regions, six were outside the Republican city wall (hence the *pomerium*): V, VII, IX, XIII, XIV, and most of I. Claudius (in A.D. 49): Tac., *Ann.* 12.23: Et pomerium urbis auxit Caesar; Gell., *NA* 13.14.7; *CIL* VI, 31537a; Vespasian: *CIL* VI, 930, 11, 14–16, utique ei fines pomerii proferre promouere, cum ex re publica censebit esse, liceat; Aurelian: S.H.A., *Aurel.* 21.9.11, in which are mentions of unconfirmed expansions of the *pomerium* under Nero and Trajan.

21. The Aurelian wall increased the area within the city circuit by some 400 hectares, half of which were in the north in Regions VI and VII; see Frézouls 1987, 373–374. According to Richmond 1971, 8, the *pomerium* was perhaps made to coincide with the Aurelian wall, although a boundary stone (*CIL* VI, 1268) dated to the time of Vespasian was found some 300 to 400 meters outside the porta Nomentana, suggesting that the *pomerium* extended beyond the city wall. See D. Boschung, "Uberlegungen zum Licinergrab," *JdI* 101 (1986) 259.

22. Lanciani 1888, 9–10.

23. *CIL* VI, 35243. See G. Gatti, "Trovamenti riguardanti la Topografia e la Epigrafia Urbana," *BullCom* 1886, 403–414. Lanciani 1888, 10–11 made reference to *CIL* VI, 4.2 as well as a funerary inscription found in this same cemetery, recording the name Sallustia Crispa, who was survived by her husband and three sons (Gatti, nr. 1664), and another from this same area naming three freedmen of Quintus Sallustius. The last two inscriptions permit the identification of the area of the columbarium "libertorum Q(uinti) Sallustii," whose contents were listed (79 cinerary urns of family servants and 37 inscriptions) in the fifteenth century but whose location was not recorded.

24. Urlichs 1871, III, 21, n. 13. "Palatium Salusti fuit ubi nunc dicitur *Pinci*, et in eo adhuc est sala Salustii."

25. See Frutaz 1962, plan LXXXVII, pl. 157 (1469) plan LXXXVIII, pl. 158 (1471), plan CIX 2, pl. 191 (Bufalini plan of 1551: Fig. 2.15), and even on later plans, i.e., Nibby's plan of 1826 [Frutaz 1963, plan XLII, pl. 84].

26. Richter 1901, 267, employed Tac., *Hist.* 3.82 (see below, n. 29), to suggest that the gardens extended to the Aurelian walls. The conflict with the forces of Vitellius could have taken place only against the north and east walls of the gardens. See Riemann 1950, 1516.

27. Lanciani 1888, 7, and Lanciani 1967, 276. See also Hülsen 1891, 123–124; Lugli 1922, 1007; and Tac., *Hist.* 3.82. It is likely that this land had once belonged to the Licinian family, whose mausoleum was found only a few meters

east of the old via Salaria: K. M. Bentz, "Rediscovering the Licinian Tomb," *Journal of the Walters Art Gallery* 55/56 (1997/1998) 63–88.

28. Discoveries near the corner of the via Sicilia and the via Lucana include polychromed marble pavements, a private house with bath (including a black and white figural mosaic), and perhaps a mithraeum (known from an inscription only): see *NSc* 1904, 43; G. Gatti, "Notizie di recenti trovamenti di antichità in Roma e nel suburbio," *BullCom* 32 (1904) 197–198; G. Mancini, "Regione VI," *NSc* 1925, 47–49; Riemann 1950, 1567; and Lugli 1922, 1008. On a graveyard not needing to hinder the expansion of private property, see Bodel 1994, 70, who discussed the Esquiline burial ground before the *horti* arrived and the possibility that private *horti* could encroach upon old graveyards and even into sacred groves. Bodel wrote that "according to Frontinus, the multitude and rapacity of landholders in Italy of his day was such that private estates encroached on sacred groves in contravention of both law and religion." This may have been particularly a problem in the suburbs where, according to one ancient writer, "private owners are accustomed to usurp pieces (of property) without any reverence for religion and to join them to their *horti*." See Champlin 1982, 101. For reused Greek gravestones from the Esquiline (gardens of Maecenas?) and others possibly to be associated with the gardens of Sallust, see M. Bell III, "Le stele greche dell'Esquilino e il cimitero di Mecenate," in *Horti Romani*, 295–314.

29. Tac., *Hist.* 3.82: "The only troops [of Vespasian] that met with serious trouble were those who had moved through narrow and slippery streets toward the left quarter of the city and the gardens of Sallust. The Vitellian forces, climbing on top of the walls that surrounded the gardens blocked their opponents' approach with a shower of stones and javelins until late in the day when they were finally surrounded by the cavalry that had broken through the Colline gate" (the gate spanning the Salarian way) (Clifford H. Moore, trans., Loeb Classical Library [London 1925]).

30. Evans 1994, 86; Säflund 1932, 76–98. See also below, p. 88.

31. Hor., *Sat.* 1.8.14.

32. Lanciani 1880(c), 437, pl. VII, nr. 8; Lugli 1930–1940, III, 323. Riemann 1950, 1516, disagreed, believing that the natural southern boundary must have been the "Servian" wall.

33. Lanciani 1990, IV, 133, related the recording in 1589 of the destruction of some "massicci" (ancient road mettle?) in this area to the possible remains of the *porticus miliarensis* (mentioned only in S.H.A., *Aurel.* 49.1) constructed perhaps over this long *piscina*. Even though Lanciani concluded it more probable that these "massicci" relate to one of the temples of Fortuna known to have been near the porta Collina, he nonetheless records on *FUR* 10 (Fig.

1.1D) the *porticus miliarensis* over the *piscina*. Lugli 1922, 1006, agreed with Lanciani; however, the identification of this *piscina* as the location of the *porticus miliarensis* is very dubious: Lehmann-Hartleben and Lindros 1935, 219. It should be noted that southwest of these remains was discovered in 1907 a large vaulted chamber covered by a mosaic of large cubes. Above this chamber was a long row of bases for a small colonnade. The precise location of these remains and their orientation are not recorded: *NSc* 1907, 521, figs. 43, 44.

Innocenti and Leotta 1996, 81–82, suggest that the remains of a rectangular colonnade found in 1886 between the via Campania and the via dell'Aurora could be the *porticus miliarensis:* see *CAR* II-E, 22, with references to R. Lanciani and G. Gatti, "Trovamenti risguardanti la Topografia e la Epigrafia Urbana," *BullCom* 1886, 81, and R. Lanciani, "Roma: Regione VII," *NSc* 1886, 123. During leveling operations for the building of the via Lombardia in 1888 (R. Lanciani, "Roma: Regione VII," *NSc* 1888, 729; C. L. Visconti, "Trovamenti risguardanti la Topografia e la Epigrafia Urbana," *BullCom* 1889, 89) were uncovered a series of brick pilasters, each carrying a rectangular block of travertine. This row of pilasters (*CAR* II-E, 35, and *FUR* 9 [Fig. 1.1C]), although not recorded as running in the same north-south direction as the colonnade found earlier to the north, is considered by Innocenti and Leotta 1996 as belonging with it. Of course, the acceptance of this colonnade as the *porticus miliarensis* would push the western boundaries of the gardens west of the present via Veneto. Astolfi 1998(a), 25, stated, without explanation, that this portico was constructed towards the eastern limits of the villa. Note in the *horti Spei Veteris* a large, probably vaulted, third-century corridor measuring 14.45 meters in width and at least 300 meters in length that Colini suggested was used for horsemen and chariots: A. M. Colini, "Horti Spei Veteris, Palatium Sessorianum," *MemPontAcc* 8 (1948) 137–177, esp. 160–162.

34. The Spithoever villa was near the intersection of via M. Pagano and the via A. Salandra (former via delle Finanze, as shown on *FUR* 10 [Fig. 1.1D]): see Frutaz 1962, plan CCVI, pl. 544 (1881 plan by G. Murray), and the Spithoever property extended eastward along the northern edge of the Quirinal at least as far as the via Servio Tullio.

35. Lanciani 1879, 436–437. Several other pertinent inscribed pipes found in the vicinity of the *horti Sallustiani* are also discussed. See *CAR* II-F, 88.

36. *NSc* 1883, 80: without reference to the position of these remains above sea level; *CAR* II-F, 87 (NB: incorrect reference to nr. 65 that is the excavation of foundations of a temple attributed to one of the *Tres Fortunae* and not the "Venere Sallustiana").

37. See Vitr., *De Arch.* 3.2.2; *Anth. Pal.* 16.40. See also *PIR* 159, n. 61: "C. Sallustius Crispus"; a grave inscription

of a freedman found in front of the porta Salaria, *CIL* VI, 25792a.

38. See *CAR* II-F 82; *NSc* 1909, 223; and *BullCom* 1909, 294. The floor of the hypocaust (a room heated from below the floor) was found eight meters below the surface of the via delle Finanze. Excavations proceeded down to the lowest level of the "Servian" wall, where a section of a circular wall (0.80 meters wide) was discovered abutting it. According to the excavation reports, this curved wall is dated to the first or second century A.D. and was built to support the old "Servian" wall from the pressure of the high embankment inside. If this is the case, the bath complex above must post-date this construction.

39. Richter 1901, 267, proposed perhaps the furthest western limit, believing that Tacitus (*Ann.* 13.47) indicated the gardens reached to the vicinity of the via Flaminia. Grimal 1969, 129–130, reported that Lanciani proposed the *via Salaria Vetus* as the western limit of the gardens. Astolfi 1998(a), 27, believed the western limit followed a line running from the vicolo di S. Nicola da Tolentino to the via Veneto.

40. Richardson 1992, 202. A private house of the Hadrianic period was discovered on the via Bissolati between the via Vittorio Veneto and the via S. Basilio: *CAR* II-F, 91, with bibliography. See Riemann 1950, 1516, who proposed the present via Toscana as the western limit of the gardens on the Pincio but who also rightly explained that both the western and eastern limits may well have increased during the Imperial period.

41. Katterfeld 1913, 92–112. According to brickstamps found during the excavation of this house, the building was likely begun as early as the middle of the first century A.D. but was rebuilt or replaced during the Hadrianic period. See Riemann 1950, 1553, who believed that this house was, from the beginning, part of the *horti Sallustiani*.

42. Likewise, on the Corso d'Italia traces of a road with sidewalks (measuring 5.34 meters for the road and .50 meters and .20 meters high for the sidewalks [note that the length is given as 3.50 meters in *CAR* II-F, 35]) were found outside and perpendicular to the Aurelian wall three meters under the street level. It is obvious that this road went out of use when the city wall was built. Although Lanciani discussed in *Cod. Vat. lat.* 13035, 67, the road under the Corso d'Italia, it seems likely that the drawing on this page indicates a trace of road perhaps near the corner of via Sardegna and via Toscana—the same section reported in *CAR* II-F, 17, as found in 1898 (see *NSc* 1898, 64, and *BullCom* 1898, 48). Katterfeld 1913, 94, fig. 2, shows this road to the west of the obelisk base and further to the east than on *CAR* II-F, 18. Katterfeld's positioning of this section of road corresponds closely enough to the location of the road mettle found further north under the Corso d'Italia to suggest they are part of the same road. In this case, the peculiar parallel roads

shown on *CAR* II-F, 1 and 5, can be reconciled into a single road as shown on *FUR* 2 (Fig. 1.1A).

43. Katterfeld 1913, 108–109; S.H.A., *Tyr. Trig.* 32, 5–7. Note that the Pincio is called here merely "collis."

44. See Grimal 1969, 126–129, for arguments in favor of a much larger expanse of the Lucullan gardens than proposed by Lanciani, *FUR* 9 (Fig. 1.1C). See Riemann 1950, 1511, 1518–1519, and *LTUR* III, s.v. horti Lucullani (H. Broise and V. Jolivet) 67–70.

45. R. Lanciani, "Miscellanea topografica," *BullCom* 1891, 153, reported that the ancient road, the *vicus Minervii* (via S. Giuseppe, via di Capo le Case, and via di Porta Pinciana), was flanked by Republican tombs and that this must constitute a primary and fundamental demarcation for the confines of the *horti Aciliorum* and *Lucullani* to the west, and the *Sallustiani* to the east.

46. Imperial gardens in the area of the Vatican and Janiculum had to contend with apparently extensive burial grounds: M. I. Pasquali, "Gli egizi nella XIV regione augustea," in *L'Egitto in Italia,* 570.

47. Excavations conducted for the building of San Isidoro recorded on *FUR* 9 (Fig. 1.1C) as "Scavi Waddington, Bartoli 35" = Bartoli *memoria,* 35 (in Fea 1790, I, 229–230): S. Isidoro nel monte Pincio. Mi fu raccontato, che facendosi li fondamenti per la facciata della chiesa di S. Isidoro, il P. Luca Wading [*sic*] direttore di essa voleva li fondamenti più profondi di quello, che si era determinato; e nel cavare più basso, si scoperse una grotta, entrovi cinque statue, le quali furono comprate dal Card. Franceso Barberini (Sant' Isidoro on the Pincio. I had been told that when making the foundations for the façade of the church of Sant' Isidoro, Father Luca Wadding, director of the church, wanted the foundations deeper than what had been proposed; and in digging lower a grotto was discovered, containing five statues, that were purchased by Cardinal Franceso Barberini). These statues are the herms now preserved in the Palazzo Altemps. B. Palma and L. de Lachenal, *I Marmi Ludovisi nel Museo Nazionale Romano* (*MNR* I,5 [Rome 1983]) mention six herms: nrs. 66 (Herakles), 68 (Dionysos), 70 (Athena), 72 (Theseus), 74 (Hermes?), 76 (Diskobolos). Note that the Collegio Irlandese, beside the church of San Isidoro, was founded in 1625 by the great Franciscan historian, Luca Wadding. See also Riemann 1950, 1550.

48. R. Lanciani, "Roma: Regione VI," *NSc* 1886, 158.

49. See *CAR* II-E, 16, with pertinent bibliography. These amphorae covered an area of 20 meters × 10 meters and were found in fourteen to fifteen layers down to a depth of 12 meters. See also E. Dressel, "Di un grande deposito di anfore rinvenuto nel nuovo quartiere del Castro Pretorio," *BullCom* 1879, pls. VII–VIII, nr. 11 = another cache of amphorae found on the via XX Settembre. NB: In the course of work undertaken in 1941 for a building at nr. 161 at the corner of the via Vittorio Veneto and the via Sicilia,

excavators uncovered tufa walls of *opus reticulatum*. This structure (with an apse) was 3.60 meters below the level of the sidewalk. In the niche they found scores of amphorae (spherical bodies with narrow, and very long necks) similar in shape to those under the Albergo Excelsior: *BullCom* 68 (1940), 225–226 (G. Gatti).

50. Grimal 1969, 130, suggested there may have been a series of small gardens in this area.

51. Lanciani 1897, 71; E. Petersen, "Satiri e Gigante," *BullCom* 17 (1889) 17–25, pls. 1, 2; Richmond 1971, 13.

52. Richmond 1971, 13, suggested (incorrectly, however) that this is where Vitellius' troops attempted to hold back Vespasian.

53. He was the author of two monographs (the *Bellum Catilinae* and *Bellum Iugurthinum)* and of the *Historiae* (surviving in only four orations and two letters as well as miscellaneous fragments). Disputed works include the *Oratio* or *Invectiva in M. T. Ciceronem* and two *Epistulae ad Caesarem*. See C. Becker, "Sallust," *ANRW* I.3 (Berlin 1973) 720–754, and W. Richter, "Der Manierismus des Sallust und die Sprache der römischen Historiographie," *ANRW* I.3 (Berlin 1973) 755–780.

54. Mart., *Ep.* 14.191.

55. Inv. A 424: J. J. Bernoulli, *Römische Ikonographie: Die Bildnisse berühmter Römer* I (Stuttgart 1882) 200–203; A. Vostchinina, *Le Portrait Romain: Album et catalogue illustré de toute la collection* (Musée de l'Ermitage) (Leningrad 1974) 155–156, nr. 28, pls. XLII–XLIII. I thank Alexander Kruglov of the Hermitage Museum for bibliographic information and for expediting the obtaining of Fig. 1.4.

56. See A. Alföldi, *Die Kontorniaten, ein verkanntes Propagandamittel der stadtrömischen heidnischen Aristokratie in ihrem Kampfe gegen das christliche Kaisertum* (Budapest 1943) 89–90, pl. 36, nrs. 1–5; Alföldi and Alföldi, I.1, 28–32; Alföldi and Alföldi, I.2, pls. 34–37. Alföldi and Alföldi list 49 examples in 1.1, 28–32; 1.2, pls. 34–37; and 2, 51, 101. Five are in the Cabinet des Médailles, Bibliothèque Nationale de France in Paris, nrs. 17175–17179. I thank Paul-André Besombes, Conservateur du Patrimoine, for permitting me to see these contorniates and for alerting me to pertinent bibliographic references. Note that Fulvio Orsini's collection of antiquities included one of these Roman contorniates with a portrait of Sallust that he published in *Imagines et elogia virorum illustrium* (Rome 1570) fig. 90. The Orsini family owned property that may have been part of the gardens of Sallust, accounting perhaps for Fulvio's interest in this Roman historian.

57. J. L. Desnier, "Salutius—Salustius," *REA* 85 (1983) 53–64.

58. Alföldi and Alföldi, 2, 51 call this image a "Bildnisfiktion."

59. The testimonia for Sallust's life and writings are listed in Kurfess 1968, xxii–xxxi, but according to Syme 1964, 4, n.

2, they are "not adequate everywhere." See also Castagnoli 1972, 383–392.

60. Hieron., *ab Abr.* 151 (this chronicle, by Eusebius of Caesarea [ca. A.D. 260–340], was translated into Latin by St. Jerome), in Kurfess 1968.

61. Syme 1964, 36, n. 36.

62. See Dio Cass., 40.63.5 (expulsion) and 42.52.2 (reason for praetorship). Ap. Claudius was among the coalition forming against Caesar, and he had family reasons—one daughter was married to Marcus Brutus, Cato's nephew, another to the elder son of Pompeius Magnus: Cic., *Fam.* 3.4.2, and Syme 1964, 334–335. See, however, B. A. Marshall, *A Historical Commentary on Asconius* (Columbia, MO 1985) 183, who explains that Appius ought to have been grateful to Sallustius in 52 for taking the side of Clodius, Appius' brother.

63. App., *BCiv.* 2.92. Sallust may have reentered the Senate through a quaestorship in 48 B.C., but this information comes only from Pseudo-Cicero, *In Sallustium* 6.17 and 8.21 (Kurfess, 1970, 18, 20), and cannot be taken as proof: see Syme 1964, 36, n. 36.

64. Dio Cass., 43.9.2.

65. See Dio Cass. 43.47.4, who stated, in general, that Caesar took bribes, and Syme 1964, 39. Pseudo-Cicero, *In Sallustium* 7.19 (Kurfess 1970, 19–20): [Sallustius] provinciam vastavit, ut nihil neque passi sint neque exspectaverint gravius in bello socii nostri, quam experti sunt in pace hoc Africam inferiorem obtinente. Unde tantum hic exhausit, quantum potuit aut fide nominum traici aut in naves contrudi: tantum, inquam, exhausit, patres conscripti, quantum voluit. ne causam diceret, sestertio duodeciens cum Caesare paciscitur. quod si quippiam eorum falsum est, his palam refelle, unde, qui modo ne paternam quidem domum reluere potueris, repente tamquam somno beatus hortos pretiosissimos, villam Tiburti C. Caesaris, reliquas possessiones paraveris. neque piguit quaerere, cur ego P. Crassi domum emissem, cum tu vetus villae dominus sis—cuius paulo ante fuerat Caesar. modo, inquam, patrimonio non comesto sed devorato quibus rationibus repente factus es tam adfluens et tam beatus? (Sallust laid waste the province, so that our allies neither suffered nor feared anything more serious in war than they experienced in peace when this man obtained lower Africa. At that time he drained as much as he was able on the promise of repayments to be transported or to be packed into ships: so much, I say, did he drain, conscript fathers, as he wished. So that he might not have to plead a case in court, he made a transaction with Caesar for 1,200,000 sestertii. But if any of these things is false, refute them publicly; since you who recently were not even able to pay the mortgage on your paternal house, suddenly, blessed as if in a dream, have bought the most expensive gardens, the villa of Gaius Caesar at Tiburtum and other possessions. Nor is it a waste of time to ask why I bought the house of

Publius Crassus, though you are the longstanding lord of the villa, of which Caesar had been lord shortly previously. So, how, I say, do you explain that you have suddenly been made so affluent and blessed, though your patrimony has been not only eaten up, but even devoured? [Translation by D. Burgess.])

66. Our only reference to his place of birth is Hieron., *ab Abr.* 151. Syme 1964, 14, pointed out that this may only explain his *patria* and that his birth could have taken place in Rome. Regardless, a hometown was a *germana patria,* as attested by the fellow townsmen from Reate who populate the pages of Varro's *De Re Rustica* and to whom this Sabine town was, according to Syme, a "true home and not only a distant cradle."

67. Julius Obsequens, 71 (during the consulships of Gaius Furnius and Gaius Silanus = 17 B.C.): "Turris hortorum Caesaris ad portam Collinam de caelo tacta," in *Livy* 14 (Loeb Classical Library), A. C. Schlesinger, trans. (Cambridge, MA, 1959) 318. See also Juvenal, *Sat.* 6.291, who mentioned a *Collina turris* and P. L. Schmidt, *Iulius Obsequens und das Problem der Livius-Epitome* (Mainz 1968).

68. Dio Cass., 42.26.3. See also *LTUR* III, s.v. Horti Caesaris (ad portam Collinam) (F. Coarelli) 55.

69. See, however, Champeau 1987, 4–17, who believed that the *Tyche Demosia* mentioned by Dio Cassius (42.26.3) as in the gardens of Caesar must be the *Fortuna Publica* on the Quirinal and not that of *Fors Fortuna* in Trastevere. This may well be the case because Dio did not specifically indicate that the Fortuna temple was in the gardens of Caesar. It is possible that the lightning strikes occurred throughout the city from the Capitol to the Quirinal and even across the Tiber to the gardens of Caesar. For an agreement as three separate places rather than two, see Purcell 2001, 555, n. 40.

70. *CIL* VI, 8671 (a marble urn): (a) C. Julius Euxinus / Medicus / ex Hortis / Sallustianis / Vixit Annis LXXX; (b) Iuvlia C L / Crata / Vix A LVI, a doctor and his wife, who were in some way associated with these gardens; *CIL* VI, 8670 (a marble slab): Dama Caseris (= Caesaris) / ex hortis Salusti / ab hortu nov, a slave of Caesar's from the *horti Sallustiani,* (now?) the new *hortus.* According to Grimal 1969, 129, n. 3, it is likely that *Caesaris* signifies probably an imperial slave and not necessarily one of Julius Caesar's slaves. Furthermore, the text implies the remembrance of an older garden, as suggested by the identification of this one as "new." Perhaps by the third century, the original gardens were expanded. Lugli 1922, 1008, suggested that this extension was perhaps near the porta Collina, where a temple of Venus stood.

71. For the third-century dating, see *LTUR* III, s.v. Horti Sallustiani (P. Innocenti and M. C. Leotta) 80.

72. Pseudo-Cicero, *In Sallustium* 7.19: see above note 65.

The sixth-century A.D. writer Lydus (R. Wuensh, ed., Ioannis Laurentii Lydi, *Liber de mensibus* [Lipsias 1898] 4.155, p. 173) names one of the seven hills of Rome Τιβούρτιος (restored), perhaps related to the Tiburtine pila mentioned by Martial as being in the environs of the gardens of Sallust (5.22.3).

For ancient references to the willing of Caesar's Trastevere gardens to the people, see Dio Cass., 44.35; Suet., *Caes.* 83. Frézouls 1987, 387–392, proposed that the property along the Tiber may have been destined for public building rather than for a public garden. Many other Romans, such as D. Junius Brutus, Antonius, Maecenas, and Varus, are known to have had villas at Tibur: C. Fulvio Giuliani, *Tibur: Forma Italiae* I, 7 (pt. 2, 1966) 14. See also Jordan and Hülsen 1871, I.3, 417, and *RE* 3 (1897) 1297, s.v. Caesaris horti (C. Hülsen).

73. I.e., G. Lugli s.v. Horti Caesaris, *Dizionario Epigrafico* III (1922) 1005.

74. Syme 1978, 295. See also Purcell 2001, 555.

75. See, for example, Richter 1901, 267; Platner 1904, 481–482; and Richardson 1992, 197.

76. I.e., Talamo 1998, 113–169.

77. Hieron., *Adv. Iovinian.* I, 48: "Cicero rogatus ab Hircio ut post repudium Terentie sororem eius duceret +, omnino facere supersedit, dicens non posse [se] et uxori et philosophie pariter operam dare. Illa [interim] congux egregia et que de [fontibus Tullianis] hauserat sapientiam nupsit Salustio inimico eius et tertio Messale Corvino, et quasi per quosdam gradus eloquentie devoluta est." – (Cicero, after he divorced Terentia and Hirtus asked him to marry his sister, refrained from doing it on any terms, saying that he could not commit himself equally both to a wife and to philosophy. His ex-wife Terentia, meanwhile, who was nobly born and had drunk wisdom from the Tullian well, married next his enemy Sallust, and third Messala Corvinus, and rolled downhill, as it were, through several levels of eloquence): R. Hanna III and T. Lawler, eds., *Jankyn's Book of Wikked Wyves* I (Athens, GA 1997) 176–177. For the life of Terentia, who died at age 103 (Pliny, *HN* 7.49), see *RE*² (Stuttgart 1934) 710–716, s.v. Terentius (95: Terentia) (S. Weinstock). Sallust did report (*Cat.* 15), however, the crimes of Terentia's sister Fabia, a priestess of the Vestals. See also Syme 1978, 291–295, who suggested that Jerome may have confused a woman named Terentia, who was married to Sallust, as the former wife of Cicero, or that he had confused Sallustius Crispus II, the adopted great nephew, who could have been married to a Terentia. In any case, the report by Jerome cannot be substantiated.

78. *RE*² (1920) 1920, s.v. Sallustius 10 (C. Sallustius Crispus) (G. Funaioli).

79. Syme 1964, 284 and n. 23.

80. Tac., *Ann.* 3.30.1, and P. de Rohden and H. Dessau, eds., *PIR* III (Berlin 1898) 159, n. 61.

81. Hor., *Carm.* 2.2. Syme 1964, 276, n. 8, suggested that rather than praise for Crispus it "is a clear note of criticism." A scholiast of Horace's *Satires* noted that there was a *Life of Sallust* by Asconius Pedianus, unfortunately completely lost: Pseudo-Acro, *Serm.* 1.2.41: "Quem Asconius Pedianus in vita eius significat," but he conflates the younger Sallust with the historian: "Sallustium Crispum adloquitur, historiographum, equitem Romanum, Augusti amicum" (*Carm.* 2.2.1). See F. Pauly, ed., *Scholia Horatiana* I (Prague 1858) 96, 168, and Syme 1986, 119.

82. Tac., *Ann.* 3.30; Syme 1958, 20.

83. Syme 1986, 160–162, n. 48, 301, n. 8. An inscription of a freedman (*CIL* VI, 23601) mentions a Sallustia Calvina, perhaps a daughter of Sallustius Crispus II, whose wife may have been a descendant of Domitius Calvinus. See also *RE²* 1A.2 (1920) 1955–1956, s.v. Sallustius (E. Stein) that makes reference to an inscription from Kos that this younger Sallust left his estate to Crispus Passienus. See *RE²* 18.4 (1974) 2097, s.v. C. Sallustius Crispus Passienus (R. Hanslik). Inscription from Kos: R. Herzog, "Nikias und Xenophon von Kos," *Historische Zeitschrift* 125 (1922) 237–238. See also an inscription from Ephesos: J. Keil, *Forschungen in Ephesos* III (Augsburg 1923) 114–115, nr. 26.

84. A *scholium* on Juvenal 4.81, related that Passienus was poisoned by Agrippina. According to Syme 1986, 160, n. 33, Passienus' death "surely occurred before early 47." This is the same Passienus Crispus who displayed a bizarre passion for a beech-tree in a grove of Diana at Tusculum, which he was accustomed to kiss and embrace, to lie under, and to water with wine: Pliny, *HN* 16.242.

85. See Tac., *Ann.* 13.47: "Nero . . . Sallustianos in hortos remeaverit." See also *CIL* XV, 7270a (from the gardens of G. Vacca), a waterpipe datable to the time of Nero: Lanciani 1880(c) 436, nr. 87.

86. *CIL* VI, 31857.

87. *NSc* 1889, 105; G. Gatti, "Trovamenti risguardanti la Topografia e la epigrafia urbana," *BullCom* 17 (1889) 151–153. See also A. Stein and L. Petersen, *PIR* IV (Berlin 1952–1966) 39, n. 202.

88. According to Riemann 1950, 1691, the small size of this base suggests that it likely carried a portrait statue (rather than an idealized image of Laco), which each *regio* would have set up to him.

89. *CIL* VI, 9005: "Genio Coeti Herodiani, praegustator divii Augusti, idem postea vilicus in hortis Sallustianis decessit non. Aug. M. Cocceio Nerva C. Vibio Rufino cos." There is no consensus regarding the dating of the two consuls mentioned in this inscription. According to *RE* 4.1 (Stuttgart 1900) 131–132, s.v. Cocceius, 14 (Jörs), M. Cocceius Nerva was from A.D. 24 until his suicide in 33 *curator aquarum* (Frontin., *Aq.* 2.102), an office bestowed on consuls; therefore, his consulship was in all probability in

A.D. 22. On the other hand, *RE²* 7A.2 (Munich 1958) 1981, s.v. Vibius Rufus (R. Helm), suggests that Vibius Rufus was consul in 39 or 40. Talamo 1998, 117, n. 24, without comment, allows for a date as late as A.D. 42. Cf. *CIL* VI, 1539 and 31674 for the mention of these two consuls.

90. Third-century waterpipes have been discovered inscribed: Ortorum Sallustianorum imp. Sev. Alexandri Aug (*CIL* XV, 7249). See also <*Panegyricus*> dictus Constantino filio Constantii IX.14.3–5 in *Panegyrici Latini: Vergilius Paladini et Paulus Fedeli Recenseverunt* (Rome 1976) 258: In Salustianos hortos ire peregrinatio et expeditio putabatur.

91. Vespasian: Dio Cass., 66.10.4; Nerva: *Chronogr. a 354; Chron. min.* I, 146: see Riemann 1950, 148.

92. Aurelian: S.H.A., *Aurel.* 49, 1–3. See W. H. Fisher, "The Augustan *Vita Aureliani,*" *JRS* 19 (1929) 125–149, who discussed three possible sources of the *Vita,* not necessarily always reliable.

93. Syme 1964, 283. Hor., *Odes* 2.2, and *Anth. Pal.* 16.40, extol his opulence and generosity. For the idea of luxury, see L. Friedländer, *Darstellungen aus der Sittengeschichte Roms in der Zeit von August bis zum Ausgang der Antonine* III (Leipzig 1910) 6–177.

94. Tac., *Ann.* 3.30.2: per cultum et munditias copiaque et adfluentia luxu propior.

95. Pseudo-Cicero, *In Sallustium* 7.19: see above note 65. Sall., *Cat.* 12.3; Syme 1964, 283, n. 38.

96. Platner 1911, 501–502.

97. Syme 1964, 42.

98. Syme 1986, 421, pointed out that "Sallust conforms to a familiar type: the senator in retirement composing an aggressive apologia."

99. For the "horti Urbi iuncti," see *Dig.* 33.9.4, 4–5: Si autem extra urbem, romae tamen sit, sed et si in ortis sit urbi iunctis, idem erit dicendum. See C. A. Maschi, "La conclusione della giurisprudenza classica all'età dei Severi: Iulius Paulus," in *ANRW* 2.15 (Berlin 1976) 667–707.

100. See App., *BCiv.* 3.14, and Cic., *Phil.* 2.109. Grimal 1969, 124, noted that Augustus' building programs—the building of his mausoleum and the Aqua Virgo—were both within these gardens. See Asconius' commentary on Cicero's *Pro Milone* 37: S. Squires, ed., *Asconius Pedianus, Quintus. Commentaries on Five Speeches of Cicero* (Bristol 1990) 61. According to Grimal (1969), the aqueduct was in the *horti Superiores,* and the mausoleum was in the *horti Inferiores.* We have no testimony for the end of the first century A.D. on the gardens of Pompey and Lucullus on the Pincio. In the second century we have mention of the *horti Aciliorum,* which Lanciani 1891(a) believed were different from those of Pompey. Grimal 1969, 127, 161, however, argued that these gardens had been formerly those of Lucullus and the upper gardens of Pompey. See also *LTUR* III, s.v. horti Aciliorum (H. Broise and V. Jolivet) 51; s.v. horti Lucullani (H. Broise

and V. Jolivet) 67–70; s.v. horti Pompeiani (V. Jolivet) 78–79.

101. See Sen., *De Ira* 3.18.4, who discussed the decapitation of some senators by Nero during an evening stroll "in xysto maternorum hortorum qui porticum a ripa separat.," and later Pliny, *HN* 86.74 mentioned "obeliscus Romae in Vaticano Gai et Neronis principum circo." According to Suetonious, *Nero* 50, Nero was buried "in the family tomb of the Domitii," which is usually located on the Pincio. It is more likely, however, that Nero was buried in the family garden near the Vatican. I will elaborate on this new interpretation of Suetonius' passage in a forthcoming publication.

102. See S.H.A., *Marc.* 1.1: "Natus est in monte Caelio in hortis" (which are probably to be identified with the *horti Anniani*), and S.H.A., *Marc.* 5.3. Waterpipes inscribed with this family name have been uncovered in various parts of the city and may suggest that the *gens Annia* owned other properties besides these on the Caelian: *LTUR* III, s.v. Horti Anniani (L. Chioffi) 53.

103. Tac., *Ann.* 11.1–3. Valerius Asiaticus had been the owner of the old gardens of Lucullus (Dio 60, 31 called them: τους του Ασιατικου κηπους). Messalina was put to death here (Tac., *Ann.* 11.37–38): see Beard 1998, 28. For the *horti Tauriani*, see Tac., *Ann.* 12.59: "Agrippinae artibus, quae . . . hortis eius inhians" and Lolliani (Tac., *Ann.* 12.22; Frézouls 1987, 387). The *horti Tauriani* were divided and given to two extremely wealthy and powerful imperial freedmen, Pallantes and Epaphroditus, and thus became known as the *horti Pallantiani ed Epaphroditiani.* After their fall from power, these properties were confiscated and again came under imperial control: see Tac., *Ann.* 14.65; Suet., *Dom.* 14; D. Mancioli, "Horti Tauriani," in *Roma Capitale,* 201–202; P. Grimal, "Les *Horti Tauriani,*" *MEFRA* 53 (1936) 254–286.

104. See *CIL* 6, 31284–31285, and T. P. Wiseman, *Talking to Vergil: A Miscellany* (Exeter 1992) 71–77.

105. See Juv., 10, 15 and Tac., *Ann.* 14.53. According to Hirschfeld 1913, 531, n. 10, both the *horti* and *suburbana* of Seneca were confiscated.

106. Tac., *Ann.* 14.57–59, 64–65, and Dio Cass., 62.13–14. See also D. Mancioli, "Horti Pallantiani," in *Roma Capitale,* 202–203, and *LTUR* III, s.v. horti Pallantiani (D. Mancioli) 77.

107. Tac., *Ann.* 15.35. During the time of the Severans, the *horti Torquatiani* on the Esquiline became known as the *horti Spei Veteris*: Frontin., *Aq.* 1.5, 2.65; Grimal 1969, 160; *LTUR* III, s.v. horti Torquatiani (D. Mancioli) 85–86; s.v. horti Spei Veteris (F. Coarelli) 85.

108. Frontin., *Aq.* 20 3–4; see also Evans 1994, 118; Hirschfeld 1913, 531 and n. 10, and D. Mancioli, "Horti Torquatiani," in *Roma Capitale,* 197.

109. S.H.A., *Heliogab.* 13.5. D. Mancioli, "Horti Variani ad Spem Veterem," in *Roma Capitale,* 197–200, mistakenly identified these gardens with the *horti Variani* (S.H.A., *Aurel.* 1.2) that probably were on the *via Flaminia,* because they were connected with the *templum Solis:* see *LTUR* III, s.v. Horti Spei Veteris (F. Coarelli) 85. The *horti Spei Veteris* were near the Porta Maggiore in the area of St. Croce in Gerusalemme. Here was an amphitheater (the absence of brick stamps, which had gone out of fashion by the early third century, suggests that Elagabalus built this) and a circus. Between these two structures was a covered (probably vaulted) corridor measuring 14.45 meters in width and at least 300 meters in length. Similar corridors have been identified in the villa of Nennig (Trier) and in that of Sette Bassi on the via Latina.

110. R. H. Darwell-Smith, *Emperors and Architecture: A Study of Flavian Rome* (*CollLatomus* 231, Brussels 1996) 44.

111. Grimal 1969, 160.

112. Pliny, *Pan.* 50.6; Frézouls 1987, 389–390.

113. Hor., *Epist.* 1.1.100.

114. Vitr., *De Arch.* 2.1.2; see J. Rykwert, *On Adam's House in Paradise* (New York 1972).

115. Jashemski II, 292–295, n. 596, fig. 328.

116. *NSc* 1907, 521, n. 1. A Parker photograph (2258) shows planting pots among a disparate group of finds in "a small Museum, founded in 1871, near Minerva Medica, to secure the fragments found there." These pots may have come from the Esquiline gardens of Maecenas: Häuber 1995, 8, fig. 3.

117. Vitr., *De Arch.* 6.6.5.

118. For example, see J. R. Clarke, "Landscape paintings in the Villa of Oplontis," *JRA* 9 (1996) figs. 15, 16 (villa of Oplontis, *caldarium* 8, and house of Livia, Room IV, respectively).

119. Purcell 1996, 144–146.

120. Neudecker 1988, 50, pl. 5: these statues may have all been set up in the theater.

121. Cic., *QFr.* 3.1.5.

122. It was possible to arrange herms in alphabetical order probably as marble representations of classical learning: Neudecker 1988, 66.

123. See V. Di Palma, "Review of A. Ballantyne, *Architecture, Landscape and Liberty: Richard Payne Knight and the Picturesque,*" *JSAH* 57:3 (1998) 338.

124. Tac., *Ann.* 15.44. Zanker 1995, 204, discussed the stagelike quality of Roman suburban villas against which real Greek philosophers, teachers, scholars, and poets would act as "props." See also Beard 1998, 23–32, who briefly discussed (among other interesting aspects) the theatrical quality of Roman gardens.

125. Transcribed by Ligorio and by Pompeo Ugonio and in a seventeenth-century anonymous sylloge: P. J. Jacks, "The *Simulachrum* of Fabio Calvo: A View of Roman Architecture *all'antica* in 1527," *ArtB* 73 (1990) 479, n. 168, and fig. 28 (Ugonio's transcription).

126. Pliny, *Ep.* 5.6.17: "ab his gestatio in modum circi." See Grimal 1969, 254–257, and Farrar 1998, 32, for a definition of a *gestatio.*

127. For the *agger* as a place of vineyards, see Wiseman 1998, 16. It was not necessary for the *agger* to extend along the Quirinal, whose northern slopes would have created a natural barrier outside the "Servian" wall.

128. Pliny, *HN* 14.11.

129. H. Mielsch, *Die römische Villa. Architektur und Lebensform* (Munich 1987) 11–12. See J. R. Patterson, "The City of Rome: From Republic to Empire," *JRS* 82 (1992) 203; H. V. Hesberg, "Publica Magnificentia," *JdI* 107 (1992) 125–147; and Purcell 1996, 135–136. For the "sterility" of *luxuria,* see the *domus* of Vedius Pollio (Ovid, *Fast.* 6.637–648; Dio, 54.23.5).

130. Pliny, *HN* 14.67. See Häuber 1995. I thank her for permitting me access to a prepublication manuscript of this article, from which much of the following information derives.

131. Olck 1905, 2034–2035, 2051, 2054.

132. Varro, *Ling.* 5.49. See Hor., *Sat.* 1.6, who compared Maecenas to Servius Tullius.

133. H. Lavagne, *Operosa Antra. Recherches sur la Grotte à Rome de Sylla à Hadrien* (*BEFAR* 72) 1988, 638–639; Richardson 1992, s.v. Lares Querquetulani, Sacellum, 233.

134. Festus, *Gloss. Lat.* 314 L: Querquetulanae virae putantur significari nymphae praesidentes querqueto virescenti (nymphs presiding over this oak grove "coming into leaf"); Olck 1905, 2049, 2052.

135. Häuber 1995, 64.

136. Keller 1913, 427; *KlPauly* 4 (1972) 207–215, s.v. Nymphai (H. Herter); Olck 1905, 2018, 2050.

137. Keller 1913, 421–608; E. Herold and K. Weiss, *Neue Imkerschule*[9] (Munich 1995) 329–330, 343–344 (on Roman beehives). See also Varro, *Antiquitates Rerum Divinarum* 3.16, where Appius Claudius Pulcher, as a result of the popular etymology of his *praenomen,* claimed to know everything about bees, *apes.* For plants used in antiquity for beekeeping, see Farrar, 134–135.

138. See Varro, *Rust.* 3, a treatise *de villaticis fructibus* in which the interlocutors were passionately interested in *fructus,* the profits to be derived from a villa, but were also devoted to its sensual pleasures. Note in this same treatise (3.2.13) Varro mentioned the example of a tiny estate of only one *iugerum* (about ⅔ of an acre) that yielded HS 100,000 per year of honey.

139. Grimal 1969, 305.

140. Häuber 1995, 17. See also Olck 1905, 2024. The blackbird as well as the magpie were also believed to be capable of human speech. See Philostr., *VA* 6.36, and J. M. C. Toynbee, *Animals in Roman Life and Art* (Ithaca 1973) 275–277, 399, n. 298.

141. Cic., *Leg.* 1.7.21.

142. Cic., *De. Or.* 3.5.18; Cic., *Leg.* 1.4.14; Macrob., *Sat.* 6.4.8.

143. Varro, *Rust.* 3.2.1–6 noted that among the speakers are five *aves*: L. Cornelius Merula ("Blackbird"), Fircellius Pavo ("Peacock"), Minucius Pica ("Magpie"), M. Petronius Passer ("Sparrow"), and Pantuleius Parra ("Owl"). G. Tossi, "La *Villa Publica* di Roma nelle fonti letterarie e numismatiche," *Atti dell'Istituto Veneto, Classe di Scienze, Morali, Lettere ed Arti* 135 (1976–1977) 413–426; Richardson 1976. For the dramatic setting of Varro's dialogue, see Linderski 1989, 119–120.

144. I. Shatzman, *Senatorial Wealth and Roman Politics* (Brussels 1975) 323, mistakenly thought that this was a real aviary and concluded that Appius "had gardens in Rome . . . in which there were aviaries." See Linderski 1989, 105–127, esp. n. 73.

145. Pliny, *HN* 12.6. See also Hor., *Odes* 2.38 and Dio Chrys., 47.14–15.

146. Stat., *Silv.* 2.3.

147. Cic., *Domo* 62.

148. *Ad malum Punicum* (Suet., *Dom.* 1.1); *Ad nucem* (*CIL* VI, 28644); *Ad pirum* (Mart., 1.108.1). See Farrar 1998, 141–143, for other possible trees.

149. Grimal 1969, 77–79, 247–249.

150. Grimal 1969, 96–97; Rawson 1985, 11.

151. Pliny, *Ep.* 5.6.35. See Grimal 1969, 88–95; Rizzo 1983, 191–194. See also J. Henderson, "P.L.I.N.Y.'s Letters: A Portrait of the Artist as a Figure of Style," *Omnibus* 4 (1982) 31–32.

152. Pliny, *HN* 12.13. Note that Pliny, *HN* 35.116, attributes to another artist of the Augustan period the invention of painted illusionism that was meant to mimic real plantings: Non fraudando et S. Tadio, divi Augusti aetate, qui primus instituit amoenissimam parietem picturam, villas et porticus ac topiaria opera, blandissimo adspectu, minimoque impendio. See also Grimal 1969, 88–95.

153. Purcell 1996, 142 and n. 29, explained this meaning but also the spelling of viridiarium, which is usually, and misleadingly, spelled viridarium.

154. Joseph., *BJ* 4.362, 468; Strab., 16.241; and E. Netzer, "The Hasmonean and Herodian Winter Palaces at Jericho," *Israel Exploration Journal* 25 (1975) 89–100.

155. S.H.A., *Tyr. Trig.* 32.5–7.

156. Lanciani 1897, 415.

157. O. Gilbert, *Geschichte und Topographie der Stadt Rom in Altertum* III (Leipzig 1890) 376, n. 1.

158. See F. Coarelli, "La situazione edilizia di Roma sotto Severo Alessandro," in *L'Urbs: Espace urbain et histoire* (*CEFR* 98, 1987) 429–456.

159. Via XX Settembre Piscina: Fiorelli, "XV. Roma, Regione VI," *NSc* 1879, 68: found in front of the Palazzo delle Finanze, in via XX Settembre, even with the ground, this piscina consists of two galleries at least 50 meters long,

2.20 meters wide, parallel to each other, divided by a row of pilasters 1.00 × 0.70 meters. The construction is brick to a height of 1.40 meters and of stone to the apex. The total height from pavement to crown of the vault is 4.05 meters. Lanciani 1897, 415, reported the restored length as 200 meters. See also Lanciani 1880(c), pl. VII, fig. 8a (plan and section drawings).

160. Lanciani 1890, cols. 459–460 and fig. 4 (plan made by Lanciani): found in the "cavallerizza dei corazzieri del Re, (barracks of the King's armed riding guards) a confine col vicolo di S. Niccola da Tolentino, dal quale è troncato a metà, quasi di rimpetto al villino Ferri (see Frutaz 1962 III, pl. 524, map of 1866), a un terzo del clivo." According to Lanciani, Uffizi 406 (Baldassare Peruzzi) is a plan of this reservoir (with indications that it is near the Terme Diocleziane and the Acqua Vergine), which Lanciani used to make his plan, fig. 4. It was very large, 6 meters wide, which in size and decoration rivaled the better-known "sette sale" on the Esquiline. Lanciani did not know what would have fed it; however, in *Relazione sulle scoperte archeologiche della città e provincia di Roma negli anni 1871–72* (Rome 1873) 30, excavations on the vicolo S. Nicola da Tolentino near the enclosure of the Villa Barberini revealed a wall covered with slabs of peperino, "il quale appartenne probabilmente ad un acquedotto." It ran north-south, forming an acute angle with the modern street and probably virtually perpendicular with a large wall of fountains.

161. Lanciani 1897, 413, stated that a reservoir "was discovered in 1888 right under the Casino dell'Aurora," but this is not recorded on *FUR* 9 nor on *CAR* II-E.

162. R. Lanciani, "Roma: Regione VI," *NSc* 1886, 158. It was divided into three compartments between two rows of arches and pilasters.

163. Lugli 1930–1940, III, Supplement 33, and G. Lugli, *Itinerario di Roma Antica* (Milan 1970) 486.

164. Lugli 1970, 486, refers the reader to *FUR* 2 and 3, but this must be incorrect, because the vicolo and via Tolentino are on *FUR* 9: Lanciani 1890, fig. 4. See *Cod. Vat. lat.* 13035 for the original sketch by Lanciani, with measurements, made probably in 1875.

165. According to *CAR* II-F 68: "Cisterna composta di tre ambienti comunicanti (ciascuno di m. 4.45 × 4); ambienti in *op. mixtum;* muri, uno dei quali in *op. latericium;* fognolo a cappuccina (0.60 × 0.45 m.); bipedale con bollo *C. Ponti/Crescentis* (in opera); graffiti e piccolo framm. di iscrizione murale di età incerta. Questi ruderi sono da identificare, almeno in parte, con le (*FUR* 9)." See also *Taccuino Gatti,* appunti e rilievi di scavo conservati nell'Archivio di Guglielmo Gatti, 910, 931 (3.V.1924); *Cartelle Gatti,* appunti e rilievi di scavo conservati nell'Archivio di Guglielmo Gatti, VI (a. 1924); *NSc* 1938, 415, n. 3.

166. See D. Cattalini, "Aqua Julia," in R. Motta, ed., *Il trionfo dell'acqua: acque e acquedotti a Roma* (Rome 1986)

62; T. Ashby, *The Aqueducts of Ancient Rome* (Oxford 1935) 151; E. B. Van Deman, *The Building of the Roman Aqueducts* (Washington, DC 1934) 163; Lanciani 1880(c), 306–308; Evans 1994, 100.

167. See Nardini 1666 (1988) II, bk. IV, ch. VII, pp. 94–95: Vidi io molti anni sono la Vigna de'Signori Verospi sul Colle (Pincio) presso le mura star tutta pensile sopra antichi anditi lunghi stretti, e bassi fatti in volte, ciascheduno de'quali o da piedi, o da capo entrava nell'altro, ed avevano di più frapposte finestrine, e condotti da comunicarsi l'acque, scoperti a caso dalla buon. mem. del Signor Ferrante Verospi, e trovati ripieni di antico sterco, furono dal medisimo fatti votare. Queste conserve d'acque è facile, che negli Atti de'SS. Ciriaco, e Compagni, ove *Ante Thermas Sallustii* si legge, vadano intese.

See also A. Fulvio, *De Urbis Antiquitatibus* II (Rome 1545) 132, 140–141: Occurrit hinc inter Quirinalem, et Viminalem, ob longa, et angusta vallis, sub hortis Sallustianis formam circi habens et spectaculorum a dextris vestigia, ubi nunc est vinea. R. D. Dominici Cardinalis Jacobatij Ro. uiri profecto integerrimi, ac multae scientiae, quid autem illic olim fuerit, non satis audeo iudicare. Imminet huic loco Templum S. Susannae. . . . Extant adhuc hortorum (Salustij) vestigia in profunda valle, parum intra portam Salariam inter montem Quirinalem et collem Hortulorum, cuius partem hi Horti cum cisternis aquarum occupabant, vnde collis nomen, accepit, locus autem nunc ab incolia dicitur corrupté Salustricum, ubi nuperrimé marmor erutum, quod nunc est in domo D. Angeli Coloti; cum inscriptione huiusmodi. M. AVRELIVS JPACORVS etc.

168. Pliny, *HN* 19.50–51. That Romans emulated Epicurus' lifestyle is clear. See, for example, Vopiscus, who lived as in the philosopher's garden in Athens: Stat., *Sil.* 5.3.93–94 and H. Cancik, "Tibur Vopisci: Statius *Silvae* I 3: Villa Tiburtina Manili Vopisci," *Boreas* I (1978) 116–134.

169. Purcell 2001, 549: *in horto* means "in a garden"; *in hortis* means "on a peri-urban estate."

170. Champlin 1982, 99; Purcell 2001, 548.

171. For example, an important feature for Pliny (*Ep.* 2.17.2 and 1.24) of his maritime villa was the ease of getting there after a busy day in the city.

172. Pliny, *Ep.* 5.6.45. For the ambivalent nature of *horti,* see A. Wallace-Hadrill, "*Horti* and Hellenization" in *Horti Romani* 1998, 3–4.

173. Symmachus, *Ep.* 3.82.

174. See M. Kretschmar, "Otium, studia litterarum, Philosophie und bios theoretikos im Leben und Denken Ciceros" (Diss. Leipzig 1937), esp. pp. 50–61; J.-M. André, *L'Otium dans la vie morale et intellectuelle romaine des origines à l'époque augustéenne* (Paris 1966). The suburban villa was not the only place for *otium,* which could be found as well in the urban *domus:* e.g., Cic., *Att.* 4.18.

175. Millar 1977, 22–27.

176. Hor., *Sat.* 2.6.77–99.

177. Neudecker 1988, 5 and 115, n. 1171.

178. Varro, *Rust.* 1.2.10; Cic., *In Verr.* 2.4.126.

179. See Pliny, *HN* 36.23 (Praxiteles) and 36.25 (Skopas); Isager 1991, 168; *LTUR* III, s.v. horti Serviliani (L. Chioffi) 84. See Grimal 1969, 157, who believed the *horti Serviliani* were near the via Ostiensis.

180. The irony is that a large portion of ancient sculpture housed in modern urban Roman museums derives from the ancient suburb and likely from ancient garden displays. Champlin 1982, 107, and n. 59.

181. See Cic., *Verr.* 2.4, for Mummius' statues beside the Temple of Good Fortune. According to Pliny (*HN* 25.125, 36.23–34), Lucullus was prepared to pay a fabulous sum (perhaps as much as one million sesterces according to one manuscript) for a statue of "Felicitas" by Arkesilaos (a Neo-Attic, contemporary sculptor), and did pay two talents for a copy of a work of the fourth-century painter Pausias, made by Dionysius of Athens.

182. Cic., *Tusc.* 5.102.

183. Rawson 1985, 194.

184. See Neudecker 1998, 78, for relevant references and discussion of this phenomenon.

185. Paus., 8.46.1.

186. Suet., *Aug.* 72.3.

187. Pliny, *HN* 36.23–25, 36.33–34.

188. Neudecker 1998, 80.

189. Cic., *Phil.* 2.42.109 and 3.12.30: "He has gutted Caesar's well-furnished house; pillaged his gardens; from them transferred to himself all their appointments (*ornamenta*)." For Verres' collection, see Cic., *Verr.* 1.51.

190. Pliny, *HN* 35.10, 36.33, 7.115. Pollio founded the first public library in which his sculptural collection may have been displayed, although Pliny did not state specifically that this was the case. According to Neudecker 1998, 80, visitors may have thought of Pollio's collection as a museum, but it had not been conceived as such.

191. Cic., *De Or.* 1.162; *Verr.* 2.4.4–5. See also G. Zimmer, "Das Sacrarium des C. Heius: Kunstraub und Kunstgeschmack in der späten Republik," *Gymnasium* 96 (1989) 493–520.

192. Rawson 1985, 114.

193. Isager 1991, 167. As Isager pointed out, since Pliny did not mention works of art on public edifices, it is noteworthy that he did comment on an arch on the Palatine (Pliny, *HN* 36.36) dedicated to Octavius, natural father of Augustus. On this arch the emperor placed images of Apollo and Artemis (carved from a single stone) by the Greek artist Lysias, displayed in a temple-like construction atop the arch.

194. Strong 1973, 254.

195. Watson 1998: *Dig.* 33.12.23: "Figures and statues fixed in place are not included in the *instrumentum* of a house but are part of it. However, those which are not fixed are equally not included . . . for they are reckoned with the furniture." *Dig.* 30.41.12: "What then is to be said of statues? If they are fixed to the walls, their removal will not be allowed; but if they stand elsewhere, there is room for doubt. But the intention of the senate is best taken as fully as possible, so that if any statues were there permanently, they should be treated as a part of the house and not be removed" (Watson 1998; see also Neudecker 1988, 116 and n. 119). Panel paintings were also seen as physically part of the wall and therefore protected by law from being removed: *Dig.* 30.41.13: "Furthermore, it must be said that pictures fixed and joined to the walls and individual images flush with the walls cannot be bequeathed either." *Dig.* 33.12.36: "Only those pictures are held to be legated which were in some sense ornaments of the villa" (Watson 1998).

196. *Dig.* 18.1.34: "For we often buy something by reason of what goes with it, say, a house by reason of its marbles, statues, or pictures" (Watson 1998).

197. Neudecker 1988, 116; see Tac., *Ann.* 1.73; Pliny, *Ep.* 10.8. It was not permissible to remove material from a town or country house except for use in a public building in the same *civitas* as the house, but it was permitted for the owner of a house to transfer material to his other house in another *civitas*. See *Dig.* 30.41.5.

198. Pliny, *Ep.* 6.2.5. It may, however, have been an unusual case for a private owner to prefer statues of himself.

199. Cicero (*Att.* 12.37) runs into problems in his attempt to purchase the gardens of Scapula (in the Vatican plain) whose heirs contemplated dividing it into four parcels for bidding among themselves or for public auction. It is likely that at least some of the sculptures there conveyed with the land.

200. For Tiberius' purchases, see Suet., *Tib.* 44; Pliny, *HN* 36.197.

201. Neudecker 1988, 116.

202. Neudecker 1988, 116, n. 1200: Saturnalia: Hor., *Carm.* 4.8; Mart., 10.87.15. Lawsuits: Tac., *Ann.* 11.1, 12.59, 13.18; Tac., *Hist.* 2.92. Plundering during fires: Sen., *contra* 2.1.12. Theft: Mart., 6.72.

203. Suet., *Nero* 11.2; Pliny, *HN* 36.197. The Seii family estate was near the porta Esquilina: see M. Corbier, "La famille de Séjan à *Volsinii*: la dédicace des Seii, Curatores Aquae," *MEFRA* 95 (1983) 719–756.

204. Neudecker 1988, 116–117; S.H.A. *Marc.* 17.4; Suet., *Tit.* 8.4.

205. Cic., *Att.* 12.29 and 33, mentioned him in 45 B.C. as splitting up *horti* on the Tiber and selling the lots at a fixed price. Elsewhere, Cicero (*ad Fam.* 7.23.2), who wishes to sell some statues, is anxious to obtain the services of Damasippus or someone like him. See also Hor., *Sat.* 2.3 16, 64, who satirizes a Damasippus for his bankruptcy, probably the

same art dealer mentioned by Cicero. According to J. J. Pollitt, "The Impact of Greek Art on Rome," *TAPA* 108 (1978) 164, "Damasippos promised to buy some unwanted sculpture from Cicero but had failed to carry through his intentions, perhaps because he was bankrupt." See also E. Rawson, "The Ciceronian Aristocracy and Its Properties," in M. I. Finley, ed., *Studies in Roman Property* (London 1976) 101, and Rawson 1985, 89, who suggested that Damasippus may have been the son of the praetor Junius Damasippus, killed by Sulla. Pollitt (above) n. 13 claimed that Damasippus had his own sculptural collection in his gardens. For the ownership of gardens along the Tiber, see Grimal 1969, 108–120. Note also that Martial (5.62) summoned his patron to brief him (*instruere*) on a newly acquired *hortus*.

206. Sen., *Ep.* 114.1: according to Bodel 1997, 5, a possible proverb may have been something like "qualis villa, talis vita." See also Neudecker 1988, 116.

207. Cic., *Brut.* 24; Diog. Laert., 3.25.

208. Cic., *Att.* 4.10.1.

209. Sen., *Ep.* 64.9: Quidni ego magnorum virorum et imagines habeam incitamenta animi et natales celebrem? Quidni ego illos honoris causa semper appellem? (Why should I not keep statues of great men to kindle my enthusiasm, and celebrate their birthdays? Why should I not continually greet them with respect and honour?), R. M. Gummere, trans., Loeb Classical Library (London 1953) 443.

210. Zanker 1995, 203, 208. For the social status of sculptural collections, see Neudecker 1988, 122 and n. 1281.

211. Wiseman 1987, 395–396. See Sallust's comment (*Cat.* 12.4): Delubra deorum pietate, domos suas gloria decorabant.

212. Fulvio 1527, fr. 24; Marliani 1544, IV, 23; Marliana 1544, V, 24; Mauro 1556, 83.

213. P. J. Osmond, "*Princeps Historiae Romanae*: Sallust in Renaissance Political Thought," *MAAR* 40 (1995) 101–143.

214. M. Verzár-Bass, "A Proposito dei Mausolei negli *Horti* e nelle *Villae*" in *Horti Romani*, 401–424.

215. Serv., *ad Aen.* 5.64, 6.152, 11.206.

216. Plut., *Luc.* 43.3.

217. See A. Kosmopoulou, "A Funerary Base from Kallithea: New Light on Fifth-Century Eschatology," *AJA* 102 (1998) 531–545; see also Neudecker 1988, 52–53, for the connections to the Dionysiac Thiasos.

218. Pliny, *Ep.* 2.1.1, 3.

219. Sen., *Ep.* 86.1: see F. Coarelli, "Il sepolcro degli Scipioni," *DialArch* n.s. 6 (1972), 74, n. 94. Cicero, in 45 B.C., considered no fewer than nine *horti* in his search for the building of a shrine to his daughter: D. R. Shackleton Bailey, *Cicero's Letters to Atticus* V (Cambridge 1966) 404–413.

220. Suet., *Caius* 59; *Galba* 20.1. Cf. Tac., *Hist.* 1.49. See

also *LTUR* III, s.v. horti Lamiani (2) (M. Cima Di Puolo) 61–64.

221. Suet., *Ner.* 50.

222. Suet., *Dom.* 1.1. See Addendum.

223. S.H.A., *Marc.* 13.3–6. According to R. P. Duncan-Jones, "The Impact of the Antonine Plague," *JRA* 9 (1996) 108–136, there was a dramatic drop in statue dedications between 166 and 180 and a complete ceasing of imperial building from 160 until after 190, all the result, apparently, of a "great plague."

224. Cicero (*Att.* 12.36), in his quest for a proper location of a shrine to his deceased daughter, did not want to build it at his house for fear of the property changing hands and with it the respect for the memory of his daughter. For the possible location of Maecenas' tumulus on the Esquiline, see R. Christine Häuber, "Zur Topographie der Horti Maecenatis und der Horti Lamiani auf dem Esquilin in Rom," *KölnJb* 23 (1990) 91, n. 270, and eadem, *Horti Romani: Die Horti Maecenatis und die Horti Lamiani auf dem Esquilin. Geschichte, Topographie, Statuenfunde* (Diss. Universität zu Köln, 1991) 12–13.

225. Pliny, *HN* 7.75; Solin., 1.88. Pliny (*HN* 37.19) and Suetonius (*Aug.* 18; *Calig.* 52) also use the word "conditorium" to refer to the casket at Alexandria of Alexander the Great, whose body could be seen.

226. Nardini 1666 (1988) II, 96, discussed that in Fauno's day (1550s), many vases of bones, among which was the head of a man of very large size, were found between the obelisk and the street leading to the porta Pinciana. See also Marliani 1544 IV, 23, and Lanciani 1990, II, 273.

227. Livy, 40.29; Pliny, *HN* 13.84–87.

228. A. Schnapp, *The Discovery of the Past,* trans. I. Kinnes and G. Varndell (New York 1997) 97–98.

229. C. L. Visconti, "Sessione VI—6 giugno 1883," *DissPontAcc* 2 (1884) 74 = *CIL* VI, 36774: FVLGVR CONDITV. See also R. E. A. Palmer, "Jupiter Blaze, Gods of the Hills, and the Roman Topography of *CIL* VI 377," *AJA* 80 (1976) 43–56, esp. 47–49, and L. Gasperini, "Sacre," in *Il Lapidario Zeri a Mentana* I (Rome 1982) 23–28. See also Talamo 1998, 115, who discussed a travertine box found in 1747, which was probably a *bidental*.

230. Obsequens (above, n. 67) 71.

231. Suet., *Nero* 38.2; *Tib.* 65.

232. See Häuber 1998, 64.

233. Hor., *Carm.* 3.29.5–11. Orosius, *Adv. Pag.* 8.6, described the tower of Maecenas as *altissima*.

234. See R. Coates-Stephens, "The Palatine from Late Antiquity to the Middle Ages," *JRS* 10 (1997) 601, and C. Wickham, "Considerazioni conclusive," in R. Francovich and G. Noye, eds., *La storia dell'alto medioevo italiano alla luce dell'archeologia* (Florence 1994) 741–759.

235. See A. Augenti, "Palatino e Celio nel Medioevo:

alcuni problemi topografici," *BullCom* 95.2 (1993 [1995]) 47–58, and idem, *Il Palatino nel Medioevo: Archeologia e Topografia (Secoli VI–XIII)* (Rome 1996).

236. *Palatium Sallustii*: Acta S. Laurentii 10, Aug. p. 519: Decius ante Caesar pergit noctu iuxta palatium Sallusti (Previously Decius Caesar proceeds by night along the palace of Sallust); Acta S. Susannae 11, Aug. p. 632: eadem hora introivit unus de servis Macedonii et nuntiavit Iovem aureum in platea, ante palatium Sallustii iacentem (At the same hour one of the slaves of Macedonia entered and announced that a golden Jupiter was in the street, lying before the palace of Sallust) (translations by D. Burgess). Acta SS. militum 25, Oct. 433; Mirabilien: Urlichs 1871, 93, 128, 157; *forum Sallustii*: Acta S. Susannae (above); baths: Acta S. Laurentii (above); Acta S. Marcelli 16, Jan. p. 372; tribunal: Acta S. Crecentii 14, Sept. p. 354; *palatium Constantini* or *Constantii*: Mirabilien (above), Jordan and Hülsen 1871, 403, 410.

237. Ligorio, *Cod. Tor.* XV, 159: "Horti Sallustiani ove sono hoggidì molte uigne tra le quali quella delli venerandi padri di santo Saluatore del Lauro, del Vescouo Muti, del Vescouo di Pauia, del Vescouo Colotio, et di Francesco Sibylla, et di uenti altri padroni." See discussion of the temples of Venus in the gardens of Sallust (pp. 82) for the location of the Muti property.

238. *Cod. Barb. lat.* 4882, c. 27: F. Ubaldini, *Vita di Angelo Colocci* (originally published in 1673 as *Vita Angeli Coloti Episcopi Nucerini*), V. Fanelli, ed., *Studi e Testi,* nr. 256 (Città del Vaticano 1969) 38: Sino del 1513 . . . comprò nel colle Pincio da Giac. Ceccarini romano un pezzo di vigna et un sito di canne CLXXII da fabricare case presso i beni di ms. Domenico de' Massimi e di ms. Matteo Bonfini e la strada pubblica . . . qui dunque egli fabricò case e giardini deliziosissimi, rinnovando in gran parte qui la magnificenza et l'amenità degli horti anticamente detti sallustiani (As early as 1513 he purchased a plot of a *vigna* on the Pincian hill from Giacomo Ceccarini, and a site of 172 canne in order to build houses near the properties of Messers Domenio de'Massimi and Matteo Bonfini and the public street . . . here, then, he built the most delightful houses and gardens, renewing in great part the magnificence and the pleasures of the gardens called in ancient days the Sallustiani). See also V. Fanelli, *Ricerche su Angelo Colocci e sulla Roma cinquecentesca* (Città del Vaticano 1979) 115–117. For the location, see *FUR* 3 (Fig. 1.1B).

239. R. Kultzen, "Die Malereien Polidoros de Caravaggio in Giardino Del Bufalo in Rom," in *Mitteilungen des Kunst-historischen Instituts in Florenz* (1960) 118: erano distinti ma confinanti. See also Aldrovandi 1556, 285–286, who comments that the "casa di M. Giacomo Colotio (è) dietro a S. Maria in Via" and the "casa di M. Stefano del Bufalo (è) dietro S. Maria in via." See also Boissard 1597, 115, who discussed the collection of sculptures in the "aedes Bufalorum."

240. See Valentini and Zucchetti IV, 429 (Leto's *Excerpta*): Intrinsecus a porta Salaria a sinistris est vallis longa, ubi fuerunt horti Sallustiani, versus ventum Libyum, circumdati pulcherrimis aedificiis, qui fuerunt non modo pomorum, sed etiam propter sumptum et ornamentum aedificiorum satis amoeni: aquae subterraneae manu factae irrigabant hortos (Within the Salarian Gate, on the left, is a long valley, turned towards the Libyan wind, where were the Gardens of Sallust, surrounded with the most beautiful buildings, which were gardens not only of fruit trees, but also were very pleasing on account of the expense and ornamentation of the buildings. Manmade subterranean irrigation watered the gardens.).

241. Brizzi 1987, 23; H. Gamrath, "Pio IV e l'urbanistica di Roma intorno al 1560," in *Studia romana in honorem Petri Krarup septuagenarii* (Odense 1976) 197–201; C. D'Onofrio, *Le Fontane di Roma*³ (Rome 1986) 210–220; C. D'Onofrio, *Acque e Fontane di Roma* (Rome 1977) 198–241. Gregory XIII (Boncompagni), predecessor of Sixtus V, perhaps had considered the restoration of the *Aqua Alexandrina,* but this was never accomplished during his pontificate (1574–1585).

242. The monumental fountain with three arches was not finished until October 1589. Flaminio Vacca, whose father owned property in the area, was one of the sculptors for the relief of "Gideon Leading His Soldiers and People over the Jordan." The Egyptian lions originally decorating the fountain of the Acqua Felice are now in the Vatican, having been substituted by copies under Pope Gregory XVI.

243. T. Tasso, *Opere* (Florence 1724) II, 560.

244. C. Garas, "The Ludovisi Collection of Pictures in 1633," *Burlington Magazine* 1967, 287–289; 339–348.

245. Schiavo 1981, 94–96.

246. F. Haskell, *Patrons and Painters: A Study in the Relations between Italian Art and Society in the Age of the Baroque* (New Haven 1980) 73–74.

247. See A. Schnapp, *The Discovery of the Past* (New York 1997) 122–126.

248. It is not surprising that in the early nineteenth-century excavations by the French in the center of classical Rome, virtually nothing of importance was discovered. See Ridley 1992, 90–91.

249. The correct name is not villa Ludovisi but rather villa Ludovisia, as recorded by a plaque at the entrance on the via Friuli: see Marchi 1980, passim and figs. 6, 7.

250. Felici 1952, 221 (Reg. 612, n. 10): I marmi duri e teneri di qualsivoglia grandezza, statue e guglie, Bassorilievi, Metalli, intagli, colonne, iscrizioni, teste, busti ed altre sculture o cose simili, che si trovassero, debbano privativamente appartenere e essere di d'o Eccmo Sig. Duca (di Sora).

251. Schiavo 1981, 102–109.

252. See, for example, the view made by the Frenchman, Israel Silvestre, who visited Rome the last years of Urban VIII (died 1644), which makes a caricature of the celebrated Ludovisi Juno that stood next to the entrance as a curiosity to passersby: Felici 1952, 240–241.

253. Felici 1952, 241.

254. For the anonymous plan of 1775–1777, see Frutaz 1962, plan CLXXIII, 4, pl. 440.

255. Ofenbach 1997. A torso of a Venus statue reportedly was found in the gardens of Sallust ca. 1859, and this could have been among the first discoveries made by Spithoever. See Part II, n. 15.

256. See Fig. 1.11 (plan of 1846), but also Frutaz 1962, plan CCV, 3, pl. 524 (plan of 1866 with the indication of the Massimi in the valley).

257. Lanciani 1906, 168. See also A. Nibby, *Itinerario di Roma e suoi dintorni*[10] (Rome 1886) 180: Si riconoscono eziandio (from the so-called circus = the valley) gli avanzi della casa, di costruzione bellissima, le finestre della quale sono conservate dal terzo piano; poi un tempio conservato molto bene, che sembra fosse quello di Venere, ricordato da un'antica iscrizione e nel catalogo di Rufo; e finalmente delle stupende sostruzioni in forma di nicchie, erette a sostegno del Quirinale. Limitrofa alla già vigna *Mandosia*, ma in situazione molto elevata ed assai deliziosa è la vigna o villa *già Barberini*, ora *Spithoever* (ingresso via Venti settembre, n. 8) in cui veggonsi avanzi dei muri di Servio, e vi si distingue perfettamente il principio dell'*Aggere*. Dirimpetto agli orti Massimo lungo la via di Porta Salara è la Villa Lodovisi.

258. Ofenbach 1997, 29, 81–83, figs. 15, 16. The villa was designed by Luca Carimini and appears to have been built on property formerly occupied by the Mandosi villa.

259. Lanciani 1897, 419.

260. Reg. 614, n. 198, according to the Piano Regolatore studied at the Comune by Felici 1952, 346, n. 2. See also Moltesen 1998, 176.

261. D. M. Smith, *Italy and Its Monarchy* (New Haven 1989). See also F. Bartoccini, *Roma nell'ottocento* (*Storia di Roma* XVI, Bologna 1985) 11–43, for the events leading up to the institution of Rome as the capital of unified Italy.

262. For a discussion of this 1883 plan as well as an earlier one of 1873, see Insolera 1971, 34–59.

263. M. Zocca, "L'urbanistica romana dal 1870 al 1945," in *Terza Roma*, 17–22; I. Insolera, *Archeologia e città: Storia moderna dei Fori di Roma* (Rome/Bari 1983) 4. See also M. Albertoni, "La necropoli Esquilina arcaica e repubblicana" in *Roma Capitale*, 140–155, figs. 3, 4.

264. Insolera 1971, 64, gave statistics for the property of the Esquiline that between 1873 and 1877 sold for 9 lire per sq. m., while between 1883 and 1887, this same property was priced between 95 and 125 lire per sq. m.

265. A. Caracciolo, *Roma capitale: Dal Risorgimento allo Stato liberale*[2] (Rome 1974) 169–205; G. Pisani Sartorio, "Tra antiquaria e archeologia," in *Roma Capitale*, 13–17; A. M. Colini, "La riscoperta dell'antico," in *Terza Roma*, 113–117.

266. For a detailed summary of these negotiations and the laws surrounding the inheritance of the estate, see Schiavo 1981, 109–111.

267. Sixty elms were cut down between the Bosco dell'Aurora and the viale del Satiro, and forty-five cypresses fell from the viale del Satiro to the citrus groves: Felici 1952, 354, n. 9. Laments over the destruction of the Ludovisi cypresses, which had even impressed the likes of Goethe, are recorded by Gabriele d'Annunzio: Tambroni, 1936, 444.

268. Lanciani 1897, 418.

269. For example, Società Generale Immobiliare stock fell from 1260 lire per share in 1887 to 114 lire in 1892: Insolera 1971, 69.

270. Felici 1952, 363–364, 367; Schiavo 1981, 110–111.

271. Felici 1952, 368–369.

272. Felici 1952, 245: le gallerie, biblioteche, ed altre collezioni d'arte o di antichità rimarranno indivise ed inalienabili fra chiamati alla risoluzione del fidecommisso, loro eredi od aventi cause. In light of this law, it is of interest that Carl Jacobsen and Edward Perry Warren in Boston were urged by Helbig to buy the whole Ludovisi collection and to split it between them: Moltesen 1990, 27–46. In 1892 Jacobsen managed to purchase some statues for the Ny Carlsberg Glyptotek in Copenhagen, and in 1896 Léon Somzée, who had earlier acquired objects from the storerooms of the Ludovisi, purchased more pieces for his collection in Belgium: Toti 1995, 120, n. 8.

273. Felici 1952, 241, n. 46. NB: MFA Archives, Boston. In 1895 the Ludovisi "Throne" (see pp. 119–130) was separated from the rest of the collection probably because it had been agreed that Warren was to purchase it.

274. Felici 1952, 246. See also Toti 1995, 120.

275. See Lombardi 1996, 131–147 (rione III), and Castelli 1988, 62, n. 44. Pope Benedict XIV made definitive boundaries of the rioni by commissioning 220 marble plaques with the names of the rioni to be put up throughout the city: I Monti, II Trevi, III Colonna, IV Campo Marzio, V Ponte, VI Parione, VII Regola, VIII Sant'Eustachio, IX Pina, X Campitelli, XI Sant'Angelo, XII Ripa, XIII Trastevere, XIV Borgo. After 1870, with Rome having become the capital of royal Italy, eight new regions were instituted: XV Esquilino, XVI Ludovisi (reducing almost by half the Rione Colonna), XVII Sallustio (formerly part of Rione Trevi), XVIII Castro Pretorio (formerly part of Rione Monti), XIX Celio (comprising the former area of Rione Campitelli between the Colosseum and the Aurelian wall), XX Testaccio (constituting the southern, uninhabited area of Rione Ripa), XXI San Saba (formerly part of Rione Ripa), and XXII Prati (a new region bound by Rione Borgo).

II. THE ARCHITECTURE OF THE GARDENS

1. Lanciani 1891(b), 167–170. I have been unable to find the present location of this drawing. Hippolyte Destailleur (1822–1893), a Parisian architect, had a collection of architectural drawings, some of which are now in the Kunstbibliothek in Berlin (formerly the Bibliothek des Kunstgewerbemuseum). Prof. Dr. Bernd Evers, Director of the Kunstbibliothek in Berlin, informed me via fax (July 22, 1999) that the Destailleur drawing of the *horti Sallustiani* is not in this library. Three albums of drawings, formerly in the Destailleur collection (sold in 1896), are in St. Petersburg: see M. A. Gukovskj, "Ritrovamento dei tre volumi di disegni attribuiti a Fra Giocondo," *Italia medievale e umanistica* 6 (1963) 263–269. According to Dr. Valery Shevchenko (via fax, May 2001), curator of drawings at the State Hermitage Museum, however, the plan of the *horti Sallustiani* is neither in the drawing department of Western European Art nor in the central library of the museum. A part of the Destailleur collection (1,328 drawings and engravings) was obtained by the Bibliothèque Nationale in Paris as a gift from the owner in 1890. In 1894, after his death, this library purchased over 3,500 more drawings and engravings, all pertaining to images of France. I thank Bernd Kulawik (via fax: June 5, 2000) for alerting me to this part of the Destailleur collection in Paris, and Kathleen Chevalier for assistance in my seeing the published indices to it. Hippolyte Destailleur published part of his collection before his death (*Catalogue de livres rares et précieux composant la bibliothèque de m. Hippolyte Destailleur, architecte du gouvernement* [Paris 1891]). It is likely that this publication alerted Lanciani to the plan of the gardens of Sallust. Lanciani 1891(b), 161, attributed the drawing to Francesco da Sangallo, but J. S. Ackerman, *The Cortile del Belvedere* (Biblioteca Apostolica Vaticana 1954) 136, n. 1, claimed that the handwriting is identical with that found on drawings of Francesco's cousin, Aristotile. For the latter reference I thank Philip Jacks.

2. Lanciani 1891(b), 168.

3. The modern via Boncompagni follows, more or less, this path. Excavations of 1888 revealed an ancient road in this same position, which Lanciani identified as an extension of the via Salaria. According to *FUR* 3 (Fig. 1.1B), excavations were on July 28, 1888, and November 8, 1888. The staircase is considered third century A.C. by Riemann 1950, 1569, who believed that this entire area on the Pincio was likely laid out under Commodus.

4. Lanciani 1891(b), 169–170. See, however, the du Pérac/Lafréry plan of 1577 (Fig. 1.7), which shows a double apsidal building on the Pincio east of the obelisk.

5. Riemann 1950, 1561–1563, 1569, with pertinent bibliography; esp. G. B. Nolli, *Nuova pianta di Roma* (Rome 1748) fol. 28.

6. The two-hundred-foot corridor may be that reported in *CAR* II-F, 33, which I associate with the cryptoporticus found on the grounds of the American Embassy (see p. 61).

7. Anon. before 1748: G. B. de Rossi, *Note per la pianta di G. B. Nolli* (Rome 1884) 18.

8. Piranesi 1756, pl. 2, 15, nr. 114: "Avanzi degli Orti Salustio inoggi ridotti a uso di sotterranei nella Villa Belloni. Quivi si troverebbono per via di scavi delle cose maravigliose, come si son trovate nella susseguente Villa [Verospi]." Piranesi 1762, pl. 3, nrs. 101 and 102: Rovine degli orti Salustiani, o sotterranei della Villa Belloni. See Wilton-Ely 1994, nr. 569.

9. Piranesi 1761, pls. 14 and pl. 17 respectively = Wilton-Ely 1994, nrs. 774 and 777.

10. See Riemann 1950, 1562–1563.

11. Talamo 1998, 131–132, and 131, n. 89, explained that the results of several test trenches opened in 1969 were never published. Note that this area is designated on her fig. 10, n. 32 (my Fig. 2.11) as "platea contenuta da muri di sostruzione (tempio di Venere Erycina?)." It is possible that the long, high wall attached to a house on the Pincio depicted on the 1577 du Pérac and Lafréry plan (Fig. 1.7: structure below 1.7B) are ancient remains of this enclosed area. See discussion (pp. 77–78) of the Temple of Venus in the Gardens, where these remains are considered in relationship to the Temple of Venus Erycina.

12. Lanciani 1888, 8, 34; Lanciani 1891(b), 170; Lanciani 1906, 167.

13. See, for example, Grimal 1969, 130. A fragment of a statue found within the structure was identified as a nymph, perhaps Amalthea (Lehmann-Hartleben and Lindros 1935, 221, pl. 12, figs. 3, 4).

14. According to Venuti 1763, 157, Piranesi "accenna gli avanzi de'Bagni, e della Casa di Salustio, vi rimangono per anco in bottini, che ricevevano gli scoli de'tetti, ed una scala dipinta a grotteschi, per cui si ascendeva ai piani superiori; come pure una fabbrica di forma ottangolare, creduto uno de'Tempj di Venere sull'indizio di una statua di questa Deità ivi trovata" (notes the remains of the Baths, and of the house of Sallust [vestiges of which] remain also in wells/basins that received the drainage from the roof, and a staircase painted with grotesques, by which one ascended to the upper stories; as [for] a building of octagonal shape, [it was] believed [to be] one of the temples to Venus, based on the evidence of a statue of this deity found there). It appears that Piranesi was describing this complex, although the possible impluvium (?) is otherwise unknown.

15. See Ligorio's small plan of Rome of 1553 (Fig. 2.39), where the vestibule is positioned in the valley and is identified as "T. DIANAE." For the finding of a statue of Venus, see Venuti 1824, I.5, 157 and 159, and Riemann 1950, 1572, with references. In the early nineteenth century, the garden pavilion was in the *vigna* Mandosi. The statue of Venus reported by Venuti in 1824 cannot be the one mentioned in

The Academy 15 (1879: January/June) 248 (March 15, 1879), which seems to have been found around 1859: "Mr Francis Marcet, F.R.S., has presented to University College, London, a cast of the torso of Venus found some twenty years ago in the gardens of Sallust. The torso itself passed through various hands, and about five years since was concealed in a cellar, whence it was bought last year by M. Duval for the Geneva Museum. Through his influence Mr. Marcet has been allowed to have a cast of the torso taken for University College, where it has been placed in the Slade School."

16. Venuti 1824, 159: *Accanto a questo Tempio a destra, ove si vedono quelle sostruzioni da me sopra accennate, nello scavarvi molti anni sono il celebre Antiquario Ficoroni, vi ritrovò una camera rivestita di bassirilievi di terra cotta d'elegantissimo lavoro, appartenendo queste o alla casa Salustiana, o all'Edituo del Tempio. Che questo fosse il Tempio di Venere, pare molto probabile; che questa poi fosse Venere Ericina, si argomenta da Ovidio, che nei Fasti collocò il Tempio di Venere Ericina fuori della Porta Collina, e descrive le feste ivi celebrati.* (Near to this temple to the right, where are seen those substructures that I noted above, many years ago the celebrated antiquarian Ficoroni excavated and found a room filled with terra cotta reliefs of the most elegant workmanship, belonging either to the house of Sallust or else to the building called a temple. That this might have been the temple of Venus appears very likely; it might even have been the Venus Erycina, as deduced from Ovid, who explained that according to the *Fasti* the Temple of Venus Erycina was located outside the porta Collina, and he described the festivals celebrated there.)

17. Nardini 1666 (1988), 58, n. 1, 96, n. 1. See Becker 1843, I, 582, 584, who also did not believe that the Venus Erycina was the same as the Venus hortorum Sallustianorum.

18. R. Lanciani, "Topografia di Roma antica: I commentarii di Frontino intorno le acque e gli aquedotti. Silloge epigrafica aquaria," *MemLinc*, ser. III, 4 (1880) 215–616, esp. 385, listed six ancient octagonal buildings identified in Rome, including one in the *vigna* Spithoever (which is, in fact, the *round* vestibule in the piazza Sallustio).

19. Lehmann-Hartleben and Lindros, 1935, 196–227; Innocenti and Leotta 1986, 356–358; Festa 1989.

20. I thank Agnese Pompei of Tecno Holding, S.p.A., for alerting me to this restoration and for sending me a copy of V. Moretti, ed., *Il Recupero dell'Aula Adrianea degli Horti Sallustiani* (Rome 2000).

21. See Pietrangeli 1977, 65, n. 62, for these measurements. The rectangular substructure is unusual for a circular building, and Boatwright 1987, 156, suggested that this may be due to the building's location near or above the Acqua Sallustiana.

22. Lehmann-Hartleben and Lindros 1935, 199, mentioned mosaics on the dome of the vestibule, which relate it to the Serapeum of Hadrian's Villa, among the few examples of such decoration on large domes until the end of the third century (unless both are later restorations). See F. B. Sear, *Roman Wall and Vault Mosaics* (Heidelberg 1977) 35. According to Boatwright 1987, 158, n. 88, two layers of stucco have been identified on the cupola, perhaps the result of later changes in the decoration of the interior.

23. Boatwright 1987, 159 and n. 93.

24. Innocenti and Leotta 1986, 358: a one-meter-long trench in front of the doorway revealed two steps of brick with traces of marble revetment.

25. Note that two fragments of marble cornices with ovolos and dentils were found in the via R. Cadorna in front of the vestibule. See *CAR* II-F 52(b): "Sottofondazioni di un casamento," and *NSc* 1894, 93: *Sottofondandosi un casamento in via Cadorna, di fronte al Ninfeo degli Orti Sallustiani, si sono rinvenuti, alla profondità di m. 13, due pezzi di cornicione intagliato in marmo, con ovoli e dentelli, di buon lavoro e benissimo conservati. Uno dei frammenti misura m. 0,55 × 0,15, l'atro m. 0,35 × 10.*

26. Blake 1947, 63, believed the consoles were later additions to adapt these niches into shrines, but Boatwright 1987, 156, n. 86, called this implausible. F. L. Rakob, "*Litus beatae Veneris aureum:* Untersuchungen am 'Venustempel' in Baiae," *RM* 68 (1961) 138–139, compared these consoles to similar examples found at the Canopus and Roccabruna of Hadrian's Villa, in the "Temple of Venus" at Baiae, and on the façades of houses in Ostia.

27. Pietrangeli 1977, 65, n. 62.

28. Festa 1989–1990, 95–98.

29. Castagnoli, 1952, 102, n. 9, listed the manuscripts of Ligorio:

(1) *Cod. Vat. lat.* 3439: this celebrated codex had belonged to Fulvio Orsini and preserves many drawings that are, according to Lanciani, by the hand of Ligorio (and with notes by Panvinio) or at least inspired by Ligorio.

(2) *Cod. Paris. ital.* 1129 (formerly *San Germ. Lat.* 86): contains the notes of seven books of the first recension (ordered by subject) of Ligorio's work on antiquity.

(3) *Cod. Bodl. Can. ital.* 138: this is the first recension of Ligorio's work (notes of eight books) and was the first manuscript to be systematically studied. T. Ashby, "The Bodleian Ms. of Pirro Ligorio," *JRS* 9 (1919) 170–201.

(4) *Cod. Napol.* XIII, B, 1–10: ten volumes containing eighteen books of the first recension.

(5) Arch. Stato, Torino, R.A. a.III: thirty volumes: the first eighteen containing the work of *Antichità* in its second recension (alphabetical), a true encyclopedia of the ancient world; volumes 19–26 contain another eighteen books compiled by subject; volumes 27–30 contain ancient geography, studies on earthquakes, ancient art, and fabricated drawings.

(6) *Cod. Ottob. lat.* 3364/3387 and *Barber. lat.* 5085 are partial copies of the Turin codices.

30. Innocenti and Leotta 1986, 356–358.

31. Note that the villa Maraini stood near the Casino dell'Aurora, which is on former Ludovisi property: Schiavo 1981, 112.

32. Lanciani 1906, 157. In earlier excavations nearby, under the via R. Cadorna, were found two fragments of marble cornices with ovolos and dentils: see note 25 above.

33. Lehmann-Hartleben and Lindros 1935, 217.

34. Innocenti and Leotta 1986, 358: a test trench uncovered the lowest brick step and at a depth of 30 cm., the foundations of concrete.

35. Lanciani 1906, 168: cloaca nel fondo della valle, parallelo all'asse della med. e perciò alquanto inclinato verso occidente (a drain in the bottom of the valley, parallel to the axis of the valley and for that reason somewhat inclined toward the west). Some "cuniculi" were reported in 1484 at the bottom of the valley, and may well be the same water conduits as these. See Lanciani 1990, I, 83. Talamo 1995, 25, also related these conduits to one mentioned by Flaminio Vacca under an oval building found on his father's property. See p. 68.

36. In notes dated January 22, 1872 (*Cod. Vat. lat.* 13035, fol. 64: Buonocore 1997, 26), Lanciani wrote that this wall of niches lay 1.80 m. to the *south* of the water channel, and so it is clear that he revised his thoughts in the later publication of 1906.

37. See Tambroni 1936, 439, who expanded on Lanciani's third-century dating of this wall of niches to include other parts of this architectural complex, which in his day were incorporated into the villino Maccari. Maccari was a painter who in 1935 had his studio in the basement of a building that stood above the ancient foundations of part of the vestibule complex. See Lehmann-Hartleben and Lindros 1935, 206, and pl. VI.1.

38. Lanciani 1906, 169. In *Cod. Vat. lat.* 13035, fol. 64, it is reported that the first section of wall contained two niches still in part revetted in marble. The second wall did not contain niches, but there were traces of marble ornament and painted stucco.

39. Lehmann-Hartleben and Lindros, 204–205.

40. On a city plan of 1884 by Romolo Bulla (Frutaz 1962, pl. 545), there appears to be a property line dividing the villa Massimi from the villa Spithoever running diagonally across the western part of the valley from the Spithoever villa to the retaining walls of the Pincio opposite (that is, more or less parallel to the present via Piemonte). This boundary may have simply continued the line of the western retaining wall above which stood the Spithoever villa.

41. Evans 1994, 86.

42. See Nash 1957, 248–249, and S. Aurigemma, "Lavori nel campo di Villa Adriana," *BdA* 39 (1954) 327–341.

43. Lehmann-Hartleben and Lindros 1935, 223; Nash 1957, 249.

44. Nash 1957, 249: "Man von einer analogen Anlage (with the Canopus of Hadrian's Villa) nicht sprechen kann."

45. F. Rakob, "Ambivalente Apsiden—Zur Zeichensprache der römischen Architektur," *RM* 94 (1987) 5, n. 7, figs. 3–5.

46. Cf. the so-called Tempio della Tossa in ancient Tibur, an impressive round structure that must have served as the vestibule to a large villa: J. J. Rasch, *Das Mausoleum der Kaiserin Helena in Rom und der 'Tempio della Tossa' in Tivoli* (Mainz 1998). See also H. Günther, "Albertis Vorstellung von antiken Häusern," in K. W. Forster and H. Locher, eds., *Theorie der Praxis: Leon Battista Alberti als Humanist und Theoretiker der bildenden Künste* (Berlin 1999) 157–202, esp. 182–183, who called this rotunda in the gardens of Sallust an "Eingangshalle."

47. *Res Gestae* 17.4.16: secutaeque aetates (after Augustus) alios transtulerunt, quorum . . . alter in hortis Sallusti . . . erecti sunt. See Iversen 1968, 128–141.

48. Valentini and Zucchetti II, 181. See Jordan and Hülsen I.3, 1907, 435, n. 116; Urlichs 1871, 71, and Valentini and Zucchetti II, 180–183: "Thermae Sallustianae et piramidem." See Lanciani 1890, 438–551, pl. 1, for a color reproduction of a page from the Einsiedeln manuscript. The assumption is that the Sallustian obelisk was standing, because the anonymous author of the Einsiedeln mentioned only this and another in the Campus Martius while ignoring those in the Circus Maximus that had surely fallen by this time.

49. Valentini and Zucchetti II, 155–162, 176–201. Walser 1987, 9–11, 144–211.

50. According to *FUR* 3 (Fig. 1.1B), these excavations occurred on August 28 and November 8, 1888.

51. *Cod. Vat. lat.* 13036, fol. 234v (= Buonocore 1997, 152). It appears from this plan and drawings that a wall was found partially crossing this street at right angles, thereby essentially interrupting, at some unknown date, its use as a main east-west artery.

52. It should be noted that there was a north-south road running to the west of the obelisk, and so one traveling north on it would see the obelisk to the right: see *CAR* II-F, 17 and 18.

53. Lanciani 1890, 460–461. See Riemann 1950, 1554, who disagreed with this identification.

54. R. E. A. Palmer, "Severan Ruler-Cult and the Moon in the City of Rome," in *ANRW* II, 16.2 (Berlin 1978) 1090.

55. Lanciani 1890, 445; Valentini and Zucchetti II, 157. Hülsen 1907, 382–424, believed this to be a confused and truncated version of a much more elaborate and detailed

itinerary to accompany a probable circular plan of the city copied from antiquity.

56. Valentini and Zucchetti II, 138, suggest that the pilgrim was not necessarily to visit each monument listed but at least to see it to his or her right or left, as indicated by the itinerary.

57. It is usually suggested that the "forma Lateranensis" must refer to the *Aqua Claudia,* even though no spur of this aqueduct is known to have gone to the Quirinal. See Lanciani 1890, 459–460, and Hülsen 1907, 395. Fauno 1548, 4, 10 (cf. *CIL* VI, 334) wrote of large aqueducts visible on the slopes of the Quirinal, but these have neither been named nor have any physical remains been identified. Lanciani pointed out a large water cistern on the vicolo di S. Nicola da Tolentino, and this could have been in use in the eighth century, although the designation as "forma Lateranensis" would be seemingly arbitrary. It may not be coincidence, however, that the Einsiedeln itinerary "A Porta Flamine usque via Lateranense" repeats several monuments "A Porta Sancti Petri usque as Portam Salariam" such as San Laurentius in Lucina, San Silvestro, and the Antonine Column and that along each route in the Campus Martius were seen remains of the *Aqua Vergine.* The "forma Lateranensis" could be the remains of the *Aqua Vergine,* but high on the Pincio, and running at this point towards the Quirinal, suggesting that these are a separate branch(?). See Bufalini's plan of 1551 (Fig. 2.15), which shows the course of the *Aqua Vergine* running in various directions.

58. B. Curran and A. Grafton, "A Fifteenth-Century Site Report on the Vatican Obelisk," *JWarb* 58 (1995) 240, n. 28; Curran 1997, 107, n. 138.

59. Hülsen 1907, 396, believed that the "pyramis" and the "obelisco" are one and the same and that its position had been mistakenly transferred in the codex from the left of the street to the right.

60. "Anonimo Magliabecchiano," *Tractatus de rebus antiquis et situ urbis Romae* (ca. 1410–1415), ch. 11, in Valentini and Zucchetti IV, 129–132. The statement that the Pincio obelisk was afterwards in the Mausoleum ("postea fuit in mausiolo") must be a mistake that was repeated a century later by Albertini 1510, fol. RIIIv. See Curran 1997, 129–131 and n. 11; Urlichs 1871, 159; and Jordan and Hülsen II, 1871, 183. See also a drawing in the *Cod. Vat. lat.* 3439, fol. 3, by Pirro Ligorio, who saw it in the vineyard of "messer Paolo Patella" about 1550, and a sketch by Carlo Fontana dated March 21, 1706, in Windsor (Vol. G I, sheet 249), showing it broken into two unequal pieces: Lanciani 1899, 171, fig. 29. According to Lanciani, Fontana's sketch "shows the way in which one of the obelisks decorating the Egyptian casino of the gardens of Sallust had fallen." This statement implies the existence of more than one obelisk and its association with a building identified as an "Egyptian casino."

In Lanciani 1906, 166, this sketch is mentioned again, with the addition that the obelisk is shown in the "vigna di Vincenzo Vittori dove già l'avevano veduto e descritto Andrea Fulvio nel 1527 e Leonardo Bufalini nel 1551, vigna incorporata nella Ludovisi l'anno 1621." The vineyard of Vincenzo Vittori is identified on Bufalini's 1551 plan (Fig. 2.15B) near the obelisk, although separated from it by a road. *FUR* 3 (Fig. 1.1B) indicates the location of the obelisk in a vineyard belonging later to the Vacca family and later still to the Verospi (where a group of Egyptian statues were excavated in 1710). In light of the above as well as Ligorio's statement of seeing it on the property of Paolo Patella, it is likely that the obelisk was not on the Vittori property and should not be associated physically with the 1710 discoveries (including the building identified by Lanciani [above] as an Egyptian casino) made on the Verospi property (see pp. 136–137). The suggestion of other obelisks is not based on any physical or literary evidence.

61. One of the earliest is the Franciscan Mariano da Firenze, whose guidebook to Rome of 1517–1518 gives the location of the Sallustian obelisk as between the porte Pinciana and Salaria, in the vineyard of the Bufalini family: "Non longe a porta Pinciana aut Salaria, in vinea Bufalorum, iacet confractus obeliscus cuius longitudo erat pedum 44." See P. Enrico Bulletti, ed., *Itinerarium Urbis Romae di Fra Mariano da Firenze (Studi di antichità christiana* II, Rome 1931) 222. See Calvo 1527, fol. Ciiiiᵛ: Circum Floralium, cuius obeliscus hodie quoque humi stratus in vineto nobilis civis Rhomani Antonii de Bubalo cernitur. See also P. Jacks, *The Antiquarian and the Myth of Antiquity: The Origins of Rome in Renaissance Thought* (Cambridge University 1993) 342, n. 134, and Jacks 1990.

62. See Marliani 1544, 89. For the name "obelisk of the moon," see Iversen 1968, 129. The hill where the obelisk lay was called by Marliani, "Gyrlus," and along the road leading to the gate were found many *hydriae* and human bones, among which were those of humans of great size identified as possibly Pusio or Secundilla: see Lanciani 1990, 273. According to Talamo 1998, 134, the area called "Gyrlus" by Marliani can be identified with a large apsidal building with parallel walls projecting from it (identified as a nymphaeum by Talamo 1998, 135) as depicted by Bufalini in 1551 (Fig. 2.15C), and du Pérac in 1577 (Fig. 1.7E). This may be the case, although the term "gyrlus" as used here by Marliani is probably due to the interpretation of the obelisk as part of a circus rather than of an apsidal building. See Nardini 1666 (1988), 94, who claimed that the term "Girlo" as used by Fulvio for the place of this obelisk was taken from "Girulus," which could derive from "Circulus."

63. Iversen 1968, 129–130. See also Mercati 1589, 256–258.

64. Fulvio 1527, fols. 24, 71.

65. See Iversen 1968, 129.

66. A. Kircher, *Oedipus Aegyptiacus* III (Rome 1654) 256–257: the entire inscription was reproduced in an engraving by Pierre Miotte, and a sketch shows the obelisk's appearance at this time. Mercati 1589, 256, had earlier suggested the Claudian date of transportation to Rome. Grenier 1989, 19, n. 30, rightly indicated that the choice of reproducing the Augustan obelisk's hieroglyphs was deliberate and significant. What technique was used for such reproduction is unclear, particularly because the Sallustian obelisk is smaller than that of the Circus Maximus.

67. A. Cassio, *Corso dell'Acque* I (1756) 333. See also Iversen 1968, 128, n. 4, who pointed out that Sallust died before any obelisk is known to have come into Rome.

68. G. Zoega, *De origine et usu obeliscorum* (Rome 1797) 619.

69. Grenier 1989, 20.

70. Maps by de Rossi of 1697 (Frutaz 1962, pl. 378), by de Fer of 1700 (Frutaz 1962, pl. 379) or by Nodot of 1706 (Frutaz 1962, pl. 380). Iversen 1968, 131–132, believed this had occurred "probably when the gardens were re-laid."

71. Lanciani 1897, 417.

72. See Iversen 1968, 133, concerning negotiations for the obelisk's delivery to the pope after the death of the princess in 1733.

73. See R. Bonfiglietti, "L'ara dei caduti fascisti eretta sul campidoglio," *Capitolium* 4 (1928) 416–418. Carlo Maderno's plan of the Ludovisi property, which had passed from the Orsini family to Ludovico, shows the position of the fallen obelisk and its base (Fig. 2.31). Even after its removal, a document dated 1744 still refers to this area as "il quarto della Guglia" in remembrance of its having been a landmark of the site: Felici 1953, 242. Giovanni Antinori had it erected on a large pedestal of white marble and placed on its top a metal cross.

74. E. Sarti, "Note Astigrafiche," *Archivio della Società Romana di Storia Patria* 9 (1886) 436. *FUR* 9 (Fig. 1.1c), because of the findspot of the base, indicated a possible position for the obelisk south of the via Boncompagni in the gardens of the present American Embassy. The reference "Scavi III, 1843" on *FUR* 9 is to the finding of the base during the digging of a hole for the planting of a tree in the Ludovisi gardens. See Nash 1957, 250.

75. Schreiber 1880, 144, n. 127: "Regelmässig zubehauener Würfel, der nach Braun um d.J. 1840 bei den Vorbereitungen zu den englischen Gartenanlagen, die sich gegen Porta Salara hin ausbreiten, aufgefunden wurde, nach der wahrscheinlicheren Angabe des Custoden dagegen in dem hinter der Colossalstatue des liegenden Silen befindlichen Theil der Villa zum Vorschein kam. . . . Nach dem Plan des Gio. Batt. Falda (*Li Giardini di Roma,* nuov. ed. Norim. tv. 15) der in die zweite Hälfte des 17 Jahr. fällt,

lad der Obelisk links neben der grossen Allee, die von dem Eingang ausgehet, etwa auf halben Wege vom Silen nach der Stadtmauer."

76. On his plan of the villa Ludovisia (Fig. 1.8), Schreiber 1880, 275, indicated the location of the Silenus north of the palazzo within the former labyrinth garden, which would place it within the modern city block bordered by the vie Sicilia and Boncompagni and the vie Marche and Toscana: *FUR* 9 (Fig. 1.1c). See also Lanciani 1897, 417, who reported the discovery as "near the gate of the villa." Note that Lanciani also believed the obelisk formed part of the same group as the Egyptian statues (see pp. 130–138), which he claimed are "clever copies of Egyptian originals."

77. Katterfeld 1913, esp. 106, where he indicated that the obelisk must belong with the raising of the ground level undertaken probably when the nearby house went out of use (perhaps soon after the Severan period) and that to this raising belongs an octagonal structure (1.20 m. per side), which must have been a nymphaeum. See also Riemann 1950, 1554; Nash 1968, 491–499, s.v. "Obeliscus Hortorum Sallustianorum"; Talamo 1998, 126. See also another octagonal structure mentioned by Vacca 1594, 109: "I remember behind the Trophy of Marius next to the street that leads to the Porta Maggiore, in the Altieri *vigna,* there was found a most beautiful Venus who is exiting from her bath, and a Hercules of marble that were displayed in an octagonal structure that I suppose could have been a fountain." (Mi ricordo dietro le spoglie di Mario accanto la via che mena a Porta maggiore, nella vigna Altieri, vi fu trovata una Venere bellissima, che esce dal bagno, ed un Ercole di marmo collocate in opera in una fabbrica ottangolare, suppongo potesse essere una fonte.) NB: F. Coarelli, *Guida Archeologica di Roma* (Rome 1980), plan of Quirinal on p. 218, incorrectly placed the obelisk two blocks to the east of the actual location. Roullet 1972, 48, still gave the possibility that it "might have stood in the centre of the depression in the garden," perhaps believing that it had been moved later to the Pincio (?).

78. For the documentation, see Felici 1952, 242, n. 48. Its whereabouts were known to Jordan and Hülsen I.3, 1907, 435, n. 119. See also Riemann 1950, 1556.

79. The present via Friuli is now merely the continuation towards the east of the via di San Basilio. Before this, the via Friuli was a street running from the via Vittorio Veneto to the via di San Basilio. This short street was later incorporated into the via L. Bissolati (after 1934) at which time, apparently, the present via Friuli was named.

80. The Kiepert and Hülsen 1912 plan as well as Lanciani's *FUR* 9 (Fig. 1.1c) displace it incorrectly some 7° towards the southeast: see Nash 1957, 247, n. 45, and Neuerburg 1965, 75.

81. Nash 1957, 247; Blake 1947, 262.

82. Nash 1957, 248, n. 49, also noted this discrepancy.

The vicolo delle Fiamme no longer exists. It was eliminated when the present via L. Bissolati was cut to link the via Veneto with the largo Santa Susanna.

83. *Beschreibung* 3.2 (1838) 380.

84. D. Faccenna, "Criptoportico decorato con pitture nel giardino della villa Boncompagni-Ludovisi," *NSc* 1951, 107–114.

85. Festuccia 1997. I thank Dr. Festuccia for showing me this cryptoporticus during her investigations and for her kindness in giving me a copy of her article as well as color photographs.

86. M. Cagiano de Azevedo, "Criptoportico in Via Lucullo: iscrizioni dipinte e graffiti cristiani," *NSc* 1952, 253–256; Festuccia 1997, 27.

87. *CAR* II-F, 33 a.

88. Suet., *Aug.* 30; Dio Cass., 50.8.7; G. Gatti, "Di un sacello compitale dell'antichissima regione Esquilina," *Bull-Com* 16 (1888) 224.

89. For example, Suet., *Caes.* 39; *Aug.* 5; *Nero* 12; *Gram.* 2. See C. Hülsen in Platner and Ashby 1929, 455, n. 1, who believed that these names never became official and that the regionary titles are not original but derive from the first listing of each region.

90. See *CIL* VI, 1956 (de regione porta Capena); *CIL* VI, 8461 ([regione] Trastiberina).

91. The catalogue of the fourteen regions presents two major problems: the aim set by its first editor and the period of its compilation. It seems clear that the lists do not follow exclusively a particular region, but in fact items overlap into adjacent regions. Secondly, the basilica, portico, and baths of Constantine, all works after 312, are listed, but not the arch of Constantine, which is dated 315–316. Thus, it could be presumed that this catalogue dates between 312 and 315. On the other hand, it is probable that the original catalogue was compiled in the period of Diocletian and that additions were made to it up to the time of Constantine.

92. Nordh 1949, 6–11, listed six manuscripts, the earliest (*Codex Vindobonensis Latinus* 162, fol. 49) dating to the ninth century: Valentini and Zucchetti I, 77–78. See also Lugli 1957, 179.

93. This is unlikely to have been the original title and is known in three principal manuscripts dating from the eighth to the twelfth centuries: *Cod. Vat. lat.* 1984, 3227, 3321. See Nordh 1949, 3–6; Valentini and Zucchetti I, 68, 74–75; Lugli 1957, 179–180.

94. A tenth-century manuscript in the Laurentian library, Florence (*Codex Laurentianus,* pl. 89, sup. 67, fols. 34v–37r: Regiones urbis Romae cum breviariis suis): Nordh 1949, 11, and Valentini and Zucchetti I, 75–76.

95. See Nordh 1949, 64–65, and Valentini and Zucchetti I, 66–71, for discussions of the evidence for the dating.

96. Valentini and Zucchetti I, 107–109.

97. The codice give "Salusti," which must be incorrect. It is named after the principal street of the region probably running from the present piazza del Quirinal to the ancient porta Collina, following the track of the modern via XX Settembre. In the last part it probably carried the name *vicus portae Collinae*: Valentini and Zucchetti I, 107, nn. 1, 3.

98. See Santangeli Valenzani 1991, 7–16; Valentini and Zucchetti I, 107, nn. 3, 4.

99. Varro, *Ling.* 5.74, affirms that Titus Tatius dedicated on the Quirinal an altar to the Sabine goddess Flora, to whom presumably was later constructed a temple: this was found not far from the Quirinal (Vitr., *De Arch.* 7.9.4) and from the incline called "Next-to-Flora" that was up towards the old Campidoglio (Varro, *Ling.* 5.158); it could have been in the vicinity of the piazza Barberini. See Valentini and Zucchetti I, 107, n. 5. Martial lived on the north slope of the Quirinal next door to the Tiburtine column and near the temple of Flora: *Epigr.* 5.22.3–4, 6.27.1.

100. According to some scholars, on the summit of the Quirinal was an ancient shrine to the triad Jupiter, Juno, and Minerva that had a cult there before that of the Capitoline: Hülsen 1891, 121; Kiepert 1903, plans 21, 22. Inscriptions (*CIL* I², 727, 728 = *CIL* VI, 373, 374, and *CIL* VI, 438: Lanciani 1889, 390), however, found in 1637 near the palazzo Barberini indicate perhaps this cult in the vicinity of the present via XX Settembre, which is on the grounds of the palazzo Barberini. See Hackens 1961, who emphasizes rightly that Varro called this a "sacellum," which is probably a small shrine rather than a tripartite temple, and who argues against the findspots of the inscriptions as indications of the site of the Capitolium Vetus. See also *RE* 24 (Stuttgart 1963) s.v. Quirinalis collis, 1304 (G. Radke), for the suggestion that this cult is not older than that of the Capitoline triad.

101. Perhaps near the present piazza del Quirinale, between the via Nazionale and the via 24 Maggio. It is recorded by Aur. Vict., *Caes.* 40.27, and Amm. Marc., 27.3.8. A restoration is recorded (*CIL* VI, 1750) in 443 under the prefect Petronius Perpenna Magnus Quadratianus. See Valentini and Zucchetti I, 108, n. 1.

102. Perhaps a statue dedicated to Veturius Mamurius, the presumed builder of the *ancili,* similar to that fallen from the sky (Ov., *Fast.* 3.383; Plut., *Vit. Num.* 13.6; Festus in *Glossaria Latina* [Paris 1930] 256 [114–116]; Varro, 6.49). This statue probably was in the curia of the Salii Collini, which was found in the vicinity of the temple to Quirinus: Valentini and Zucchetti I, 108, n. 2.

103. This temple to the deified Romulus was vowed by L. Papirius Cursurus and dedicated by his son in 293 B.C. (Livy, *Epit.* 10.46.7; Pliny, *HN* 7.213). It was damaged by lightning and then in 49 B.C. almost destroyed by a fire. It was almost immediately restored, but the definitive restoration was

completed in 16 B.C. under Augustus (*Res Gestae* 4.5, 6.32; Dio Cass., 54.19.4). It was probably located in the southeast of the Quirinal gardens (*CIL* VI, 475, 565 = *CIL* I², 803; see C. Hülsen in Platner and Ashby 1929 I.3, 407–410). It seems that this temple lent its name to the district (*CIL* VI, 9975, 31895). See also *NSc* 1921, 87, 109–110 (G. Mancini); and Valentini and Zucchetti I, 108, n. 3.

104. The place of the *horti Sallustiani* seems always to have been known: Flavio Biondo's *Roma instaurata* probably written in 1444 to 1446 (dedicated to Eugenius IV; printed editions listed by Schudt 1930, 362–364). "Magnae autem et obstupendae sunt (Salustiani horti) ipsorum hortorum quas adhuc extare videmus murorum fornicumque reliquias quae a Viminali olim nunc Sanctae Agnetis porta in collinam nunc Salariam ad Sanctam Susannam propemodum extenduntur." Quoted from Scaglia 1964, 145, n. 43. On Biondo's career, see B. Nogara, *Scritti inediti e rari di Biondo Flavio* (Rome 1927).

105. A temple that Domitian erected in the location of the house in which he was born (Suet., *Dom.* 1). According to Valentini and Zucchetti I, 108, n. 5, it must have been south of the Alta Semita near the present via delle Quattro Fontane; but see my addendum for an alternative location.

106. Maximianus decreed the construction of these baths in the northern part of the Viminal after his return from Africa in the autumn of 298, consecrating them to Diocletian. They were dedicated to the Roman people between May 1, 305 and July 25, 306 (*CIL* VI, 1130 = 31242). *CIL* VI, 1131, seems to allude to a later restoration. The damage of the aqueducts during the invasion of the city in 410 by Alaric probably put the baths out of use. The name survived in a bull of Honorius I in 625 and in Medieval tradition. Valentini and Zucchetti I, 108–109, n. 6.

107. Valentini and Zucchetti I, 171–172.

108. An area ("of the Pomegranate") where Suetonius (*Dom.* 1) claimed Domitian was born. According to J. C. Rolfe, *Suetonius* (London 1914) 339, n. b, "Ad Malum Punicum" was a street probably corresponding to the modern via delle Quattro Fontane.

109. "et Constantinianas" must be, as in the *Curiosum*, after the "Capitolium Antiquum," for the baths of Constantine did not stand near to those of Diocletian: Valentini and Zucchetti I, 171, n. 2. It was not unusual for monuments of similar type or function to be placed together in these early itineraries, even though they may not have been physically near each other. For example, in Regio XIIII is mentioned Naumachias II, which must indicate one northwest of the Castel San Angelo, and the second on the other side of the Janiculum hill in the area of Trastevere.

110. See Valentini and Zucchetti I, 193–206; IV, 421. Preserved today in *Cod. Vat. lat.* 3394 and in an inexact copy in *Cod. Barb. lat.* 28. The basis for Leto's manuscript

was the *Notitia* preserved in a manuscript belonging to the Laurentian family, which was published after Leto's death sometime between 1502 and 1506 under the title *P. Victoris de regionibus Urbis Romae libellus aureus:* Valentini and Zucchetti I, 201. Giulio Sanseverino (Leto) was a professor of rhetoric and leader of the "Roman Academy," a group of humanists (among whom were Angelo Colocci, and Bartolommeo Sacchi [who went by the Latinized name "Platina"]) who paid homage to the ancient past by their mastery of Latin and their enthusiasm for archaeological remains. See V. Zabughin, *Giulio Pomponio Leto, Saggio critico,* 2 vols. (Rome 1909); J. D'Amico, *Papal Humanism in Renaissance Rome: Humanists and Churchmen on the Eve of the Reformation* (Baltimore 1981) 91–97; and I. D. Rowland, *The Culture of the High Renaissance: Ancients and Moderns in Sixteenth-Century Rome* (Cambridge 1998) 10–25.

111. Valentini and Zucchetti I, 216; *CIL* VI, 2235: "in domo Pomponii Laeti patris." We do not know precisely where Leto's house stood, but it survived his death and was described by his "pupil" Andrea Fulvio (Fulvio 1513, Bk. II, c. L 1ʳ), as near the house of Platina: The manuscript was given to Pope Leo X (it is now in the Biblioteca Laurenziana, cod. 33, 37), and it was printed by Mazzocchi in Rome near the end of 1513. Angelo Colocci is reported to have obtained Leto's property on the Quirinal, apparently having inherited it from Leto: V. Fanelli, *Ricerche su Angelo Colocci e sulla Roma cinquecentesca* (Città del Vaticano 1979) 113. Colocci did not, however, inherit Leto's (other?) home, which was on the Esquiline.

112. It was assumed that this temple stood on a hill opposite that of the Capitolium Vetus and was called Mons Apollinis et Clatrae, but this topographical identification is purely hypothetical. See Hackens 1961, 80, and T. Hackens, "Mons Apollinis et Clatrae: Note de topographie romaine," *RendPontAcc* 33 (1960–1961) 185–196. In the *Excerpta* 60, l. 29 (see below, n. 118), the toponym *Clatiae et Apollinis* is found, but above *Clatiae* (probably a misspelling of Clatrae) is written *lunae,* suggesting that a follower of Leto may have had doubts about its meaning. It is possible that this interpolator was Sabellicus, a member of Leto's Academy and later prefect of the library of San Marco in Venice. See De Rossi 1882, 71–72.

113. This circus of Flora appears to be derived from a misinterpretation of "Lud. in circo Florae," which is in the *Fasti Venusini* (*CIL* I², p. 221). Hackens 1961, 133, explained that the *Fasti Venusini* were not discovered until 1488, yet the games of Flora were cited earlier as a toponym. According to Valentini and Zucchetti I, 216, n. 7, it is also possible that the interpolator having before him the *Fasti Allifani* (*CIL* I², p. 217) could have confused the "templum Florae" on the Quirinal with that near the Circus Maximus, not listed in his Region XI. The Flora temple near the Circus Maximus,

which had been founded by Lucius and Marcus Publicius in about 240 B.C., was rebuilt by Tiberius, according to Tac., *Ann.* 2.49. But see Varro, *Ling.* 5.158: "The Incline Next-to-Flora is up towards the old Capitol, because there is in that place a chapel of Jupiter, Juno, and Minerva, and this is older than the temple which has been built on the Capitol": R. G. Kent, *Varro on the Latin Language* I (London 1938) 149.

114. Note that between the sanctuaries of Flora and Quirinus Vitruvius (*De Arch.* 7.9.4: Eae autem officinae sunt inter aedem Florae et Quirini) places some "officinae minii": cinnabar manufacturing, which Lanciani believed were on the north side of the Alta Semita, under the southern wing of the Quirinal palace, but which Hülsen 1894, conjectured must be on the northern slopes of the Quirinal outside the "Servian" wall because this location would be away from the residential areas and would give access to water, a necessity for this industry. See H. Blümner, *Technologie und Terminologie der Gewerbe und Künste* IV (Hildesheim 1969) 490–499, and Rodríguez-Almeida 1986, 52–54.

115. Perhaps the interpolator is presenting here information from the *Fasti Esquilini* (*CIL* I², p. 211). On the Quirinal near the porta Collina were three temples to Fortuna, as reported by Vitr., *De Arch.* 3.2.2: "A temple is called *in antis* when its façade includes the ends of the walls which enclose its cella, and in between these two ends (antae) are two columns, on top of which a gable should be set in place according to the symmetries that shall be laid out in the present book. An example of this type of temple may be found at the sanctuary of the Three Fortunae of the three temples, it is the one closest to the Porta Collina": I. D. Rowland, *Vitruvius: Ten Books on Architecture* (Cambridge 1999) 48. This may refer to a temple of Fortuna Primigenia vowed in 204 by P. Sempronius Sophus before the battle of Croton with Hannibal and dedicated on the Quirinal hill by Quintus Marcius Ralla in 194 B.C. See Livy, 29.36.8, 34.53.5.

116. In the Acts of Santa Susanna (Acta Ss., p. 632) this piazza is indicated in front of the *Statio ad duas Domos* where there rose the church of Santa Susanna. See Duchesne 1916–1917, 33–35. In the *Excerpta* 60 (see below, n. 118) the piazza is indicated after the church of Santa Susanna where there was another church, that of San Gabinus. See C. Hülsen, *Le chiese di Roma* (Rome 1927) 511–512.

117. S.H.A., *Heliogab.* 4.3: "He also established a *senaculum,* or women's senate, on the Quirinal Hill." *Senaculum* denotes a place where senators waited while in session. This name was applied here for the gathering of matrons to give it a quasi-political importance: D. Magie, *The Scriptores Historiae Augustae* II (London 1924) 112, n. 6. S.H.A., *Aurel.* 49.6: "He had planned to restore to the matrons their senate, or rather *senaculum,* with the provision that those should rank first therein who had attained to priesthoods with the senate's approval." A. Pasqui, "Antico edificio riconosciuto

per la sede del Senaculum mulierum," *NSc* 1914, 141–144, identified the remains of an ancient structure found near the via XX Settembre, 38.5 meters from the corner of the via di Porta Salaria as the *senaculum.* Two female statues (headless) and two columns were recovered (all now in the Museo Nazionale delle Terme?). Cf. the *senaculum* near the porta Collina mentioned by Fest., 347.

118. Valentini and Zucchetti IV, 421–422: the *Excerpta* are contained in a codex in the Biblioteca Marciana in Venice, nr. 3453. It was said that this was a transcription of Leto himself as he was guiding a stranger through the monuments of Rome, beginning at the amphitheater, considered the center of the city, and passing to the Roman forum and the areas adjacent to it, the forums of Nerva and Trajan, the Pantheon, the Campus Martius, Santa Maria del Popolo, and the Pincio. It continues on the hills of Rome—the Quirinal, the Viminal, the Esquiline, the Celio, the Aventine, the Palatine, and finally the Capitoline. See also Valentini and Zucchetti I, 196, and De Rossi 1882.

119. Valentini and Zucchetti IV, 428: "Inter collem Quirinalem et [H]ortulorum est locus depressus: ubi nunc est vinea, quae appellatur Pila Tiburtina: prope quam Pilam fuit domus Mar[tia]lis." Martial also had gardens high on the Janiculum hill with views of the Tiber and the Via Flaminia: Mart., 4.64.

120. Valentini and Zucchetti IV, 428: Exeundo a domo Pomponij per dorsum montis Quirinalis, versus septentrionem, sunt duo equi cum statuis marmoreis. Fuerunt missi a Tiridate rege Armeniae ad Neronem imperatorem. Sunt tres statuae marmoreae Constantinorum. Sunt duo statuae marmorae sedentes, cornu copiae manu sinistra tenentes, eae sunt statuae fluminum deorum: significant rerum copiam. Cibele sedens super duobus leonibus turrita quia preest turribus et castris.

A statue of Cybele seated on a single lion was in the collection of the Villa Doria Pamphili as early as 1666 and is believed to have been found at Anzio where the Pamphili owned property: J. Garms, *Quellen aus dem Archiv Doria Pamphilj zum Kunsttätigkeit in Rom unter Innocenz X* (Rome 1972) 341, fol. 30; R. Calza, ed., *Antichità di Villa Doria Pamphilj* (Rome 1977) 93–95, nr. 117 (B. Palma). Palma refers the reader to G. Lugli, "Saggio sulla topografia dell'antica Antium," *RivIstArch* 7 (1940) 153–188, for the discovery, but the Cybele statue is not mentioned. The findspot is not recorded specifically, although according to F. Lombardi, *Anzio antico e moderno: opera postuma* (Rome 1865) 234, "una Cibele, o Giunone Tiria sedente sopra un leone" was found at Anzio. The link between Lombardi's listing of this statue type with the Pamphili is indeed enticing but not assured. The Pamphili statue, however, is unlikely to have been the one on the Quirinal.

121. Mistakenly transcribed as "dextris" by Albertini 1510, fol. D iii r°–v°: P. Murray, *Five Early Guides to Rome and*

Florence (Westmead 1972). For the relationship among the different works concerning the antiquities of Rome after Leto to 1527, see R. Weiss, "Gli studi antiquari in Italia dal dodicesimo secolo al sacco di Roma di 1527," *Rinascimento* 9 (1958) 141–201, esp. 168–174. For a listing and dates of the numerous editions of Leto, see Schudt 1930, 364–367.

122. This house is that of Oliviero Caraffa who had rented it from Francesco Orsini *in Agone* (now the Palazzo Braschi): see Valentini and Zucchetti IV, 428, n. 5; Lanciani 1990 I, 106, and Hülsen 1917, 85–88: this had been the property of Leonardo Boccaccio, and the present vicolo del Boccaccio still recalls this ownership.

123. The Quirinal was a chain of separate *colles* linked by saddles lower than the summits but higher than the valleys separating the ridges of both the Viminal to the south and the Pincio to the north. See J. Poucet, "L'importance du term <collis> pour l'étude du développement urbain de la Rome archaïque," *AntCl* 36 (1967) 101–115.

124. Fulvio 1513, fol. H i. r°:

Haud longe mons clatrae et apollinis eminet altus . . .
Concava vallis ubi clamosi more theatri extat
In qua lascivo floralia rustica motu scorta celebrabunt
populo spectante togato.

(Not far off towers the lofty mountain of Clatra and Apollo. . . . There remains a hollow valley like a noisy theater in which prostitutes will celebrate naughtily floral rituals with a rustic dance, with the toga-wearing population looking on.)

125. It had been believed that Publius Victor was the pseudonym of the Neapolitan humanist Giano Aulo Parrasio, who published in 1503 or 1504 for the first time a catalogue of the fourteen regions (derived from the *Notitia* compiled by Leto) entitled *De regionibus Urbis Romae libellus aureus* and attributed to P. Victor. See Valentini and Zucchetti I, 201, and Burns 1988, 23. Jacks 1990, 456, however, believed that not Parrasio but Bernardo Rucellai may have invented this fictitious author, although Ermolao Barbaro has six references to P. Victor in his *Castigationes Plinianae*, written in Rome in the years 1490 to 1492: see Ferrary 1996, 140, n. 13. Later publications would attribute this regionary catalogue to Fabius Victor, Paulus Victor, or P. Aurelius Victor: Valentini and Zucchetti I, 203. Flavio Biondo's *Roma Instaurata* I, 18 (written between 1444 and 1446) records finding in Monte Cassino an (illustrated?) manuscript, *Urbis Romae descriptio,* which he attributed to Sextus Rufus and identified as an example of the *Regiones urbis Romae* discovered in 1436 in Speyer and copied (*Oxford, Bodl.* 19854, formerly *Canon. misc. lat.* 378) by Pietro Donato, bishop of Padua: R. Sabbadini, *Le Scoperte dei Codici Latini e Greci ne' Secoli XIV e XV* (Florence 1905) i, 119–120, and

Ferrary 1996, 140, n. 14. See Valentini and Zucchetti I, 200, and Scaglia 1964, 153, n. 94, who suggested that the Monte Cassino codex was illustrated—Donato's signature on the codex copied in Speyer states it was "cum picturis": Scaglia 1964, 153, n. 95. It was reprinted numerous times, such as in the 1558 publication of *Reipublicae Romanae commentariorum libri tres* of *Sexti Rufi V.C. De Regionibus Urbis liber* by Onofrio Panvinio. Both names, Publius Victor and Sextus Rufus, are used as authors of this *Regionary,* although by the nineteenth century they were seen to be merely amplifications of the more ancient and genuine regionary catalogues. See Valentini and Zucchetti I, 206. Note that Ligorio possessed a manuscript of this regionary (*Cod. Vat. lat.* 3427), which was used by Panvinio in 1553 and later passed into the possession of Fulvio Orsini: Valentini and Zucchetti I, 204–205; Ferrary 1996, 140–142.

126. Fulvio 1527, published by March 1527 (just before the publication of Calvo's plan) and a few weeks before the sack of Rome in which he and the almost eighty-year-old Calvo perished. Fulvio's work was imitated by three popular antiquarian works in Rome: Marliani 1534 (improved in a Roman edition of 1544 [*Urbis Romae Topographia*] and reprinted numerous times down to the eighteenth century); Fauno 1548 (frequently reprinted down to 1735); Mauro 1556 (reprinted in 1558 and 1562 and bound with Aldrovandi 1556, a pocket guide to ancient statues preserved in contemporary Roman collections). See Schudt 1930, 370–375, 387; Mandowsky and Mitchell 1963, 19; and S. Tomasi Velli, "Gli antiquari intorno al Circo Romano, riscoperta di una topologia monumentale antica," *AnnPisa* 20 (1990) 61–168, esp. 88–98. Of interest is Pirro Ligorio's invective towards Fauno, whom he called "il maestro sciocco," and Mauro, who was referred to as Fauno's "discipulo" (*Cod. Ottob. lat.* 3373, fol. 3v). See R. Weiss, "Andrea Fulvio Antiquario Romano," *AnnPisa* 28 (1959) 1–44. A summary of the study of Roman archaeology before Fulvio is R. Weiss, "Il primo Rinascimento e gli studi archeologici," *Lettere Italiane* 11 (1959) 89–94. See A. Momigliano, "Ancient History and the Antiquarian," *JWarb* 13 (1950) 285–315, and Hackens 1961, 135–136, nn. 28–30 for specific references.

127. Calvo 1527; a 1556 edition gives the name "Antonij de Bubalo." See C. Scaccia Scarafoni, *Le Piante di Roma* (Rome 1939) 21–22, pl. 1, and P. N. Pagliara, "La Roma antica di Fabio Calvo: Note sulla cultura antiquaria e architettonica," *Psicon* 8–9 (1976) 65–87. Calvo, a learned physician from Ravenna, honored by Raphael in whose house he lived, surely collaborated with Raphael's never-completed project to make a graphic reconstruction of the ancient city of Rome, and it is from this research that the *Simulachorum* derives. For the evidence of Raphael's project, see Goltzio 1936, 82–92, and of his devotion to Calvo, who was perhaps a guiding force of this project, see Goltzio 1936, 282. The schematic and simplified character of Calvo's

Roman topography seems to have been, according to Burns 1988, 39–40, a desire "to represent Rome as a late antique artist might have done."

128. On Bufalini and his plan, see F. Ehrle, *Roma al tempo di Giulio III: La pianta di Roma di Leonardo Bufalini del 1551, riprodotta dall'esemplare esistente nella Biblioteca Vaticana* (Rome 1911); C. Hülsen, *Saggio di bibliografia ragionata delle piante icnografiche e prospettiche di Roma dal 1551 al 1748* (Florence 1933) 38–41; Frutaz 1962, I, 168–170 and pls. 189–221. His plan was made with the aid of a surveying instrument, similar to that described supposedly by Raphael in his *Letter to Leo X* (for this letter, see Goltzio 1936, 82–92) and shown by Bufalini at the bottom of the plan, next to his self-portrait. See Burns 1988, 22.

129. Ligorio was clearly influenced by Bufalini's map, which places the Praetorian camp at the top and the Vatican at the bottom left, as Marliani had done earlier in 1544. This orientation is different from Medieval plans that have north at the bottom, for example, the miniatures by Pietro del Massaio of ca. 1453–1471 and the plan of 1474 by Alessandro Strozzi (Frutaz 1962, pl. 159), all of which seem to be derived from an unknown archetype. Note, however, that the Strozzi plan indicates the position of the *horti Sallustiani,* while the slightly earlier plans of Massaio do not. It is argued persuasively by Scaglia 1964 that the prototype of Strozzi's plan goes back to *Roma instaurata,* which indeed discusses the location of the *horti Sallustiani* (p. 171).

130. *Paradosse di Pyrrho Ligori Napolitano: Il primo libro delle Antichità di Pyrrho Ligori Napolitano nel quale paradossamente confuta la comune oppinione sopra varii et diversi luoghi della città di Roma,* a work composed of two opuscules, the first entitled *Libro di M. Pyrrho Ligori napolitano, delle antichità di Roma, nel quale si tratta de' circi, theatri, et anfiteatri* (Venice 1553):

Fol. 2 v°: Il terzo circo era alla porta Collina dentro le mura, à canto à gli horti di Salustio, là dove hoggidi si vede uno obelisco in terra, intagliato a caratteri Hierogliphici. Et se bene io non posso affermare [non ne havendo più che tanto] che questo havesse forma di circo murato con gran fabrica; tuttavia per lo spatio che quivi si vede et per l'historie che ne parlano, parmi d'esser assai chiaro, che cotal luogo serviva al corso de' cavalli et de' givochi Apollinari . . . ; fol. 3 v°: Eravi di più ancora il nono circo, chiamato da P. Vittore il Circo di Flora, perche vi si facevano i Florali; et questo era su 'l colle Quirinale, et secondo la commune opinione, tra la vigna stata de i signori Carrafi et che hora è dell' illustrissimo Hippolito secondo Cardinal di Ferrara, et quella del Boccacio che è al riscontro (Hackens 1961, 138, n. 38).

(The third circus was at the porta Collina inside the walls, next to the gardens of Sallust, where today one sees an obelisk lying on the ground, carved with hieroglyphic characters. It may well be, although I cannot be sure [not

having anything more than this obelisk] that this place once took the shape of a walled circus with large constructions; yet by the space that one sees there and by documents pertinent to it, it appears to me to be quite clear that such a place served as a racecourse for horses and for the games of Apollo . . . There was even still a ninth circus, called by P. Victor the Circus of Flora, because the Floralia were played there. This was on the Quirinal hill, and according to common opinion, it is acknowledged to have been between the vigne of the Carafi [today it is of the most illustrious Hippolito, second Cardinal of Ferrara], and that of Boccacio.)

131. See Madonna 1980, 257–271. Ligorio's alphabetical dictionary of antiquities comprises fifty-one "libri" that are preserved among manuscripts in libraries in Oxford, Paris, Naples, and Turin: see Mandowsky and Mitchell 1963, 35, and Vagenheim 1987, 267–268. The first copies date to the seventeenth century: one executed on the orders of Cassiano Dal Pozzo, another for Cardinal Barberini, and a third for Queen Christina of Sweden. Fourteen volumes copied by various hands for Christina of Sweden are in the Vatican Library (*Cod. Ottob. lat.* 3364–3377), and part of these was published in *De re vehiculari* by J. Schefferus (Johannes Scheffer) in 1671: see Vagenheim 1987, 252–253, and Mandowsky and Mitchell 1963, 38. For a listing of all the Ligorian manuscripts, see n. 29 above, and Vagenheim 1987.

132. *Cod. Ottob. lat.* 3374, fol. 261 v°: TEMPLUM FLORAE, cioe il tempio di Flora Dea delli Fiori à cui si sacrificava et si facevano i giuochi Florali sul colle Quirinale fu in quella parte della Valle che si volge alla parte settentrionale nella parte piu alta soprastatite [sic] al circo d'essa Flora situato eminentemente del quale infino ai giorni nostri erano rimasti i vestigi della Testa d'esso tempio d'opera laterizia incrostato di marmo, et nell'edificar de giardini del Sig. Hippolito Cardinal di Ferrara sono finiti di guastare ogni memoria, et del Circo et della particella del Tempio nel vero, come cose caduche, ne più buone ad uso alcuno. (Templum Florae, that is the temple of Flora, goddess of flowers, to whom sacrifices were given and games were played, the Floralia, on the Quirinal hill. It was in a valley that faced north into, and at a higher level than, the circus. This temple of Flora, situated prominently even up to our day had remains at the head of the valley of brickwork encrusted with marble. But with the building of the gardens by Hippolito, Cardinal of Ferrara, every memory of it has been lost, and of the Circus and of the remaining part of the temple; in truth, as a decaying object, it is no longer of any use.)

133. Hülsen 1917, 87.

134. R. Lanciani, "Il Panorama di Roma delineato da Antonio van der Wyngaerde circa l'anno 1560," *BullCom* 23 (1895) 81–109, esp. 105–106, n. 34; Lanciani 1990 III, 234; Talamo 1998, 127; Ligorio in *Cod. Paris. ital.* 1129, fol. 335: Nella regione Altasemita era il circo da fare i giuochi

florali il quale luogo tutto ad un tempo è stato disordinato della forma sua che vi rimaneva col suo tempio rotondo in una testa del circo, che per essere in una valle del colle è stato ripieno del terreno cavato dalla via pia Nomentana in maniera che ogni memoria è sparita da ogni parte all'antiche memorie. (In the region of the Alta Semita was the circus for the games of the Floralia. The entire area at one time had been transformed from its original shape where once had been a round temple at the head of the circus. The valley had been filled by soil excavated from the via Nomentana in such a way that every memory of any of the ancient remains has been lost.) For criticism by Ligorio of the porta Pia, see Coffin 1964, 191–210, esp. 198.

135. The 1561 plan was designated by Ligorio himself, as well as several of his contemporaries, as "Roma grande" in contrast to the small plan of 1553 (a bird's-eye view of Rome showing antique features based on the regionaries of Publius Victor and Sextus Rufus). Ligorio was to abandon his reliance on the above regionaries for his 1561 plan for, according to *Cod. Ottob. lat.* 3368, s.v. Ferrara, Pomponius Laetus and Flavio Biondo "non conobbero neanche i colli di Roma" (knew not even the hills of Rome).

The 1553 plan was essentially a pictorial supplement to his *Paradosse* of the same year: the only publication during the lifetime of Ligorio (issued in only this single edition) that displayed his wealth of classical knowledge, which is otherwise preserved in various manuscripts. See A. Schreurs, "Das antiquarische und das kunsttheoretische Konzept Pirro Ligorios," *KölnJb* 26 (1993) 57–82, esp. 74–76. The *Paradosse* of 1553 was written in response to opinions published by Marliani 1544, in which Marliani reacted against the innovations of Ligorio, who is hidden under the pseudonym of Strepsiades (a character of ridicule in Aristophanes' *Clouds*) and by L. Fauno in *De antiquitatibus Urbis Romae ex antiquis novisque auctoribus excerptis,* published in Venice in 1549: Vagenheim 1987, 271–272. See also G. Vagenheim, "La Falsification chez Pirro Ligorio," *Eutopia* 3 (1994) 67–113, esp. 76–77; Ferrary 1996, 84–86. The manuscript version of the *Paradosse* is found in the Paris codex: Vagenheim 1987, 272.

Note that Ligorio was unable to take advantage of perhaps the most useful information for the study of Roman topography—the fragments of the Severan marble plan—which were not discovered until 1562: Valentini and Zucchetti I, 50; Lanciani 1990 II, 208; III, 222; G. Carettoni, A. M. Colini, L. Cozza, and G. Gatti, *La Pianta Marmorea di Roma antica* (Rome 1960). Eight years later, the publication of Ligorio's large plan was seen by contemporaries as an achievement unmatched by previous undertakings: Castagnoli 1952, 102, n. 9.

136. It is possible that Ligorio based the round shape of the Temple of Venus in the Gardens of Sallust on a coin, as he (mistakenly) did for the Temple of Mars Ultor in the Forum of Augustus, despite the physical remains visible in his day that indicated an octastyle peripteral temple. See I. Campbell, "Pirro Ligorio and the Temples of Rome on Coins," in R. W. Gaston, ed., *Pirro Ligorio Artist and Antiquarian* (Milan 1988) 93–106, esp. 100–101. There are seven large codices by Ligorio filled with drawings of coins and medals, often accompanied by extensive commentaries. Three are in Naples: BNN XIII.B.1 (Greek and East Hellenistic); XIII.B.5 (Roman before Caesar); XIII.B.6 (Caesar to Byzantine). Four in Turin: AST (Archivio di Stato, Turin) J.a.II.6 (Vol. 19: "Fameglie Romane" up to Augustus); J.a.II.8 (Vol. 21: Tiberius to Commodus); J.a.II.9 (Vol. 22: Elagabalus to period of the Thirty Tyrants); J.a.II.15 (Vol. 27: Non-Roman coins).

137. Boissard 1597, 114: Inde sub Quirinalis radices progrediendum est, donec venies sub hortos Carpenses, ubi plurimae sunt camerae et fornices obscuri et longo ordine producti: hos nonnulli volunt esse officinas, in quibus conficiebatur et elaborabatur minium: alij malunt eum locum assignare habitaculis meretricum quae eo se recipiebant tempore Floralium ludorum qui celebrabantur in circo Florae fornicibus his adiacente: nihilominus constat officinas minii prope hunc circum exstitisse (Hackens 1961, 141, n. 56). (From there one ought to proceed along the foot of the Quirinal until you come beneath the Carpensine gardens where there are many vaults and shaded arcades and arches drawn out in a long line. Some want these to be factories in which cinnabar was manufactured and worked. Others prefer to assign this place to the residences of prostitutes who betook themselves there during the time of the Floral Games which were celebrated in the Circus of Flora adjacent to these arches. In any case, it is established that there existed workshops for cinnabar in this vicinity. [D. Burgess.])

138. An engraving of 1619 by Giovannoli shows large blind arches supporting the northern wing of the Sforza palace, and these are identified as remains of the Cerchio di Flora: Hülsen 1917, 47, fig. 32.

139. Donati 1638, 365, 532. The date of 1617 derives from an inscription found at the corner of the Quattro Fontane, reproduced by G. Vasi, *Delle magnificenze di Roma antica e moderna* (Rome 1758) Bk. X, vol. 4, p. (XXVII).

Donati 1638, 365: Caeterum Tiburtinae pilae, in regione septima viae latae, finitimus erat Circus Florae, in regione Altae Semitae. Erat hic circus in valle media inter Quirinalem et Pincium eiusque caveam et vestigia sedilium subiecta aedibus Barberinis vidimus aliquot ante annis antequam ea vallis novis aedificiis impleretur. Immo veteres substructionum reliquiae quibus fulta eius palatii moles Septentrionem versus fontem erigit, cryptoporticus, muríque arcuati erant, aut ego fallor, ad gradus exterioresque circi porticus sustinendas. (Moreover, the Circus of Flora was adjacent to the Tiburtine pillar, on a broad road in the seventh district in the area of the Alta Semita. This Circus was in the middle of a valley between the Quirinal and the Pincio, and we have seen its hollow and the vestiges of seats under the buildings of the Barberini. This valley was filled in with new buildings some years previously. Indeed, there are old remains of foundations by which the mass of this palace, propped up, rose toward the northern fountain, there was a cryptoporticus, and there were walls of niches and galleries of the Circus which had to be supported toward the exterior stairs. [Translation by D. Burgess.])

Donati 1638, I.4 c. 12 p. 399: Aucti horti adiacentes (from the Quirinal palace); obstabat obiectus collis, subiecta vallis. Asportantes multorum manus ille secutus decrevit in planitiem: vallicularum replevit iniecta et aggesta humus, cui sustinendae directa ingenti mole substructio est. In fine hortorum as remittendas interdum curas adiuncta domus. Horti vero aequata planitie iam in immensum excurrunt" (Jordan and Hülsen, 395, n. 2: according to Hülsen, the "vallicula" is precisely where the modern Quirinal tunnel stands). (The adjacent gardens were expanded. A nearby hill stood before and a valley beneath. The successor decreed that the hands of many men be bringing in [dirt?] for a level space. And dirt, heaped up and thrown in, filled up the little valley, for supporting this there is a substructure arranged with a huge mass. On the border of the gardens an adjoining house meant that these works had to sometimes be abandoned. The gardens, with a very level plain, run along now to great extent. [Translation by D. Burgess.])

140. Nardini 1666 (1988) 189: Sotto nella valle, che piazza Grimana si dice, fu il circo di Flora. (Below in the valley, which is called the piazza Grimani, was the circus of Flora.) See also Venuti 1824, I, V, 156, who continued to promote this view.

141. Nardini 1666 (1988), II, 93–94. See also Donati 1638, 335. The shape of the large valley appears to have changed over the years, perhaps as a result of large-scale earth movings, several of which are known, but others that probably have gone unrecorded. The 1544 plan by Marliano (Frutaz, 1962, plan XII, pl. 21) as well as that by Oporino of 1551 (Frutaz 1962, plan XV, pl. 24) show the head of this valley (at the east) not rounded but wedge shaped. Panvinio's 1565 plan (Frutaz 1962, plan XX, pl. 35) shows a rather undefined valley, yet he reconstructs within it a circus with long, straight sides and a half-round end, probably following Ligorio's plan of 1552 (Fig. 2.38) and his later reconstruction of 1561 (Fig. 2.40), which shows a definite curving head at the end of the valley. Cartaro's 1576 plan (Fig. 2.2) reveals a definite circus shape, but like his predecessors, it is identified not as a circus but rather as the "Horti Salustiani." Perhaps the earliest identification of the large valley between the Pincio and Quirinal hills as a circus is in a codex entitled *Horti Barberini Quirinales illustrati,* according to C. Cecamore, "Una

pianta della VI Regione augustea nel codice Barberiniano Latino 1950," *BullCom* 93 (1989–1990) 53, possibly a copy after an original by Donati 1638, who uses virtually identical words to describe this valley. Furthermore, a plan in this codex (fol. 3) shows by dotted lines the extent and shape of this circus, identified as *Circus Hortorum Sallustianorum,* as well as that of the *Circus Florae* to the west (below on this plan). The latter is of interest, for this Circus of Flora is rotated 90 degrees with respect to earlier and contemporary plans. According to Cecamore (p. 54), this new orientation is probably the result of the identification of ancient structures near the piazza Barberini as those of a circus. Blaeu's later 1663 plan (Frutaz 1962, plan XIX, pl. 63) likewise identifies the valley between the Pincio and Quirinal as the "Circus Sallustii." Where earlier plans had added a circus or hippodrome around the obelisk on the Pincio, Blaeu's shows neither obelisk nor circus/hippodrome but inexplicably includes an obelisk in the valley. In fact, Blaeu's drawing corresponds so closely with Nardini's observations that they must be related. It is possible that Blaeu was aware of Nardini's views before their publication in 1666, and these influenced his placement of the "Circus Sallustii," complete with Pincio obelisk, within the large valley. Grimal 1969, 250, mistakenly reported that the hippodrome in the valley is that referred to as the Circus of Flora by the humanists and that this is likely to be a garden hippodrome of the 1st century A.D.

142. P. Rolli and B. van Overbeke, *Degli avanzi dell'antica Roma* (London 1739) 176; F. Ficoroni, *Vestigie e rarità di Roma antica* (Rome 1744) 128: Rovine d'edificij non rimangono nel Quirinale, se non che alcune nel declivio dopo il giardino Barberini e la chiesa della Madonna della Vittoria, le quali possono appartenere al Circo di Flora, e principiano orbicolari nel basso della valle col proseguimento delle mura. (Ruins of buildings do not remain on the Quirinal, except for some on the slopes following the gardens of the Barberini, and the church of the Madonna della Vittoria. These ruins could belong to the Circus of Flora where the curving parts begin at the bottom of the valley and continue to the city ["Servian"] wall.)

143. Becker 1843, I, 673–675: Becker questioned that the walls on both sides of the valley were for a circus.

144. Jordan and Hülsen I, 3, 433–434. Although Hülsen had spoken against the existence of a circus, the idea of an actual circus rather than a garden hippodrome was included in Kiepert and Hülsen 1912. As pointed out by Nash 1957, 247–248, a circus here is impossible, given that there would have been a drop of 18.5 meters in the level of the ground from east to west.

145. Note that the large valley was seldom called the Circus of Flora, save for the indication by Bufalini in 1551 (Fig. 2.15D) that this was the place for the "Ludi Florales

Meretricum nudarum," and the 1618 plan by Greuter (Frutaz 1962, pl. 287), which places the name Temple of Flora in the valley, which takes the shape of a long rectangle.

146. For example, Lugli 1930–1940 III, 332–335; Santangelo 1941, 179; Lugli and Gismondi 1949 show a circus in the valley but using the wall at the Pincio as its northern boundary. The southern boundary is shown as a dotted line running along the lower edge of the Quirinal, for which there is no evidence.

147. The Kiepert and Hülsen 1912 plan as well as *FUR* 9 (Fig. 1.1C) locate this wall incorrectly. It is, as seen by Nash 1957, 247, n. 45, almost parallel to the via Lucullo, displaced about 2° towards the southwest, while Lanciani (*FUR* 9) shows it displaced some 7° towards the southeast.

148. Nash 1957, 297–298.

149. See Nash 1957, 248; Pietrangeli 1977, 46; F. Coarelli, *Guida archeologica di Roma*⁵ (Milan 1989) 223–225. Talamo 1998, 129, believed that a tholos temple of Venus Sallustiana stood at the head of this garden stadium and that in the center flowed a canal fed by the *amnis Petronia*.

150. See Montfaucon 1725, 72, where begins the Roman part of the Italian Diary in which Flaminio Vacca's *Memorie* (Vacca 1594) were used as a guide for his twenty-day tour of Rome; according to Montfaucon, Vacca's work had not yet been made "public." Vacca was buried in Santa Maria Rotunda (the Pantheon) in Rome, his tomb carrying the inscription: Flaminio Vaccae Sculptori Romano, qui in operibus quae fecit, nunquam sibi satis fecit.

151. Vacca 1594, n. 58: [n]ella Vigna di Gabriel Vacca mio Padre, accanto Porta Salara dentro le mura, vi è un fondo, dove si dice gli Orti Salustiani; cavandoci trovò una gran fabrica di forma ovata, con portico attorno ornato di Colonne gialle, lunghe palmi diecidotto scannellate, con capitelli, e basi Corintie; detto ovato aveva quattro entrate con scale, che scendevano in esso al pavimento fatto di mischj con belli scompartimenti, ed a ciascuna di dette entrate vi erano due Colonne di Alabastro Orientale trasparente. Vi trovammo certi condotti sotto a dett'ovato grandi, che vi caminava un uomo in piedi, tutti foderati di lastre di marmi greci, come anche due condotti di piombo longhi dieci palmi l'uno, ed il vano di essi era più di un palmo, con le seguenti lettere NERONIS CLAVDIVS. Vi si trovarono ancora molte medaglie di Gordiano di metallo, e di argento della grandezza d'un quattrino, e quantità di mosaici. Il Cardinale di Montepulciano comprò le Colonne gialle, e ne fece fare la balaustrata alla sua Cappella in S. Pietro Montorio: comprò ancora quelle di Alabastro, una delle quali essendo intera la fece lustrare, e delle altre rotte ne fece fare tavole, e con altre anticaglie le mandò a donare al Re di Portogallo; ma quando furono in alto Mare, l'impetuosa Fortuna, trovandosele in suo dominio, ne fece un presente al Mare.

152. These lead pipes seem to be related by Lanciani 1888, 3, to one found in the villa Verospi, recorded by Lanciani 1879, 437, n. 93: AQVAPINCIANA/DNFLVALENTINIA/NIAVG, and recorded in a letter from Bracci to Lami dated February 5, 1757, in *Nov. lett. ior.* 18, 197, a. 1757; see also Bianchini, *Cod. Veron.* CCCLXII, f. 52.

153. Lanciani 1888. Vatican 3439 is a collection of Ligorian drawings copied from Naples XIII.B.7 and other sources, which were united with other material from Fulvio Orsini (1529–1600: librarian and keeper of the Farnese collections) in the seventeenth century. See Mandowsky and Mitchell 1963, 32 and 140 (dating "between 1564–5 and sometime before 1570"). The drawing discussed measures 23 cm. × 16 cm.

154. Lanciani 1888, 4.

155. Lanciani 1888, 5, read "venate."

156. Hülsen 1889, 272, n. 3, read "spirae," while Lanciani 1888, 5, did not offer a transcription.

157. According to Lanciani 1888, 5: "vel."

158. A "+" is written near the fifth small column from the top, indicating that the following information concerns the interior.

159. According to Lanciani 1888, 5, eight more words follow, not easily decipherable, but according to Hülsen 1889, 272, n. 3, this reads: "Etiam solum. a pavimento ascensus tribus gradibus circum circa."

160. G. B. De Rossi, "Delle sillogi epigrafiche dello Smezio e del Panvinio," *Annali dell'Instituto di corrispondenza archeologica* 34 (1862) 220–244. Lanciani 1888, 3–11. In 1558 Panvinio printed, without Ligorio's knowledge, his manuscript (*Cod. Vat. lat.* 3427) of Publius Victor's *Regionary,* which Panvinio (1529–1568) seems to have obtained five years before from Agustín (1517–1586): Ferrary 1996, 141–142. See Burns 1988, 24–25, and Mandowsky and Mitchell 1963, 19, 29–34, for Ligorio's associates in Rome, including Panvinio and Agustín. It is possible that the drawing is also by the hand of Panvinio, who copied an original by Ligorio: see Hülsen 1889, 270–274. I thank Ingrid Rowland for aiding in the transcription of this passage.

161. Hülsen 1889, 271, proposed that a large part of *Cod. Vat. lat.* 3439 was created by Panvinio for his private use. See Vagenheim 1987, 208.

162. The Paris manuscript had passed to Saint-Germain-des-Prés in 1718 and then to the Bibliothèque Nationale in 1795–1796. It includes books 1–4, 6–7 and is the only one of all the preserved Ligorian manuscripts to transmit books 4 and 7. The first book is dedicated to Ippolyto D'Este II (1618–1714: therefore, the dedication cannot be by Ligorio, who died in 1583), as is that of the first book of the Naples manuscript. Ligorio's script is categorized in three "hands" by the letters a, b, c. In the Paris manuscript, hand "b" dominates, including fols. 307–310, with which we are concerned: Vagenheim 1987, 271–273. See also Castelli 1988, 55. According to Riemann 1950, 1564, T. Ashby indicated there

is another unpublished drawing in Berlin, Kunstgewerbe-mus., nr. 3832.

163. *Cod. Paris. ital.* 1129, fol. 309: In una testa della piazza, o vogliamo dire, Foro Sallustiano fu un Tempio di cinquantadui piedi (di) diametro con tutto il perittero e circuitioni di colonne, le quali erano di dui piedi grosse del marmo caristio gialle svenate di alcune macchie rosse, erano striate il portico era di vano sei piedi. I muri dentro del tempio era grosso tre piedi senza le parastase (a incasso?) delle colonne che sportavano in fuori un quarto di palmo. Le spire delle colonne ciò è basi, non haveano il plinto o vogliamo dire zocco, erano alte un piede senza intagli, dell' ordine composito esser i capitelli i quali erano alti dui piedi e un quarto, i fusi delle colonne piedi deciotto manco un quarto di piede. I nicchi di fori erano larghi tre piedi e mezzo, quelli di dentro al tempio piedi dui e mezzo questi erano ornati di colonnette picciole dui terzi di piede del marmo alabastrino, che posavano sopra a certi modelletti e ornavano essi nicchi, de quali non havemo demostrata altezza alcuna per esser stati già rovinati. Per li tempi passati e quel che v'era remesto sotto delle rovine ce ha insegnato la forma di quanto ho scritto e demostrato in questa pianta circolare, era di dentro e di fuori incrostato di tavole sottili di alebastro di porphidi, serpentini e d'altri marmi come anche era fatto il suo piano del pavimento suo di fuori e di dentro del Tempio in cui s'ascendeva per tre gradi che attorno tutto il circuivano. certamente opera picciola ma di grandissima spesa e di vaghezza mirabile. di cui fanno inventione nei buoni testi scritti a penna Publio Vittori e Sesto Rufo. L'architravi e le cornici sue tutte per altri tempi furono portati via. Fu trovata una inscrizzione che diceva VENERI HORTORVM SALLVSTANORVM C SALLVSTIVS DVRDVS AEDITVVS D D Furono gli horti prima fatti da Sallustio che scrisse le cose di Catelina, e dopo dalla fameglia mantenuti e nobilitati dall'imperatori. I thank my colleague Magda Ferretti for discussing this passage and for aiding in its transcription.

164. Lanciani 1888; Hülsen 1889, 272, n. 4. Hülsen 1889, 272, n. 3, also pointed out that on Lanciani's plan between the cella and the outer colonnade "statt des unverständlichen Lᴬ PALMI zu berichtigen *4ᵃ palmi.*" Translation of measure-ments: braccio = 0.5836 m.; palmo (romano = 0.2234 m.; 10 palmi = 1 canna); piede (antico = 0.297 m.): from H. Wurm, *Baldassarre Peruzzi: Architekturzeichnungen* (Tübingen 1984) XV, who refers the reader to two essays on the subject: W. Lotz, "Sull'unità di misura nei disegni di architettura nel Cinquecento," *Bolletino del Centro Internazionale di Studi di Architettura* 22 (1979) 223–232; H. Günther, "Die Rezeption eines antiken Maßes in der Renaissance," *Sitzungsberichte der Kunsthistorischen Gesellschaft Berlin* (Dez.) 1982.

165. Riemann 1950, 1564, pointed out this discrepancy, although without further explanation.

166. Vacca 1594, n. 38: "I don't recall if this temple was round or oval in plan."

167. See Castagnoli 1952, 100–101, fig. 3, who discussed the plan of another round building in *Cod. Vat. lat.* 3439, fol. 25r, which is perhaps mistakenly identified by Panvinio as the temple of Isis and Serapis.

168. *CIL* VI.5, 667. The condemnation of Ligorio as a falsifier of inscriptions goes back to his contemporary, Agustín: Vagenheim 1987, 253, and n. 182.

169. TEMPLUM VENERIS HORTORUM SALUSTIA-NORUM. Fu ancor esso piccolo Tempio ma ornatissimo tutto del marmo pario con colonne striate bianchissime dell'Ordine Corintio di forma rotonda col peryptero attorno, cioè circondato di portico come havemo posto nel disegno delli Horti Sallustiani lo quale era un poggio soprastante al Foro Sallustiano in testa della Valle verso l'Oriente (that is, Ligorio's 1561 plan of Rome [Fig. 2.40]) dove appunto havemo veduto cavare delle sue rovine pretio-sissime et d'ammirabile diligentia lavorate, et quivi in circa fu trovata questa dedicazione, la quale hebbe Monsignore Agnelo Colotio (Angelo Colocci [1474–1549] president of the Roman Academy) in una base di marmo di quelli dedi-corono à Diana, che havea un'altro Tempio nelli medesimi horti ci vi era quello delle Ninfe (the vestibule on the slopes of the Quirinal), che ancor si vede in un cantone d'opera laterizia.

Note that Ligorio mentioned only columns of white marble, not yellow as in *Cod. Vat. lat.* 3439, fol. 28r.

170. For the discovery by Fulvio, see Fauno 1548 (1552) 122; and A. Manuzio, *Orthographiae Ratio* (Venice 1566) 427. Montfaucon's 1725, 157, translation is: "M. Aurelius Pacorus, and M. Cocceius Stratocles, Overseers of the Temple of Venus, in the Salustian Gardens, dedicated the Marble Pavement, and what it stands on, to the Goddess," believing that "Basem" means the foundations under the pavement.

171. For references to its discovery in the gardens of Angelo Colocci or near the church of Santa Susanna, see *CIL* VI.4, 30699. The belief that the brick vestibule was dedicated to the Nymphs was due to reported discoveries of three statues of the nurses of Zeus, including Amalthea with a goat and the infant god, and two others pouring water. Also discovered in this same area was a statue base inscribed with the name Minerva: *Cod. Paris. ital.* 1129, fol. 310. Note that a statue of Minerva, wearing an aigis (lacking head, arms and feet), was found in 1885 during construction of a house on the via Quintino Sella, under the Palazzo Moroni: *NSc* 1885, 42; *CAR* II-F, 89 II, and Jordan and Hülsen I, 3, 429, n. 99. I am unable to securely identify this statue.

172. *CIL* VI.4, 32451.

173. *CIL* VI.4, 32468. Lugli 1957, 240, nrs. 261, 262. Others are cited incorrectly by Pace 1945, 636, n. 7 as *CIL*

VI, 3241, 5667, 324551. See also Lanciani 1888, 11, who also included *CIL* VI.2, 4327; however, this inscription mentions only a temple to Venus, without indicating its location; Hülsen 1889, 270; Platner and Ashby 1929, 552. Note that the hill on which the villa Patrizi was built is partially created from earth excavated near the Aurelian wall and therefore objects found there could be associated with the gardens of Sallust.

174. See Coffin 1991, 68–69. In 1554 this former bishop of Paris purchased land on the Viminal Hill that included the large exedra and the northern tower of the Baths of Diocletian, which lay opposite the church of Santa Susanna on the Alta Semita (the later [1560] via Pia and the present via XX Settembre). The following year, within these ancient ruins, as depicted by Dupérac in 1577 (Fig. 1.7), formal gardens were planted, and, according to Boissard 1597, pt. 1, p. 90 and pls. 120–131, these were decorated by ancient statues, statuettes, and busts. According to Coffin 1991, 69, the inscription over the entrance portal, *Horti Bellaiani,* recalling to a sixteenth-century visitor the names of ancient gardens such as the *Horti Sallustiani,* may be the first Roman garden since antiquity to be so designated. This inscription mentioning the ancient gardens, therefore, may have carried great significance for this sixteenth-century garden.

175. Gruter 1707, 102, n. 1; B. d'Overbeke, *Les restes de l'ancienne Rome* III (The Hague 1763) 19. Note that during the time of the Severans, the *horti Torquatiani* on the Esquiline became known as the *horti Spei Veteris:* Grimal 1969, 160.

176. The *aeditui* were usually public slaves, some who merely opened and closed doors, others who carried more responsibility. See Strong 1973, 247–264. On the various categories of the *aeditui* and their social standing, see J. Marquardt, *Römisches Staatsverwaltung*[2] 3 (Leipzig 1885) 214–218. The first dialogue of Varro's *Res Rusticae* takes place over dinner at the temple of Tellus at the invitation of L. Fundilius, the *aedituus,* who may well be the individual listed as a member of the *consilium* of the consul Cn. Pompeius Strabo. See *CIL* I[2], 709 and Linderski 1989, 126, n. 96.

177. Ov., *Fast.* 4.871: Collinae proxima portae; Ov., *Rem. Am.* 549: prope Collinam portam. According to Castelli 1988, 53, Livy, 30.38 (ita abundavit Tiberis, ut ludi Apollinares circo inundato extra portam Collinam ad aedem Erucinae Veneris parati sint) seems to contradict himself. He reported that in the year 551 (203 B.C.), when the Tiber had flooded, it was necessary to transfer the Ludi Apollinares to outside the porta Collina near the temple of Erycina. Yet this Erycina temple did not exist until nineteen years *after* that time. Livy is merely specifying, however, the location of these games using contemporary topographical markers, and so there is no contradiction regarding the

foundation and dedication dates of the temple: see O. Gilbert, *Geschichte und Topographie der Stadt Rom im Altertum* III (Leipzig 1890) 91, n. 2. Pace 1945, 636, cited Livy, 22.9: aedes Veneri Erycinae ac deae Menti vovendas esse; 23.30, 23.31 as well as Suet., *Calig.* 7 and *Galb.* 18 as the earliest references. According to App., *BCiv.,* 1.93.428, in 82 B.C. the *aedes Erycinae* is mentioned as the place near where Sulla brutally liquidated the last resistors of Italy, killing 40,000 Samnites (Sanniti), but it is unclear to which temple (the one outside the Colline gate or the one on the Capitoline) Appian refers.

178. Livy, 40, 34.4.

179. Livy, 22.9–10 (vow), 23.30–31 (dedication). Note that Pace 1945, 636, gave the incorrect date of 212 B.C. for the dedication of the Capitoline Venus temple. There are other such errors throughout Pace's work, as noted by Schilling 1982, 257, n. 1.

180. Livy, 23.9.

181. Pace 1945, 636.

182. For the dedications, see, for example, *IGS* 281, 285; *CIL* X, 7253, 7254, 7255, 7257; Pace 1945, 634; Schilling 1982, 247. For the connection of Aeneas to Venus Erycina, see Wilson 1990, 283.

183. Diod., 4.83.6–7. See also J. Serrati, "Garrisons and Grain: Sicily between the Punic Wars," in C. Smith and J. Serrati, eds., *Sicily from Aeneas to Augustus: New Approaches in Archaeology and History* (Edinburgh 2000) 132.

184. Strab., 4.272. See also Diod., 4.83; Tac., *Ann.* 4.43; Suet., *Claud.* 25; cf. Hülsen, *RE* 1907, 103.

185. Pace 1945, 633; Schilling 1982, 237; see also Kienast 1965, 478–489.

186. Inscription on a marble offering table from Herculaneum: R. S. Conway, *The Italic Dialects* I (Cambridge 1897) 82, nr. 87; Pozzuoli inscription: *CIL* X, 8042. See Schilling 1982, 51 and 239. Another inscription from Potentia (*CIL* X, 134) dated to A.D. 210 is also dedicated to Venus Erycina. Note that Pace's 1945, references, 635, nn. 7–9, to these inscriptions are incorrect.

187. *Ov., Fast.* 4.865–900. See Schilling 1982, 91–155, for the cult of the Vinalia. Note that Tiberius in 27 B.C. received the toga virilis on April 23, and on this date in A.D. 22, he and his mother Livia dedicated the "sig(num) Divo Augusto patri ad theatrum Mar(celli)." See also T. P. Wiseman 1998, 16, who pointed out that Venus Lubentina was also honored during the Vinalia festival on April 19 and that like Venus Erycina, this cult stood outside the *agger.*

188. *CIL* I[2], p. 316.

189. Castelli 1988, 53; Wilson 1990, 283–284.

190. The suggestion that Cato must have been responsible for the temple being built *extra pomerium* was made first in *RE* 8A (1955) s.v. Venus 7: V. Erucina extra portam Collinam, 855 (C. Koch). See also Galinsky 1969, 185, and

E. M. Orlin, "Why a Second Temple for Venus Erycina?" *Studies in Latin Literature and Roman History* (*CollLatomus*) 10 (2000) 70–90, who pointed out that the dedication of this temple reaffirmed Senate control over religious matters.

191. Castelli 1988, 53; cf. Ov., *Fast.* 4.865 and Strab., 4.2.5.

192. Ov., *Fast.* 4.873–876.

193. For the possible ceasing of the cult at Erice in the first century A.D., see Wilson 1990, 285.

194. Strab., 6.2.6: ἀφίδρυμα [the Ἀφροδίτη of Eryx] δ' ἐστὶ καὶ ἐν Ῥώμῃ τῆς θεοῦ ταύτης τὸ πρὸ τῆς πύλης τῆς Κολλίνης ἱερὸν Ἀφροδίτης Ἐρυκίνης λεγόμενον, ἔχον καὶ νεὼν καὶ στοὰν περικειμένην ἀξιόλογον. ("There is a reproduction of this goddess in Rome, I mean the temple before the Colline Gate, which is called the temple of Venus Erycina. It is remarkable for its shrine and the surrounding colonnade."): Galinsky 1969, 184. According to Galinsky, the word ἀφίδρυμα means "copy" or "reproduction," but in this context it probably signifies not a direct copy of the architecture but a reproduction of the cult practices and of the image of the goddess from Eryx.

195. G. Cultrera, "Il 'temenos' di Afrodite Ericina e gli scavi del 1930 e del 1931," *NSc* 1935, 294–328.

196. *CIL* VI, 2274 (preserved in the gardens of the Palazzo Barberini): D(is) M(anibus) / C. Stiminius / Heracla / sortilegus / ab Venere Erycina et / Iulia Melanthis / parentes/ Mercuriali / f(ilio) pientiss(imo) / fecerunt / vix(it) ann(os) XIII / m(enses) III d(ies) XX. According to Wiseman 1998, 22, this inscription may be associated with the Three Fortunes whose temples stood *in colle Quirinale*.

197. E. Babelon, *Description historique et chronologique des monnaies de la république romaine* I (Paris 1885) 376, nr. 1; Grueber 1910, 473, nrs. 3830, 3831, 3832, pl. XLVII, 21; Mirone 1918.

198. Grueber 1910, 471, n. 1, pl. XLVII, nr. 18.

199. Ov., *Fast.* 4.865–870. According to Montfaucon 1725, 157, this statue may be recognized in the Vatican (in the corner of the Belvedere court), carrying an inscription: VENERI FELICI SACRUM SALLUSTIA HELPIDUS D.D.

200. Only Santangelo 1941, 138, n. 98, suggested that it represents the temple near the porta Collina in Rome. Pace 1945, 642–644, and n. 6, believed that the temple represented on the coin is round, but Mirone (1918, 193–194, 198) and Wilson (1990, 284) believed it is a tetrastyle temple and is definitely representing the temple in Sicily and not that at Rome.

201. Lanciani 1888. See A. Nibby 1838–1841, II (Rome 1839) 355–356, who believed Vacca's description was that of the vestibule in the piazza Sallustio.

202. *NSc* 1924, 61–62 (G. Mancini).

203. *AnnEpig* 1924, 34, nr. 118.

204. *NSc* 1924, 62 (G. Mancini).

205. See *RE* 15 (Stuttgart 1955) 701–702, s.v. Venerii servi (H. Habermehl), and *RE* 15 (Stuttgart 1955) 855–856, 873, s.v. Venus III 7: V. Erucina extra portam Collinam, and III 22b: V. Hortorum Sallustianorum (C. Koch).

206. DeGrassi 1963. Schilling 1982, 261, wondered what function a freedwoman would serve in the temple. He identified C. Stiminius Heracla, *sortilegus ab Venere Erucina,* as probably pertaining to the cult in the temple near the porta Collina because of the foreign surname, and he cited another inscription *CIL* VI, 32468: T. Claudius Apollinaris minister al(mae) Veneris ex ho(rtis) Sallustian(is).

207. Pugliese Carratelli 1979, 478–479.

208. Pugliese Carratelli 1979, 479.

209. I. C. Love, "A Preliminary Report of the Excavations at Knidos, 1972," *AJA* 77 (1973) 424.

210. I. C. Love, "A Preliminary Report of the Excavations at Knidos, 1971," *AJA* 76 (1972) 402. Note also that a large crack in the podium was filled by mortar perhaps at a much later period, for the line of this fault appears in Byzantine structures northwest of the podium. See also I. C. Love, "Excavations at Knidos, 1971," *TürkArkDerg* 20.2 (1973) 97–142, esp. 105–109.

211. H. Bankel, "Knidos: Der hellenistischen Rundtempel und sein Altar. Vorbericht," *AA* 1997, 51–71. I thank B. S. Ridgway for this reference.

212. Talamo 1998, 124, fig. 10, nr. 32 (see my Fig. 2.11): "Platea contenuta da muri di sostruzione (tempio di Venere Erycina?)." In his 1850 plan, Canina (Fig. 2.51) depicted an oval building having four entrances near the porta Salaria, which must be his interpretation of Vacca's report of the finding of such a structure in his father's vineyard. Canina's location of it near the porta Salaria may have influenced Lanciani's assertion that the Vacca vineyard lay against the porta Salaria and the placement of his round structure on *FUR* 3 (Fig. 1.1B).

213. La Rocca 1997, 44; see also Coarelli 1996, 335–338, for a discussion of a similar terraced structure in the gardens of Lucullus on the Pincio.

214. Coarelli 1983.

215. Coarelli 1983, 274, fig. 10.

216. For example, Hülsen's incorrect plan is published by Galinsky 1969, 183, and by Castelli 1988, 55, fig. 8.

217. Venuti 1824, 159–160, rightly identified the difference between the porta Salaria of the Aurelian wall and the porta Collina along the via Porta Pia.

218. Note in Ligorio's earlier plan of 1553 that the general location (without the depiction of a structure) of the AED. VENERIS ERYCINA is indicated *inside* the circuit of the Aurelian wall east of the porta Pinciana, and two temples of Fortuna are indicated on the opposite side of this gateway. It seems clear that Ligorio had confused the porta Pinciana—called in his day the porta Collatina—with the porta Collina of the "Servian" wall, near where Vitruvius (3.2.1) reported three temples of Fortune. Furthermore, on this

same plan, the round structure near the two temples of Fortune, usually identified as a temple of the Sun, was believed
at this time by Ligorio to be a temple to Fortune (although
not identified on this plan), thus completing the Vitruvian
triad of temples to this goddess. See C. Burroughs, "Palladio and Fortune: Notes on the Sources and Meaning of the
Villa Rotonda," *Architectura* 18 (1988) 76, fig. 19.

219. Castelli 1988, 53; La Rocca 1997, 43, agreed with
Castelli's placement of Vacca's round building in the
valley.

220. The Verospi also owned an elegant palazzo on the
Corso (nr. 300): see R. Krautheimer, *The Rome of Alexander
VII, 1655–1667* (Princeton, 1988) 22. According to the 1551
Rome plan by Bufalini (Fig. 2.15B), before the ownership by
the Verospi this property was in the possession of Vincenzo
Vittoria (who had a collection of antiquities).

221. Vacca 1594, n. 24 = Nardini 1666 (1988) n. [a].

222. G. Manca di Mores, "Terrecotte architettoniche e
problemi topografici: contributi all'identificazione del tempio di Quirino sul colle Quirinale," *AnnPerugia* 20 (1983–
1983) 340. R. Giordani, "Note sul significato di <iuxta> nel
Liber Pontificalis," in *Vetera Christianorum: Bari, Istituto di
Letteratura cristiana antica* 15 (1979) 203–219. Castelli 1988,
57, pointed out that Piranesi's description of his engraving
of the interior of the vestibule on the Quirinal (Piranesi
1748) states that it is "vicino all'antica Porta Salara" even
though it is some distance from it.

223. Vacca 1594, n. 59 = Fea 1790, 79: Mi ricordo, che il
sig. Carlo Muti nella sua vigna poco lontano dagli Orti Sallustiani, trovò un Fauno maggiore del naturale con un puttino in braccio, ed un vaso grande con Fauni, e Baccanti, che
ballano, con cembali in mano; che oggi sta nel suo giardino.
Trovò anche molte statue ritrovate sparse molto disordinatamente, *le quali si può credere fossero in quella fabrica trovata
nella vigna di mio padre* (my italics); mentre vi si vedono
muraglie piene di nicchie, e che fossero trasportate nella
vigna del sig. Carlo Muti.

224. Lanciani 1906, 159.

225. Lanciani 1897, 417.

226. Venuti 1763 I, 115: Vi (near the "Temple of
Venus") ha osservato (Piranesi) un piccolo avanzo delle sostruzioni, o siano rivestimenti, che erano alle falde (lower
slopes) del Quirinale per assicuare le mura Urbane, anteriori
al nuovo circondario d'Aureliano, che ricorrevano sopra le
medesime falde: questo rimane negli orti della Madonna
della Vittoria verso la Villa Barberini. Altro avanzo delle
medesime sostruzioni consistente in un lungo muraglione
munito di spessi barbacani della cima al fondo si osserva:
questo avanzo rimane nella Villa Mandosi vicino alla Porta
Salara. Fra lo stesso muraglione, e il Circo indicato, era la
via, che conduceva al Foro di Salustio. Vedevasi in questi
Orti, che occupavano ambedue i Colli, un Portico detto
Migliarense: crede il Sig. Piranesi (pag. 148. 109); d'aver
trovato avanzi di questo Portico nella Villa Cesi. (There

[near the "Temple of Venus" Piranesi] observed a small
remnant of the substructures, or perhaps of revetments
that were at the foot of the Quirinal to support the city
wall that ran above these very same slopes before the later
circuit of the Aurelian wall. The remains of substructures
consist of a long wall supplied with thick buttresses from
the top to the bottom. These are in the villa Mandosi near
the porta Salaria. Between this wall and the Circus [the valley between the Quirinal and Pincio] was the street that
went to the forum of Sallust. There was seen in these gardens, that occupied both hills, a Portico called Migliarense,
remains of which, according to Piranesi, were found in the
villa Cesi.)

227. See Montfaucon 1725, 157 who stated that a fluted
transparent alabaster column in the Vatican Library could
be from this temple.

228. Bartoli, *mem.* 33 in Fea 1790, I, 229–230.

229. Lanciani 1888, 3, and *Beschreibung* 3.2 (1838) 378.

230. Hülsen 1889, 271, n. 1. Castelli 1988, 55, agreed
that the Vacca and Bartoli reports must indicate different
buildings.

231. Vitr., *De Arch.* 3.2.2. Wiseman 1998, 22, made the
suggestion that the Venus Erycina was at the northern end
of the *agger* on the Quirinal, while her sister temple, that of
Venus Lubentina, was near its southern end on the Esquiline. If this were the case, Venus Erycina would not have
been in the gardens of Sallust.

232. A. Nibby in Nardini 1666 (1988), 96, n. 1, and *Beschreibung* 3.2 (1838) 576: "Man möchte auf Bäder schliessen."

233. Hülsen 1889, 273, compared Ligorio's round building to fragment 59 of the *Forma Urbis Romae*, which
had been interpreted by H. Jordan, *Forma Urbis Romae*
(Rome 1874) 60, pl. 12, as a *lavachrum*, that is, a small,
private thermal building. Nash 1959, 134–137, demonstrated that this fragment was in fact part of a circular plan
for a temple, that of Minerva Chalcidica in the Campus
Martius, and that the preserved letters "VACH" that had
been read [LA]VACH[RUM] are to be read "[MINER]VA
CH[ALCIDICA]." He was able to give this reading because
of a joining of a small fragment to the plan which indicated
clearly that the inscription began with the letter "M": see
his pl. 33 and *La Pianta Marmorea di Roma Antica* (1959)
97–100, pl. 31. Note that the fragment containing the plan
of this building is lost but was recorded by Bellori, who had
already published it in 1673: I. P. Bellori, *Fragmenta vestigii
veteris Romae* (Rome 1673) 23, pl. 5. It was later "joined" to
the plan by E. Nash, "Porticus Divorum und Serapeum im
Marsfelde," *RM* 18 (1903) 39, pl. 1, placing it next to the
"DIVORUM." Although Nash effectively refuted Hülsen's
premise for the identification of the building as a *lavachrum*,
he left open the question of identifying the *horti Sallustiani*
building as a temple of Venus. See Richardson 1976 and F.
Castagnoli, "Minerva Calcidica," *ArchCl* 12 (1960) 91–95.
Note that the plan of this circular building does not indicate

a colonnade, and so it is difficult to identify it as a tholos or a temple. See also Riemann 1950, 1564, who, following Hülsen, identified this building as a *lavachrum.*

234. Ovid, *Rem. Am.* 549–554.

235. S.H.A., *Gord.* 32, 5–7.

236. See Jacks 1990, 474–480.

237. Piranesi 1748: Tempio di Venere appresso il Circo Apollinare negl'Orti di Sallustio vicino all'antica Porta Salaria; Piranesi 1762, pls. XLI, XLIII. See Venuti 1763, 87, in which Piranesi's 1748 prints (having been reprinted in 1752) were employed. Venuti's descriptions persisted into the nineteenth century, with new editions of his work, such as Venuti 1824, 158–159, and Nibby 1838–1841, I, 356, 647.

III. SCULPTURAL FINDS

1. A. L. Cubberley, ed., *Notes from Rome by Rodolfo Lanciani* (British School at Rome 1988) 1 (= *The Athenaeum,* vol. 2516, January 15, 1876, 96–97): "The Municipal Archaeological Commission decided in 1872 on publishing periodically a Bulletin, intended to keep the public informed of the discoveries made while enlarging the city. After appearing regularly for four years, the *Bulletin* has not yet got through the topographical discoveries made in the last six months of 1872. . . . The difficulty is, that the discovery of today loses its interest tomorrow in the presence of some fresher and more interesting find."

2. R. Lanciani, *NSc* 1886, 230, 272; Visconti 1886.

3. Visconti 1886, 390–392, pls. 14–15.

4. Lanciani 1906, 173–175. Immediately thereafter, A. Furtwängler, "Die neue Niobidenstatue aus Rom," *Sitzungsberichte der philosophisch-philologischen und der historischen Klasse der K.B. Akademie der Wissenschaften zu München* (1907) 208, reported this discrepancy. See also *CAR* II-F 58(I).

5. Ludwig Pollak and Matthew Stewart Prichard visited the villa Spithoever in 1897, where they reportedly saw "fragments of a large deer." These may well be pieces of the hind that were not included among fragments of this sculpture group purchased by Jacobsen in 1888. Perhaps they were not known in 1888, or else they were thought not pertinent. For Pollak's remarks, see Moltesen 1998, 185.

6. Visconti 1886, 299. Cf. fragment of an Artemis-hind group from the via Principe Umberto: Mustilli 1939, 136, pl. LXXXV, 320, nr. 12 (Inv. nr. 923).

7. Jacobsen 1892, nr. 1048/49. See Studniczka 1926, 17, and fig. 8, for the original displaying of the torsos. Jacobsen was in Rome in 1887 and at this time came into contact with Wolfgang Helbig. Helbig became his trusted counselor and for the next decade acted as Jacobsen's agent in the purchasing of these torsos as well as many other antiquities. See Poulsen 1951, 7–8.

8. A. Furtwängler, *Meisterwerke der griechischen Plastik* (Leipzig 1893) 558, A.4. Furtwängler later accepted that the two figures belong together, remarking to Studniczka that the group dated to the late Hellenistic period and that the Artemis, which he had believed was Praxitelean, was a copy after an earlier work: Studniczka 1926, 143.

9. Studniczka 1926, 22–23, figs. 10, 11 (showing both arms of Artemis). See *CAR* II-F 58(I, c), which lists incorrectly a "statua acefala di fanciulla che corre (Niobide)."

10. Studniczka 1926, 1.

11. Shortly before World War I Eugen von Mercklin and Hans Nachod measured the depth of this still-existing basement at the request of Studniczka: Studniczka 1926, 5. L. Savignoni, "IV. Roma. Nuove scoperte nella città e nel suburbio: Regione VII," *NSc,* 1901, 247, reported that this excavation reached 13.30 meters below the modern street level, but according to Studniczka (who cited incorrectly G. Gatti as the author of the above report), this measurement seems to have been calculated from the basement level. Worth noting is the earlier report in Studniczka 1904, 224, giving a depth of 15 meters below the present ground level, which Studniczka did not address in his 1926 publication.

12. The definitive analysis of the 1901–1902 excavations occurred twenty-five years later (Studniczka 1926), but brief reports appeared earlier: Studniczka 1904; F. Studniczka, "Verlorene Bruchstücke Iphigeniengruppe zu Kopenhagen," *AA* 22 (1907) cols. 273–275; F. Studniczka, "Artemis und Iphigenie: Marmorgruppe der Ny Carlsberg Glyptothek, gefunden in den Gärten des Sallust in Rom" in *Festblatt zum Winckelmannstage 1912 für das Archäologische Seminar der Universität Leipzig* (Leipzig 1912) n.p.n.: three photographs and a single page description only. See also *CAR* II-F 58 (III).

13. Studniczka 1926, 5, 6: there is a discrepancy with the recorded measurements of the width of the chamber.

14. See Moltesen 1998, 181, fig. 5.

15. Studniczka 1926, 2, 20 and pl. 25 (p. 30).

16. The whereabouts of this altar were not known until it appeared in a 1966 auction: Park-Bernet Galleries, New York, *Egyptian, Western, Asiatic, Greek and Roman Antiquities, Pre-Columbian Art, Public Auction Friday January 28, 1966,* 36, nr. 121 (with photograph). For bibliography prior to 1966, see F. Matz, *Ein römisches Meisterwerke: Der Jahreszeitensarkophag Badminton–New York (JdI-EH* 19 [1958]) 41–45, n. 44. It was purchased by the University of Würzburg for the Martin von Wagner-Museums, Würzburg (Inv. nr. H 5056), and was published (dated to the Claudian period) soon thereafter by E. Simon, *Der Vierjahreszeitenaltar in Würzburg* (Stuttgart 1967). See also E. Simon, "Neuerwerbungen des Martin von Wagner-Museums Würzburg," *AA* 83 (1968) 154–159 and E. Simon, *Augustus: Kunst und Leben in Rom um die Zeitenwende* (Munich 1986) 127, figs. 165–168. The altar was attached to a column base when sold,

but it is clear that these were not originally together. It is possible, as Simon speculated (*AA* 155), that the altar and base were put together in antiquity as reused material, but the 1886 photograph shows only the altar and therefore speaks against such a combination. The altar is elaborately carved with four winged putti identified as the seasons. Separating these personifications are identical baluster-like pillars supporting amphorae and with swags of drapery between. These pillars are likely references to Apollo Aygeius, as suggested by Simon (*Vierjahreszeitenaltar,* 26–28) and acknowledged in *LIMC* II (1984) 329, s.v. Apollo Aygieus (E. di Filippo Balestrazzi) 329, nr. 15, pl. 281. See also O. Dräger, *Religionem Significare. Studien zu reich verzierten römischen Altären und Basen aus Marmor* (*RM-EH* 33 [1994]), 265, nr. 116, and 141, for a discussion of the appropriateness of altars in garden settings. See also Cain 1985, 79, 110, n. 580, 185.

17. Bardini, who later bequeathed a museum to his native town, made plaster casts of these for Studniczka, and later Jacobsen purchased the marble fragments. Studniczka 1926, 19, n. 2, reported having seen later at Bardini's the marble altar, but he was unaware of its location at the time of his publication. This base was published by Visconti 1886, 299, 314, pl. 10.

18. Studniczka 1926, 9–10.

19. See Studniczka 1926, 12, n. 4, and V. Visconti, "Degli avanzi di un ninfeo di casa privata," *BullCom* 5 (1877) 59–65, pls. 1–2, and 3 (a color restoration of part of the wall). Lanciani cited this in *FUR* 22 as "Domus Avidiorum" because five waterpipes were found carrying the name Titus Avidius Quietus.

20. Evans 1994, 86.

21. Studniczka 1926, 7 and 9: it could not be determined if the pavement was meant to hold water.

22. Visconti 1886, 344.

23. Lehmann-Hartleben and Lindros 1935, 217, explained that this discrepancy may have been the result of the fill of earth still covering the floor from which Lanciani recorded his measurement on *FUR* 10 (Fig. 1.1D).

24. Visconti 1886, 344: Nei cavi dei piloni per la nuova fabbrica si osservarono anche altre parti del medesimo fabbricato, ma più malconce e spogliate.

25. Studniczka 1926, 12, 17.

26. English translation of original German text of Studniczka 1926, 13. According to Visconti 1886, 344, an exact colored drawing of the decoration of this nymphaeum was made through the kindness of Joseph Spithoever, but Studniczka 1926, 13, was unable to find it, even with the aid of the Spithoever heirs.

27. Visconti 1886, 344.

28. Studniczka 1926, 14–15, indicated that his information concerning the whereabouts of these architectural pieces came from E. von Mercklin, who in 1914 attempted, unsuccessfully, to see and photograph them. A piece of a column base was also noted by Studniczka 1926, 9, who believed it could have come from an upper story.

29. *CAR* II-F 58(I, c); Visconti 1886, 299. This statuette was reported in 1903 by Ludwig Pollak to be on the art market, but its present location is unknown: Studniczka 1926, 15, n. 3. It is Pollak's photograph that S. Reinach employed for his drawing in *Répertoire de la statuaire grecque et romaine* 4 (Paris 1910) 30.3. Shrines of Silvanus could be in private gardens, as attested by an inscription found on the Pincio to a *vilicus* in the gardens of the Glabrioni, Tichico, who dedicated to Silvanus an inscription that may have been fixed to a sacred shrine of this *numen* (R. Lanciani, "Sugli orti degli Acilii," *BdI* [1868] 119–128, esp. 119–120). Such shrines must have been very simple, however, and likely without any significant sculpture. Neudecker 1988 does not have a single example of an image of Silvanus in his extensive listing of sculptures found in the context of Roman villas.

30. Studniczka 1926, 15, n. 1. Some of this material has been published: E. Paul, *Antike Welt in Ton: Griechische und römische Terrakotten der archäologischen Instituts in Leipzig* (Leipzig 1959) 104–105, nrs. 376–388 = Inv. nrs.: T 924–T 936.

31. Studniczka 1926, 15.

32. Studniczka 1926, 9 and n. 4. Lanciani, *NSc* 1886, 272, recorded peperino slabs, as did Savignoni, *NSc* 1901, 247. Studniczka 1886, 343, correctly recorded these peperino paving slabs, but Visconti never mentioned stamped brick pavers.

33. Studniczka 1926, 9. H. Block, *I Bolli laterizi e la storia edilizia Romana* (Rome 1947) 184–185, n. 155. Savignoni, *NSc* 1901, 247. *CIL* XV.1, 1075–1076 (100–125 A.D.), 319, 847 (A.D. 123), 1051 (after A.D. 132). See also *CAR* II-F 58 (IIa, c); *CAR* II-F 58 (III).

34. F. Studniczka, *Fra Ny Carlsberg Glyptoteks Samlinger* II (Copenhagen 1922) 60; Studniczka 1926, 142–145, believed it could be an earlier work of the unnamed sculptor of the Niobid group represented by figures in Florence and the Vatican: *RE* 9 (1916) 2621, s.v. Iphigenia (L. Kjellberg).

35. G. Lippold, *Antike Skulpturen der Glyptothek Ny Carlsberg* (Basel 1924) 22, fig. 22; Poulsen 1951, 82–83.

36. Moltesen 1998, 181.

37. B. Sismondo Ridgway, *Hellenistic Sculpture I: The Styles of ca. 331–200 B.C.* (Madison, Wisc. 1990) 283; B. Sismondo Ridgway, *First Century Styles in Greek Sculpture* (Madison, Wisc. 2002) 83, 105, n. 43; *LIMC* II (1984) 837–838, nr. 337, s.v. Artemis/Diana (E. Simon); E. Simon, "Kriterien zur Deutung 'Pasitelischer' Gruppen," *AA* 1987, 291–304, esp. pp. 291–292 and n. 5. For an example of a wall painting with this subject, see *LIMC* I (1981) 265, nr. 41, s.v. Agamemnon (O. Touchefeu).

38. Studniczka 1926, 17, 45. For discussion of repairs to sculptures as a normal practice in antiquity, see Neudecker 1988, 116.

39. M. Bieber, *The Sculpture of the Hellenistic Age*[2] (New York 1961) 77, figs. 268–271; Simon 1984, 838.

40. Apart from those discussed the remains of a possible replica were found in Roman ruins near the village of Muletarevo in Bulgaria. See B. S. Ridgway, *First Century Styles in Greek Sculpture* (Madison, Wisc. 2002), and T. Stoyanov, "Artemis and Iphigenia: A Fragmental Part of a Statuary Group from the Strymon Valley. An Attempt at Reconstruction," in *Akten* 1988, 384–385, pl. 57.4 for a reconstruction drawing.

41. Martini 1984, 204–206, pl. 29.

42. Freyer-Schauenburg 1988, 382–384; and Freyer-Schauenburg, "Iphigenie und Artemis," in C. Bayburtluoğlu, ed., *Festschrift Akurgal* (*Anadolu* 23 [1984–1997]) 37–56. A study of this group will be published in *Samos* XIII.

43. Martini 1984, 233–235 (Phases 1 and 2), 252 (Phase 3), 261–262 (Phase 4), 264 (Ending).

44. Martini 1984, 235, and Beilage: state plan. This room continued in use through the fourth building phase and, in fact, by the addition of a doorway in the south wall, became an entry room into the complex. It is possible that the sculptural group was displayed here only at this final stage, having been moved from another room in the bath or even from another building entirely.

45. Freyer-Schauenberg 1988, 383. It is possible that the use of dark and light stone for the statue was to harmonize with the dark and light stone of the walls of the bath, suggesting a common date for both.

46. Freyer-Schauenberg 1988, 383; J. Inan, "Eine hellenistische Tänzerin aus Perge," *Akten* 1988, 347–348, pl. 50:3–4: Perge statue in the Antalya Museum, Inv. nr. 10-29-81. It is one of ten replicas and twelve variants known; Inan dated it to the Hadrianic period, after an original of the second quarter of the second century B.C.

47. Studniczka 1926, 45.

48. Freyer-Schauenberg 1988, 383.

49. Artemis sanctuary: K. Tsakos, "ΕΝΑ ΙΕΡΟ ΤΗΣ ΑΡΤΕΜΙΔΟΣ ΣΤΗ ΣΑΜΟ," *AAA* 13 (1980) 305–318 (summary in German); Cybele votives: F. Naumann, *Die Ikonographie der Kybele in der phrygischen und der griechischen Kunst* (*IstMitt-BH* 28, Tübingen 1983) 218, Beilage 5.

50. Freyer-Schauenberg 1988, 383–384 and n. 7, pointed out that the Artemis sanctuary was in the vicinity of the Roman bath, implying a connection between the two. The connection can be, however, only serendipitous rather than significant.

51. Rome, Museo Capitolino, Inv. nr. 9778. For the excavation report, see Colini 1935, esp. 150, pl. I. Also D. Velestino, "Restauro del gruppo di Giove Dolicheno sul toro," *BullCom* 95 (1993) 196–201. The earliest evidence for a sanctuary to Jupiter Dolichenus in Rome is an inscription dated precisely to July 31, A.D. 191. See S. Settis, "'Esedra'

e 'ninfeo' nella terminologia architettonica del mondo romano. Dall'età repubblicana alla tarda antichità," *ANRW* 1.4, 729.

52. Simon 1984, 838, nr. 338, pl. 621; O. Brendel, "Archäologische Funde," *AA* 50 (1935) cols. 552–556, fig. 10. Colini 1935, 157 believed the figure has the hairstyle of Julia Soaemias and dated the statue to about A.D. 220.

53. Simon 1984, 838.

54. Besides the statues mentioned below, it should be noted that a relief of Niobids is reported by J. J. Winckelmann, *Storia delle arti del disegno presso gli antichi di Giovanni Winckelmann* (translated from the German, corrected and supplemented by Carlo Fea, Rome 1783) II, 202: "Nelle ruine degli orti di Sallustio a Roma sono state trovate alcune figure in basso-rilievo esprimenti la favola stessa (Niobids), e Pirro Ligorio, che ciò narra ne'suoi manoscritti che serbansi nella biblioteca Vaticana, ci assicura che bellissimo n'era il lavoro. Lo stesso soggetto esprime un basso-rilievo nella galleria del conte di Pembroke a Wilton in Inghilterra, il quale da chi ha fatto l'indice di quella galleria sembra essere stato stimato a peso, poichè ci avvisa che pesa tre mila libbre inglesi." (In the ruins of the gardens of Sallust in Rome have been found some figures in relief of the myth of Niobe. According to Pirro Ligoro, in his manuscript preserved in the Vatican Library, he certifies that the work was most beautiful. The same subject is in a relief in the gallery of the Count of Pembroke in Wilton, England, for which whoever did the inventory of that gallery seems to have estimated the weight, because he advises us that it weighs 3,000 English pounds.)

55. Moltesen 1998, 176, gave the year 1888 for the purchasing of these statues. See pages 25–27 for a discussion of Josef Spithoever.

56. Lanciani 1906, 176: "Come il lettore facilmente avrà notato, le notizie da me racolte ed esposte non danno molta luce sul ritrovamento dei Niobidi. Rimangono solo accertati questi punti: . . . che una delle due figure, oggi nella collezione Jacobsen, fu trovata a 15 m. di profondità sotto la casa Bai nell'agosto 1886: e che la seconda proviene dal nascondiglio scoperto sotto la casa stessa nell'ottobre seguente." See Moltesen 1981, 363, who interpreted "nell'ottobre seguente" as meaning 1887.

57. Lanciani 1906, 173: Fu trovata nel cavo per il pilone angolare della casa di Cesare Bai, quasi incontro la fronte del Ninfèo, alla profondità di 15 metri insieme a frammenti importanti di una replica della Diana di Versailles e della cerva che l'accompagna. Vi era anche una scoltura che il Visconti ebbe a chiamare rarissimo monumento, descrivendolo a questo modo: "Statua acefala mancante delle gambe delle braccia rappr. una fanciulla nell'atto di correre nello stadio (Niobide). Appartiene ai tempi dello stile elegante." (It [one of the Niobids in the Ny Carlsberg Glyptotek] had been found in the pit made for a corner pylon of the Bai

house, almost opposite the front of the Nymphaeum [the "vestibule"] at a depth of 15 meters together with important fragments of a replica of the Diana of Versailles and of a hind that accompanies her. There was also a sculpture that Visconti had called a most rare monument, describing it this way: "A headless statue missing parts of the legs and arms representing a young girl in the act of running in the stadium [a Niobid]. It belongs to the period of the elegant style.") It is noteworthy that Lanciani's quote of Visconti 1886, 299, is not completely accurate. Visconti described the statue as "una fanciulla spartana." The identification as a Niobid, placed in parentheses, is Lanciani's opinion, not Visconti's. See Furtwängler 1907, 208, who reported Lanciani's misidentification.

58. Lanciani 1906, 174–175; for the month of October, see p. 173.

59. R. Lanciani, "IV. Roma: Regione VI," *NSc* 1886, 272, and Visconti 1886, 390.

60. See Visconti 1886, 343–344; Visconti, *NSc* 1886, 272; Lanciani 1906, 174.

61. Lanciani 1906, 175, made it clear that this information was reported to him: "Io non posso parlarne che sulla testimonianza altrui."

62. Lanciani 1906, 175: Queste sculture furono trasferite in una stanza terrena del Casino Spithoever, nel quale il Visconti ed io potemmo esaminarle, in parte, nella primavera del 1888. (These sculptures had been transported to a ground floor room of the Spithoever villa, where Visconti and I were able to examine them, in part, in the Spring of 1888.)

63. Talamo 1998, 145 and n. 148. I have been unable to see this report to confirm or refute, to my complete satisfaction, Talamo's dating of 1882.

64. Lanciani 1906, 172: La statua rinventa nella vigna Spithoever è di giovanetto ravvolto in parte nel manto è alto m. 1,30 ed è mancante del solo braccio sinistro. Fu rinveuta nello sterro che si viene facendo per la nuova via (Flavia) che partendo da quella di porta Salaria deve arrivare sino al nuovo Museo Agrario (via delle Finanze). L'area della strada è ancora di proprietà Spithoever, non avendo il Comune stipulato ancora il contratto. Gli operai dell'impresa avevano rinvenuta la statua fino da sabato, ma però l'avevano nascosta, e quantunque si sospettasse di qualche cosa, pure non fu potuta rinvenire dal ricordato proprietario prima di ieri mattina. (Quoted by Lanciani from a report of Inspector Buonfanti.) (The statue found in the Spithoever gardens is of a young man, 1.30 meters high, wrapped in part by a mantle and lacking only the left arm. It had been found during the excavations for the new street [Flavia] that beginning at the porta Salaria, will extend up to the new Museo Agrario [via delle Finanze]. The area of the street is still the property of Spithoever, the Municipal authorities not having yet settled the terms of a contract. The workers of these operations found the statue on Saturday, but they

had hidden it, and although someone may have suspected something, yet it was not brought to light by the previously mentioned owner until yesterday morning.)

65. Talamo 1998, 145.

66. Poulsen 1951, 341, nr. 475.

67. Moltesen 1998, 186.

68. Piranesi 1756, I, 15, nr. 115, pl. 2: delle statue e de' bassirilievi, de' pezzi di colonne e molti capitelli di varie sorte con altre rarità.

69. Venuti 1763, 116: molte statue, che sono nella Villa Ludovisi, *particolarmente il Fauno* [my italics], furono trovati in questi Orti, come quelle de'Palazzi Verospi. See also Fea 1790, 201, who noted that statues in the courtyard of the palazzo Verospi had been found near the new church of San Agnese.

70. Schreiber 1880, 17–18.

71. Arndt 1912, 65.

72. Text to *BrBr* 712–714.

73. Rizzo 1906, 446.

74. Inv. nr. 520 (Moltesen 1981); Arndt 1912, 81–82 (cat. nr. 1047).

75. Arndt 1912, 67.

76. Arndt 1912, 81: "Marbre d'un grain assez grossier, probablement de provenance grecque" (Dying Youth). Arndt 1912, 65: "Marbre blanc" (Fleeing Maiden).

77. M. Moltesen, *Greece in the Classical Period* (Ny Carlsberg Glyptotek 1995) 43, 46.

78. Inv. nr. 72274; H.: 1.49 meters; the left arm has been reattached; found near the piazza Sallustio, near the corner of via Collina (depth of 11 meters). *NSc* 1906, 434–435; *CAR* II-F 61(b); B. Germini, "Statua di Niobide," in *Palazzo Massimo delle Terme* (Rome 1998) 74–75.

79. Moltesen 1981, 364.

80. Ramieri 1983, 25.

81. See C. Häuber, "I Vecchi Ritrovamenti (Prima del 1870)," in Cima/La Rocca 1986, 195, n. 13.

82. Rizzo 1906, 434–446.

83. Riemann 1950, 1562.

84. Moltesen 1981, 364.

85. For an example of the complete type and its pertinence as villa decoration, see L. J. Roccos, "The Citharode Apollo in Villa Contexts: A Roman Theme with Variations," in Gazda 2002, 273–293.

86. H.: 1.10 meters: *BullCom* 1888, 419; *CAR* II-F, 24, II.

87. *NSc* 1888, 497; Lanciani 1906, 175; *CAR* II-F, 32: "la stessa di cui al n. 24, II."

88. Candilio 1990, 206, n. 98; Candilio 1998, 70.

89. Lehmann-Hartleben and Lindros 1935, 221, n. 3 (Ins. Neg. 55.112).

90. Mansuelli 1958, 101–110, 121, n. 82; Geominy 1984, 117–124; 309–320.

91. Charbonneaux 1963, 72; Geominy 1984, 129–133, fig. 143.

92. Poulsen 1951, 340, n. 472; Geominy 1984, 117–124, fig. 123. See also P. G. Huebner, "Detailstudien zur Geschichte der antiken Roms in der Renaissance" *RM* 26 (1911) 288–328, esp. 322–328: "Der Niobidenpaedagoge." The Copenhagen replica is considered the best stylistically: Candilio 1990, 208.

93. The Louvre replica was found in Soissons together with a male Niobid that may reflect the original juxtaposition of pedagogue protecting a youth: Candilio 1990, 208.

94. Grimal 1969, 146–147; H. Weber, "Zur Zeitbestimmung der Florentiner Niobiden," *JdI* 75 (1960) 112–133.

95. W. Klein, *Praxiteles* (Leipzig 1898) 326–342; Mansuelli 1958, 101–122.

96. Mansuelli 1958, 101.

97. Moltesen 2002, 26, no. 83.

98. A. Furtwängler, *Sitzungsberichte der philosophisch-philologischen und der historischen Klasse der K.B. Akademie der Wissenschaften zu München* (1899) II, 2, 279–296, and A. Furtwängler, "Griechischer Giebelstatuen aus Rom," *Sitzungsberichte der philosophisch-philologischen und der historischen Klasse der K.B. Akademie der Wissenschaften zu München* (1902) 443–455.

99. Lanciani 1906, 177. Furtwängler 1907, 207–225, addressed the Terme Niobid in relationship to his earlier theory and believed that it, in fact, confirmed his opinion.

100. K. Schefold, *Meisterwerke griechischer Kunst* (1960) 76–78, 241, Abb. 294–296. In 1960 the Apollo/Theseus, the Terme Niobid, and the Berlin Torso (identified four years earlier by Moltesen 1981 as the so-called lost Niobid mentioned by Lanciani) were brought together for the Jubilee of the Basle Museum: K. Vierneisel, "Ein neuer Niobide," *Pantheon* 32 (1974) 123–126.

101. La Rocca 1985, 71–72. G. Hafner, "Die beim Apollotempel in Rom gefundenen griechischen Skulpturen," *JdI* 107 (1992) 17–32, believed these sculptures likely were never pedimental, but see G. Despinis, "Sculture architettoniche greche a Roma," *BullCom* 97 (1996) 255–258. See also an unusual archaistic statue identified as Odysseus (Boston, Isabella Stewart Gardner Museum, Inv. nr. S5s23) that was found near the vestibule. It is considered by most scholars to have originally decorated a small pediment: *CAR* II-F 59 (I); *NSc* 1885, 341; *BullCom* 15 (1887) 274; Lanciani 1906, 183; V. Poulsen, "Odysseus in Boston," *ActaArch* 25 (1954) 301–304, B. Sismondo Ridgway, *The Archaic Style in Greek Sculpture* (Princeton 1977) 314; C. Vermeule, *Sculpture in Stone in the Isabella Stewart Gardner Museum* (Boston 1977) 12, nr. 14; M. D. Fullerton, *The Archaistic Style in Roman Statuary* (Leiden 1990) 177. I thank Richard Lingner for discussing this statue with me and for allowing me to see the pertinent archives in the Isabella Stewart Gardner Museum.

102. E. Langlotz and M. Hirmer, *Die Kunst der Westgriechen in Sizilien und Unteritalien* (Munich 1963) 83–84, text to pls. 115–117.

103. Moltesen 1981, 362.

104. W. B. Dinsmoor, "The Lost Pedimental Sculpture of Bassai," *AJA* 43 (1939) 27–47, believed that the Copenhagen Niobids decorated the pediments of the Temple of Apollo at Bassai.

105. W. H. Schuchhardt, "Die Niobidenreliefs vom Zeusthron in Olympia," *AM* 1 (1948) 95–137, esp. 135.

106. E. Pfuhl, "Attische und Ionische Kunst des fünften Jahrhunderts," *JdI* 41 (1926) 129–175, esp. 142–143.

107. B. Sauer "Alte und neue Niobiden," in *Zeitschrift für bildenden Kunst* 22 (1911) 129–138, attributed the Copenhagen Niobids to the master of the sculptures for the Hephaisteion in Athens.

108. La Rocca 1985, 71.

109. La Rocca 1985, 72.

110. A. Corso, "Prassitele: Fonti epigrafiche e letterarie. Vita e opere," I, *Xenia*, Quaderni 10 (Rome 1988) 104–106, and in particular n. 597, speculated that statues by Praxiteles could have occupied niches inside the temple of Apollo Sosianus.

111. B. Sismondo Ridgway, *Fifth Century Styles in Greek Sculpture* (Princeton 1981) 54–59; La Rocca 1985, 71.

112. Inv. 840; H.: 0.69 meters; Parian marble. C. Visconti, "Trovamenti di oggetti d'arte e di antichità figurate," *BullCom* 16 (1888) 417–418, first published this but did not recognize it as an Amazon. See E. Talamo, "Statua di Amazzone," in M. Cima, ed., *Restauri nei Musei Capitolini* (Verona 1995) 73–76. See also a copy of the Amazon Sciarra type found two years earlier in the via Nicola da Tolentino and now in Berlin, Staatliche Museen, Antikensammlung, Inv. nr. Sk 7: R. Bol, *Amazones Volneratae* (Mainz 1998) 173–174, pls. 2, 3, 22, 23, 133–134.

113. E. Petersen, "Sitzungsprotocolle," *RM* 4 (1889) 86–88. Hafner (above, n. 101), 18, n. 8, suggested that this statue may not have been pedimental.

114. La Rocca 1985, 76–78.

115. Auberson and Schefold 1972, 113–121, figs. 22–24; E. Touloupa, Τὰ ἐναετια γλυπτὰ του ναου του Απόλλωνος Δαφνηφορου στην Ερετρια (Athens 1983) 101.

116. A fifth-century temple in Eretria is only recognized by a small fragment of a cornice for a window; otherwise, there is no other physical evidence: see Auberson and Schefold 1972, 121.

117. The cutting in the back of this statue may not be original, and it was initially reported by Visconti 1888a, 418, as perhaps modern ("sembra moderno").

118. Rolley 1999, 178.

119. But even public works of art, carrying sometimes complex iconography, may have been less visible and therefore less discussed than works in garden settings. P. Veyne, "Conduct without Belief and Works of Art without Viewers," *Diogenes* 143 (1988) 1–22, esp. 10, believed that such "works of art only function at ten percent of their capacity"

and that they are part of "the urban decor" to which no one pays much attention.

120. Candilio 1990, 210, n. 106.

121. Felici 1952, 236–237: Un Gladiatore di marmo che misura lungo palmi 10 in circa, con un piedistallo di legnio dipinto e dorato, con un'arme del S.r Card.le intagliata e dorata (Archivio Boncompagni Ludovisi in the Archivio Segreto Vaticano, Arm XIX, prot. 611, n. 43).

122. Felici 1952, 237: una statua di un gladiatore ferito grande del naturale antico, sopra il suo piano di marmo con un corno e spada appresso colcato, con piedistallo di legnio finto di pietra velata, corniciato d'oro con l'arme del sig. Cardinale dorata (Archivio Boncompagni Ludovisi in the Archivio Segreto Vaticano, Arm IX, prot. 325, n. 1).

123. Franceschini 1987, 159, n. 1. See also Felici 1952, 238. NB: B. Palma, *I Marmi Ludovisi dispersi* (*MNR,* I.6 [Rome 1986]) 94, gave the years 1688–1689 for the transfer of the statue to Livio Odeschalchi.

124. Mattei 1987, 4.

125. Franceschini 1987, 157–160.

126. Stuart-Jones 1912, 338–340, pl. 85.

127. U. Aldroandi [*sic*], *Delle statue antiche, che per tutta Roma, in diversi luoghi, & case si veggono* in Mauro 1556, 123–124: ne' portici del cortile [in the house of Cesi near St. Peter's] si vede gittato à terra un torso di gladiatore: un putto che dorme: una sepoltura antica con due teste iscolpite, & altri frammenti: e presso ogni colonna del portico del palagio vi ha pezzo di marmo antico con epitafi antichi assai belli.

128. P. A. Maffei, *Raccolta di statue antiche e moderne* (Rome 1704) 62, pl. 65.

129. C. G. Heyne, *Sammlung antiquarischer Aufsätze* II (Leipzig 1779) 236–237.

130. C. Fea, *Nuova descrizione de' monumenti antichi ed ogetti d'arte contenuti nel Vaticano e nel Campidoglio* (Rome 1819) 223: "si pretende, che parte della base, e del braccio destro sia ristauro di Michelangelo Bonarroti." That Michelangelo had restored the right arm was a common belief in the eighteenth century: see Stuart-Jones 1912, 340.

131. C. Friederichs, *Bausteine zur Geschichte der griechisch-römischen Plastik* (Berlin 1868) 326, nr. 579 = C. Friederichs and P. Wolters, *Die Gipsabgüsse antiker Bildwerke in historischer Folge erklärt: Bausteine zur Geschichte der griechisch-römischen Plastik* (Berlin 1885) 523, nr. 1412.

132. Schreiber 1880, 12. See Mattei 1987, 2–4, 17–19. It is likely that it was restored by Ippolito Buzzi in 1621 or 1623, according to payment documents: Y. Bruand, "La restauration des sculptures antiques du Cardinal Ludovisi (1621–1632)," *Mélanges d'archéologie et d'histoire* 68 (1956) 398–399.

133. Palma 1983(b), 149. Marius and his daughter: *RE* 24.2 (Stuttgart 1930) s.v. Marius 28 (Stein) 1821; Pyramus and Thisbe: Ovid, *Met.* 4.55; Paetus and Arria: Mart., *Epigr.*

1.13: "When virtuous Arria was handing her Paetus the sword she had drawn from her own flesh, she said: 'I swear the wound I have dealt does not hurt, but the wound you will deal, Paetus, *that* hurts me.'" J. Sandrart, *Sculpturae veteris admiranda* (Nürnberg 1680) first proposed this identification. See Palma 1983(a), 60, figs. 70, 71 (Sandrart's tav. h and tav. c). Macareus and Canace: Ovid, *Her.* 11.

134. Visconti 1831, 325–326.

135. H. Brunn, "I doni di Attalo," *JdI* 46 (1870) 292–323.

136. A. Schober, "Das Gallierdenkmal Attalos I. in Pergamon," *RM* 51 (1936) 104–124; "Epigonos von Pergamon und die Früh pergamenische Kunst," *JdI* 53 (1938) 126–149; and *Die Kunst von Pergamon* (Vienna 1951) 53–55 believed it stood on the circular base in the center of the piazza of the sanctuary of Athena Nikephoros. E. Künzl, *Die Kelten des Epigonos von Pergamon* (Würzburg 1971) 7–9, 26 (Abb. 6: reconstruction drawing) proposed it stood on a long inscribed base at Pergamon dedicated by Attalos I. See also S. Howard, "The Dying Gaul, Aigina Warriors, and Pergamene Academicism," *AJA* 87 (1983) 483–487.

137. See Marszal 1991, 478, who dated these sculptures to the second century A.D.

138. Coarelli 1978, 234; first suggested by Visconti 1831, 325–326.

139. Neudecker 1988. Marszal 1991, 480–488, identified several statues of Gauls that *could* have come from garden settings.

140. Mattei 1987, 133–134, n. 9. There are also other possible Roman repairs to the base: see Mattei 1987, 134. Note that the comparable torso in Dresden (Mattei, pl. XXIX) seems to have had a head attached at precisely the same join to the neck as the Capitoline Gaul, where a torque would be. The Dresden torso, formerly in the Chigi collection, may have been found in Hadrian's Villa at Tivoli: P. R. von Bienkowski, *Die Darstellungen der Gallier in der hellenistischen Kunst* (Vienna 1908) 6, following F. A. Sebastiani, *Viaggio a Tivoli* (Fuligno 1828) 280, who mistakenly believed that the Ludovisi *Dying Gaul* was found in Tivoli.

141. Stuart-Jones 1912, 338.

142. Felici 1952, nr. 43.

143. Visconti 1831, 325: (G)uerriero in riposo. Statua sedente. Un giovane guerriero di robuste forme siede in terra colle gambe incrocicchiate, colle braccia posate sulle gambe, e col dorso alquanto incurvato, onde prendere riposo. La mano destra posta sulla gamba sinistra, tiene una spada: un lembo della sua clamide distesa a terra si avvolge alla coscia sinistra. See F. Capranesi, *Description des sculptures anciennes qui existent dans la galerie de la villa de S. E. Antoine Boncompagni Ludovisi* (Rome 1842) n. 55; perhaps the same figure as Schreiber 1880, 139–140, n. 118: of Pentelic marble, but the head is of another, finer marble; called a "Ruhender Krieger" = 1633, fol. 32.

144. M. Marvin, "The Ludovisi Barbarians: The Grand

Manner," in Gazda 2002, 205–223; I thank the author for sending me a prepublication copy of her article. See also I. M. Ferris, *Enemies of Rome: Barbarians through Roman Eyes* (Stroud, Gloucestershire 2000).

145. Vacca 1594, 59: "Mi ricordo, che il sig. Carlo Muto nella sua vigna poco lontano dagli Orti Sallustiani, trovò un Faun maggiore del naturale con un puttino in braccio, ed un vaso grande con Fauni, e Baccanti, che ballano, con cembali in mano; che oggi sta nel suo giardino. Trovò anche molte statue ritrovate sparse molto disordinatamente, . . . mentre vi si vedono muraglie piene di nicchie, e che fossero trasportate nella vigna del sig. Carlo Muti." See also V. E. Q. Visconti, *Illustrazioni de'Monumenti scelti Borghesiani* (Rome 1821) I, pl. VI.

146. B. Palma, "Appunti preliminari ad uno studio sul piccolo donario pergameno," in *Alessandria e il mondo ellenistico-romano: Studi in onore di Achille Adriani* (*Studi e materiali* 5, Pisa 1984) 774–782. Lanciani 1897, 417; Lanciani 1906, 159, gave a 1566 date for excavations near Santa Susanna and stated that "circa questi tempi" (although elsewhere) were found the faun and the vase.

147. G. B. de'Cavalieri, *Antiquarium Statuarum Urbis Romae Tertius et Quartus Liber* (Rome 1594) pl. 75.

148. Lanciani 1897, 417. This is the area designated on *FUR* 9 as "Villa Cesi d'Acquasparta poi Massimo di Rignano." See also Lanciani 1990 (V: 1994), 38.

149. See Schreiber 1880, 10, who recognized the connection of Vacca's report with the location of the Muti property on Bufalini's plan.

150. Lanciani 1906, 159, added in parenthesis "dal ninféo degli."

151. *CAR* II-F, 127, nr. 45.

152. Scipione Francucci, *Galleria dell'Illustris. e Reverendis. Signor Scipione Cardinale Borghese* (1613) Manuscript, ASV, Fondo Borghese, IV, 102: Saturno con un figlio in braccio; see Kalveram 1995, 218.

153. Kalveram 1995, 218: Jacobi Manilli, Romani, *Villae Burghesiae Vestiario Praefecti, Descriptio Villae Burghesiae extra Portam Pincianam* (1650); W. Fröhner, *Notice de la sculpture antique* (1870) nr. 250. In the Louvre archives is a document for proposed restorations, dated Versailles December 25, 1863, and signed by P. Pons; but it is unclear whether these proposals were indeed carried out. See also Montfaucon 1725, 157, who reported that the Silenus with Dionysos was in the Pincian gardens of the Medici.

154. Paris, Louvre, Ma 922 9880212 AGR. The comments on the state of preservation are from personal observations as well as the report by Kalveram 1995, 217–218, nr. 105, pl. 58. There is nothing in the Louvre archives concerning the "état de conservation." It should be noted that the Louvre archives give the present height of the statue as 2.01 meters, but Kalveram's measurement is approximately 10 centimeters shorter (1.90 meters).

155. Flavian date proposed by Vierneisel-Schlörb 1979 447, n. 3, but questioned by Grassinger 150, n. 11.

156. Replica listing in F. P. Johnson, *Lysippos* (Durham, N.C. 1927; repr. New York 1968) 184–185. See also Vierneisel-Schlörb 1979, 446–452, esp. 447.

157. Paris, Louvre, Inv. nr. 985-N 275 (MA 86). Truszkowski 1988, 3–16; Grassinger 1991, 181–183, nr. 23, pls. 83–90, 221; M. Hamiaux, *Les sculptures grecques* II (Paris 1998) 199–201, nr. 217.

158. W. Fuchs, *Der Schiffsfund von Mahdia* (Tübingen 1963) 11 (100 B.C.); F. Coarelli, "Classe dirigente e arti figurative," *DialArch*, nr. 4/5 (1971) 245 (120 B.C.); and D. Grassinger, "Die Marmorkratere," in G. Hellenkemper Salies, H.-H. von Prittwitz, and G. Bauchhenss, eds., *Das Wrack: Die antike Schiffsfund von Mahdia* (Cologne 1994) I, 259–283.

159. Truskowski 1988, 14. F. Hauser, *Die neu-attischen Reliefs* (Stuttgart 1889) 55–60, was the first to identify this krater, and others like it, as Neo-Attic works.

160. Truskowski 1988, 14–15.

161. W. Fuchs, "Die Vorbilder der neu-attischen Reliefs, *JdI-EH* 20 (1959) 108–118.

162. Grassinger 1991, 144.

163. Grassinger 1991, 144–146.

164. See D. Michel, "Pompejanische Gartenmalereien," in H. A. Cahn and E. Simon, eds., *Tainia für Roland Hampe zum 70. Geburtstag* (Mainz am Rhein 1980) 373–404, esp. 390–91.

165. Grassinger 1991, 150; W. Jashemski, *The Gardens of Pompeii* (New Rochelle 1979) 311, fig. 480; S. de Caro, "The Sculptures of the Villa of Poppaea at Oplontis: A Preliminary Report," in *Ancient Roman Villa Gardens* (Dumbarton Oaks Colloquium on the History of Landscape and Architecture 10, 1984) 1986, 96–101, nrs. 11,12.

166. Neudecker 1988, 47–54, esp. 47.

167. In 1893 the Ny Carlsberg Glyptotek acquired marble theater masks from the villa Spithoever in Rome; they may have been discovered within the confines of the ancient gardens of Sallust. See J. S. Østergaard, *Imperial Rome: Catalogue of the Ny Carlsberg Glyptotek* (Copenhagen 1996) nrs. 120–123; and Talamo 1998, 154–156, figs. 24–26.

168. Grassinger 1991, 150; W. Elliger, *Die Darstellung der Landschaft in der griechischen Dichtung* (Berlin 1975) 254; 443–444 (on the characterization of the stopping place of the Maenads in the Bacchae [l. 1051] of Euripides as a "locus amoenus"), 258–259, 332–333, 357–358, 362–363 (on the "locus amoenus" in Hellenistic writings, for example Theokrites). See also Pandermalis, 196 (on the *hortus* of the Villa of the Papyri, which was thought to have been inhabited by Satyrs); and P. Zanker, *Augustus und die Macht der Bilder* (Munich 1987) 35–41.

169. *NSc* 1882, 301; Lanciani 1906, 175; *CAR* II-F 50: "nel ninfeo."

170. Poulsen 1951, 341, nr. 475.

171. In 1890 a herm of a bearded Hercules was found near the corner of the via Lucullo and the via Friuli. It could be the bearded pugilist reported by Pollak: *CAR* II-F 55; Talamo 1995, 39, n. 66.

172. Neudecker 1988, 194, nr. 39.38 (villa of the Quintilii), 231, nr. 66.29 (villa of Cassio).

173. Rome, Museo Nazionale (Palazzo Massimo); 0.65 meters × 0.25 meters. Dated to the second century A.D. *NSc* 1908, 347 and fig. 1 (p. 348); *CAR* II-F, 83–85 (III.b): "Lavori edilizi."

174. Note that 43 meters from the via Flavia were found traces of a north-south wall in *opus reticulatum*.

175. Dimensions: 0.585 meters × 0.32 meters. *NSc* 1908, 348–350, and figs. 2, 3 (p. 349); *CAR* II-F, 83–85 (III.b).

176. A. Sogliano, "Casa degli Amorini dorati," *NSc* 1907, 549–593: results of excavations made from December 1902 through March 1905.

177. Rome, Museo Nazionale, Inv. nr. 72; dimensions: 0.40 meters × 0.12 meters. *NSc* 1908, 382, fig. 1 (headless); CAR II-F, 83–85 (III.b); *MNR* I.2, 344, nr. 46.

178. *NSc* 1909, 7; *CAR* II-F, 83–85 (III.c).

179. New York, Metropolitan Museum of Art, Acc. nr. 10.151; dimensions: 0.37 meters × 0.40 meters. G. M. A. Richter, *Catalogue of Greek Sculptures in the Metropolitan Museum of Art* (Oxford 1954) nr. 232, pl. 160b: she did not, however, recognize that this was the same sculpture as reported by Vaglieri in *NSc* 1908, 382, fig. 2; *CAR* II-F, 83–85 (III.b); Moltesen 1998, 185. Cf. A similar piece (in mirror image) in the Vatican collection: G. Kaschnitz-Weinberg, *Sculture del Magazzino del Museo Vaticano* (Città del Vaticano 1937) 175.

180. Ligorio, *Cod. Paris. ital.* 1129, c. 309. A head of Zeus was found at the end of the eighteenth century near the vie Sallustiana and Quintino Sella (in the villa Verospi on the Pincio). It is now in the Vatican's Museo Pio-Clementino: E. Q. Visconti, *Il Museo Pio-Clementino* VII (Milan 1822) 178–185, pl. 37.

181. Lanciani 1906, 159; Lehmann-Hartleben and Lindros 1935, 221, pl. 12, figs. 3, 4.

182. G. Winkelmann [*sic*], *Notizie di antichità scavate in Roma, e nella sua campagna tratte dalle opere dell'Ab. Giovanni Winkelmann in C. Fea, Miscellanea Filologica, Critica e Antiquaria dell'avvocato Carlo Fea* (Rome 1790) 202. See also *Werke* VI, 268–269.

183. *Die Skulpturen der Sammlung Wallmoden* (Göttingen 1979) 43–46, n. 12 (H. Döhl); *A Description of the Collection of Ancient Marbles in the British Museum; with Engravings* 1.2 (London 1812) pl. 28; *Werke* VI.1, 267–268. Schreiber 1880, 17, quoted Winckelmann: "neben dem labrum einer antiken Fontäne" (near the basin of an ancient fountain). Döhl (above) quoted Winckelmann that the two figures were lying in "ihrer Gruft neben einander. Der Ort scheint ein Zimmer gewesen zu sein; aus dem Schutte der Trümmer aber ist kein deutlicher Begriff zu ziehen" (in their grave next to each other. The place appears to have been a room, but from the rubble of the ruins there is no clearer idea to draw). Winckelmann, letters to Moltke (November 5, 1765); to Paciaudi (November 8, 1765); to Heyne (December 1 (more likely 5), 1765, and December 28, 1765 (more extensively published in *GGA* 1766, 109–111); J. Winckelmann, *Anmerkungen über die Geschichte der Kunst des Altertums* (1767) 117; C. Küthmann, *Provinzial-Museum Hannover: Katalog der antiken Skulpturen und kunstgewerblichen Geräte der Fideicommiss-Galerie des Gesamthauses Braunschweig-Lüneburg...* (Hannover 1914) 19–20; G. Lippold, *Die Plastik der Griechen, HdA* III, 1 (Berlin 1950) 347, n. 1.

General: H. Heydemann, *Die Knöchelspielerin im Palazzo Colonna* (Halle 1877). Berlin statue: C. Blümel, *Römische Bildnisse* (Berlin 1933) 31–32, R. 75, pl. 47. Terracottas: F. Winter, *Die Typen der figürlichen Terrakotten* (Berlin 1903) Type II, 134–136. Painting on marble: C. Robert, *Die Knöchelspielerinnen des Alexandros* (Halle 1897); *A Guide to the Exhibition Illustrating Greek and Roman Life*[3] (London 1928) 200, fig. 220.

Plinth: F. Coarelli in *I Galli e l'Italia* (Rome 1978) 233–235.

Restored primarily by Cavaceppi: head and neck; a large part of the left shoulder; the right foot and the toes of the left; index and middle fingers and end of the little finger of the left hand; thumb, index and middle fingers of the right hand, as well as the ends of the others (restored in plaster). Much weathering, particularly at the back (perhaps water damage). Total H.: 0.675 meters; plinth H.: 0.09 meters; L: 0.68 meters.

184. B. Cavaceppi, *Raccolta d'antiche statue* I (1768) pl. 60.

185. See Cain 1985, 187, who gave an incorrect date of discovery as 1756 and repeated this apparently false report regarding a fountain.

186. A. H. Smith, *A Catalogue of Sculpture in the Department of Greek and Roman Antiquities* III (London 1904) 80–82, nr. 1710.

187. Berlin: Clarac 1850, 57–58, pl. 578, nr. 1249; Heydemann 1877, 25; Naples: figure found at Tyndaris (Heydemann 1877, 3, 24); Louvre: from the Villa Borghese (Clarac 1850, 128, nr. 1425, pl. 323).

188. Rome, Vatican, Galleria dei Candelabri, Inv. nr. 2667: E. Q. Visconti, *Il Museo Pio-Clementino* VII (Milan 1822) 178–185, pl. 37; Cain 1985, 187, cat. nr. 103, pls. 76.4, 83.1.

189. *CAR* II-F 59 (I); *NSc* 1885, 341.

190. Property of the Sisters of St. John. Operations for the enlargement of a building. Found with pieces of colored marble columns and amphorae as well as a brickstamp (*CIL* XV, 1410 b): *CAR* II-F 77c; *NSc* 1901, 247; 421; *BullCom* 1901, 72. Cf. the lion's feet for a candelabrum in Naples:

Museo Nazionale (Storeroom), Inv. nr. 6858: Cain 1985, 164, cat. nr. 49, pl. 51.1, 2; and another example in London, British Museum (Storeroom) Inv. nr. 2510: Cain 1985, 161, cat. nr. 36, pl. 52.1–3.

191. *NSc* 1908, 382; *CAR* II-F, 83–85 (III.b): monopode: 0.55 meters; oak leaves and acorns: 0.20 meters × 0.15 meters. Cf. London, British Museum (storeroom; lower diameter 0.155 meters), Inv. nr. 2516: better-preserved example of perhaps the same type as ours, dated first century A.D.: Cain 1985, 161, cat. nr. 38, pl. 88.2.

192. Studniczka 1926, 15.

193. Cain 1985, 12–22.

194. Visconti 1887, 267: "di recente diseppellito nella Villa Ludovisi."

195. Petersen 1892, 67; Lanciani 1897, 414.

196. Felici 1952, 220, explained that the area in question was formerly owned by the Frati della Traspontina, called also the villa Capponi.

197. Lanciani 1906, 176. There were only two guards to oversee a vast area.

198. Nash 1959, 110; Felici 1952, 360–363.

199. Lanciani 1906, 175. See Visconti 1887, 267. See also Petersen 1892, 32.

200. Riemann 1950, 1557; E. Langlotz, *Das Ludovisische Relief* (Mainz 1951) 23, n. 1.

201. Nash 1959, 110.

202. Pollak 1994, 46.

203. Petersen 1892, 67.

204. E. Simon, "La Scultura di Locri Epizefirii," in *Locri Epizefiri: Atti del sedicesimo Convegno di Studi sulla Magna Grecia, Taranto 1976* (Taranto 1977: published 1980) 463–477. See also G. Gullini, "Il trono Ludovisi: un'ipotesi," in *Aparchai: Nuove ricerche e studi sulla Magna Grecia e la Sicilia antica in onore di P. E. Arias* (Pisa 1982) I, 305–318.

205. See Studniczka 1911, 87, fig. 22; R. Carpenter, "Observations on Familiar Statuary in Rome," *MAAR* 18 (1941) 41–61, 105, pls. 17–19 ("Ludovisi Throne").

206. An intriguing letter of 1920 written by T. Homolle to E. P. Warren preserved in the archives of the Museum of Fine Arts, Boston, declares that the writer has in his possession an archaeological monument from his excavations in Erice that can support the authenticity of the relief on the Boston "throne." If such evidence exists, the association of both "thrones" with the sanctuary of Venus Erycina in Rome would be very strong indeed.

207. Pollak 1994, 46; La Rocca 1997, 36. In a typed report (probably by John Marshall) in the archives of the Museum of Fine Arts, Boston, it is stated that the relief first appeared on the market, probably in September of 1894, and it is at that time Hartwig first saw it. It is clear, however, from Pollak's report that Hartwig knew about the relief at least a month before he saw it.

208. Nash 1959, 110, concluded that it was found 160 to 180 meters northwest of the findspot of the *Ludovisi "Throne,"* between the vie Romagna, Sicilia, Puglia and Boncompagni. See also Gerkan 1929, 161–163; Riemann 1950, 1560.

209. Archives, Museum of Fine Arts, Boston: Marshall reported that Warren first saw the relief in March 1895 in Francesco Martinetti's magazine near the Arch of Septimius Severus in Rome.

210. Ashmole and Young 1968; H. Jucker, "Sachlisches zur Echtheit des 'Bostoner Throns,'" *MusHelv* 22 (1965) 117. Perhaps the most skeptical of the recent scholars has been J. M. Eisenberg, "The Ludovisi and Boston Thrones," *Minerva* 7 (1996) 29–41, who claimed that both "thrones" are modern forgeries.

211. Guarducci 1987, 54.

212. Pollak 1994, 46–48, 232; L. Musso, "'Römische Memorien' di Ludwig Pollak: l'archeologo, il conoscitore, il commerciante d'arte antica," *Studi Germanici* 33.1 (1995) 95–110, esp. 103–104; La Rocca 1997, 35.

213. Guarducci 1987, 49–62; Pollak 1994, 46–47, n. 18; La Rocca 1997, 36.

214. L. D. Caskey, *Catalogue of Greek and Roman Sculpture, Museum of Fine Arts, Boston* (Boston 1925) 30–48; Studniczka 1911.

215. Petersen 1892, 32.

216. For example, E. A. Garner, "The Boston Counterpart of the 'Ludovisi Throne,'" *JHS* 33 (1913) 74–83; W. Klein, "Zur Ludovisischen Thronlehne," *JdI* 31 (1916) 231–257; Gerkan 1929, 125–172. See Guarducci 1987, 52, for a more complete listing.

217. For a cogent review of this evidence, see Guarducci 1987, 54–55.

218. P. Cellini, "Appunti: *Ne sutor ultra crepidam*," *Paragone* 6, nr. 65, May 1955, 44–47; Nash 1959, 107.

219. Nash 1959, 107: "(q)uesto sarcofago veniva dal cortile dei frati Cappuccini di Via Sicili e Via Romagna, dove era piazzato al muro." Jandolo stated that the relief was found around 1896; however it is clear that it was already on the market in 1895.

220. Nash 1959, 108.

221. J. J. Herrmann, Jr., "Thasos and the Ancient Marble Trade: Evidence from American Museums," in *Marble: Art Historical and Scientific Perspectives on Ancient Sculpture* (Malibu 1990) 73–100; M. Cristofani, "Due frammenti di marmo insulare da Locri," *BdA* 51 (1966) 3–4, 167–168.

222. Rome, Museo Capitolino, H.: 1.39 meters. *BullCom* 14 (1886) 51–52, 418, n. 6: discovery; Lanciani 1906, 173; *CAR* II-F 58(I, b): "Construzione di una casa (prop. Bai)"; Talamo 1995, 83–86; Talamo 1998, 139–141.

223. Colin 1946.

224. Petersen 1892, 32–33.

225. Mertens-Horn 1997(a); Mertens-Horn 1997(b). See also Guarducci 1985; H. Prückner, *Die lokrischen Tonre-*

liefs (Mainz 1986) 89–91; Costamagna and Sabbione 1990, 187–210. D. Mertens' reconstruction in Guarducci 1987, 53, fig. 4, and Costamagna and Sabbione 1990, 198, fig. 278.

226. Mertens-Horn 1997(a), 217; Guarducci 1985, 5–6.

227. Mertens-Horn 1997(a), 217, 221.

228. Mertens-Horn 1997(a), 217–219; M. Mertens-Horn, "La nascita di Pegaso e la nascita di Afrodite" in *Corinto e l'Occidente: Atti del trentaquattresimo convegno di Studi sulla Magna Grecia, Taranto 1994* (Taranto 1998) 257–289. According to Mertens-Horn 1997(a), the realistic aspect of the lifting of the "goddess" by the grasping of the armpits is also more appropriate for a cultic ritual rather than for a mythological scene.

229. La Rocca 1997, 40–41.

230. G. Rodenwaldt, "Drei Miscellen," *AA* 1946/47, cols. 41–43 (*Ludovisi* and *Boston "Thrones"*).

231. Studniczka 1911, 92; Gerkan 1929, 152; F. Krauss, "Uber die ursprüngliche Gestalt des Ludovisischen Reliefs, seine Veränderung und deren Beziehung zum Relief in Boston," *JdI* 62–64 (1948–1949) 40–69; Costamagna and Sabbione 1990, 210.

232. Curtius 1938, 214.

233. La Rocca 1997, 41.

234. P. Irdi Coretti, *Greece and Italy in the Classical World* (Acts of the XI International Congress of Classical Archaeology, London, 3–9 Sept. 1978) abstract, p. 243. I thank B. S. Ridgway for alerting me to this theory.

235. Bakalakis 1955. See also Herrmann and Newman 1995, 105, fig. 4; La Rocca 1997, 40, fig. 4.

236. See Bakalakis 1955, p. 51, fig. 8; Herrmann and Newman 1995, 105, fig. 3.

237. N. Sevinç, "A New Sarcophagus of Polyxena from the Salvage Excavations at Gümüşçay," *Studia Troica* 6 (1996) 251–264.

238. N. Sevinç, C. B. Rose, D. Strahan, and B. Tekkök-Biçken, "The Dedetepe Tumulus," *Studia Troica* 9 (1998) 305–327. Thanks to Brian Rose for this information.

239. B. Barletta, *Ionic Influence in Archaic Sicily: The Monumental Art* (Gothenburg 1983).

240. See Ashmole and Young 1968; J. J. Herrmann, "Exportation of Dolomitic Marble from Thasos:. Evidence from European and North American Collections," in M. Waelkens, N. Herz, and L. Moens, eds., *Ancient Stone: Quarrying, Trade and Provenance* (ActaArchLov, Monographiae 4, 1992) 93–104; and J. J. Herrmann, "The Exportation of Dolomitic Marble from Thasos: A Short Overview," in C. Koukoule-Chrysanthake, A. Muller, and S. Papadopoulos, eds., *Thasos: Matières premières et technologie de la préhistoire à nos jours* (Athens 1999) 57–74. Other studies by John Herrmann on Thasian marble are published (listed in his 1999 article), and I thank him for sending me copies of these.

241. *NSc* 1887, 447; C. L. Visconti, "Trovamenti di Oggetti d'arte e di antichità figurata," *BullCom* 15 (1887) 336–344; Lanciani 1906, 175; *CAR* II-F, 23(b).

242. Moltesen 1998, 184.

243. Schneider 1986, 188–195: KO 1 (Naples Inv. nr. 6117); KO 2 (Naples Inv. nr. 6115); KO 3 (Copenhagen Inv. nr. 1177), and pl. 1; R. Cantilena, E. La Rocca, U. Pannuti, and L. Scatozza, *Le Collezioni del Museo Nazionale di Napoli* (Rome 1989) 164, nrs. 67, 69.

244. Talamo 1998, 132.

245. Castelli 1988, 53. I have not been able to identify this statue in the Terme Museum.

246. Schneider 1986, 188–191.

247. Rome, Musei Capitolini, *NSc* 1888, 699; *CAR* II-F 40; Talamo 1995, 34, fig. 9.

248. G. C. Picard, *Les Trophées romains* (Paris 1957) 282–283.

249. Bodel 1997; E. Rawson, "The Antiquarian Tradition: Spoils and Representations of Foreign Armour," in *Staat und Staatlichkeit in der frühen römischen Republik, Akten eines Symposiums, 12.–15. Juli 1988, Freie Universität Berlin* (Stuttgart 1990) 158–173 = E. Rawson, *Roman Culture and Society* (Oxford 1991) 582–598.

250. L-A. Touchette, "Two Nikai with a Trophy—Two Women with a Herm: Public and Private in Roman Copies of the Nike Parapet," in *Horti Romani*, 325.

251. Colin 1946. Colin believed that the *Boston "Throne"* was sculpted in Tiberian times (because it is believed the gardens passed to the imperial family under Tiberius) and that this was an attempt by that emperor to relate himself directly to the *gens Iulia,* his divine origins. Cf. La Rocca 1997, 46, who made a similar suggestion.

252. P. Veyne, "The Hellenization of Rome and the Question of Acculturations," *Diogenes* 106 (1979) 1–27, esp. 26.

253. Inv. nr. 39.602. First published by F. W. Robinson, "A Greek Marble Head of a Horse," *Bulletin of the Detroit Institute of Arts of the City of Detroit* 19 (1940) 83–85.

254. William Peck kindly relayed bibliographic information as well as the letter by Otto Brendel in the archives of the museum.

255. F. Brommer, "Studien zu den Parthenongiebeln IV," *AM* 73 (1958) 110–111. B. S. Ridgway, who has seen this piece, expressed to me that the head is probably correctly labeled as fifth century.

256. P. Alessandro Mazzoleni, *Vita di Monsignor Francesco Bianchini Veronese* (Verona 1735), S. Rotta, s.v. Francesco Bianchini in *Dizionario Biografico degli Italiani* 10 (Rome 1968) 187–194, and more recently, F. Uglietti, *Un erudito veronese alle soglie del Settecento: Mons. Francesco Bianchini 1662–1729* (Verona 1986) esp. 60–66 (archeological excavations, although no mention of those on the Pincio). Bianchini was an astronomer and antiquarian who published (among other works) *La Istoria Universale provata con monumenti e figurata con simboli degli antichi* in

1697, which is based on the conviction that archaeological evidence makes a firmer basis for history than literary evidence—in the spirit of the seventeenth century as "the century of numismatics." See A. Momigliano, "Ancient History and the Antiquarian," *JWarb* 13 (1950) 299. Also L. Piastra, "Due novità nello studio dei disegni di antichità di Francesco Bianchini," *BullCom* 96 (1994–1995) 165–172. Bianchini's manuscripts and library went to the Biblioteca Capitolare in Verona in 1765 after the death of his inheritor and nephew, Padre Giuseppe Bianchini. Some of Bianchini's correspondence is preserved in the Biblioteca Vallicelliana in Rome.

257. B. Montfaucon, *L'Antiquité expliquée et représentée en figures* Supplement 2 (Paris 1724) 126, quotes Bianchini: "Hae statuae ex terra eductae sunt anno 1710 ad Septentrionale latus vinae Verospiorum sitae prope circum Sallustii versus portam Salarium." The villa Verospi (later Belloni-Cavalletti) did not belong to the Ludovisi family until 1825; therefore these statues were never part of the Ludovisi Collection. Immediately after their discovery, two statues (Inv. nr. 22 [*Touya*] and Inv. nr. 29 ["*Ptolemaic Princess*"]) were put into the Museo Capitolino. Two others (Inv. nr. 25 [*Arsinoe II*] and Inv. nr. 27 [*Ptolemy Philadelphos*]) stood temporarily in the portico of the Palazzo dei Conservatori until 1714, when Clement XI officially transferred them to the Consiglio Comunale for restoration and display. Two statues (although see below, n. 260) are included in the catalogue of the Capitoline museum by Bottari 1755, 150–152, fig. 76 (my Fig. 3.37): *Touya,* and fig. 77 (my Fig. 3.40): copy of *Arsinoe*—both identified as genuine Egyptian works. In 1838 all four statues were moved to the Vatican with other Egyptian sculptures on the Campidoglio: Pietrangeli in Botti and Romanelli 1951, 136–137.

258. Roullet 1972, n. 153, fig. 117, n. 179, 180, 181, figs. 202–204, 220; M. Malaise, *Inventaire préliminaire des documents égyptiens découverts en Italie* (*EPRO* 21, Leiden 1972) 183. They are in the Vatican, Museo Greg. Egizio (Helbig I, 482c); Botti and Romanelli 1951, 18–25, 33–34, nrs. 28, 31–33 (Inv. nrs. 22, 25, 27, 29); Toti 1995, 146–153 (M. P. Toti). (1) *Touya, Queen of Seti I* (Inv. nr. 22678); black granite; H.: 3.00 m. (with plinth), Nineteenth Dynasty, inscribed; (2) *Arsinoe, Queen of Ptolemy II* (Inv. nr. 22681), red granite, H.: 2.70 m. (with plinth), Ptolemaic period, inscribed; (3) *Ptolemy II* (Inv. nr. 22682), red granite, H.: 2.66 m. (with plinth), Ptolemaic period; inscribed; (4) "*Ptolemaic princess,*" red granite, H.: 2.70 m. (with plinth), Roman copy with incomplete hieroglyphs of Inv. nr. 22681. Grenier 1989, 30–31, pointed out the reasons for identifying the "Ptolemaic princess" (Inv. nr. 22683) as a Roman copy: (1) heavier carving and with a different face; (2) the inscription is incomplete, although it is clearly an adaptation, by one versed in the reading of hieroglyphics, of the Arsinoe inscription (Fig. 3.41); (3) the top of the head of the Arsinoe statue is flat for the addition of her separately made

crown of Lower Egypt (missing), which was a specific type consisting of a solar disk and two feathers; the head of the "copy" does not have this platform on which to place such a crown. These characteristics speak for the Arsinoe statue not having her crown when the "copy" was made or for the copyist's deliberate exclusion of it. Another example of a Roman copy of an Egyptian original is a green porphyry sphinx from the Iseum Campense (discovered in 1856 and now in Memphis), which is virtually identical to a sphinx of the Eighteenth Dynasty in the Museo Barracco, Rome. See Roullet 1972, 132–133, nrs. 277–278; and K. Lembke, *Das Iseum Campense in Rom: Studie über den Isiskult unter Domitian* (Heidelberg 1994) 225 (nr. 15), 242 (nr. 45): Curran 1997, 86–87, n. 62. See also J. Quaegebeur, "Kleopatra VII und der Kult der ptolemäischen Königinnen," in *Kleopatra, Ägypten um die Zeitenwende* (Ausstellung in München, 18 Juni–10 September 1989) Mainz 1989, 45, who believed that the statues of Arsinoe and Ptolemy were originally cult objects at Heliopolis.

259. Montfaucon 1724, 127 quotes Bianchini: Quinta statua ex marmore & ipsa quoque nigro erat, aliisque minor, sed peritioris artificis. Nescio an uspiam visa sit Aegyptiaca Statua, tam exquisiti laboris. Virum illa repraesentabat staturae vulgaris septem vel octo palmorum; sed & caput & pedes exciderunt. (The fifth statue was also of black marble, smaller but better quality than the others. I do not know whether I have ever seen an Egyptian statue of such exquisite workmanship. It represents a man of normal stature, seven or eight palms in height, but the head and the feet are missing.) It is listed by Roullet 1972, 120, nr. 220, as "present whereabouts unknown." Grenier 1989, 21, suggested that the fifth figure may not be identified because it was not well preserved when found (although, according to Bianchini's description, only the head and feet were missing). De Felice 1982, 24–29, proposed that this "fifth statue" of black stone had been used for the restoration of *Touya* because (1) it could have represented a female figure; *Touya* is mistakenly mentioned as male in the documents of 1714; (2) only four statues are mentioned as having been restored; (3) red granite is reported to have been purchased for the restoration of *Arsinoe,* but there is no mention of acquiring black granite for the restoration of *Touya;* (4) black granite was difficult to obtain; and (5) *Touya* is restored in small pieces of black granite. According to Castelli 1988, 62, n. 55, together with the Ptolemaic statues was found a bust of a Pharaoh in grey basalt, formerly in the Ludovisi Collection (not identified by Castelli, and his reference to Lanciani 1906, 166–167, did not mention it, but it is presumably Schreiber 1880, nr. 99) and today in the Museo Nazionale Romano (Palazzo Altemps) Inv. nr. 8607: Helbig[4] III, 242, nr. 2323 [K. Parlasca]. F. Lenormant, "Frammento di Statua d'uno dei Pastori d'Egitto," *BullCom* 1877, 100–112, pl. 9, thought it came from the *horti Sallustiani,* and was origi-

nally from Tanis. It is clear, however, that Bianchini did not discover this figure, for not only did the Ludovisi not own this property until 1825 but it appears in a drawing by Pirro Ligorio and is listed in a Ludovisi inventory of 1641: see Toti 1995, 132–134 (M. P. Toti). On p. 134, Toti reported that Ligorio (no specific reference by Toti), gave the findspot as "nel Pantheon di Agrippa. Era già in più pezzi" and, therefore, Toti suggested that it may have remained in this area until Ludovico, who financed the nearby building of San Ignazio, brought it to his collection. Schreiber 1880, 120, compared the hairstyle to an unspecified, over-life-sized female figure of basalt found in the eastern portion of the park (which had been the property of the Verospi) but did not elaborate. It is difficult to see how this unusual hairstyle could be relevant to any of the figures reportedly found by Bianchini.

260. Schreiber 1880, 18: (1) Isis (Bottari 1755, 76); (2) Isis (Bottari 1755, 77); (3) Isis (P. Righetti, *Descrizione del Campidoglio* I [Rome 1833] pl. 97 [identified as the goddess Neith]; Montagnani-Mirabili 1804, 122); (4) Priest (Bottari 1755, 86); (5) Ptolemy (Montagnani-Mirabili 1804, 108); and (6) Arsinoe (Montagnani-Mirabili 1804, 107). Several of these citations are incorrect: nr. 3, identified by Schreiber as Isis is, in fact, the figure of Arsinoe (Schreiber nr. 6). Note that Felici 1952, 222, stated, without explanation, that Schreiber listed five statues rather than six, probably because he was aware of this overlapping of nrs. 3 and 6. Note also that the references in Schreiber to nrs. 5 and 6 are not to these figures: the correct plate numbers are 123 and 122 respectively. These last two (nrs. 5 and 6) are hesitantly added to the group because, according to Schreiber, their findspots were reported vaguely as "in den Trümmern der Gärten des Sallust." It is possible that Schreiber's hesitation originated from, or at least shared with, Montagnani-Mirabili's 1804 statement (p. 99) that the figure of Ptolemy "fu parimenti ritrovato negli Orti di Sallustio." Nr. 4, identified as a Priest, appears to be very similar to the figure of Ptolemy (Nr. 5), and it is considered by Botti and Romanelli 1951, 25, to be the same statue. Yet there is a difference in the recorded heights (2.40 meters without plinth: Botti and Romanelli; "minor del naturale": Bottari), material ("granito rosso": Botti and Romanelli; "basalt": Bottari), and the engraving in Bottari does not carry any indication of hieroglyphic inscriptions (which are prominently displayed separately on the engravings in Bottari of Arsinoe and her "copy"). Finally, it is unlikely that Bottari in 1775 would include the Ptolemy statue in his catalogue of sculptures in the Capitoline Museum, when it had been moved in 1714 to the Consiglio Comunale (see above, n. 257). It is possible, therefore, that Schreiber 1880, nr. 4 (Priest) is, in fact, not the same statue as Schreiber 1880, nr. 5. According to Talamo 1998, 130, n. 77, in 1838 four statues passed to the Vatican Museums, and a female figure is now in the Louvre, which I have been unable to confirm.

261. Grenier 1989, 21.

262. Montfaucon 1724, 126, who quotes Bianchini, and Braschi 1724, I, 4–5: VI: Bina haec Signa palmos undecim cum dimidio sua altitudine excedunt. Reperta fuerunt Anno 1710 in praedio Urbano nobilis familiae de Verospiis, ubi olim erant Horti Sallustiani propè Forum eiusmet Sallustii, non longe à Porta Quirinali, vulgò Salaria. Indeque in Capitolium traducta fuerunt, et seorsim ibi posita, tum ad ornatum, tum ad tutelam, nè novum aliquod discrimen incurrerent, et progressu temporis interirent. Nàm tametsì aspectu quodammodo ridicula, et significatione contemptibilia forte aliquibus videantur, suae ipsius vetustatis et raritatis ratione nihilominus commendantur, et Archeographis ac antiquae eruditionis studiosis magnopere in pretio sunt. (These two statues exceed eleven palms with half their height. They had been discovered in 1710 in the urban estate of the noble family of Verospi where once had been the Gardens of Sallust by the Forum of that same Sallust, not far from the Quirinal Gate commonly called the Salarian Gate. And these had been brought into the Capitoline and placed there apart both for their adornment and their protection, so that they might not incur any further new danger and that they might not perish through the progress of time. For even if to some they seem perchance ridiculous, so to speak, in their appearance and contemptible in their significance, they are, nevertheless, protected by reason of their own age and rarity, and they are especially of value to epigraphers and to those who study ancient learning. [Translation by D. Burgess.])

VII: Aliqui opinantur, haec bina Signa, non Idola, non Averuncos esse Deos sed sacerdotum speciem praeseferre, Numinum Egyptiorum cultui addictorum. Et ut ex ipso intuitu apparet, unum marem, alterum faeminam exhibet, lineamentis tantummodò vultuum, ac prominentia pectoris differentes, in reliquis valde cosimiles. Dorso utriusque Signi impressa cernuntur ab imo usque ad verticem varia hieroglyphica Aegyptia . . . (Others believe these two statues to bear before themselves not Idols and not to be the Averuncian Gods but the image of priests dedicated to the cult of Egyptian Divinities. And, as is evident from autopsy, it will show one to be male, the other female, differing in the lineaments only of the faces and in the prominences of the chest. In other respects they are very similar. On the back of each statue various Egyptian hieroglyphs are seen to be carved from the base to the top. [Translation by D. Burgess.])

263. Posterla 1725, 5.

264. F. Ficoroni, *Notizie di antichità ricavate dalle opere* nr. 15 in Fea 1790, 124–125: Nell'anno 1714 nella villa Verospi presso gli Orti Sallustiani prima di arrivare alla porta Salara si trovarono due statue egizie di non ordinaria grandezza; una di marmo nero durissimo con macchie gialle, con torre sul capo, nella mano sinistra un ramo di palma, e nella des-

tra un volume, e geroglifici dietro alle spalle, che spiego il P. Melchiore Briga Gesuità in un libretto intitolato: *Fascia Isiaca statuae Capitolinae*. L'altra statua era di granito rosso con un fiore di loto in capo. Ora sono nel Museo Capitolino. Nello stesso luogo, e nello stesso anno, si trovarono altre due statue egizie, dello stesso granito, che ora stanno nel portico del palazzo dei Conservatori. (In the year 1714 in the villa Verospi near the gardens of Sallust before arriving at the porta Salaria two over-life-sized Egyptian statues were found; one of very hard black marble with yellow spots, with a tower on the head and behind on the support hieroglyphs that Father Melchiore Briga, S.J., explained in a pamphlet entitled *Fascia Isiaca statuae Capitolinae*. The other statue was of red granite with lotus flowers on the head. Now they are in the Capitoline Museum. In this same place, and in the same year, were found two other Egyptian statues, of the same granite, that now are in the portico of the Conservatori palace.)

265. Lanciani 1906, 167, cites Braschi 1724, and Ficoroni in Fea 1790, as reporting a date of 1720 for the finding of two of the statues, but this is not the case. The 1720 date appears to have its origins in C. Fea's remarks to Ficoroni (Fea 1790, 125, n. a): "Monsig. Braschi, che ne parla de *Trib.stat.in Capit. er.* cap. 1, n. 5, e le dà nella tavola premessavi, le dice trovate nel 1720." Two statues reportedly moved in 1714 to the Consiglio Comunale, and two others remaining in the Capitoline Museum negate a 1720 date of discovery.

266. Montfaucon 1724, 126; de Felice 1982, 24, believed Posterla's dating of 1711. Regardless, these statues must have been found before October 1713: see de Felice 1982, 25, n. 7.

267. Lanciani 1906, 166–167.

268. Pietrangeli in Botti and Romanelli 1951, 136, nr. 28, who added that the restorations of the sculptures were by Francesco Maratta, called il Padovano.

269. de Felice 1982, 25, n. 8: the official act was made on October 26, 1714.

270. *Werke* III, 119, 124–125, 339, and Winckelmann 1764, 51, 54, 63–64. Note that the Italian translation of *Geschichte* (Winckelmann 1769), edited by C. Fea, does not mention these statues. See also G. Winckelmann, *Monumenti antichi inediti*² II.1 (Rome 1821) 101: "Una testa di basalto nella villa Altieri ha la chioma arricciata con più centinaja d'anelli, che le cadono dinanzi al petto, ed una statua portataci dal Pococke (*Desc.of the East*, T. 1, p. 212), ha la chioma nella stessa guisa acconciata" (A basalt head in the villa Altieri has curly hair with more than one hundred ringlets, that fall in front of the shoulders, and a statue reported by Pococke [*Description of the East*, T. 1, p. 212] has its hair in the same style), and Schreiber 1880, 17–19.

271. See Toti 1995, 117, n. 1, who also made this suggestion.

272. Canopic jar: Schreiber 1880, 16; Winckelmann 1764, 64. According to Winckelmann 1769 I, 117, there were two canopic jars in the Albani collection: "il più bello dei quali fu trovato sul promontorio Circeo." This one must be villa Albani, nr. 691 (Hadrianic date), said to have been discovered near Circeo: S. Curto, *Le Sculture Egizie ed Egittizzanti nelle ville Torlonia in Roma* (Leiden 1985) 46–51, nr. 13, and pls. XVI–XVII; Bol 1994, nr. 537, pp. 439–444 (M. de Vos). It is possible the other jar (not in the Albani collection: Curto, above, 442) came from the Borioni collection and was discovered within the confines of the gardens of Sallust, as Schreiber implied. Statue of Macrinus: Winckelmann 1769, 320; E. Q. Visconti, *Il Museo Pio-Clementino* III (Milan 1819) 54–56, nr. 12; Schreiber 1880, 16, reported it was in the Sala de'busti, nr. 398. After the death of Antonio Borioni, the Macrinus sculpture passed to his heirs from whom it eventually was acquired for the Vatican museum. Note that Schreiber 1880, 16, mentioned a "sturz [*sic*] eines Löwen" of green basalt, formerly in the Borioni collection, that must be the "Löwenkopf" in Bol 1994, 447, nr. 539. See also S. A. Morcelli, C. Fea, and E. Q. Visconti, *Description de la Villa Albani* (Rome 1869) nr. 654.

273. Suggested by Riemann 1950, 1568; see also Venuti 1736, 1–2, pl. 1.

274. Lanciani 1906, 175; Poulsen 1951, 137, n. 187; Moltesen 1998, 181. The purchase of the *Hippopotamus* was made from the Regnicoli brothers, building contractors in Tivoli, who apparently acquired sculptures from various construction sites: see Moltesen 1993, 230–231.

275. Lanciani 1906, 175: "Il sig. Giuseppe Spithoever mi parlò di un andito angusto e profondo nel quale sarebbero state nascoste alquante opere di scultura, fra le quali una Leda, un Endimione, una figura di Niobide, una replica del Fauno di Prassitele, e un montone in rosso antico."

276. A sleeping figure identified as "Genius of Death," now in Ny Carlsberg Glyptotek (Inv. nr. 501) was purchased as early as 1886 and was said to have been found in 1884 in the Sallustian gardens in Rome, a year the Spithoever property was being excavated (see Poulsen 1951, 132, nr. 174; Arndt 1912, 220, text to pl. 156). According to Moltesen 1998, 188, it is possible this is the otherwise unidentified figure of Endymion mentioned by Lanciani 1897, 421.

277. Lanciani 1897, 421. According to Moltesen 1998, 185, and fig. 9, this statue may be Copenhagen, Ny Carlsberg Glyptotek (cat. nr. 237), which was acquired in 1901 from Paul Arndt in Munich. Ludwig Pollak had earlier bought this statue from Bardini in Florence.

278. Lanciani 1897, 421. Lanciani's notes in *Cod. Vat. lat.* 13035, fol. 63r: "Scavi Spithoever: Statua rapp. Leda; statua rapp. Endimione; statue rapp. Fauno Prasitele, cane di rosso antico. . . ." The dog has not been identified.

279. Merkel Guldan 1988, 137–139. Photographs were said to have been taken during this visit in 1897, but I have been unable to discover whether these still exist.

280. Nardini 1666 (1988) II, 93. Montfaucon 1724, 128 (for Bianchini quote). Note that Bianchini stated specifically that he relied on Nardini and others for his topographical descriptions of the city.

281. Note that Lanciani 1906, 167, and Nash 1957, 249, called this building a "casino di stile egizio," while Lehmann-Hartleben and Lindros 1935, 223, referred to it as a "diaeta egiziana." These designations can cause confusion because Nash 1957, 249, used the term "diaeta egiziana" for the round vestibule on the Quirinal slope. Lehmann-Hartleben and Lindros placed it on the slopes of the Pincio opposite the vestibule, while Nash said it was on top of the hill and sited it 110 meters from the north wall of the valley. Old city plans show ancient remains on the Pincio and these could be identified with this building. However, according to Nardini, 1666 (1988) II, 95, during his day the vineyards of the Verospi on the Pincio hung over long, narrow ancient corridors with many small openings and conduits to carry water, which he believed were likely the "Ante Thermas Salustii" recorded in the Acts of SS. Ciriaco, Largo and Smeraldo. See also Lanciani 1906, 167, and Talamo 1998, 130 and n. 76. See also Piranesi 1761, pl. 7, fig. 1, pls. 11 and 14 respectively: a Corinthian corner capital, found in 1754 in the villa Verospi; a column base and a Tuscan capital = Wilton-Ely 1994, nrs. 767, 771, and 774. Riemann 1950, 1565, called this building found by Bianchini a palace in Egyptian style.

282. *Cod. Veron.* 347, fol. 152v [137v]: OPUS DOLIAREXPREDDOM•N•AUG / EX FIGLINIS DOMITIA (due palme); OPDOLI EX PR DOMINI N AUG / EX FIGLIN TAURIANUS (Serapis sia alia fig.ª). The former is very similar to *CIL* 15.1, nr. 155 dated to the reign of Commodus. H. Bloch, *I Bolli Laterizi* (Rome 1947), did not report the latter.

283. Grenier 1989, 22, n. 42.

284. Grenier 1989, 28 and nn. 44, 45, and 47. Tacitus (*Ann.* 2.60) reported that Germanicus (and perhaps his young son, Caligula) visited the temple of Karnak and was told by a Theban priest about the exploits of Ramses II. Furthermore, Diodorus Siculus (1.47.3) mentioned in his description of the Ramesseum some statues of the mother (Touya) and one "of black stone" that stood next to a seated statue of her son and reaching only to the height of his knees. Grenier (1989, n. 48) suggested that with a height of 3 m., the *horti Sallustiani* statue might well be this very figure mentioned by Diodorus. This seems unlikely, not only because of the highly suspect coincidence of the preservation of text and image but because the Ramesseum statues of Ramses and his mother were probably carved from a single block.

285. For the brick stamps see above, n. 282. See Palmer 1976.

286. See *FUR* 3B: This road is designated as "Diverticulum a Via Salaria vetere ad Portam Collinam." Ligorio, *Cod. Paris.* 1129, c. 309, recorded the discovery of two statues of nymphs with urns pouring water which Lanciani 1897, 417, claimed were found in the villa Mandosi. Although Lanciani 1906, 159, was later dubious about this report, Lehmann-Hartleben and Lindros 1935, 221, pl. 12, figs. 3, 4, found near the circular nymphaeum a fragment of a marble statue identified as a nymph, and they explained that Ligorio's recording of nymphs from this vicinity may well be true. Palmer 1976 also believed Ligorio and claimed these statues of nymphs confirm that the street passing through the later property of the villa Mandosi was what he called the *vicus Nympharum.*

287. For a reasonable approach to the equating of sculpture with cult, see L. Bongrani, M. Ciceroni, and M. I. Pasquali, "Gli egizi nella XIV regione augustea: Le testamonianze culturali (M. Ciceroni)," in *L'Egitto in Italia,* 565–569.

288. Rome, Palazzo dei Conservatori. *RT,* IV, p. 356, report n. 39 from 31/VIII/1888, n. 793: "aquila grande al vero mancante del becco." According to the *Catalogo annuo delle Sculture depositate nei Musei Capitolini,* this was displayed in the "sala dei nuovi Fasti" in the Palazzo dei Conservatori on 3/IX/1888. See Talamo 1998, 157, n. 183.

289. Rome, Palazzo dei Conservatori: recomposed from 37 fragments. H. 0.81–0.89 meters: *NSc* 1888, 497; *BullCom* 1888, 332; Mustilli 1939, 104, nrs. 1–3; *CAR* II-F, 32; Viscogliosi 1996, 136–137, figs. 163, 164a, 164b, 225.

290. Viscogliosi 1996, 136–137.

291. Inventory of November 2, 1623: see Palma 1983(a), 41; and Schreiber 1880, 12.

292. Above, n. 291 (Palma 1983(a), 61). See also M. Vasi, *Itinerario istruttivo di Roma* (Rome 1794) I, 274 = Palma 1983(a), 150–151.

293. See Palma 1983(b), 84–89: Inv. nr. 8604; H. of Electra: 1.92 meters; H. of Orestes: 1.70 meters, including the plinth.

294. Palma 1983(b), 84.

295. C. L. Visconti, *I monumenti del museo Torlonia* (Rome 1885), pl. 24.

296. A. Furtwängler, *Die Sammlung Sabouroff* I (Berlin 1883–1887) 50–51.

297. M. Fuchs, *In Hoc Etiam Genere Graeciae Nihil Cedamus* (Mainz 1999) 82, n. 115.

298. L. Curtius, "Review of G. Lippold, *Kopien und Umbildungen griechischer Statuen* (Munich 1923)," *DLZ* 45 (1924) 428.

299. Zanker 1974, 51.

300. Zanker 1974, 58: "Die Nennung des berühmten Names braucht kein direktes Lehrer-Schüler-Verhältnis zu bedeuten, sie ist vielleicht auch verständlich als Werkstattempfehlung."

301. *RE* 15 (1931) 835 s.v. Menelaos (G. Lippold).

ADDENDUM

1. It is not assured Vespasian and Titus were buried there, although it is certain that Julia, daughter of Domitian, and Domitian himself were entombed there. See Suet., *Dom.* 17.3; Mart., 9.35.8; Stat., 5.1.237–241.

2. Mart., 9.3.12, 34.8, 93.5–6. See also R. H. Darwall-Smith, *Emperors and Architecture: A Study of Flavian Rome* (*CollLatomus* 231, Bruxelles 1996) 159–165.

3. Paris 1994, 18. See also Gazda and Haeckl 1996.

4. For the Roman remains see Krautheimer, Corbett, and Frankl 1970, 259–262.

5. The house of Caius was perhaps near the church of San Caio that was located near the present via Firenze and XX Settembre (it was demolished in 1885 to make room for the building of the via Firenze). The house of Gabinius is thought to have been located near the present church of Santa Susanna or perhaps where the church of San Bernardo now stands: see C. Cecchelli, *Le chiese di Roma* (Rome 1953) 145. See, however, A. Bonanni, s.v. Duae Domus in *LTUR* II, 217, who suggested that the two homes may refer to those of the Ceionii and the Nummii that were located in this region.

6. See Krautheimer, Corbett, and Frankl 1970, 255.

7. Paris 1994, 21.

8. Paris 1994, 21–25.

9. *CIL* VI, 29788 = *ILS* 5988.

10. Lanciani 1889, 385. Paris 1994, 23, wrote incorrectly that this is now the *via* San Nicola da Tolentino, which does not cross the XX Settembre.

11. Lanciani 1889, 386.

12. Note in *Ottob.* 3374, 267 Ligorio wrote (presumably in error) that in the "Domus Titi Flavii Sabini incontro gli'Horti Carpensi" (that is in the *vigna* Sadoleto on the Quirinal) "vi fu trovata la immagine dell'Apollo che hora si vede in Belvedere . . . con atto di tirare l'arco." See Castagnoli 1952, 102, n. 12.

13. Lanciani's location of the Sadoleto gardens relied on his interpretation of Ligorio's and Vacca's remarks and ignored a document (although published by Lanciani 1889, 386–387) in which Cardinal Giacomo di Sadoleto left to his nephew Camillo a *vigna* with "casa, giardino e altre fabbriche, posta presso la chiesa di S.ta Susanna."

14. *CIL* XV, 7451; *NSc* 1893, 418 (G. Gatti): found 18 meters from the via Firenze at a depth of 1.5 meters. The length of the pipe is recorded as 1.3 meters. Near this pipe was recovered a marble fragment of the leg of a child. Cf. a *fistula plumbea* with the name T. Flavius Salinator (*CIL* XIV, 7452) and two inscriptions with the name of Flavia Sabina (*CIL* VI, 29788 and 31021) found near the Palazzo delle Esposizioni, both of whom are mentioned together on an inscription (provenance unknown) in the Museo Capitolini in Rome (G. L. Gregori, "Pedanii Flavii Salinatores,"

ZPE 62 [1986] 185–189). These individuals were tied to the Flavians and may have had property and a tomb near that of the Flavian imperial family: M. Verzár-Bass, "A Proposito dei Mausolei negli *Horti* e nelle *Villae*," in *Horti Romani*, 418.

15. Torelli 1987, 568, indicated that this pipe was found only a short distance from the caserma dei Corazzieri. G. Manca di Mores, "Terrecotte architettoniche e problemi topografici: contribuiti all'identificazione del Tempio di Quirino sul colle Quirinale," *AnnPerugia* 20 (1982–1983) 337, added that it was turned in the direction of the ancient remains discovered under the caserma dei Corazzieri, which was located immediately to the west of Santa Susanna. She employed this information as support for the pertinence of these two remains, and directed the reader to Coarelli 1980, 245, who, however, expressed his opinion that this inscribed pipe "si dirigeva *probabilmente* [my italics] proprio in direzione del nostro edificio." The contemporary report in the *NSc* 1893, 418, does not indicate the position of this pipe.

16. M. de Vos, *Dionysus, Hylas e Isis sui Monti di Roma: Tre monumenti con decorazione parietale in Roma antica (Palatino, Quirinale, Oppio)* (Rome 1997) 57–98.

17. Coarelli 1984, 147–155; Torelli 1987, 568; Paris 1994, 24–25. A cistern and fountains were recorded east of San Nicola da Tolentino. R. Lanciani, *Relazione sulle scoperte archeologiche della città e provincia di Roma negli anni 1871–72* (Rome 1873) 30, reported on excavations on the vicolo San Nicola Tolentino near the enclosure of the villa Barberini where a wall was found covered with slabs of peperino, "il quale appartenne probabilmente ad un acquedotto." It ran north-south, forming an acute angle with the modern street and was probably virtually perpendicular with the large wall of fountains. This possible aqueduct reported by Lanciani was near enough to the caserma dei Corazzieri and its possible aqueduct to be the same conduit. See Coarelli's positioning of the mosaic fountain on the Grande-Scagnetti plan (p. 148; designated by an asterisk) and the location of the cistern flanking the vicolo di San Nicola da Tolentino on *FUR* 9. See the discussion of water on pp. 15–16.

18. See A. F. Caiola, "Occasioni per la 'Piazza di Termini'" in Paris 1994, 97–105, who explained that with the recovery from the economic crisis at the end of the nineteenth century, the city of Rome began in haste to complete building projects that had been interrupted such as the north arm of the exedra. Consequently, systematic archaeological excavations were abandoned in order to complete building as efficiently as possible.

19. Paris 1994, 23.

20. Torelli 1987, 569; Paris 1994, 26, fig. 14.

21. E.g., Paris 1994, 21.

22. See *NSc* 1907, 504–525 for excavations near Santa Maria della Vittoria and the discovery of sections of the "Servian" wall. Many pieces of architectural terracottas were

recovered, and these could have been part of the temples of Fortuna (p. 517, n. 3). Also found were marble sculptures: the head of a beardless man, a head of Castor, part of an inscribed herm of Socrates, and other fragments.

23. *NSc* 1882, 301; 411; Lanciani 1906, 169; Lugli 1930–1940, 338. See Talamo 1998, 114, n. 3 and 115, n. 115, who equated the *Fortuna Publica* mentioned by Dio 42.26.3 (perhaps in the *horti Caesaris*) with the *in antis* temple reported by Vitruvius (3.2.2) near the porta Collina. Talamo suggested that these foundations are for this temple. See also Champeau 1987, 4–17, who believed that the *Tyche Demosia* (*Fortuna Publica*) mentioned by Dio was in the gardens of Caesar and must have been the *Fortuna Publica* on the Quirinal and not that of *Fors Fortuna* in Trastevere. I agree with Champeau that the temple mentioned by Dio was likely that on the Quirinal; Dio did not state specifically, however, that this temple was in the gardens of Caesar. Indeed, Dio described a violent earthquake and thunderbolts that struck from the Capitol and the Quirinal (the temple of *Fortuna Publica*) to the gardens of Caesar. There is nothing explicit that these gardens of Caesar and the temple of Fortuna were in the same location. Indeed, the point may be that the thunderbolts extended throughout the city from the northwest (Quirinal) to across the Tiber at the southeast (the gardens of Caesar).

24. See my discussion of this series of rooms with regard to the southern limits of the gardens, pp. 6–7.

25. Lanciani 1897, 421. These, as well as the Faun by Praxiteles, are listed in Lanciani's notes: *Cod. Vat. Lat.* 13035, f. 63r: "Scavi Spithoever: Statua rapp. Leda; statua rapp. Endimione; statue rapp. Fauno Prasitele, cane di rosso antico." Note that Lanciani and Visconti visited Spithoever in the spring of 1888, when Lanciani 1906, 175, recorded they saw sculptures that had been found in "un andito angusto e profondo nel quale sarebbero state nascoste alquante opere di scultura, fra le quali una Leda, un Endimione, una figura di Niobide, una replica del Fauno di Prassitele, e un montone in rosso antico."

26. See H. Bloch, *I Bolli Laterizi* (Rome 1947) 184 [180]. It is perhaps of interest to note that according to Venuti 1824, 160: "sopra alla Villa Mandosi verso le mura si vedeva un antico edifizio mezzo diruto, chiamato dal volgo il Tempio Scelerato, dentro del quale si vedevano delle stanze, le quali vogliono che servissero di carceri alle Vestali." Although it is clear that this identification cannot be correct, the remains reported by Venuti could be those completely uncovered later by Spithoever.

27. Talamo 1998, 114, n. 3, stated, however, that the entire podium was dynamited after the archaeological excavations were completed, as indicated in *Archivio Vittoriano*, P 875, preserved by the Soprintendenza Arch. di Roma.

28. *Beschreibung* 3.2, 378.

29. Krinagoras, *Epigr.* XLVIII (*Anth.Pal.* 16.40). O. Jahn, "Satura," *Hermes* 2 (1867) 245–246, attempted to relate the three Tyches mentioned by Krinagoras with a temple to the three Fates mentioned by Procopius (*B. Goth* 1.25) as standing in the Roman Forum. Because Krinagoras indicated that the three Tyches were located near the house of Sallust, Jahn suggested that this house is not a reference to the one in the famous gardens but to an otherwise unrecorded *domus* near the Roman Forum. K. Zangemeister, "Zur römischen Topographie," *Hermes* 2 (1867) 469–470, disagreed with Jahn that the "Three Tyches" mentioned by Krinagoras are the Fates and was the first to connect them to the *tres Fortunae* mentioned by Vitruvius as having sanctuaries near the porta Collina. Zangemeister speculated that the "Three Tyches" could be related to a temple to Tyche "dedicated by Trajan in the Homeric way" according to Lydus, *de mens* IV, 7.

30. Liv. 29.36.8: consul principio pugnae (by Croton) aedem Fortunae Primigeniae vovit, si eo die hostes fudisset: composque eius voti fuit; 34.53.5: aedem Fortunae Primigeniae in colle Quirinali dedicavit Q. Marcius Ralla, duumvir ad id ipsum creatus: voverat eam decem annis ante Punico bello P. Sempronius Sophus consul, locaverat idem censor. Livy erroneously attributed the dedication to P. Sempronius Sophus who was consul in 268 and censor in 252: Coarelli 1995.

31. A. Ziolkowski, *The Temples of Mid-Republican Rome and Their Historical and Topographical Context* (Rome 1992) 40–45; Coarelli 1995.

32. *Cal. Antiat.* = *NSc* 1921, 117; *Cat. Arval.* = *CIL* I, p. 215.

33. T. P. Wiseman, "The God of the Lupercal," *JRS* 85 (1995) 10; M. Guarducci, "La Fortuna e Servio Tullio in un'antichissima <sors>," *RendPontAcc* 25–26 (1951) 23–32.

ABBREVIATIONS OF PERIODICALS AND SERIES

AA = Archäologischer Anzeiger

AAA = Athens Annals of Archeology

AbhLeip = Abhandlungen der Sächsischen Akademie der Wissenschaften su Leipzig, Philologisch-historische Klasse

ActaArch = Acta archaeologica (København)

ActaArchLov = Acta archaeologica Lovanensia

AJA = American Journal of Archaeology

AJAH = American Journal of Ancient History

AJP = American Journal of Philology

AM = Mitteilungen des Deutschen Archäologischen Instituts, Athenische Abteilung

Anadolu = Anadolu. Revue annuelle des études d'archéologie et d'histoire en Turquie

AnnEpig = L'Année épigraphique

AnnPerugia = Annali della Facoltà di lettere e filosofia, Università degli studi di Perugia

AnnPisa = Annali della Scuola normale superiore di Pisa

ANRW = H. Temporini ed., *Aufstieg und Niedergang der römischen Welt* (Berlin 1972–)

AntCl = L'Antiquité classique

AntW = Antike Welt

ArchCl = Archeologia classica

ArtB = Art Bulletin

BdA = Bollettino d'arte

BdI = Bullettino dell'Istituto di corrispondenza archeologica

BEFAR = Bibliothèque des Ecoles françaises d'Athènes et de Rome

BMFA = Bulletin of the Museum of Fine Arts, Boston

BMonMusPont = Bollettino. Monumenti, musei e gallerie Pontificie

BrBr = H. Brunn, *Denkmäler griechischer und römischer Sculptur in historischer Anordnung* (Munich: Bruckmann 1888–1911)

BullCom = Bullettino della Commissione archeologica comunale di Roma

CEFR = Collection de l'Ecole française de Rome

CIL = Corpus inscriptionum latinarum

CollLatomus = Collection Latomus

CP = Classical Philology

CQ = Classical Quarterly

CRAI = Comptes rendus des séances de l'Académie des inscriptions et belles-lettres (Paris)

DialArch = Dialoghi di archeologia

DissPontAcc = Atti della Pontificia Accademia romana di archeologia. Dissertazioni

DLZ = Deutsche Literaturzeitung

EA = P. Arndt and W. Amelung, *Photographische Einzelaufnahmen antiker Skulpturen* (Munich 1893–1940)

EPRO = Etudes préliminaires aux religions orientales dans l'empire romain

GGA = Göttingische gelehrte Anzeiger

HdA = Handbuch der Archäologie (Handbuch der Altertumswissenschaft, Berlin 1931–)

Helbig⁴ = W. Helbig, *Führer durch die öffentlichen Sammlungen klassischer Altertümer in Rom*, 4th ed. supervised by H. Speier (Tübingen 1963–1972)

ILS = H. Dessau, ed., *Inscriptiones latinae selectae* (1892–1916)

IstMitt-BH = Istanbuler Mitteilungen. Beiheft

JdI = Jahrbuch des Deutschen Archäologischen Instituts

JdI-EH = Jahrbuch des Deutschen Archäologischen Instituts. Ergänzungsheft

JHS = Journal of Hellenic Studies

JRA = Journal of Roman Archaeology

JRS = Journal of Roman Studies

JSAH = Journal of the Society of Architectural Historians

JWarb = Journal of the Warburg and Courtauld Institutes

KlPauly = Der kleine Pauly. Lexicon der Antike

KölnJb = Kölner Jahrbuch für Vor- und Frühgeschichte

LIMC = Lexicon iconographicum mythologiae classicae (Zurich and Munich 1974–)

LTUR = E. M. Steinby, ed., *Lexicon topographicum urbis romae* (Rome 1993)

MAAR = Memoirs of the American Academy in Rome

MEFR = Mélanges d'archéologie et d'histoire de l'Ecole française de Rome

MEFRA = Mélanges de l'Ecole française de Rome, Antiquité

MemLinc = Memorie. Atti della Accademia nazionale dei Lincei, Classe di scienze morali, storiche e filologiche

MemPontAcc = Memorie. Atti della Pontificia Accademia romana di archeologia

MonAnt = Monumenti antichi

MusHelv = Museum Helveticum

NSc = Notizie degli scavi di antichità

ÖJh = Jahreshefte des Österreichischen archäologischen Instituts in Wien

OpArch = Opuscula archaeologica

Pantheon = Pantheon. Internationale Zeitschrift für Kunst

PIR = Prosopographia imperii romani

PP = La parola del passato

RA = *Revue archéologique*

RE = Pauly-Wissowa, *Real-Encyclopädie der klassischen Alter-tumswissenschaft* (1893–)

REA = *Revue des Etudes anciennes*

RendPontAcc = *Atti della Pontificia Accademia romana di archeologia. Rendiconti*

RIN = *Rivista italiana di numismatica e scienza affini*

RivIstArch = *Rivista dell'Istituto nazionale d'archeologia e storia dell'arte*

RM = *Mitteilungen des Deutschen Archäologischen Instituts, Römische Abteilung*

RM-EH = *Mitteilungen des Deutschen Archäologischen Instituts, Römische Abteilung. Ergänzungsheft*

SkrRom = *Skrifter utgivna av Svenska Institutet i Rom*

StEtr = *Studi etruschi*

StRom = *Studi romani*

TAPA = *Transactions of the American Philological Association*

TürkArkDerg = *Türk arkeoloji dergisi*

Xenia = *Xenia. Semestrale di antichità*

BIBLIOGRAPHIC ABBREVIATIONS

Albertini 1510 = F. Albertini, *Opusculum de Mirabilibus Novae et Veteris Urbis Romae* (Rome 1510). This was reprinted several times: in 1515 in Rome, in 1519 in Basle, in 1520 in Lyons, and again in Rome in 1523.

Akten 1988 = Akten des XIII. Internationalen Kongresses für klassischer Archäologie, Berlin 1988 (Mainz ca. 1990).

Aldrovandi 1556 = U. Aldrovandi, *Delle statue antiche* in Mauro 1556, 285–286.

Alföldi and Alföldi = A. Alföldi and E. Alföldi, *Die Kontorniat-Medaillons* I.1–2 (Berlin 1976); 2 (Berlin 1990).

Arndt 1912 = P. Arndt, *La Glyptothèque Ny-Carlsberg* (Munich 1912).

Ashmole and Young 1968 = B. Ashmole and W. J. Young, "The Boston Relief and the Ludovisi Throne," *BMFA* 66, nr. 346 (1968) 124–166.

Astolfi 1998(a) = F. Astolfi, "Gli Horti Sallustiani: Prima Parte," *Forma Urbis* 10 (October 1998) 21–26.

Astolfi 1998(b) = F. Astolfi, "Gli Horti Sallustiani: Seconda Parte," *Forma Urbis* 11 (November 1998) 19–29.

Auberson and Schefold 1972 = P. Auberson and K. Schefold, *Führer durch Eretria* (Bern 1972).

Bakalakis 1955 = G. Bakalakis, "Γωνιακὸ ἀκρωτήριο ἀπὸ τὴ Μαρώνεια." *Hellenika* 14 (1955) 3–22.

Beard 1998 = M. Beard, "Imaginary *Horti:* Or up the Garden Path," in *Horti Romani,* 23–32.

Becker 1843 = W. Becker, *Handbuch der römischen Alterthümer* (Leipzig 1843).

Beschreibung = C. Bunsen, *Beschreibung der Stadt Roms* (Stuttgart 1829–1842).

Blake 1947 = M. E. Blake, *Ancient Roman Construction* (Washington, D.C. 1947).

Boatwright 1987 = M. T. Boatwright, *Hadrian and the City of Rome* (Princeton 1987).

Bodel 1994 = J. Bodel, *Graveyards and Groves: A Study of the Lex Lucerina* (Cambridge, Mass., 1994).

Bodel 1997 = J. Bodel, "Monumental Villas and Villa Monuments," *JRA* 10 (1997) 5–35.

Boissard 1597 = J. J. Boissard, *Romanae Urbis topographiae* I (Frankfort 1597).

Bol 1994 = P. Bol, ed., *Forschungen zur Villa Albani: Katalog der antiken Bildwerke* IV (Berlin 1994).

Bottari 1755 = G. G. Bottari, *Del Museo Capitolino* III (Rome 1755).

Botti and Romanelli 1951 = G. Botti and P. Romanelli, *Le sculture del Museo Gregoriano Egizio* (*Monumenti Vaticani di archeologia e d'arte,* IX, Vatican City 1951).

Braschi 1724 = G. B. Braschi, *De tribus statuis in romano Capitolio erectis anno MDCCXX* (Rome 1724).

Brizzi 1987 = B. Brizzi, *Le Fontane di Roma* (Rome 1987).

Buonocore 1997 = M. Buonocore, ed., *Appunti di Topografia Romana nei Codici Lanciani della Biblioteca Apostolica Vaticana* II (Vatican City 1997).

Burns 1988 = H. Burns, "Pirro Ligorio's Reconstruction of Ancient Rome: the Antiquae Urbis Imago of 1561," in R. W. Gaston, ed., *Pirro Ligorio Artist and Antiquarian* (Milan 1988) 19–92.

Cain 1985 = H.-U. Cain, *Römische Marmorkandelaber* (Mainz am Rhein 1985).

Calvo 1527 = F. Calvo, *Antiquae urbis Romae cum regionibus Simulachrum* (Rome 1527).

Candilio 1990 = D. Candilio, "Statua di pedagogo dagli Horti Sallustiani," *BdA* 1–2 (1990) 206–211.

Candilio 1998 = D. Candilio, "Gli Horti Sallustiani," in *Palazzo Massimo alle Terme* (Rome 1998).

CAR = Carta archeologica di Roma I (Florence 1962); II (Florence 1964); III (Florence 1978): Ministero per I Beni Culturali e Ambientali: Ufficio Centrale per i Beni Ambientali, Architettonici, Archeologici, Artistici e Storici.

Castagnoli 1952 = F. Castagnoli, "Pirro Ligorio topografo di Roma antica," *Palladio* 2 (1952) 97–102.

Castagnoli 1972 = F. Castagnoli, "Appendice," in I. Mariotti, ed., *Gaio Sallustio Crispo, Opere* (Rome 1972) 383–392.

Castelli 1988 = M. Castelli, "Venus Erycina e Venus hortorum Sallustianorum," *BdA* 73 (1988) 53–62.

Champeau 1987 = J. Champeau, *Recherches sur le culte de la Fortune à Rome et dans le monde romain des origines à la mort de César II: Le transformation de Fortuna sous la République* (CEFR 64, Rome 1987).

Champlin 1982 = E. Champlin, "The *Suburbium* of Rome," *AJAH* 7 (1982) 99–117.

Charbonneaux 1963 = J. Charbonneaux, *La sculpture grecque et romaine au Musée du Louvre* (Paris 1963).

Cima and La Rocca 1986 = M. Cima and E. La Rocca, eds., *Le tranquille dimore degli dei: La residenza imperiale degli horti Lamiani* (Venice 1986).

Cipriani 1982 = G. Cipriani, *Horti Sallustiani*[2] (Rome 1982).

Clarac 1850 = F. M. de Clarac, *Musée de sculpture antique et moderne* IV (Paris 1850).

Coarelli 1978 = F. Coarelli, *I Galli e l'Italia* (Rome 1978).

Coarelli 1980 = F. Coarelli, *Roma*[2] (Rome 1980).

Coarelli 1983 = F. Coarelli, "Architettura sacra e architettura privata nella tarda repubblica," *CEFR* 66 (1983) 191–217.

Coarelli 1984 = F. Coarelli, *Roma Sepolta* (Rome 1984).

Coarelli 1995 = F. Coarelli, s.v. Fortunae Tres, Aedes, in *LTUR* II (Rome 1995) 285–287.

Coarelli 1996 = F. Coarelli, *Revixit Ars: Arte e ideologia a Roma, dai modelli ellenistici alla tradizione repubblicana* (Rome 1996).

Coffin 1964 = D. R. Coffin, "Pirro Ligorio on the Nobility of the Arts," *JWarb* 27 (1964) 191–210.

Coffin 1991 = D. R. Coffin, *Gardens and Gardening in Papal Rome* (Princeton 1991).

Colin 1946 = J. Colin, "Les Trônes Ludovisi-Boston et les Temples d'Aphrodite Erycine." *RA* 25 (1946) 23–42: part 1; 139–172: part 2.

Colini 1935 = A. M. Colini, "La Scoperta del santuario delle divinità Dolichene sull'Aventino," *BullCom* 63 (1935) 145–159.

Colini 1977 = A. M. Colini, *L'isola della purificazione a piazza Barberini* (Rome 1977).

Colini 1984 = A. M. Colini, "Nei primi venti anni di Roma capitale," *Bollettino della Unione Storia ed Arte* (January–June 1984) 3–20.

Costamagna and Sabbione 1990 = L. Costamagna and C. Sabbione, *Una città in Magna Grecia: Locri Epizefiri* (Reggio Calabria 1990).

Curran 1997 = B. A. Curran, *Ancient Egypt and Egyptian Antiquities in Italian Renaissance Art and Culture* (Ph.D. Diss. Princeton University, 1997).

Curtius 1938 = L. Curtius, *Die antike Kunst* II (Berlin 1938).

de Felice 1982 = M. de Felice, *Miti ed allegorie egizie in Campidoglio* (Bologna 1982).

DeGrassi 1963 = A. DeGrassi, "Veneria," *Latomus* 22 (1963) 436–439.

De Rossi 1882 = G. B. De Rossi, "Note di Topografia Romana raccolte dalla bocca di Pomponio Leto e testo pomponiano della *Notitia Regionum Urbis Romae*," *Studi e documenti di storia e diritto* 3 (1882), 49–87.

Di Manano 1989–1990 = P. Di Manano, "Regione VI: Via Venti Settembre," *BullCom* 93 (1989–1990) 100.

Donati 1638 = A. Donati, *Romae vetus ac recens* (Rome 1638).

Duchesne 1916–1917 = L. Duchesne, "Les légendes de l'Alta Semita," *MEFR* 36 (1916–1917) 27–56.

Evans 1994 = H. B. Evans, *Water Distribution in Ancient Rome: The Evidence of Frontinus* (Ann Arbor 1994).

Excerpta = *Excerpta a Pomponio dum inter ambulandum cuidam domino ultramontano reliquias ac ruinas Urbis ostenderet* found in a codex in the Biblioteca Marciana di Venezia nr. 3453 (ms. Lat. cl. X, n. 195) at cc. 25a–31b.

Farrar 1998 = L. Farrar, *Ancient Roman Gardens* (Gloucestershire 1998).

Fauno 1548 = L. Fauno, *Delle antichità della città di Roma* (Venice 1548 and 1552).

Fea 1790 = C. Fea, *Miscellanea filologica critica e antiquaria* I (Rome 1790).

Felici 1952 = G. Felici, *Villa Ludovisi in Roma* (Rome 1952).

Ferrary 1996 = J. L. Ferrary, *Onofrio Panvinio et les antiquités Romaines* (Rome 1996).

Festa 1989–1990 = F. Festa, "Regione VI: Horti Sallustiani," *BullCom* 93 (1989–1990) 95–98.

Festuccia 1997 = S. Festuccia, "Un criptoportico sotto gli Horti Sallustiani," *Forma Urbis* 9 (September 1997) 23–27.

Franceschini 1987 = M. Franceschini, "L'Acquisto del *Gladiatore Ludovisi* per il Museo Capitolino," in Mattei 1987.

Frazer 1998 = A. Frazer, ed., *The Roman Villa, Villa Urbana* (Philadelphia 1998).

Freyer-Schauenburg 1988 = B. Freyer-Schauenburg, "Zur Artemis-Iphigenie-Gruppe," *Akten des XIII. Internationalen Kongresses für klassische Archäologie* (Berlin 1988) 382–384.

Frézouls 1987 = E. Frézouls, "Rome Ville Ouverte: Réflexions sur les Problèmes de l'Expansion Urbaine d'Auguste à Aurélien," in *L'Urbs: Espace Urbain et Histoire* (CEFR 98, Rome 1987) 373–392.

Frutaz 1962 = A. P. Frutaz, *Le piante di Roma* I–III (Rome 1962).

Fulvio 1513 = A. Fulvio, *Antiquaria Urbis* (Rome 1513).

Fulvio 1527 = A. Fulvio, *Antiquitates Urbis* (Rome 1527).

FUR = R. Lanciani, *Forma Urbis Romae* (Milan 1893–1901).

Furtwängler 1907 = A. Furtwängler, "Die neue Niobidenstatue aus Rom," *Sitzungsberichte der philosophisch-philologischen und der historischen Klasse der K.B. Akademie der Wissenschaften zu München* (1907) 207–225.

Galinsky 1969 = G. Karl Galinsky, *Aeneas, Sicily and Rome* (Princeton 1969).

Gazda 2002 = E. Gazda, ed., *The Ancient Art of Emulation* (Ann Arbor 2002).

Gazda and Haeckl 1996 = E. K. Gazda and A. E. Haeckl, *Images of Empire: Flavian Fragments in Rome and Ann Arbor Rejoined* (Ann Arbor 1996).

Geominy 1984 = W. A. Geominy, *Die Florentiner Niobiden* (Diss. Bonn University 1984).

Gerkan 1929 = A. v. Gerkan, "Untersuchungen am Ludovisischen und Bostoner Relief," *ÖJh* 25 (1929) 125–172.

Goltzio 1936 = V. Goltzio, *Raffaello nei documenti* (Vatican City 1936).

Gjerstad 1954 = E. Gjerstad, *The Fortifications of Early Rome* (*Acta Instituti Romani Regni Sueciae* 18, Rome 1954).

Grassinger 1991 = D. Grassinger, *Römische Marmorkratere* (*Monumenta Artis Romanae* 18, Mainz am Rhein 1991).

Grenier 1989 = J. C. Grenier, "Notes isiaques," *BMonMusPont* 9.1 (1989) 5–40.

Grimal 1969 = P. Grimal, *Les Jardins romains à la fin de la*

République et aux deux premiers siècle de l'Empire[2] (Paris 1969).

Grueber 1910 = H. A. Grueber, *Coins of the Roman Republic in the British Museum* I (London 1910).

Gruter 1707 = J. Gruter, *Corpus Inscriptionum, ex recensione et cum annotationibus Joannis Georgii Graevii* (Amsterdam 1707).

Guarducci 1985 = M. Guarducci, "Due pezzi insigni del Museo Nazionale Romano: Il 'Trono Ludovisi' e l'Acrolito Ludovisi," *BdA* 70 part 33–34 (1985) 1–20.

Guarducci 1987 = M. Guarducci, "Il cosidetto trono di Boston," *BdA* 72 part 43 (1987) 49–62.

Hackens 1961 = T. Hackens, "Capitolium vetus," *Bulletin de l'Institut Historique Belge de Rome* 33 (1961) 69–88.

Häuber 1995 = C. Häuber, "The *horti Romani*: Amidst Forest, Sacred Grove and Arbor," unpublished manuscript for *Gardens of the Roman Empire,* a symposium at the University of Pennsylvania, November 18–19, 1995.

Häuber 1998 = C. Häuber, "The Esquiline Horti: New Research," in Frazer 1998, 55–64.

Herrmann and Newman 1995 = J. J. Herrmann, Jr., and R. Newman, "The Exportation of Dolomitic Sculptural Marble from Thasos: Evidence from Mediterranean and Other Collections," in Y. Maniatis, N. Herz, Y. Basiakos, eds., *The Study of Marble and Other Stones Used in Antiquity, ASMOSIA III Athens* (London 1995), 73–86.

Heydemann 1877 = H. Heydemann, *Die Knöchelspielerin im Palazzo Colonna zu Rom* (Halle 1877).

Hirschfeld 1913 = O. Hirschfeld, *Kleine Schriften* (Berlin 1913).

Horti Romani = M. Cima and E. La Rocca, eds., *Horti Romani. Atti del Convegno Internazionale, Roma, 4–6 maggio 1995* (*BullCom,* Supplement 6, Rome 1998).

Hülsen 1889 = C. Hülsen, "Der Aufsatz Lanciani's 'La Venus Hortorum Sallustianorum,'" *RM* 4 (1889) 270–274.

Hülsen 1891 = C. Hülsen, "Jahresbericht über Topographie der Stadt Rom: Collis hortorum," *RM* 6 (1891), 123–124.

Hülsen 1894 = C. Hülsen, "Zur Topographie des Quirinals," *Rheinisches Museum für Philologie* 49 (1894) 407–408.

Hülsen 1907 = C. Hülsen, "La pianta di Roma dell'Anonimo Einsidlense," in *Dissertazioni della Pontificia Accademia Romana di Archeologia,* ser. II, vol. IX (1907) 382–424.

Hülsen *RE,* 1907 = *RE* 6.1 (1907) 602–604, s.v. Eryx (C. Hülsen).

Hülsen 1917 = C. Hülsen, *Römische Antikengärten des XVI. Jahrhunderts* (*Abhandlungen der Heidelberger Akademie des Wissenschaften* 4, Heidelberg 1917).

Innocenti and Leotta 1986 = P. Innocenti and M. C. Leotta, "Il cosiddetto ninfeo degli Horti Sallustiani," *BullCom* 91.2 (1986) 356–358.

Innocenti and Leotta 1996 = P. Innocenti and M. C. Leotta in *LTUR* III, s.v. Horti Sallustiani: Porticus Miliarensis, 81–82.

Insolera 1971 = I. Insolera, *Roma Moderna: Un secolo di storia urbanistica* (Rome 1971).

Isager 1991 = J. Isager, *Pliny on Art and Society: The Elder Pliny's Chapters on the History of Art* (London 1991).

Iversen 1968 = E. Iversen, *Obelisks in Exile* I (Copenhagen 1968).

Jacks 1990 = P. Jacks, "The *Simulachrum* of Fabio Calvo: A View of Roman Architecture *all'antica* in 1527," *ArtB* 72 (1990) 453–481.

Jacobsen 1892 = C. Jacobsen, *Ny Carlsberg Glyptotek: Nyt tillæg til fortegnelse over Kunstvækerne* (Copenhagen 1892).

Jashemski 1993 = W. F. Jashemski, *The Gardens of Pompeii* II (New York 1993).

Jordan and Hülsen 1871 = H. Jordan and C. Hülsen, *Topographie der Stadt Rom im Alterthum* I. 1–2 (Berlin 1878); I.3 (Berlin 1907); II (Berlin 1871).

Kalveram 1995 = K. Kalveram, *Die Antikensammlung des Kardinals Scipione Borghese* (Worms am Rhein 1995).

Katterfeld 1913 = E. Katterfeld, "Ein roemisches Haus auf dem Pincio," *RM* 28 (1913) 92–112.

Keller 1913 = O. Keller, *Die Antiketierwelt* (Leipzig 1913).

Kiepert 1903 = H. Kiepert, *Formae orbis antiqui* (Leipzig 1903).

Kiepert and Hülsen 1912 = H. Kiepert and C. Hülsen, *Forma Urbis Romae Antiquae* (Berlin 1912).

Kienast 1965 = D. Kienast, "Rom und die Venus vom Eryx," *Hermes* 93 (1965) 478–489.

Krautheimer, Corbett, and Frankl 1970 = R. Krautheimer, S. Corbett, and W. Frankl, *Corpus Basilicarum Christianarum Romae: The Early Christian Basilicas of Rome (IV–IX Cent.)* IV (Vatican City 1970).

Kurfess 1968 = A. Kurfess, ed., *C. Sallusti Crispi. Catilina, Iugurtha, Fragmenta Ampliora*[3] (Leipzig 1968).

Kurfess 1970 = A. Kurfess, ed., *Appendix Sallustiana* (Leipzig 1970).

Lanciani 1879 = R. Lanciani, "Silloge epigrafica aquaria," *MemLinc* 3 (1879) 436–437.

Lanciani 1880(c) = R. Lanciani, "Topografia di Roma antica: I commentarii di Frontino intorno le acque e gli aquedotti. Silloge epigrafica aquaria," *MemLinc* 4 (1880) 215–616.

Lanciani 1888 = R. Lanciani, "La 'Venus Hortorum Sallustianorum,'" *BullCom* 16 (1888) 3–11.

Lanciani 1889 = R. Lanciani, "Ara dell'incendio Neroniano scoperta presso la chiesa di S. Andrea al Quirinale," *BullCom* 17 (1889) 379–391.

Lanciani 1890 = R. Lanciani, "L'Itinerario di Einsiedeln e l'Ordine di Benedetto Canonico," *MonAnt* 1 (1890) 438–551.

Lanciani 1891(a) = R. Lanciani, "Gli Horti Aciliorum sul Pincio," *BullCom* 1891, 132–155.

Lanciani 1891(b) = R. Lanciani, "Quatre Dessins inédits de la collection Destailleur rélatifs aux ruines de Rome," *Mélanges d'archéologie et d'histoire* 11 (1891) 159–178.

Lanciani 1897 = R. Lanciani, *The Ruins and Excavations of Ancient Rome* (Boston 1897).

Lanciani 1899 = R. Lanciani, *The Destruction of Rome* (New York 1899).

Lanciani 1906 = R. Lanciani, "Il gruppo dei Niobidi nei giardini di Sallustio," *BullCom* 1906, 157–185.

Lanciani 1967 = R. Lanciani, *Pagan and Christian Rome* (New York 1967).

Lanciani 1990 = R. Lanciani, *Storia degli scavi di Roma* I–IV (Rome 1902–1912); reprinted with different pagination and an additional volume (Rome 1990–1994).

La Rocca 1985 = E. La Rocca, *Amazzonomachia: Le sculture frontonali del tempio di Apollo Sosiano* (Rome 1985).

La Rocca 1997 = E. La Rocca, "I Troni degli horti Sallustiani ed il santuario di Venere Erycina: alcune proposte," in *Troni*, 35–47.

L'Egitto in Italia = N. Bonacasa, M. C. Naro, E. C. Portale, and A. Tullio, eds., *L'Egitto in Italia dall'antichità al medioevo* (Atti del III Congresso Internazionale Italo-Egiziano Roma, CNR-Pompei, 13–19 Novembre 1995; Rome 1998).

Lehmann-Hartleben and Lindros 1935 = K. Lehmann-Hartleben and J. Lindros, "Il palazzo degli Orti Sallustiani," *OpArch* I (1935) 196–227.

Leto 1560 = Pomponio Leto, *De antiquitatibus urbis Romae* in *Antiquit: Variarum auctores* (Ludguni 1560).

Linderski 1989 = J. Linderski, "Garden Parlors: Nobles and Birds," in R. I. Curtis, *Studia Pompeiana & Classica in Honor of Wilhelmina F. Jashemski* II (New Rochelle, N.Y. 1989) 105–127.

Lombardi 1996 = F. Lombardi, *Roma: Le Chiese scomparse* (Rome 1996).

Lugli 1922 = G. Lugli, s.v. Horti Sallustiani, in *Dizionario Epigrafico di antichità romane* (Rome 1922) 1005–1009.

Lugli 1930–1940 = G. Lugli, *I monumenti antichi di Roma e suburbio* I–IV (Rome 1930–1940).

Lugli 1957 = G. Lugli, *Fontes ad Topographiam veteris urbis Romae pertinentes* IV (Rome 1957).

Lugli 1970 = G. Lugli, *Itinerario di Roma Antica* (Milan 1970).

Lugli and Gismondi 1949 = G. Lugli and I. Gismondi, *Forma urbis Romae imperatorum aetate* (Novara 1949).

Madonna 1980 = M. L. Madonna, "L' 'Enciclopedia del mondo antico' di Pirro Ligorio," *Quaderni de 'La Ricerca Scientifica'* 106 (Rome 1980) 257–271.

Mandowsky and Mitchell 1963 = E. Mandowsky and C. Mitchell, *Pirro Ligorio's Roman Antiquities* (Studies of the Warburg Institute 28, London 1963).

Marchi 1980 = C. Marchi, *Palazzo Margherita: The Embassy of the United States of America in Rome* (Rome 1980).

Marliani 1534 = B. Marliani, *Topographia antiquae Romae* (Lyon 1534) = *Antiquae Romae Topographia libri septem* (Rome 1534).

Marliani 1544 = B. Marliani, *Urbis Romae Topographia* (Roma 1544).

Mansuelli 1958 = G. A. Mansuelli, *Galleria degli Uffizi, Le Sculture* I (Rome 1958).

Marszal 1991 = J. R. Marszal, *The Representation of the Gauls in the Hellenistic and Roman Imperial Periods* (Ph.D. Diss. Bryn Mawr College 1991).

Martini 1984 = W. Martini, *Das Gymnasium von Samos* (*Samos* 16, Bonn 1984).

Mattei 1987 = M. Mattei, *Il Galata Capitolino* (Rome 1987).

Mauro 1556 = L. Mauro, *Le antichità della città di Roma* (Venice 1556).

Mercati 1589 = M. Mercati, *De gli obelischi di Roma* (Rome 1589).

Merkel Guldan 1988 = M. Merkel Guldan, *Die Tagebücher von Ludwig Pollak: Kennerschaft und Kunsthandel in Rom 1893–1934* (Vienna 1988).

Mertens-Horn 1997(a) = M. Mertens-Horn, "Bilder heiliger Spiele. Zur Deutung der sog. 'Throne' aus Marmor in Rom und Boston," *AntW* 1997, 217–231.

Mertens-Horn 1997(b) = M. Mertens-Horn, "Rappresentazioni di scene sacre," in *Troni*, 94–106.

Millar 1977 = F. Millar, *The Emperor in the Roman World* (London 1977).

Mirone 1918 = S. Mirone, "Il tempio di Afrodite Ericina sul denario di L. Considio Noniano," *RIN* 31 (1918) 189–198.

MNR = *Museo Nazionale Romano* (Catalogues of the collection).

Moltesen 1981 = M. Moltesen, "Two Fleeing Niobids," *Apollo* 114 (1981) 362–365.

Moltesen 1990 = M. Moltesen, "Una nota sul Trono Ludovisi e sul Trono di Boston: La 'Connection' danese," *BdA* 64 (1990) 27–46.

Moltesen 1993 = M. Moltesen, "Lapis Albanus: A Group of Hellenistic Sculptures in Peperino," in P. Guldager Bilde, I. Nielsen, and M. Nielsen, eds., *Aspects of Hellenism in Italy: Towards a Cultural Unity?* (*Acta Hyperborea* 5, Copenhagen 1993).

Moltesen 1998 = M. Moltesen, "The Sculptures from the Horti Sallustiani in the Ny Carlsberg Glyptotek," in *Horti Romani*, 175–188.

Moltesen 2002 = M. Moltesen, ed., *Imperial Rome III, Statues: Ny Carlsberg Glyptotek* (Copenhagen 2002).

Montagnani-Mirabili 1804 = P. P. Montagnani-Mirabili, *Il Museo Capitolino colla descrizione delle antichità e pitture che sono nel Campidoglio* II (Rome 1804).

Montfaucon 1724 = B. Montfaucon, *L'Antiquité expliquée et représentée en figures*, Supplement 2 (Paris 1724).

Montfaucon 1725 = B. de Montfaucon, *The Antiquities of Italy, Being the Travels of the Learned Bernard de Mont-*

faucon from Paris through Italy, in the Years 1698 and 1699[2] (English version from the Paris edition of the Latin original) revised by Montfaucon and edited by J. Henley (London 1725).

Mustilli 1939 = D. Mustilli, *Il Museo Mussolini* (Rome 1939).

Nardini 1666 = F. Nardini, *Roma Antica*[4] (Rome 1818). First published in 1666 after the death of the author. Republished in 1704 with Flaminio Vacca's *Memorie di varie antichità trovate in diversi luoghi della città di Roma* (Rome 1594). A third edition appeared in 1771 with notes by Antonio Nibby, and this was republished in 1818. A reprinted facsimile of this 1818 edition appeared in 1988 in two volumes as *Roma Antica di Famiano Nardini*, from which all references in this text are derived.

Nash 1957 = E. Nash, "Obelisk und Circus," *RM* 64 (1957) 232–259.

Nash 1959 = E. Nash, "Über die Auffindung und den Erwerb des 'Bostoner Thrones,'" *RM* 66 (1959) 104–137.

Nash 1968 = E. Nash, *Pictorial Dictionary of Ancient Rome*[2] (London 1968).

Neudecker 1988 = R. Neudecker, *Die Skulpturen-Ausstattung römischer Villen in Italien* (Mainz am Rhein 1988).

Neudecker 1998 = R. Neudecker, "The Roman Villa as a Locus of Art Collections," in Frazer 1998, 77–91.

Neuerburg 1965 = N. Neuerburg, *L'architettura delle Fontane e dei Ninfei nell'Italia Antica* (Naples 1965).

Nibby 1838–1841 = A. Nibby, *Roma nell'anno MDCCCXXX-VIII* (Rome 1838–1841).

Nordh 1949 = A. Nordh, ed., *Libellus de regionibus urbis Romae* (Skrifter Utgivna av Svenska Institutet, ser. 2, vol. 3 (Rome 1949).

Ofenbach 1997 = E. Ofenbach, *Josef Spithöver: Ein westfälischer Buchhändler, Kunsthändler und Mäzen im Rom des 19. Jahrhunderts* (Regensburg 1997).

Olck 1905 = *RE* 5.2 (1905) s.v. Eiche (und Eichel) 2013–2076.

Pace 1945 = B. Pace, *Arte e civiltà della Sicilia antica 3: Cultura e vita religiosa* (Genoa 1945).

Palma 1983(a) = B. Palma, *I Marmi Ludovisi. Storia della collezione,* (*MNR, Le Sculture* I, 4, Rome 1983).

Palma 1983(b) = B. Palma, *I Marmi Ludovisi nel Museo Nazionale Romano* (*MNR, Le Sculture* I, 5, Rome 1983).

Palmer 1976 = R. E. A. Palmer, "Jupiter Blaze, Gods of the Hills, and the Roman Topography of *CIL* VI 377," *AJA* 80 (1976) 43–56.

Panvinio 1558 = O. Panvinio, *Reipublicae Romanae commentariorum libri tres* (Venice 1558).

Paris 1994 = R. Paris, ed., *Dono Hartwig. Originali ricongiunti e copie tra Roma e Ann Arbor: Ipotesi per il Templum Gentis Flaviae* (Rome 1994).

Petersen 1892 = E. Petersen, "Aphrodite," *RM* 7 (1892), 32–80.

Pietrangeli 1977 = C. Pietrangeli, "Quirinale e Viminale dall'antichità al Rinascimento," in *Il Nodo di S. Bernardo* (Milan 1977) 13–68.

Piranesi 1748 = G. B. Piranesi, *Varie vedute di Roma antica e moderna* (Rome 1748).

Piranesi 1756 = G. B. Piranesi, *Le Antichità Romane* (Rome 1756).

Piranesi 1761 = G. B. Piranesi, *Della Magnificenza ed Architettura de'Romani* (Rome 1761).

Piranesi 1762 = G. B. Piranesi, *Il Campo Marzio dell'antica Roma* (Rome 1762).

Platner 1904 = S. B. Platner, *The Topography and Monuments of Ancient Rome* (Boston 1904).

Platner 1911 = S. B. Platner, *The Topography and Monuments of Ancient Rome*[2] (Boston 1911).

Platner and Ashby 1929 = S. B. Platner and T. Ashby, *A Topographical Dictionary of Ancient Rome* (Oxford 1929).

Pollak 1994 = L. Pollak, *Römische Memoiren* (Rome 1994).

Posterla 1725 = F. Posterla, *Roma Sacra e Moderna già descritta dal Pancirolo ed accresciuta . . .* (Rome 1725).

Poulsen 1951 = F. Poulsen, *Catalogue of Ancient Sculpture in the Ny Carlsberg Glyptotek* (Copenhagen 1951).

Pugliese Carratelli 1979 = G. Pugliese Carratelli, "Testi e Monumenti," *PP* 34 (1979) 442–481.

Purcell 1996 = N. Purcell, "The Roman Garden as a Domestic Building," in I. M. Barton, ed., *Roman Domestic Buildings* (Exeter 1996) 121–151.

Purcell 2001 = N. Purcell, "Dialectical Gardening," *JRA* 14 (2001) 546–556.

Ramieri 1983 = A. M. Ramieri, "L'archeologia in Roma capitale: le scoperte, i metodi e gli studi," in *Roma Capitale*, 18–29.

Rawson 1985 = E. Rawson, *Intellectual Life in the Late Roman Republic* (London 1985).

Richardson 1976 = L. Richardson, jr., "The Villa Publica and the Divorum," in L. Bonfante and H. von Heintze, eds., *In Memoriam Otto Brendel: Essays in Archaeology and the Humanities* (Mainz 1976) 159–163.

Richardson 1992 = L. Richardson, jr., *A New Topographical Dictionary of Ancient Rome* (Baltimore 1992).

Richmond 1971 = I. A. Richmond, *The City Wall of Imperial Rome* (College Park, MD, 1971).

Richter 1901 = O. Richter, *Topographie der Stadt Rom* (*HdA* III.3.2, Munich 1901).

Ridgway 2002 = B. S. Ridgway, *Hellenistic Sculpture III: The Styles of ca. 100–31 B.C.* (Madison, WI 2002).

Ridley 1992 = R. T. Ridley, *The Eagle and the Spade: Archaeology in Rome during the Napoleonic Era* (Cambridge 1992).

Riemann 1950 = *RE* 20.2 (1950) 1483–1603, s.v. Pincius mons (H. Riemann).

Rizzo 1906 = G. E. Rizzo, "Statua di una Niobe, scoperta nell'area degli orti Sallustiani," *NSc* 1906, 434–446.

Rizzo 1983 = S. Rizzo, "L'<ars topiaria>," in *Roma Capitale*, 191–194.

Rodríguez-Almeida 1980–1981 = E. Rodríguez-Almeida, "Di Virgilio e Marziale, a proposito del nome <Alta Semita>, *BullCom* 87 (1980–1981) 75–82.

Rodríguez-Almeida 1986 = E. Rodríguez-Almeida "Alcune notule topografiche sul Quirinale di epoca domizianea," *BullCom* 91.1 (1986) 49–60.

Roma Capitale = *Roma Capitale 1870–1911: L'archeologia in Roma capitale tra sterro e scavo* (Venice 1983).

Roma instaurata = F. Biondo, *Roma instaurata* (Rome 1446; Venice 1511, Basel 1531). Lucio Fauno translated this into Italian (Venice 1542).

Rolley 1999 = C. Rolley, *La sculpture grecque, 2: La période classique* (Paris 1999).

Roullet 1972 = A. Roullet, *The Egyptian and Egyptianizing Monuments of Imperial Rome* (Leiden 1972).

RT I–III = *Registri dei Trovamenti*, Vol. I, 1872–1874; II, 1875–1876; III, 1877–1896. (Currently housed at via del Portico di Ottavia, 29.)

Säflund 1932 = G. Säflund, *Le mura di Roma repubblicana* (*Acta Instituti Romani Regni Sueciae* I, Rome 1932).

Santangeli Valenzani 1991 = R. Santangeli Valenzani, "ΝΕΩΣ ΥΠΕΡΜΕΓΕΘΗΣ Osservazioni sul tempio di piazza del Quirinale," *BullCom* 94 (1991) 7–15.

Santangelo 1941 = M. Santangelo, "Il Quirinale nell'antichità classica," *MemPontAcc* 5.2 (1941) 77–210.

Scaglia 1964 = G. Scaglia, "The Origin of an Archaeological Plan of Rome by Alessandro Strozzi," *JWarb* 27 (1964) 137–159.

Schiavo 1981 = A. Schiavo, *Villa Ludovisi e Palazzo Margherita* (Rome 1981).

Schilling 1982 = R. Schilling, *La Religion romaine de Vénus* (Paris 1982).

Schneider 1986 = R. M. Schneider, *Bunte Barbaren* (Worms am Rhein 1986).

Schreiber 1880 = T. Schreiber, *Die antiken Bildwerke den Villa Ludovisi in Rom* (Leipzig 1880).

Schudt 1930 = L. Schudt, *Le Guide di Roma: Materialien zu einer Geschichte der römischen Topographie* (Vienna 1930).

Simon 1984 = *LIMC* II (1984) 837–838 s.v. Artemis/Diana (E. Simon).

Strong 1973 = D. E. Strong, "Roman Museums," in D. E. Strong, ed., *Archaeological Theory and Practice* (London 1973) 247–264.

Stuart-Jones 1912 = H. Stuart-Jones, *A Catalogue of the Ancient Sculptures Preserved in the Municipal Collections of Rome*, Vol. 1: *The Sculptures of the Museo Capitolino* (Oxford 1912).

Stuart-Jones 1926 = H. Stuart-Jones, *A Catalogue of the Ancient Sculptures preserved in the Municipal Collections of Rome*, Vol. 2: *The Sculptures of the Museo Conservatori* (Oxford 1926).

Studniczka 1904 = F. Studniczka, "Archäologische Gesellschaft zu Berlin: Dezembersitzung," *AA* 19 (1904) cols. 224–225.

Studniczka 1911 = F. Studniczka, "Das Gegenstück der Ludovisischen 'Thronlehne,'" *JdI* 26 (1911) 50–192.

Studniczka 1926 = F. Studniczka, "Artemis und Iphigenie: Marmorgruppe der Ny Carlsberg Glyptotek," *AbhLeip* 37.5 (1926) 1–160.

Syme 1958 = R. Syme, "Obituaries in Tacitus," *AJP* 79 (1958).

Syme 1964 = R. Syme, *Sallust* (Berkeley 1964).

Syme 1978 = R. Syme, "Sallust's Wife," *CQ* 28 (1978) 292–295.

Syme 1986 = R. Syme, *The Augustan Aristocracy* (Oxford 1986).

Talamo 1995 = E. Talamo, "Gli originali greci degli Horti Sallustiani," in M. Cima, ed., *Restauri nei Musei Capitolini* (Verona 1995) 17–39.

Talamo 1998 = E. Talamo, "Gli *horti* di Sallustio a Porta Collina," in *Horti Romani*, 113–169.

Tambroni 1936 = F. Tambroni, "Rione XVI–XVII: Ludovisi-Sallustio," in *Roma nei suoi Rioni* (Rome 1936) 431–445.

Terza Roma = S. De Paolis and A. Ravaglioli, eds., *La Terza Roma: Lo sviluppo urbanistico edilizio e tecnico di Roma capitale* (Rome 1971).

Torelli 1987 = M. Torelli, "Culto imperiale e spazi urbani in età flavia," in *L'Urbs: Espace urbain et Histoire* (CEFR 98, Rome 1987), 563–582.

Toti 1995 = O. Lollio Barberi, G. Parola, and M. P. Toti, *Le Antichità Egiziane di Roma Imperiale* (Rome 1995).

Troni = *Il Trono Ludovisi e il Trono di Boston* (Convegno di studio, Istituto Veneto di Scienze, Lettere ed Arti. 12 settembre 1996; Venice 1997).

Truszkowski 1988 = E. Truszkowski, "Sur la date du cratère Borghèse," *Histoire de l'Art*, nr. 3 (October 1988) 3–16.

Urlichs 1871 = C. L. Urlichs, *Codex Urbis Romae Topographicus* (Würzburg 1871).

Vacca 1594 = F. Vacca, *Memorie di varie antichità trovate in diversi luoghi della città di Roma* (Rome 1594).

Vagenheim 1987 = G. Vagenheim, "Les inscriptions ligoriennes, notes sur la tradition manuscrite," *Italia Medioevale e Umanistica* 30 (1987) 199–309.

Valentini and Zucchetti = R. Valentini and G. Zucchetti, *Codice topografico della città di Roma* I–IV (Rome 1940–1953).

Venuti 1736 = R. Venuti, *Collectanea Antiquitatum Romanarum Antonii Borioni* (Rome 1736).

Venuti 1763 = R. Venuti, *Descrizione topografica delle antichità di Roma* I (Rome 1763).

Venuti 1824 = R. Venuti, *Accurata e Succinta Descrizione Topografica delle Antichità di Roma*[3] (Rome 1824).

Vierneisel-Schlörb 1979 = B. Vierneisel-Schlörb, *Klassische Skulpturen des 5. und 4. Jahrhunderts v. Chr. (Glyptothek München, Katalog der Skulpturen* II, Munich 1979).

Viscogliosi 1996 = A. Viscogliosi, *Il Tempio di Apollo in Circo e la formazione del linguaggio architettonico augusteo* (*BullCom* Supplement 3, 1996).

Visconti 1831 = E. Q. Visconti, *Opere varie, italiane e francesi* IV (Milan 1831).

Visconti 1886 = C. L. Visconti, "Trovamenti di oggetti d'arte e di antichità figurate," *BullCom* 14 (1886) 299, 343–344, 390–392.

Visconti 1887 = C. L. Visconti, "Un singolare monumento di scultura ultimamente scoperto negli Orti Sallustiani," *BullCom* 15 (1887) 267–274.

Visconti 1888(a) = C. L. Visconti, "Trovamenti di oggetti d'arte e di antichità figurate," *BullCom* 16 (1888) 415–425.

Visconti 1888(b) = C. L. Visconti, "Elenco degli oggetti di arte antica scoperti per cura della Commissione archeologica comunale dal 1º gennaio a tutto il 31 dicembre 1888 e conservati nel Campidoglio, o nei magazzini comunali," *BullCom* 16 (1888) 479–505.

Walser 1987 = G. Walser, *Die Einsiedler Inschriftensammlung und der Pilgerführer durch Rom (Codex Einsidlensis 326),* (*Historia* 53, Stuttgart 1987).

Watson 1998 = A. Watson, ed., *The Digest of Justinian* (Philadelphia 1998).

Werke = J. J. Winckelmann, *Werke,* Vols. I–VII, C. L. Fernow, H. Meyer, and J. Schulze, eds. (Dresden 1808–1820).

Wilson 1990 = R. J. A. Wilson, *Sicily under the Roman Empire: The Archaeology of a Roman Province 36 BC–AD 535* (Warminster, England 1990).

Wilton-Ely 1994 = J. Wilton-Ely, *Giovanni Battista Piranesi: The Complete Etchings* (San Francisco 1994).

Winckelmann 1764 = J. J. Winckelmann, *Geschichte der Kunst des Alterthums* (Dresden 1764).

Winckelmann 1769 = J. J. Winckelmann, *Storia delle arti del disegno presso gli antichi* II, C. Fea, ed., (Rome 1769).

Wiseman 1987 = T. P. Wiseman, "*Conspicui Postes Tectaque Digna Deo:* The Public Image of Aristocratic and Imperial Houses in the Late Republic and Early Empire," in *L'Urbs: Espace Urbain et Histoire* (*CEFR* 98, Rome 1987), 393–413.

Wiseman 1998 = T. P. Wiseman, "A Stroll on the Rampart," in *Horti Romani,* 13–22.

Zanker 1974 = P. Zanker, *Klassizistische Statuen* (Mainz am Rhein 1974).

Zanker 1995 = P. Zanker, *The Mask of Socrates: The Image of the Intellectual in Antiquity,* trans. A. Shapiro (Berkeley 1995).

ILLUSTRATION CREDITS

Fig. 1.1: *FUR* 2, 3, 9, 10 (digitized images and details).

Fig. 1.2: Plan of ancient Rome, by Martin Boss (digitized image [with additions and subtractions], after E. Simon, *Augustus: Kunst und Leben in Rom um die Zeitenwende* (Munich 1986) 6.

Fig. 1.3: Plan of modern Rome (photo: AAR, Fototeca unione 4346 bF).

Fig. 1.4: Portrait bust of Sallust, Hermitage, St. Petersburg, Inv. A 424 (photo courtesy of the State Hermitage Museum, St. Petersburg).

Fig. 1.5: Contorniate. Obverse, portrait of Sallust. Cabinet des Médailles, Bibliothèque Nationale de France, Paris, Nr. 17175 (photo: BN 99.A.79143).

Fig. 1.6: Acqua Felice, engraving by G. B. Falda, *Fontane di Roma* (Istituto Centrale per il Catalogo e la Documentazione; Neg. series F, Nr. 814).

Fig. 1.7 with details A–F: Perspective plan of Rome, by Stefano du Pérac, edited by Antonio Lafréry, 1577: detail (digitized images after Frutaz 1962, plan CXXVII, 7, pl. 254).

Fig. 1.8: Original plots of Ludovisi property, by T. Schreiber 1880, with additions by Felici 1952, N.1 (photo: Avery Architectural and Fine Arts Library, Columbia University).

Fig. 1.9: Plan of the gardens of the Ludovisi, by G. B. Falda (Istituto Centrale per il Catalogo e la Documentazione; Neg. series E, Nr. 14658).

Fig. 1.10: Casino di Villa Lodovisi presso Porta Pinciana, engraving by G. Vasi (photo from Schiavo 1981, fig. 19).

Fig. 1.11: Plan of Rome, by E. Salandri, 1846: detail (digitized image after Frutaz 1962, plan CXCIX, pl. 511).

Fig. 1.12: Plan of Rome, by M. Gregorio de Rossi: detail (digitized image after Frutaz 1962, plan CLVII, 1, pl. 351).

Fig. 1.13: Plan of Rome of 1878, edited by the Spithoever bookstore: detail (digitized image after Frutaz 1962, plan CCXIV, 2, pl. 541).

Fig. 1.14: Palazzo Piombino (later villa Margherita), elevation by G. Koch (photo from Schiavo 1981, fig. 108).

Fig. 1.15: Stemma of Rione XVII: Sallustiano (Fratelli Palombi Editori).

Fig. 2.1: Plan of Rome, by B. Marliano, 1544: detail (digitized image after Frutaz 1962, plan XII, pl. 21).

Fig. 2.2: Plan of Rome, by M. Cartaro, 1576: detail (digitized image after Frutaz 1962, plan CXXVI, 2, pl. 240).

Fig. 2.3: Valley of the Sallustian gardens showing slopes of the Pincio: "Le Marché de Salluste," engraving by B. van Overbeke, *Les restes de l'ancienne Rome* (Amsterdam 1709) III, nr. 10, pp. 19–20 (photo: Avery Architectural and Fine Arts Library, Columbia University).

Fig. 2.4: Valley of the Sallustian gardens, engraving by J. B. Piranesi, from Piranesi 1762, pl. XLI.1 (photo: AAR Fototeca unione 3073 F).

Fig. 2.5: Valley of the Sallustian gardens, engraving by J. B. Piranesi, from Piranesi 1756, pl. XVI, fig. 1.A

Fig. 2.6: Valley of the Sallustian gardens, engraving by L. Rossini, 1828, from *I Sette Colli di Roma* (Rome 1828/1829) pl. X

Fig. 2.7: Primitive fortifications, Quirinal, Parker 153 (DAI, Inst. Neg. PK 153).

Fig. 2.8: So-called Destailleur plan of the gardens of Sallust, probably by Aristotile da Sangallo, sixteenth century (photo: AAR, Fototeca unione 3211 F).

Fig. 2.9: Plan of Rome, by G. B. Piranesi, 1756: detail (digitized image from Frutaz 1962, plan XXXV, pl. 69).

Fig. 2.10: Various capitals, by G. B. Piranesi in Piranesi 1761 (photo from J. Wilton-Ely, *Giovanni Battista Piranesi: The Complete Etchings* [San Francisco 1994]).

Fig. 2.11: Plan of area of the gardens of Sallust, with indications of archaeological discoveries from Talamo 1998, 124, fig. 10.

Fig. 2.12: House of Sallust(?), Parker 1020 (photo: DAI, Inst. Neg. PK 1020).

Fig. 2.13: So-called Nymphaeum (vestibule), Piazza Sallustiana (photo: DAI, Inst. Neg. 55.112).

Fig. 2.14: Ruins of the Vestibule, Piazza Sallustiana (photo: AAR, Fototeca unione 3231 F).

Fig. 2.15 with details A–F: Plan of Rome, by L. Bufalini, 1551 (digitized images after photograph, Archivio delle Stampe FV 29137).

Fig. 2.16: "Del Tempio dela Luna Sallustiana" (plan and cross-section) *Cod. Paris. ital.* 1129 (formerly St. Germaine 86), fol. 311r (photo: Bibliothèque Nationale, Paris).

Fig. 2.17: "Del Tempio dela Luna Sallustiana" (three-dimensional elevation) *Cod. Paris. ital.* 1129 (formerly St. Germaine 86), fol. 312 (photo: Bibliothèque Nationale, Paris).

Fig. 2.18: "Del Tempio dela Luna Sallustiana" (Ionic capital) *Cod. Paris. ital.* 1129 (formerly St. Germaine 86), fol. 313 (photo: Bibliothèque Nationale, Paris).

Fig. 2.19: "Del Tempio dela Luna Sallustiana" (plan and

Fig. 3.6: *Artemis, Iphigenia, and a Hind* from the Sanctuary of Jupiter Dolichenus on the Aventine, Museo Capitolino, Rome, Inv. 9778 (photo: Musei Capitolini).

Fig. 3.7: *Fleeing Maiden,* Ny Carlsberg Glyptotek, Copenhagen, Kat. 398 (photo: Ny Carlsberg Glyptotek).

Fig. 3.8: *Dying Youth,* Ny Carlsberg Glyptotek, Copenhagen, Kat. 399 (photo: Ny Carlsberg Glyptotek).

Fig. 3.9: *Resting Satyr,* Ny Carlsberg Glyptotek, Copenhagen, Inv. 474 (photo: Ny Carlsberg Glyptotek).

Fig. 3.10: *Wounded Niobid,* Museo Nazionale delle Terme, Rome, Inv. 72274 (photo: DAI, Inst. Neg. 62.533).

Fig. 3.11: "Frammento di Niobide del Celio" from unpublished notebook of Rudolpho Lanciani, *Cod. Vat. lat.* 13035, fol. 110r (photo: Biblioteca Apostolica Vaticano).

Fig. 3.12: Striding *Apollo Kitharoidos:* Fragment of draped leg, Museo Capitolino, Rome (photos: author).

Fig. 3.13: *Pedagogue* of the children of Niobe, Museo Nazionale delle Terme, Rome: Palazzo Massimo (photo: Museo Nazionale delle Terme).

Fig. 3.14: *Crouching Amazon,* Conservatori Museum, Rome, Inv. 840 (photos: author).

Fig. 3.15: *Dying Gaul,* Musei Capitolini, Rome (photo: DAI Inst. Neg. 70.2122).

Fig. 3.16: *Suicidal Gaul and "Wife,"* Museo Nazionale delle Terme, Rome: Palazzo Altemps, Inv. 8608 (photo: DAI, Inst. Neg. 56.349).

Fig. 3.17: *Silenus with the Baby Dionysos,* Louvre, Paris, Inv. 9880212 AGR: Ma 922 (photos: Museum [cliché C. Larrieu]).

Fig. 3.18: *Borghese Krater,* Louvre, Paris, Inv. 985-N 275: MA 86 (photos: Louvre, Paris [cliché P. Lebaube]).

Fig. 3.19: *Resting Satyr,* Ny Carlsberg Glyptotek, Copenhagen, Inv. 2237 (photo: Ny Carlsberg Glyptotek).

Fig. 3.20: *Papposilenus,* Museo Nazionale delle Terme, Rome: Palazzo Massimo (photo: Museo Nazionale delle Terme).

Fig. 3.21: Double-sided *Marble Slab Sculptured in Relief* with A: heads of a maenad and a silenus, and B: dancing fauns, Inv. 5668 (photos: Museum of Fine Arts, Budapest, Negs. A.27831, 27832 [G. Fittschen-Badura]).

Fig. 3.22: *Faun Seated on a Wineskin,* Museo Nazionale, Rome, Inv. Nr. 72 from *EA* 5004: Panisk auf Schlauch sitzend (photo: Visual Resource Center, Art History and Archaeology, Columbia University).

Fig. 3.23: Statuette of *Faun on a Large Goat* (photo: *NSc* 1909, 7 [Avery Architectural and Fine Arts Library, Columbia University]).

Fig. 3.24: *Goat Tied by Its Hooves,* Metropolitan Museum of Art, New York, Acc. No. 10.151 (photo courtesy of Metropolitan Museum of Art [Elizabeth Milliker]).

Fig. 3.25: *Nymph,* Wallmoden Collection, Archäologisches Institut, Göttingen, courtesy H.R.H. The Prince of Hannover, Duke of Brunswick and Lüneburg (photo: Stephan Eckardt, courtesy of Archäologisches Institut, Göttingen).

Fig. 3.26: *Nymph,* British Museum, London, Inv. 145689 (photo © The British Museum).

Fig. 3.27: *Candelabrum,* Galleria dei Candelabri, Vatican, Inv. 2667 (photo: Musei Vaticani, Archivio Fotografico, Neg. Nr. XXXII.54.30).

Figs. 3.28: *Ludovisi "Throne."* A: front; B: left side; C: right side. Museo Nazionale delle Terme, Rome: Palazzo Altemps (photos by Rossa: DAI Inst. Neg. 72.2043–2045).

Figs. 3.29: *Boston "Throne."* A: front; B: left side; C: right side. Museum of Fine Arts, Boston, Inv. 08.205 (photos: Henry Lillie Pierce Fund, © Museum of Fine Arts, Boston).

Fig. 3.30: *Nike,* Museo Capitolino, Rome: ACEA, Montemartini (photo: author).

Fig. 3.31: Archaic marble *Sarcophagus* from Asia Minor, detail: mourning woman [Hecuba] (photo: N. Sevinç, C. B. Rose, D. Strahan, and B. Tekkök-Biçken, "The Dedetepe Tumulus," *Studia Troica* 9 [1998] fig. 19).

Fig. 3.32: *Kneeling Barbarian,* Ny Carlsberg Glyptotek, Copenhagen, Inv. 1177 (photo: Ny Carlsberg Glyptotek).

Fig. 3.33: *Kneeling Barbarian,* Museo Nazionale, Naples, Inv. 6117 (photo by Schwanke: DAI, Inst. Neg. 83.2149).

Fig. 3.34: *Kneeling Barbarian,* Museo Nazionale, Naples, Inv. 6115 (photo by Schwanke: DAI, Inst. Neg. 83.2161).

Fig. 3.35: *Trophy,* Museo Capitolino, Rome (photo: author).

Fig. 3.36: *Head of a Horse,* fifth-century B.C. Greek, Detroit Institute of Arts, Acc. Nr. 39.602: Founders Society Purchase, General Membership Fund (photo © 2002 The Detroit Institute of Arts).

Fig. 3.37: *Touya, Queen of Seti I,* Musei Vaticani, Inv. 22678 (photo: Musei Vaticani, Archivio Fotografico, Neg. XXXIII.54.40).

Fig. 3.38: *Ptolemy II,* Musei Vaticani, Inv. 22682 (photo: Musei Vaticani, Archivio Fotografico, Neg. XXXIV.35.38).

Fig. 3.39: *Arsinoe,* Musei Vaticani, Inv. 22681 (photo: Musei Vaticani, Archivio Fotografico, Neg. I.1.19).

Fig. 3.40: Roman copy of statue of *Arsinoe,* Musei Vaticani, Inv. 22683 (photo: Musei Vaticani, Archivio Fotografico, Neg. XIX.25.17).

Fig. 3.41: Hieroglyphic inscription on back of Fig. 3.40, Musei Vaticani (photo: Musei Vaticani, Archivio Fotografico, Neg. XXXII.37.29).

Fig. 3.42: *Hapy,* god of the Nile, Musei Vaticani, Inv. 22809 (photo: Musei Vaticani, Archivio Fotografico, Neg. XXXIV.30.39).

INDEX